MONEY
TALES

First published 2007

Printed in France 2007

Translated from Mythes et Légendes économiques
First published by Ed. Economica, Paris, 2007

Alessandro Giraudo

Money Tales

ISBN 978-2-7178-5349-0

Cover: "Allegoria dell'Abbondanza", Valerio Castello (1624-1659)
Courtesy of the Carige Collection – Genova (Cassa Risparmio di
Genova e Imperia)

Alessandro GIRAUDO

MONEY TALES

Translation: Lindsay Lighfoot
Editing: Michael Westlake

ECONOMICA

49, rue Héricart, 75015 Paris

ACKNOWLEDGEMENTS

I am indebted to my former teachers Michele Molineris and Carlo Maria Cipolla for having instilled in me a lasting passion for economic history. I would like to thank Nicholas Brown, Philippe Chalmin, Pascale Gaillot-Rosset, Caroline Hugo, Richard Hudson, Jeanine Hutellier, Emilio Molinari, Jovan Pavlevski, Stefano Pitto, Cristina Vasilescu and Marialuisa Viglione, as well as Patrick Combes and Farid Belkacemi (respectively CEO and General Manager of the Viel Tradition Group), and of course my family, without whose encouragement this work would never have seen the light of day.

CONTENTS

To Régine
« sine qua non... »

INTRODUCTION
`VIAGGIARE RENDE CURIOSI!´
(CHRISTOPHER COLUMBUS)

Travel makes one curious! Columbus was certainly right, even if
he made the luckiest mistake in history. It was curiosity that led
me to write this book. Consisting of a kaleidoscope of short chapters on a variety of subjects, it makes no claim to be comprehen-
sive. It invites the reader to discover the myths, legends and truths
behind the economic facts of history. The scope is very wide: from
the pre-Bronze Age obsidian trade to the development of container transport spurred on by the Vietnam War; from coins
minted by the temple at Delphi to the pieces of eight which
financed the golden age of the Spanish Empire; from Venice's
turbulent struggles to maintain the monopoly in spices and glassware to the espionage surrounding map-making; from the Silk
Road – along which the Black Death also travelled – to the first
great global economic crises at the end of the 19th century; from
the strategic role played by pirates and privateers in the economic
war in the Caribbean to the Chicago slaughterhouses that inspired
Henry Ford. A number of short chapters cover the Renaissance
period and the great geographical and scientific discoveries made
then, when the earth finally became round. It was unquestionably
one of the most fertile epochs in history: men fought against
fanatical dogmatism and ignorance with even greater determina-
tion, they risked their lives in the search for gold and spices, they
showed renewed curiosity in science and technology, they organized new systems for promoting international trade... but, regret-
tably, they also managed slavery on a vast scale until it became

almost an industrial system and laid down the foundations for western colonialism!

Economic history teaches us that highly developed and powerful civilizations can collapse once the management of empires becomes too bureaucratic and centralized and the cult of the personality is allowed to take over government. Shortsightedness is the enemy of intellectual curiosity and progress. The opulence of the late Roman Empire, the pampered life of the Caliphates and the occupants of the Topkapi palace, the isolation of the Chinese emperors inside the gilded cage of the Forbidden City, the luxurious comforts of the palaces lining the Grand Canal, the silver of old Peru and the woes it brought to the Spanish Empire, the monolithic power structures in pre-Columbian civilizations – all of these are so many instances of blindness, leading to the decline and fall of great powers which had never foreseen their eventual collapse.

Ego, love of power, ignorance, mistakes both large and small, all played their part in fueling wars (hot and cold), economic wars, stock exchange battles and massive speculation, economic and social crises which brought suffering to millions. For all that, Penelope carried on working patiently; she unceasingly wove and then unpicked her tapestry of History and Economics... many of the events of recent years recall those of the past, both distant and not so distant... *sic transit gloria mundi*[1]!

---

1. Thus passes away the glory of the world

A NUMBER OF CIVILIZATIONS COLLAPSE ONE AFTER THE OTHER 6000 YEARS AGO

Around six thousand years ago the principal civilizations of the period suddenly collapsed, one after the other. They were located around the eastern end of the Mediterranean, north of the Saudi Arabian peninsula and in western India. In the case of Egypt the disintegration was partial; the texts of the period speak of `drought and sandstorms...´. In Greece, there are numerous traces of fires in various regions, including Poliochni and Lerna. On the islands of Crete and Cyprus flourishing ports fell into ruins, for example Pygros and Enkomi in Cyprus. There is further evidence of catastrophe in Western Anatolia: Troy (a strongly fortified, Bronze Age town which should not be confused with the Troy of Priam's era and the Trojan Wars) was entirely destroyed. Other Turkish towns suffered substantial damage. In Palestine, life in the town of Jericho was completely wiped out, despite its very strong fortification, and evidence of fierce fires can still be seen. The towns Megiddo and Beth Shan were also destroyed. The large towns of Ouera, Nagar, Nabada and Tuttul in the Upper Valley of the Euphrates were suddenly abandoned. In Mesopotamia, the great kingdom of Sargon of Akkad fell – this had been an early example of empire building. In the Indus valley, rich farming civilizations which had developed around the large towns of Harappa and Mohenjodaro disappeared leaving no sign of population migration.

Researchers have for a long time been trying to find the cause of these events. The most likely explanation is that they were caused by a meteorite falling 10 miles north of the confluence of the Tigris and Euphrates. This natural phenomenon would have produced severe earthquakes, fires and floods. The meteorite created a crater nearly two miles in diameter which is still visible in Iraq, clearly showing the violence of its impact on the earth's surface. Researchers are still trying to date this crater in the knowledge that many archaeologists have already found evidence of a severe drought in the region's history and the abandonment of several large towns.

In 1948 an archaeologist put forward the hypothesis of a huge natural catastrophe, but the idea was discarded in favor of that of the fall of civilizations, in view of the large area concerned and also a marked rise in the birth rate at the time. This explanation has now been challenged. Studies are under way to pinpoint the events, which all happened more or less at the same time, and in this way to find a possible link with the fall of the meteorite. Historians have already found a clear link between the fall of civilization on the island of Crete and the serious crisis in Northern Egypt, following the eruption of the volcano on Santorini (probably around 1640 BC, though the date is still disputed amongst the experts), which gave rise to earthquakes, tidal waves and volcanic ash rain throughout the Eastern Mediterranean. The inhabitants of Thira (in the southeast of Santorini Island) even had to abandon their homes, which were buried under a couple of dozen feet of volcanic ash.

THE OBSIDIAN ROAD: MEDITERRANEAN BLACK GOLD

Obsidian is a very hard rock of volcanic origin related to pumice but with a glass-like quality, which can be used for cutting. It is a type of lava which has cooled rapidly, releasing its gases very quickly. Pumice stone, on the other hand, comes from almost the same type of lava, but it has cooled and released its gases much more slowly; it is light in weight and has a sponge-like appearance, and is used as an abrasive (for toothpaste, abrasive pastes, preparing denim, etc.). The word obsidian is derived from the name of the Roman citizen who found this stone in Ethiopia. Before the age of metals, people needed tools for cutting, slicing, and sharpening arrows. They used hand-chipped pieces of stone (flint), but these were not very effective or precise. So an alternative had to be found. In the Mediterranean Basin, there are obsidian deposits in the Aeolian Islands (northeast of Sicily), in the Island of Pantelleria (to the south of Sicily, between Tunisia and Malta), in Sardinia, (especially in the volcanic region of Mount Arci), in the Island of Palmarola (to the west of Naples), in some of the Peloponnesian Islands (Giali and Melos), in Turkey (Cappadocia), in the Carpathian Mountains (southeast Slovakia and northeast Hungary) Georgia, Armenia and Iran. The most sought-after obsidian, because of its hardness, came from the Aeolian Isles (mainly Lipari, where it could be picked up off the ground) and Pantelleria, where the Sesi and Mursia civilizations developed. Trade in obsidian was conducted mostly by sea, and this naturally favored islands rather than places where obsidian seams were located in remote mountain areas.

MARITIME TRADE ROUTES PROVIDE CLEAR INSIGHTS INTO EARLY HISTORY

Many of these obsidian stones have been discovered at archaeological sites throughout the Mediterranean, continental Europe, the Middle East and even North Africa. The trade routes originate in the islands and merchant sailors set out to exchange the obsidian for other products – particularly textiles, vases and livestock – throughout the Mediterranean. Caravan merchants then transported the stones to other destinations in the continental interiors. All these islands and centers of stone production benefited enormously, becoming wealthy and well developed in comparison with other manufacturing centers or regions with only agricultural or mining economies. Obsidian from Lipari and Sardinia has been found in Italy as far north as Trieste and in France as far west as Toulouse. The stones traveled far and wide; not only were they of practical use – for cutting, making knives, and sharpening arrows and spears – but they were also used in luxury products, such as mirrors polished with goat's milk, statuettes, funerary and ritual objects, and amulets to bring good luck. Obsidian was very valuable, especially in areas remote from the deposits. The stone's value was increased by two factors: the first according to the distance traveled by the merchants, the second and more important depending on the expertise of the mariners, who were able to navigate to islands (especially Pantelleria and Lipari) that were distant and invisible from the coast. It took considerable skill to orientate oneself and set a course ...over 6000 years ago!

Even in the Bronze Age, obsidian remained irreplaceable, and only when iron and other alloys were introduced, did it lose its economic value and thus led to the decline, steady in some places and more abrupt in others, of the centers of production, which now specialized in making jewelry and other small household objects and ornaments.

THE KEY ROLE OF OBSIDIAN IN PRE-COLUMBIAN CIVILIZATIONS

In pre-Columbian civilizations such as the Mayan, Aztec and Inca, obsidian was also valuable, but over a much longer period of time, for although these civilizations used metallurgy in a very sophisticated manner for the treatment of precious metals, their mastery of it for ordinary metals was moderate and primitive. The abundance of obsidian throughout the Andean *Cordillera* reduced the need to produce base metals. Moreover, for certain civilizations, obsidian was a symbol of power and good fortune. The knives used in human sacrifice – opening the thorax, fracturing the skull and so on – were made of the hardest obsidian, which also often had some golden sheen and was highly prized. The Moon and Sun temples at Teotihuacán, near Mexico City, were built in a region that was rich in obsidian quarries. The legendary town of Machu Picchu in Peru owes its good fortune to the presence of the obsidian quarries at the foot of the volcanic dome which towers above the town. The Apaches long used the obsidian they found in the Utah desert to make arrow heads for hunting animals and for fighting American soldiers and settlers.

SALT: GIFT FROM THE GODS
AND REFRIGERATOR OF THE ANCIENTS

In Timbuktu, around 1000 AD, salt had the same value, ounce for ounce, as gold. One of the strategic reasons behind Caesar's conquest of Gaul was the will to control salt production in the west on the Atlantic coast, as well as to gain access to the region's mines, particularly its silver and gold mines. Roman soldiers received part of their pay in the form of salt, which came to Rome along the *via salaria* or salt road. In fact the word for remuneration in English – salary – and other European languages derives from the Latin for salt. All the princes and kings of the late medieval period owned salt-boxes or stores as part of their treasury. Indeed, the great Renaissance sculptor Benvenuto Cellini produced a remarkable salt-cellar as one of his masterpieces. Henry VIII gave the future Queen of France, Catherine de Medici, an exquisite salt-cellar. For a long time salt was the white gold of our civilizations, even if, today, you can buy a pound in the supermarket for less than a dollar, depending on its quality and its packaging.

THE BEST WAY OF PRESERVING FOOD THROUGHOUT HISTORY

Salt was the 'refrigerator' of the past: fish, meat, vegetables and many other fresh foodstuffs can be preserved for long periods by salting, which protects them from the spread of bacteria, since the salt absorbs the water in them and so prevents their putrefaction. All civilizations have required salt for use in food, medicine and early industries, and they obtained it either locally from mines or salt pans, or by means of trade or war. Salt is essential for food; used as a condiment, in food preservation, in beer, wine, cheese and even bread. It is beneficial to the human body; low concentration salt solutions help to reduce swelling in mucous membranes and can help treat sinusitis, tonsillitis and pharyngitis. The Romans were familiar with the use of salt baths for treating rheumatism. Many people brush their teeth with salt solution. Following the introduction of coffee and tobacco in Europe, men and women used to try and remove the nicotine and coffee stains from their teeth with salt water. Many popular remedies involve rubbing of salt on the affected part of the body; the Greeks believed that eliminating salt from their diet reduced men's potency. During the 16th and 17th centuries it was common for ladies to rub their lovers with salted water to increase their vigor!

THE INFLUENCE OF SALT ON TRADE AND POLITICS

Salt trade routes developed across every continent: donkeys, mules climbed mountains, camel trains made up of ten thousand animals crossed deserts, llamas traversed the Andes, barges were hauled up and down rivers by men and animals, boats sailed the high seas, all transporting this precious merchandise. In Europe, the Hallstatt culture of the Austrian Alps developed thanks to the `gem salt´ mines (gem as in gemstone, whence the expression `white gold´) and supplied a trade that extended throughout central Europe from Bosnia to Spain. It was salt that helped to foster the rise of Celtic and Etruscan cultures. Scandinavian countries in Northern Europe were obliged to import salt due to the low salinity of their seas and the cool climate which was unfavorable to evaporation. So they traded wood, animal skins and, later, metal for salt coming from southern and central Europe. Even today, mines are still being worked in the Libyan Sahara that have been in existence for several centuries, supplying the caravans that followed the trade routes from the southern Mediterranean basin into the heart of Africa. Salt was used as currency in Africa: a block of salt would purchase a sheep; in Congo three goats would were worth two baskets of salt. In Timbuktu, one of the great trading posts of the past, a slave could be bought for a plaque of salt the size of his foot. The great European merchant cities – Venice,

Genoa, Antwerp, Amsterdam and others – tried to control the salt trade, as they had done with pepper and other spices. The trade was very lucrative and price speculation fuelled the fears of people dependent on salt in their daily lives. Through its control of the production and trade of salt, Venice was able to force ships with salt cargoes to go via Venice on their way from the production area to their final destination. Since salt was carried only on Venetian ships, this trade provided considerable work for their merchant fleet and generated large tax revenues for the city. Indeed one of the Doges said: `Il sale è il vero fondamento del nostro stato´ (`Salt is the real basis of our state´). There was even a special, and very powerful, body (Collegio del Sal) for managing the production, storage and trade of salt.

In China and India, the maritime regions produced salt, which they sold to the people of the interior. In India salt was traded for spices, in China for horses and arms. The highly organized Chinese salt trade was noticed by Marco Polo, who commented that salt was the main product traded on the Yang Tse river, along which it was transported from the coast (predominantly the city of Hangchou) to cities inland. In North America, the native population found it very difficult to obtain salt, which came from the coast or salt lakes. The inhabitants of South America depended essentially on salt coming from maritime regions on the two coasts and from the biggest salt desert in the world, at a height of more than 11,000 feet in the Andes – the immense Salar de Uyuni in Bolivia and the terraced salt mines of Saras were playing a strategic role for the Inca imperial city of Cuzco and the fortress of Ollantaytambo.

Governments were quick to understand that a salt tax, on a commodity that everyone needed, would help fill the empty coffers of their treasuries. In the USA the state of New York financed the Erie Canal with salt taxes. According to Pliny, kings obtained more revenue from the salt tax than from the gold tax. Salt became the prerogative of kings and princes: the first legal document concerning salt dates from 715, decreed by Liutprand, the king of Lombardy. From the end of the Renaissance in Europe, with the appearance of the great nation-states, the sale of salt became a state monopoly; salt consumption was taxed, in certain instances becoming compulsory (a minimum sum per family per year). In England, Queen Elizabeth I was concerned about the country's dependence on foreign salt, mainly from France, which was an enemy at the time. Colbert, the French Minister of Finance exploited this source of revenue to the maximum and the peak came in 1680... the *gabelle* or salt tax weighed particularly heavily on families and fuelled social unrest. The term *gabelle* comes from the Arab word *kabala* which means tax. In every country the smuggling of salt became a means of earning a livelihood; governments tried to combat this by passing strict laws and by specifying different shaped salt cake for different regions in order to make people use the state salt rather than contraband salt.

GANDHI AND SALT

`You are the salt of the earth´, Jesus told his Apostles. For the Early Greeks it was quite simply a divine gift, since Thetis, daughter of the god of the sea, gave Peleus a gift of salt when they were married, a union which produced Achilles. Salt was believed to protect you against evil spirits... at the time of the Inquisition many innocent women confessed under torture to having eaten without salt and were burned at the stake as a result. In 1790 the Constitutional Assembly of the newly formed French Republic, decided to abolish the *gabelle*. During the American Civil War, northern troops attempted to destroy southern salt pans and salt storage facilities in order to cause problems in the supply of salt for their soldiers, cattle and horses. Salt played an important role at a crucial moment in the struggle for Indian Independence when, on the 5th April 1930, Mahatma Gandhi refused to respect the salt monopoly imposed by the British and launched a civil disobedience campaign in which everyone started producing their own salt. This was the first successful action of the movement which was to bring about Indian Independence some twenty years later.

THE TROJAN WAR: FOUGHT OVER A WOMAN OR FOR ECONOMIC REASONS?

Homer in the Iliad and Virgil in the Aeneid both drew on the myth of Menelaus's wife Helen and her abduction, to account for a war that lasted for at least ten years. But in fact, behind the confrontation between the Greeks and Trojans lies another reality, that of an unrelenting commercial war over the control of trade and the passage between the Eastern Mediterranean and the Black Sea.

PRIAM, HELEN, MENELAUS, AGAMEMNON, ACHILLES

Paris, one of Priam's sons, was promised by the goddess Aphrodite that he would have the most beautiful wife in the world. He seduced and then abducted Helen, the wife of Menelaus, King of Sparta. Menaleus's brother, Agamemnon, united the leaders of the small kingdoms of Greece and challenged Troy, in the form of an expedition to retrieve the beautiful Helen – who seemed to be enjoying Paris's ardor and the splendors of Troy. Such is the romanticized version that Homer gives us with all its intrigues and pathos. But there is probably a far more prosaic explanation hidden behind this tale of love and jealousy. Helen's alluring eyes were not the only *causus belli* – and there was probably no abduction, only a fierce and ruthless war for the control of one of the most important trade route of ancient times.

During this period, around 1200 BC, the Eastern Mediterranean was dominated by three powers: the still powerful Egyptian Empire, the Hittite Empire now in a vulnerable state of decline, and the Greek world of the Mycenaeans. Recall that some centuries earlier there had been the terrible eruption of the volcano on Santorini (in the archipelago of small volcanic islands that form the Cyclades, between the Peloponnese and the island of Crete). The volcano exploded and millions of cubic yards of dust and ash were deposited on the fertile soils of Crete, the southern part of latter-day Turkey, Cyprus and northern Egypt. The Cretan civilization, which also was subjected to the effects of a tidal wave, was swept away and the palace at Knossos was seriously damaged. Crops and livestock far across the Mediterranean also suffered considerable damage.

TROY: THE CITY THAT CONTROLLED ACCESS TO THE DARDANELLES (HELLESPONT)

Troy enjoyed a truly strategic position. The city, close to the Dardanelles Strait, controlled all shipping and trade in the Sea of Marmara, through which ships must pass to enter to the Black Sea by way of the Bosphorus. Trade was not very highly developed at this period, but in practice some four-fifths of goods were transported by sea, which was hazardous because of piracy. Nevertheless, ships could transport goods in far greater quantities than pack animals or carts, especially in view of the state of the roads, which were even less safe than the sea and poorly maintained. It would take at least another thousand years and the rise of Rome to establish a reliable, well organized and well maintained network of roads. Trade in merchandise between the Mediterranean and the Black Sea was comparatively simple at this time: wine, raisins, citrus fruits, oil, spices (from the Red Sea), textiles (Egyptian cotton), dyes (produced by the Phoenicians) and certain metals were exported from the Mediterranean. From the Black Sea came animal hides, wheat, metals (Carpathian gold), salt (from the salt mines of what is modern Romania), honey and high quality wood, for the most part. Troy levied a tax on all these goods, whilst its merchants were responsible for their trade. The city had a pastoral economy and obtained much of its wealth from pillage – in which its sailors became specialists. Moreover, the tribes and minor potentates of the nearby Greek communities had to cope with a mountainous and rugged terrain and the absence of large plains suitable for intensive cultivation. The Achaeans – the name of the Greeks who took part in the war against the Trojans – began to look for alternative ways to expand, and some coastal areas of Asia Minor (in western Turkey) fell under Greek control. They cannot yet be referred to as colonies, a term better applied to areas in southern Italy at the height of Athens' splendor (5th century BC), and should rather be seen as trading posts.

THE EXPANSION OF THE GREEK KINGDOMS INTO THE EASTERN MEDITERRANEAN

Accustomed to local conflicts, the Greek leaders launched themselves into the conquest of Troy. According to the tablets found at Mycenae, Pylos and Knossos, the Trojan War appears to have been a straightforward attempt by local monarchs to extract themselves from their economic difficulties and re-establish their prosperity by seizing the rich prize of Troy, putting an end to the Trojan monopoly over the trade route in a strategic zone, and replacing the Trojan pirates with their own sailors. The Siege of Troy lasted at least ten years (probably between 1193 and 1184 BC): the town possessed water, wells and walls; the Greeks were not well armed and they depended on their bases in Greece and the islands for all their supplies. After the city – the remains of which can still be seen – was destroyed, the Achaeans placed the whole region around Troy under their control. The Romans would later adopt the same approach with Carthage, their greatest enemy, at the end of the Punic Wars. Thus a simple act of pillage, just a little more organized, gave birth to a civilization of conquerors and allowed the Greeks to extend their hegemony across the Eastern Mediterranean, taking advantage of the decadence of the Hittites and the monolithic structure of the Egyptian Empire. Egypt was in any case much more preoccupied with the conquest of the lands to the south (for the gold and slaves of Sudan) and protecting itself from the Black Pharaohs of Nubia.

USURY: FROM DRACON TO CLEOPATRA, FROM CALVIN TO ROOSEVELT

The first evidence for legal and economic principles of usury is found in Aristotle's *Nichomachean Ethics*, where he defines the usurer or money-lender as one who gives a little but demands a lot. Naturally, in an essentially rural economy, based above all on barter, the calculation of usury is difficult to make; but it can be assumed that the wealthy might rent out or lend seedlings, animals or dwellings and that they would be reimbursed in kind. The cost of these loans would be closely linked to the harvest and to the incidence of diseases affecting animals, people or crops.

THE MONEY REVOLUTION

From the time the first coins were minted in Asia Minor, the economy underwent radical change. Initially coins were very small and made from white gold, a naturally occurring alloy of gold and silver. A handful of these coins was equivalent in value to several harvests, large quantities of livestock, or even land. In Sparta though, the legislator Lycurgus, who sought equality for all citizens, forbade the circulation of these coins, replacing them with an iron bar weighing a little more than eight pounds; the metal soon became unusable, however, because it was first immersed in vinegar. Lycurgus achieved his goal at the cost of excluding his city-state from the trade in the Aegean Sea, but was unable to prevent the concentration of wealth into the hands of around two hundred families.

In Athens, another legislator, Dracon (to whom we owe the term `draconian´) envisaged a system of laws that were intended to be favorable to all citizens and produce economic equality among them. He set a fixed rate for usury for the first time: the repayment (capital plus interest) must be no greater than five-sixths of the annual harvest. It was a measure which heavily penalized the debtor and indirectly favored the oligarchs, who were already very wealthy. A generation later, in 597 BC, the Archon Solon was elected: he introduced a constitution in which citizens' rights were based on their income. Many of Dracon's laws were subsequently repealed or relaxed. Solon outlawed the practice of loans in which the individual was offered as security. Then Peisistratos very substantially reduced interest already accrued and awarded state loans to craftsmen and shopkeepers at zero per cent (sic!), using the revenue from the silver mines. But the experiment ended badly: he was obliged to devalue the coins, the weight of which was reduced from 1/70 mine to 1/100 mine (1 mine = 14 ounces).

THE GROWTH OF BANKING IN ATTIC GREECE

The first appearance and spread of banks in Greece allowed the cost of credit to be significantly reduced. Competition between different banks wishing to work in the many towns, as well as that between the towns themselves, brought the balance between supply and demand into play in a more transparent world – the principle of the stock exchange – and little by little credit came to reflect risk value. The highest rate was charged by merchant shippers: 3% a month, or 36% a year (the principle of compound rate did not yet exist). This rate took into account the high risk of these activities, constantly threatened by piracy, the weather and the fortune of the seas. The banks offered credit to towns and to the kings at a rate of 10-15% for political reasons, even if the risks were high. Craftsmen, shopkeepers and farmers could obtain loans at rates of less than 10%. On the other hand, the banks created the principle of penalizing borrowers who were unable to repay their debts, with rates varying between 10 and 12%.

TEMPLES AND OTHER RELIGIOUS SITES LOWER THE INTEREST RATES STILL FURTHER

Many religious centers began to mint coins for the faithful; these were in circulation at the site and pilgrims were obliged to exchange their currency for that provided by the religious center. People exchanged their money when they arrived; when they left they were obliged to resell any remaining coins and to pay a 7% commission to cover the exchange risk and finance the activities at the site. The temples also minted coins for towns which had no mint of their own. These included Delos, Ilion Apollonia in Pontus, Aegina and Delphi. Religious sites thus became issuing banks as well as having the function of commercial banks; their rates were lower than private banks, thanks to the 7% commission, income from the sale of animal hides after the pilgrims' sacrifices, offerings (in kind and in cash), revenue from their crops and livestock, and the charges levied for consulting the oracle. The temples also received income from fines pilgrims had to pay for offences committed against the religion. Loans were made on trust; the name of any borrower failing to pay back his loan was circulated throughout the network of banks and temples, and he would be unable to take out further loans. The rates in use ranged from a maximum of 20% for distant towns and kings to a minimum of 10% for the leaders of towns nearer the religious site. A 10% rate was charged on loans to pay ransoms on people captured by pirates, the same as for consumer credit, and loans of 300 drachmas were available to anyone requiring them. With few disputes, it was known for loans to be paid back over a period of three generations.

Among the Greeks, the phenomenon of usury was considerably restrained by the economic functions of the temple, with money being lent at the market rate or even lower. After the Roman conquest, this type of organization lost its power due to the spread of Roman coinage, which became the monetary standard and the international currency throughout the Mediterranean basin and the Empire, to the furthest northern and eastern regions of Europe.

CREATION OF THE FIRST CENTRAL BANK... IN EGYPT!

In ancient Egypt, banking was a royal monopoly, even if hitherto the Jews and Greeks settled there had issued maritime loans at higher rates than those offered for other purposes because of the significant dangers of sea trade. In Ptolemy's era interest rates fell, but they peaked at an annual rate of 24%. Ptolemy I Soter reorganized the credit system and created the first central bank, providing the model on which the Bank of England would eventually be founded. It is based on two activities: on the one hand, issuing money, and on the other, receiving savings and taxes. Loans made to kings and towns had to have the authorization of the pharaoh, which was granted largely on the basis of political considerations. The banking monopoly applied only to the Egyptian interior, since Alexandria – the leading Mediterranean financial center at the time – benefited from a completely unrestricted system. Here credit was received and issued in a highly competitive `international´ market. Egyptian rates fell only after Egypt's conquest by the Roman legions, when Rome set up an extensive network of public and private banks.

CARTHAGE WAS UNABLE TO FIND THE MONEY NEEDED TO FIGHT ROME

In its early years, Rome adopted the economic practices and customs of the Etruscans (to the north) and the Greeks (to the south). We have few details about banking during the first centuries of Roman life. We do know that during the first Punic war – Carthage and Rome were fighting for control of shipping in the Mediterranean and over economic and territorial expansion – the pharaoh Ptolemy refused to lend Carthage 2000 talents of silver (40 tons of the metal) with which to continue the war. Although he wished to retain his neutrality, he indirectly favored Rome. `Republican´ Rome went through a difficult period and money-lending became widespread – and people with bad debts were sold as slaves! In fact, senators, who by law were only allowed to undertake economic activities linked to the land (crops, livestock and mining), were the main sponsors. They remained hidden behind banking fronts which lent their names to the senators, increasing their rates in so doing, in order to compensate for the risk of detection. As a result, the rate for money-lending remained very high. Only in 357 BC did the Republic take strict measures to fix the rate of money-lending at 8.33%, on the basis of the *faenus unciarium*. This notion refers to the monetary pound, sub-divided into 12 ounces, each ounce being sub-divided into 12 'scruples' – whence the term still used today to refer to minimal moral values.

THE PROPERTY BOOM

Property speculation was once again responsible for the rise in money-lending rates, especially after a price crisis which increased the number of unpaid loans. Only when Sulla became dictator, was the important decision made to fix the rate of usury at 1% per month. Another reality lying behind this decision was the struggle between limiting or increasing the amount of money in circulation. Senators, owners of large estates and oligarchs were in favor of strict monetary controls; ranged against them were shopkeepers, soldiers, small-holders, noblemen and legionaries, all of whom thought that a large amount of money in circulation was good for the economy. Roman magistrates were no longer able to hold money-lending rates in check in a Republic which had degenerated. For example, Marcus Junius Brutus, son of Servilia (one of Caesar's favorite mistresses), lent money at 48% to anyone in need throughout the Roman provinces and in the town of Salamine, Cyprus. Pompey (Pompeius Magnus) granted loans to the kings of Cappadocia at rates high enough to pay the wages of four legions. Even Cicero loved money so much that he left his wife to marry a girl of eighteen in order to administer her wealth and especially his father-in-law's.

THE CONQUEST OF EGYPT: NOT FOR CLEOPATRA BUT FOR WHEAT AND GOLD

With its legions and wealth, Rome acquired a position of prominence in Europe: it led the way 'internationally' as the center for financiers, speculators, brokers and bankers from the countries of the west and the Mediterranean basin. Business also attracted many wealthy women and major political figures such as the King of Cyprus and Ptolemy XII Aulete, who became impoverished following failed speculation. It would seem that there was only one honest banker and that was Marcus Licinius Crassus, who lent money to his friends at ridiculously low rates or sometimes even for nothing. Caesar benefited hugely from this at the time when he was no more than a minor patrician encumbered with debts, and had even been held prisoner by pirates. But he was very strict about repayment. Once Caesar came to power, he tried to apply standards to limit usury, but it was not until the arrival of Augustus and the economic boom which lasted forty years that interest rates finally dropped. The monetization of plunder from Egypt allowed interest rates to fall to less than 4%, thanks to the abundance of liquidity which favored the economic situation. The Roman expedition to conquer Ancient Egypt was not for the sake of Cleopatra's beautiful eyes; rather it was to lay hands on the immense wealth of a large grain-producing country which also possessed gold mines in the Sudan – the cause of the celebrated war against the Black Pharaohs –, and controlled silk and spice routes through its Mediterranean and Red Sea ports. Thanks to resulting increase in liquidity, loans became progressively cheaper and the usury system went into decline.

The economic stability characterizing the period from Augustus to Commodus was further strengthened through reforms carried out by Nero – better known for having burnt Rome – which altered the relation between the value of gold and silver. The system was flooded with liquidity: maximum rates were 6%, against the official rate of lending, fixed at 12%; the Empire's finances were often in surplus and large cash deposits were placed with banks, which had a major impact on interest rates.

CLAUDIUS INTRODUCES MARINE INSURANCE

The Emperor Claudius brought down marine interest rates by introducing marine insurance, enabling the economic risks involved in shipping to be offset. Under the Antonine dynasty, the Empire continued to benefit from extremely favorable conditions in terms of loans and credit, but usury began to reappear.

Legislation was becoming more complex, and indeed allowed individual clauses to be included in commercial contracts, which bordered on usury. However, the creation of Christian banks limited the damage caused by usury: these banks gave loans to those in need, at rates which were often little more than symbolic, on condition that they were repaid on time.

But the profession was evolving. The bank owned by Callistus, who later became Bishop of Rome, also lent money to the wealthy and to Jews – at the market rate, of course. From the 2nd century AD onwards, especially under Septimus Severus, the state concentrated the means of production in its hands and proceeded widely to distribute its revenues among the population: wheat, salt, salted meat, clothing, shoes and medicines were distributed for free. The Empire began to live beyond its means. Banks disappeared, leaving only the money-changers which managed the relatively unimportant exchange of non-Roman coins with those of the Empire, which were in general circulation everywhere. The decline of the banks contributed to the resurgence of usury. The financial crisis of the 3rd century, with its monetary chaos and successive inflation-driven devaluations, brought about an explosion in usury. Inflation encouraged usury on goods in kind, as confidence in the currency fell to a low point. There was galloping inflation throughout the 4th century: the price of a pound of gold rose from 7500 deniers to 560,000 deniers, or at a rate of 7% per annum. Justinian, who moved the capital of the Empire to Constantinople, tried to halt this process by fixing the usury rate at 6%, but these measures failed to curtail the spread of usury, where rates of up to 50% per annum were the norm!

THE MEDIEVAL PERIOD: MONEY IN DECLINE

In Europe, the fall in trade, shipping and regional commerce limited the use of money; cash was no longer so functional since many commercial transactions were was carried out on a barter basis, within every narrower geographical zones.

Romans and Barbarians tried nonetheless to apply Justinian's norms: the *Lex Romana Visigothorum* and *Lex Romana Burgundiorum* protected the borrower from usury, but economic difficulties gave power to those possessing capital (both monetary and in kind) and usury spread once more. The Church was the only institution which tried to oppose it: it strongly condemned the principle of interest and those who profited from it. In his *Ammonitio Generali* in 789, Charlemagne forbade Christian citizens from lending money with interest and declared monetary commerce `immoral´. In Charlemagne's Empire, minting currency was no longer a royal prerogative, and many individuals specialized in producing coins intended for princes, the nobility and religious institutions; some abbeys minted their own coins. During the Merovingian period, there were 5000 master craftsmen working in 1200 mints scattered throughout the land.

Later, under the Carolingian kings, each earldom produced coins to the value of six pounds weight of silver per year, provided by the king who retained one *sou* per pound (1/20). This was known as the *droit de seigneur* or feudal levy. The master craftsman received a further *sou* in payment, a practice that led the earls to add copper to the coins to make good the levies. Counterfeit coins were rife and usury continued, if only on a small scale, up until the first millennium.

Contrary to what is often believed, Charlemagne did not achieve any important reforms in the monetary sector. It was his father, Pepin the Short, who tried to bring some order to the monetary chaos. Charlemagne abandoned the 'Roman' monetary system, altered a few parities and tried to strengthen the currency in a period when monetary stability was relatively unimportant in comparison with the physical availability of coins. Very little money was exchanged during this period: local economies were `autonomous´ and had little contact with other regions. Goods were in such short supply that Charlemagne introduced fasting twice a week! In 829, the Council of Paris condemned usury unequivocally, but the feudal lords and church officials were all able, with their different methods, to lend at rates over 100%. There were no banks; only non-Christians (Jews and others) could practice usury and loans without risking divine punishment.

THE CRUSADES AND THE NEED FOR TRANSFERABLE MONEY

The crusades created a need for new money and for its availability in large amounts in distant lands. The Church applied the rules of usury, with a certain tolerance, as ships from Venice, Pisa and Genoa carried the crusaders across the Mediterranean; merchants provided guarantees of the transfer of their money. But the Council of Lyon in 1274 hit out strongly against these practices: it condemned usurers, any clergy accepting inheritances from a usurer, and anyone trading with Arabs and other infidels. The Italian banker, Francesco Datini, invented letters of exchange, in which interest was camouflaged by the valuation of the *denaro* and the *lettera*. The principle of compensatory interest was established, though it should be distinguished from other types of interest, for example, usury. Bankers began to set up special accounts, such as the `Our Lord's Account´, with its percentage of concealed interest, paid to the Church (*Gottes Geld*). Moreover, some bankers offered loans at `relatively´ low interest rates (8-10%) to the Church, kings and to towns, in exchange for which they were granted free concessions and the right to collect taxes and to hold mining or transport monopolies.

CALVIN AND THE EXPANDING WORLD

The growth of shipping sailing to the west coast of Africa and the rediscovery of islands in the Atlantic Ocean through Italian and Portuguese explorers seeking gold and spices, changed the economic order. Trade between the Levant and the Italian maritime cities and the Champagne fairs – a succession of six fairs in the towns of Champagne and Brie, which changed location every two months from January to December, and linked the cloth-producing cities of the Low Countries with the Italian dyeing and exporting centers – also had a great effect on the money markets. The Church relaxed its attitude toward the principle of a rate of interest, but still condemned usury. Calvin was one of the first preachers to deny the sterility of money and thus to admit its essential role in the world of economics. The climate of opinion evolved and the Church's position radically altered, enabling it to finance its princely expenditure; loans for the purpose of `doing good´ were increasingly accepted, as long as the interest rate was moderate (in this way the rate remained unfixed, the `type´ of loan defining the interest rate instead). The Spanish galleons, laden with silver from Mexico and Peru (from the Potosi mines, now in modern Bolivia), could no longer satisfy the money demands of the military – continually at war in Europe following the discovery of the New World – and of the towns and cities which needed to build fortifications to protect themselves from enemy artillery. Inflation in the 16th century and the increasing threat from the Ottoman Empire, which was making inroads into Venetian possessions and now occupied the Balkans, both contributed to a rise in interest rates. European markets were flooded with `black´ money: silver coins containing lead in ever-increasing quantities, which had a marked effect on their color and above all reduced their value.

SELF-FINANCING LEADS TO A DECLINE IN INTEREST RATES

With the exception of Italy and the Low Countries where the banking system was very highly developed, interest rates remained very high: for example, Italian and Jewish bankers lent at a rate of 20% in England. Public borrowing and that of towns was only possible at a rate of more than 10%. The beginnings of industry permitted the accumulation of financial-industrial capital, thanks to self-financing, and this practice put downward pressure on interest rates. In 1821 the Vatican's *Sagra Congregazione del Santo Ufficio* allowed that granting a loan was not contrary to ecclesiastical laws, and that therefore it came under the jurisdiction of commercial law. Economic development meant that the middle classes were better off and had less need to borrow money. On the other hand, the spread of co-operatives and pawnbrokers made it possible to finance the more minor needs of the less well-off, who were also helped by the Church and private charitable institutions.

ROOSEVELT AND INTEREST RATES

Usury became once more a current and very widespread phenomenon following the First World War, but the policy of low interest rates, adopted by Roosevelt and followed by other countries, enabled usurious interest rates to be kept in check. The practice re-arose in the 1970s following monetary chaos, inflation and the weakness of many economies. The central banks' monetary policies, aimed at curbing inflation, had a damaging effect on interest rates and encouraged the return of usury, which was fuelled by massive speculation on currencies, stock markets and raw materials. Since the end of the 1990s, with the decision by the world's central banks to maintain high liquidity in order to avoid the most serious economic problems, usury has remained confined to the legal arsenal, even if it is still a continuing and significant feature of the `black market´ in most countries and a major source of revenue for organized crime.

DELPHI: A RELIGIOUS CENTER AND A GREEK MINT

For twelve centuries the Oracle of Delphi gave directions and advice to legislators, citizens and philosophers on many subjects – matters of State, affairs of finance and sex, military and strategic decisions. For a long time it was thought that the Pythias, or priestesses who predicted the future, were under the influence of aphrodisiacal leaves which they chewed and/or divine inspiration. Now we are almost certain that it was ethylene vapor that affected the women. The ground at Delphi is composed of limestone rock which contains tar and oils, with cracks in the strata that allow for ethylene vapor to escape; this is a sickly sweet gas which was used in the past as an anesthetic and which in small doses can induce a state of euphoria. Plutarch explicitly refers of the euphoric state of the Pythias.

As for the history of the Temple of the Oracle, we know that the Greeks built a temple very close to Corinth, on the slopes of Mount Parnassus, around 1200 BC. Thereafter the temple assumed such an important role for the Greeks that they considered it to be the center of the world. Dedicated to the goddess Gaia, around the 8th century BC it became a center of worship to Apollo, god of prophecy. During the ceremonies the prophetess would go down into an underground cave and inhale the sacred vapors. Today we know that there is a large fault line of volcanic origin which crosses the Corinth region and emits traces of the gases methane, ethylene and ethane, and that it is ethylene which induces an altered mental state in people who inhale it, manifested by euphoria and pleasurable sensations.

The legend asserts that Zeus himself had decided to free two eagles from diametrically opposed points on the circumference of the earth's disc, from where they flew toward one another. The birds met at Delphi, at a point marked by a conical stone, surmounted by two gold eagles. This ancient stone, over which the temple was later built as a reliquary, was the famous *omphalos*, the earth's navel, from which the glory of Delphi radiated throughout Greece and the Mediterranean for more than a thousand years. Those who have visited this magical spot may repeat with Plato: `...for surely the place is holy...'[1]

During the 4th century AD the oldest Panhellenic institution, the Amphictyonic League, started to mint its own new coins. An *Amphictyon* was a religious and political confederation bringing together representatives of various peoples; the most renowned was at Delphi and was made up of the main Greek states (Thessalians, Beotians, Dorians, Spartans, Ionians, Athenians, Phocidians, Malians, etc). This coin issue was unusual since it was not initiated by a state institution and was relatively short lived.

A TRANSNATIONAL COINAGE

The coins were minted by the body with the task of managing Delphi from the economic standpoint. The *stater* was worth two *eginetic* drachmas – one of the first monetary systems, from the island of Egina in the Peloponnesus – and theoretically weighed 13.4 grams of silver. It is thought that some 200,000 coins were minted in all.

There were at least three reasons for this operation. The prime reason is probably that the finances of this great religious center of antiquity benefited from having a single currency, which was acceptable everywhere, rather than having many different coins circulating, brought to the center by the many pilgrims who came to worship and consult the Oracle. The money changers working there would obviously have been penalized, for at the time their profession was not well thought of (especially at religious sites), and they had little political influence.

---

1. From *Phaedrus* by Plato, translated B. Jowett

The second reason is much more complex and modern. It is likely that the leaders of the League wished to introduce a currency that would be accepted throughout the Greek world of the time, one that could replace the Attic coinage (largely Corinthian and Athenian) which was the true `dollar´ of the period – exchanged by everyone and used as the standard. The main coin was the *tetradrachme*, minted in Athens and in circulation throughout Greece and accepted beyond its borders in neighboring countries by merchants, sailors and caravaneers.

However, the Delphic coin contained 13% less metal than the Corinthian money, according to the calculations of numismatists, although it was accorded exchange parity by the authorities. The lower metal content is explained by the fact that the coins were minted from the other, melted-down coins. There is usually some wastage in this process, but it is minimal. So at least a part of this *agio* or charge was deliberate and confirms that the men of Delphi and the League intended giving their coin a greater value than those circulated by the center, thereby enhancing their charisma in comparison with religious power.

PHILIP OF MACEDONIA BACKS THE NEW COINS

A further reason for this new coin can be found in the desire of the League to issue `souvenir´ coins for visitors to Delphi, like the Santiago de Compostela scallop shells distributed to medieval Christian pilgrims visiting St James's shrine, and many other similar medals and coins, which are partly devotional in intent, or simply for display or collection.

On the other hand, in terms of its overall success, this coin issue was disappointing since its circulation was very limited. But the history of the League and in particular the power of Philip of Macedonia, which was at its height, must be born in mind. Philip probably wanted to break the monetary monopoly of Athens and Corinth, and to this end played the *amphictyon* card. Clearly, after the great battle of Chaeronea (338 AD), which Philip won with the invaluable help of his son Alexander (the future Alexander the Great), who commanded the cavalry against the Greek States, the balance was altered in a dramatic fashion and power passed into the hands of the northeastern Greeks. Philip and Alexander were preparing to attack the Persians and the League coin was no longer minted. After that came the great conquests of the Middle East and the expedition through which Alexander led his phalanxes and cavalry as far as India.

ROME OF THE CAESARS: HOW TO FEED ONE MILLION INHABITANTS

At the time of the Caesars, Rome had a population of less than a million, but at its height this rose to 1.2 million, including visitors, traders, students and other temporary residents. This population had to be fed and controlled. It was an enormous administrative task calling for a very smooth-running organization, similar to modern models, to avoid the problems of the period such as famine, unrest, disease and rebellion. The region around Rome supplied fruit, vegetables, cheese and wine, but in insufficient quantities. So livestock had to be imported from elsewhere in Italy, as well as grain, which came mostly from Sicily and, later, Egypt – the two great granaries of the Roman Empire.

THE EGYPTIAN WHEAT ROUTE

All Roman emperors had one overriding priority (if they wished to retain their popularity): avoiding famine. Frequently they organized the free distribution of wheat, imported to Rome and stored in large warehouses near the Eternal City. Egypt became the principal supplier and the Alexandrian fleet was the most secure means importing thousands of tons of grain every year. The emperors persuaded the senators (who were also wealthy merchants) to help build this very large fleet. The ships could not come all the way to Rome, since it is not on the coast, but anchored at Pozzuoli, near Naples, a deep enough harbor to take heavily laden merchant ships. The wheat was unloaded and stored or transported by other smaller boats to the port of Ostia, where the enormous warehouses and even the quarters of the many fire fighters of the period may still be seen. It took at least 800 large shiploads of grain to supply Rome with wheat. Some small boats were able to navigate up the river Tiber to Rome itself. But it took two weeks to complete a return journey from Pozzuoli to Rome and, on top of which navigation became particularly hazardous in winter – so the large quantities of wheat stored in the grain sheds at Pozzuoli sometimes failed to arrive on time in the capital. As a result Rome suffered from occasional food shortages, with all the political risks this entailed for the position of those in power.

Oil, wine and fish – a story of amphorae.

Oil was also an essential commodity in the life of the Romans – for food and its conservation, beauty products and lamps. Oil came from Spain in particular, in immense amphorae which were broken on landing so that the liquid could be decanted into smaller containers that were easier to transport. The debris of these huge amphorae formed, like a slagheap, Mount Testaccio (on average more than 100 feet high with a volume of 870,000 cubic feet). It is estimated that 260,000 large amphorae arrived in Rome to supply sufficient oil for an average consumption of 28 US gallons per person per year!

Wine was also brought to Rome by ship. This was produced in large quantities in the region around Narbonne in Gaul, in Southern Spain, in Sicily, in Greece and in coastal North Africa. The Roman diet included a large amount of fish, and fishing was developed to an almost industrial scale. The centers where the fish was salted, especially tuna and mackerel, were scattered throughout the Mediterranean as far as Portugal. Archaeological remains have been found that reveal the existence of a very sizeable network which collected and salted the fish, before storing it in large amphorae and shipping it to Rome. The city also required large quantities of building materials for the construction of dwellings and public buildings. Tuff and travertine were both available from quarries around Rome (where the rocks are sedimentary and volcanic in origin), but marble was also needed – and was brought from quarries in Carrara (near Pisa), Spain, the Greek islands and Turkey.

THE WORLD OF LUXURY AND BLACK AFRICA

Nor should we overlook the luxury goods which the nobility, senators, aristocracy and newly wealthy were particularly partial to. Exotic hardwoods, precious stones, metals, Indian and even Chinese silks, works of art – many Greek statues were discovered in the ruins of Pompeii and Herculaneum –, pearls and spices; all these arrived from the four corners of the Empire, but especially from Africa, the Indian Ocean and China. The trade routes crossed the deserts of the Middle East, developed with the opening up of the Indian Ocean and with increased access to the hitherto unknown world of Equatorial Africa, from where gold was brought to pay for the whims of the patrician class and especially those of the Roman matrons. Africa also supplied the wild animals used in the Roman Games. It was a very lucrative trade, and one can still admire the villa built for a friend of Diocletian in Piazza Armerina in Sicily: an architectural jewel with twenty or so large rooms of which the floors are adorned with huge mosaics, still almost intact...not to be missed when visiting Sicily!

THE AMBER ROAD
AND THE ROMAN EMPIRE

Amber is fossilized resin, produced particularly by conifers to protect against plant parasites, animals and sudden changes in temperature. The oldest amber dates from around 300 million years ago and the most recent from about 40 million. Amber younger than 140 million years old frequently has well preserved insects or plant material trapped in it. It was used from the Neolithic period onward to make jewelry and amulets and in the preparation of healing potions. Amber objects have been found from the Bronze Age in many tombs in Northern Europe and the Mediterranean basin. Various Mycenaean archaeological sites and Egyptian, Phoenician, Etruscan and Mesopotamian tombs all point to the widespread distribution of amber, especially amongst the wealthy and in more developed cultures. Amber from the Baltic has been discovered in China, where it was particularly prized by the Han dynasty. It reached them through what is now Russia and Kashmir on the Silk Road to the Empire of the Middle Kingdom. There are many stories and legends surrounding amber. Ovid wrote in his *Metamorphosis* that Phaeton, son of Helios, drove his chariot around the earth and lost control of the horses and nearly burnt the planet; his father struck him with lightning, and the Heliades, his sisters, were inconsolable and wept tears of amber and were gradually transformed into trees.

THE ROMAN ROAD FROM 2ND CENTURY BC

The Romans bought amber from Germanic traders at Carnuntum (near modern-day Bratislava in Pannonia), who in turn procured it from the Aestii tribe, inhabitants of the Baltic littoral, where 90% of the world's amber is still produced. Rome and its empire were the main customers for the `gold of the North´ from the Baltic amber hunters. Wealthy Roman matrons and even the well-off middle classes cried out for amber as a luxury product. Roman women were given amber ornaments and jewelry, such as earrings, necklaces and beads, which they wore around their necks or woven in their hair. Pieces of amber were thought to bring good luck. Pliny the Elder wrote: `The women from the region of Gallia Transpadana (Lombardy) wear amber necklaces. As well as being ornamental, amber has medicinal properties; indeed it is thought it can ward off illnesses of the throat and tonsils´. This belief was also held by the Roman physicians, Celsius (1st century AD) and Galen (2nd century AD), and lasted throughout medieval times. Tacitus (in *Germania*) and Ptolemy (in the *Geography*) wrote at some length on amber and its uses and trade.

The demand in Rome was so great that a veritable Amber Road was created, following an existing route between the Baltic and the Adriatic. Along this road merchants transported and traded hides and furs, honey and wax. Destined for Rome and the Mediterranean basin, these products were paid for mostly with spices, but also with gold (from Sudan and Mali), wine, oil, glassware, coral and Roman silver and gold coins, many examples of which have been found in digs in the Baltic region. The amber was transported via the estuary and valleys of the Oder and Vistula, in southern Poland, and the River Moravia; the route crossed Slovenia and ended at Aquileia, where there were large workshops in which the amber was prepared, sculpted and polished. The principal centers of the trade were Adyga, Atria, Spinea and Aquileia. Traffic on this route was for the most part river-borne. But there was also another road which forked off on the plains of the modern-day Czech Republic, over the Brenner Pass, across Po valley to Rome and the western Mediterranean basin, and from the port of Brindisi, to the eastern basin as well. The Roman traders gradually tried to cut out the Germanic intermediaries, taking advantage of their position as the major customers for amber. In 12 BC the Romans reached the areas of amber production in the north. Nero (56-64 AD), who organized the imperial games, sent a Roman merchant to negotiate directly with the producers, accompanied by a number of Roman cavalry units. The merchant returned to Rome with an enormous cargo. One block of amber weighed as much as thirteen pounds, and the emperor had the canopies of his amphitheatres and his gladiators and their weapons all decorated with pieces of amber!

THE MONOPOLY OF THE TEUTONIC KNIGHTS

The fall of the Roman Empire led to a sharp reduction in the demand for amber, and its market became concentrated mostly within the Baltic region. However, the demand from the Middle East remained buoyant and trade continued along the Amber Road, even if it was no longer on the same scale. Evidence of the interest that the Arabs have always had in this product from northern Europe can be found in the origin of the word `amber´, which derives from the Arabic *anbar*, meaning `an ashy substance with the perfume of musk, which comes from whales´ stomachs and floats in the sea…both grey and black amber float in the sea' – hence the confusion between the two words, amber and ambergris, the second of which is described above. Since the Arab world is such a great distance from where amber is produced, the error is understandable. On the other hand the Greeks and the Romans called it *Elektron, Electrum* or *succinum,* the last still occurring in the term *Succinum acidum,* a homeopathic remedy for hay fever. Amber was in any case well known to the Arabs: the well-known 11th century scholar Abu Rayhan Biruni viewed amber as a remedy for `the man who sees everything in a bad light´, and the philosopher-physician Avicenna used it as one of his preferred ingredients at the court of the Caliph in Baghdad.

The renewal of the amber trade in Europe was due to the Teutonic Knights, whose glory and power originated in the Crusades. In the 13th century they conquered northern Poland and amber once again became a traded commodity, being used extensively for making rosaries. The Knights established a monopoly for the collection and sale of amber in 1312, with Bruges becoming a major center for its crafting and distribution, in competition with Lübeck. Guilds were established in these two cities, with the number of guilds in Bruges soon rising to seventy, together with three centers for teaching apprentices. The city was very well placed on trade routes and maintained links with Venice, which took care of distribution to the Middle East. With fall from power of the Teutonic Knights at the battle of Tannenberg in 1410 the monopoly was transferred to Poland, where and the city of Gdansk became the main center for the production and distribution of amber. But it faced competition from the guild in the city of Königsberg (today's Kaliningrad). The two cities rose to the height of their powers when amber became fashionable as one of the diplomatic gifts that would be presented on official visits and at receptions of European sovereigns. Many crowned heads of state were seduced by the charms of amber. Peter the Great and Catherine the Great II, Frederick-William, Elector of Brandenburg, Frederick of Prussia and Louis XIV were all major customers of the amber cutters. Even Kant possessed a piece of amber containing a fly... the great philosopher said `If thou couldst but speak, little fly, how much more we would know about the past´. Many collectors also wanted pieces of amber for their scientific showcases. Amber marquetry may be found on church altars and in châteaux and palaces, especially in Russia where the celebrated Amber Room was a decorative feature of St Petersburg Palace, but was destroyed, probably during the Second World War.

INDUSTRIAL PRODUCTION, THE SOVIET CRISIS AND RUSSIAN EXPANSION

Production from the Kaliningrad region was restarted with the introduction of new mining techniques and the transfer of the monopoly to the company of Stantien and Becker in 1860; control then passed to the German state in 1898. In 1945, production was incorporated into the Soviet mining system, which developed it until the end of the 1980s. The fall of the Soviet empire led to the liberalization of production and trade, and from 1993 amber hunters began clandestine operations giving rise to an influential black market in amber. The political future of the Kaliningrad enclave will be crucial for the amber industry in the region.

THE ECONOMIC CRISIS THAT RUINED
THE ROMAN EMPIRE

The extent of Ancient Rome's power and influence still impresses us today. The army was hierarchical and well structured and highly efficient in maneuvering on the battlefield; it was a perfectly adapted instrument of conquest and dominance. Pax Romana was founded on a rigid control of the imperial territories, an extensive road and communications network which allowed for the rapid transfer of troops, and an efficient postal system. Moreover, a single common language, or *lingua franca*, and a system of common law both helped to create a single entity and to unite the empire, even if local customs and usages were still tolerated. Trade developed because it could rely on a well organized road system and on navigation that was largely secure. The empire specialized in regional production: wheat from Sicily, Egypt and the lands of the Danube valley; oil from the southern regions of France, Spain and Italy; wine from the south of France; wool and hides from England, Germany and Spain; wood, wax and pitch from the Black Sea region; various metals and ores mined in Tuscany, Germany, France and England; and marble from the Aegean Sea in particular. But this supremacy was founded essentially on military conquest and on agriculture, relying on large estates worked by slaves. When the army was no longer able to produce new sources of revenue (from territorial conquest, slaves and plunder) the state coffers emptied rapidly and the emperors were obliged to raise the level of taxes dangerously high, hitting farmers particularly heavily.

A FIFTY YEAR CRISIS

For half a century, from 235-284 AD, the Roman Empire hung precariously in the balance. Some twenty emperors followed one another in rapid succession, most of them powerful generals who were proclaimed emperor by their soldiers. Often they did not even have the time to reach Rome in order to put into place the reforms necessary to sort out the immediate problems. The origin of the crisis basically lay in a profound military crisis that upset the balance of power and unity in the army whilst at the same time pressure from the barbarians at the borders of the empire, 6000 miles from Rome, was intensifying and gravely threatening the frontier. In 235, the Emperor Alexander Severus was murdered by his soldiers during a military campaign against the Sassanids in Persia. In 260 the Emperor Valerian was severely defeated in battle, once more against the Sassanids, and taken prisoner; Rome could not even muster an expedition to rescue him. The victory of Claudius the Goth over the Goths, in the battle of Naissus in 268, marked a turning point in the crisis, and Claudius's successor Aurelius regained control of Gaul and the kingdom of Palmyra. But the economy was highly vulnerable to the instability of the Roman system. There were no new conquests bringing fresh plunder with which to replenish the empire's coffers. The treasury had to finance state expenditure (especially for paying its 400,000 soldiers) through a heavy increase in taxes which hit farmers, shopkeepers, the poor and minor state functionaries especially hard. Many farmers and shopkeepers had to sell their lands and shops to pay their taxes and avoid ending up as galley slaves. But the pressure from raised taxes also badly affected senators, who traditionally had been exempt, as well as the aristocracy, who were obliged to leave the towns and take refuge in the country. Roads became more dangerous and the tax administration had to rely increasingly on soldiers to raise taxes, with an accompanying deterioration of the tax system, which relied on abuses to extract the tax monies due. Furthermore, the mints were producing silver coins with so little silver content that after a few months in circulation they turned brown and were no longer accepted as currency. Soldiers refused to be paid in these coins and demanded payment in kind (livestock, cereals, salt and gold). Tax collectors too refused to accept these coins any longer and, like the soldiers, demanded payment in kind (even land) in lieu of taxes. Such were the ingredients that led to uncontrollable hyperinflation and destabilization of the economy. When Diocletian came to power the monetary system was on the verge of collapse.

A COMMERCIAL CRISIS AND ITS SOCIAL CONSEQUENCES

The safety of transported goods was no longer assured and trade suffered: traffic within and beyond the empire regressed and the economy became increasingly localized and regional. Owners of estates and big agricultural producers no longer found it worth their while to cultivate large areas of land to produce saleable products because the markets were changing and the volume of demand was reduced. Cholera and plague pandemics were recorded, and a number of occurrences of food shortages; these were infrequent phenomena in the Roman Empire, which had always been able to ensure food supplies and had organized and promoted both personal and public hygiene. But this crisis also had a strong impact on the Roman class structure, traditionally divided into three: senators, wealthy cavalry officers and plebeians. Senators and cavalry officers (mainly high ranking soldiers and wealthy landowners) now formed a highly privileged class known as *honestiores*. Craftsmen and small traders were generally part of the class known as *humiliores*, consisting of less well-off city dwellers and rural smallholders. The former of these two classes retained many of their privileges, whereas the latter saw their privileges steadily eroded and sought protection from the rich landowners, particularly to avoid military service. Indeed the army had ever greater need of soldiers, and the risks were also much increased because there were permanent wars, often on several different fronts. These men who asked for protection from the *honestiores* progressively lost part of their freedom and became `colonized´ – the embryonic stage of the medieval system of feudal serfs and tithes.

Large cities also suffered and lost a portion of their population who went to live in the small towns and villages that were growing up around large farms; these small semi-urban centers needed to protect themselves and often erected defensive walls, especially if they were in the frontier regions of the empire, which was in constant danger of being overrun by barbarians, against whom Rome was now powerless, often having to pay tributes to `buy peace´. Some Germanic tribes were much more belligerent, stronger and better organized than the Romans. In Armenia, Mesopotamia and Syria on the eastern frontier, military pressure from the newly resurgent Persian Empire was unrelenting. Nor was Rome itself exempt: the Emperor Aurelian had a defensive wall built to protect the capital, which after many centuries of security, was again threatened by barbarians.

THE ARRIVAL OF DIOCLETIAN, AND CONSTANTINE'S *SOLIDUS*

Following the Emperor Valerian's fall from power in 260, the Emperor Gallien agreed to allow the partition of the Empire into three large regions for the period of 14 years; this was probably Rome's most difficult moment of the 3rd century. But emperors, mainly Balkan (Illyrian) in origin, such as Claudius and Aurelian, managed to keep the empire united through their military skills and armies. Such emperors were no longer Italian or Iberian, generally cultured or of noble birth; rather they were professional soldiers who had often risen through the ranks and had a talent for leadership. The economic situation was worsening and for at least ten years trade and the economy were limited to the production of basic materials and their barter, on an essentially regional basis. Only Aurelian (270-275) was successful in fully reuniting the Empire and again began minting coins of good quality, but for half a century the state revenues and soldiers' pay was rendered in kind. Between 275 and 277, the frontiers of Upper Germania and Rhetia province were abandoned and the Rhine became the new limit (*limes*) of the empire.

Diocletian (284-305) reorganized the empire; he introduced the principle of tetrarchy which was founded on the establishment of four divisions, each subdivided into dioceses which grouped together several provinces. The frontiers were better protected by defense systems which the Emperor Constantine (306-336) later developed. The Diocletian reforms, which penalized the large estate owners, relaunched the economy and the general climate became more positive with a notable improvement in security. Diocletian tried to bring stability to the value of money; he had a new coin minted, called the *follis*, which enabled inflation to be partially brought under control. Constantine also introduced major reforms to the empire, dividing it into two huge regions: the eastern empire, the capital of which he named Constantinople and undertook its construction, and the western empire, with Rome as the capital. He began minting the *solidus*, which weighed 4.5 grams of gold: a coinage that radically stabilized the monetary system and strengthened the economy. The *solidus* long underpinned the monetary system of the eastern empire and remained a standard reference point well into the medieval era. The economy and political structures had achieved a sufficient level of viability, and two further centuries were to pass before the final crisis of the empire; but the seeds of this were already sown. The system had received a severe blow to its functioning and the army was no longer the conquering war machine of its prime in the 2nd century. Soldiers were reluctant to go off and defend a frontier far distant from their own region, which itself was also often under threat. The enrolment of `barbarian troops´ became the norm in the Roman army and the number of mercenaries constantly grew. Thus the offensive capacity of the army was greatly reduced and its role became largely defensive; this new state of affairs called into question the very fundamentals of the Roman economic system. The problem was now one of knowing how best to manage decline and how long this might take.

THE END OF THE EMPIRE: MILITARY ANARCHY AND THE BARBARIANS

During this period of military anarchy (235-284), there were constant struggles between the armies allied to the senators and those led by the cavalry elite. This situation encouraged incursions made by Rome's enemies along the imperial frontier regions, many of whom were experiencing marked demographic expansion. Soldiers demanded a larger and larger `cut´ (salary plus bonus) for protecting the empire and went so far as to influence the election of emperors, thereby gaining ground in the political and administrative spheres. Farmers, craftsmen and shopkeepers steadily lost their power and even the power and influence of the `greybeard´ senators declined strongly. From 250 onwards barbarian incursions were so frequent that they succeeded in paralyzing all traffic and communications in certain regions. With Pax Romana no longer able to guarantee the peace, many barbarian tribes agreed to refrain from invading Roman territory in return for Roman gold; this caused permanent hemorrhaging from the imperial finances.

VERDUN: A MAJOR CENTER
OF THE EUROPEAN SLAVE TRADE

From the 7th to 11th century, Verdun was an important European commercial center, thanks to its geographical position and to the rivers which allowed easy transport of goods. The town was also one of the principal slave markets, together with Kiev, Regensburg, Prague, Constantinople, Samarkand, Zabid (Yemen), Venice (later) and Malta (from 1530) …exactly like the island of Delos, the main slave market of the Roman Empire, where up to ten thousand slaves were sold every day! During the 6th century, Europe was hit by a massive plague epidemic (the other major outbreak claimed even more victims – a third of the population – in the mid-fourteenth century). As a result, the availability of manpower dropped considerably and wages increased rapidly. In Europe, the spread of serfdom, the decline in economic activity and above all the new wage conditions, all led to the revival of slavery, which had been in decline since the fall of the Roman Empire. Its geographical position enabled Verdun to become pivotal to the slave trade, with all its associated activities – collecting people, castration, and redistributing this human livestock. On this topic, Engels wrote that according to the bishop Liutprand of Cremona in the 10th century, Verdun specialized in the castration and export of eunuchs to Spain to supply the Moorish harems. The slaves came from the Germano-Slavic regions to the east of the rivers Main and Saal – there were organized raids – and northern Europe. The ‘merchandise’ was destined for the whole of western Europe and especially Muslim countries from the Caliphate of Cordoba, with its capital in Andalusia, to Damascus, Antioch,

Constantinople and Baghdad, which were all high growth areas. Slaves coming from Kiev – the word `slave´ derives from `Slav´ – to Verdun, would go on to Narbonne and from there, on foot, down to southern Spain and across to Fez, or by boat to Cairo and the harbors of the Mediterranean Levant.

THANK YOU, CHARLEMAGNE!

Following Charlemagne's victories against the Saxons these slave markets grew rapidly, while southern Spain with its large Muslim market became a massive importer. Slaves were also a major `European exports´, being transported to the Middle East. At the time, western Europe had a large trade deficit, for although it exported fabrics, furs, hides, honey, some base metals and a few arms (the famous Frankish swords), it also imported gold, spices, fruit, silk, glass and other luxury goods (too many expensive things). The slave trade allowed the balance to be redressed. Even if canonical law of the period considered slaves as livestock and property, the Church was not entirely at ease with this trade – which explains why many of the traders in this sector were Jewish. Though the Gospels, the Acts of the Apostles and the Epistles of Saint Peter and Saint Paul sought neither to explain nor to justify slavery, Augustine and Thomas Aquinas said that slavery was the consequence of original sin. We must not forget, however, that many abbeys and convents had slaves and that slaves in large numbers were often among the gifts that the Frankish kings presented to the Church.

VERDUN AND THE MAMELOUKS

The decline of Verdun as a center of the slave trade and of trade in general, came about slowly, especially following the decision of Al-Hakam (796-822) to build an army of 5000 slaves, none of whom could speak Arabic. These were the Mamelouks – the name means `white slave´. In 980, one of his successors, Almanzor, replaced the Mamelouk slaves, who had become too powerful, by slaves from Africa. This essentially political measure had severe economic repercussions for Verdun; the town began to decline commercially by the late 11th century, before recovering some two centuries later as a result of the Champagne Fairs. But the slave trade continued, as is evident, for example, from the fate of the Children's Crusade in 1212. The shepherd Etienne de Cloyes led thousands of children to Marseille, promising them that they were going to liberate the Holy Land, where their elders had failed. A high proportion of this army, made up of children under 12 years old, was kidnapped by slave traders and sold in Egypt.

WORLD CLIMATE CHANGE: ITS IMPACT ON ECONOMIES AND CIVILIZATIONS

`Quintili Vare, legiones redde´`: Varus, give me back my legions! According to Tacitus, this was Augustus's bitter comment when he learned that Publius Quincilius Varus had lost his three legions in a fierce battle against the Cherusci, led by Arminius. The confrontation took place in a wood at Teutberg, in northern Germany, and lasted three terrible days in September, 9 AD. In the course of the battle more than 20,000 well armed Roman soldiers lost their lives. Varus, who was leading the soldiers, committed suicide: he was one of the great Roman generals with a distinguished military career in Africa behind him and an important politician – he had even married Augustus's niece. Handel composed his opera *Arminio* in 1730, and it was performed at Covent Garden in London; but the work was unsuccessful and withdrawn after six performances. At Teutberg extreme weather conditions caused the Romans' defeat; three divisions, six cohorts and three battalions of heavy cavalry were annihilated by the northern warriors, who had neither the preparation nor the military organization of the Romans. At the end of the first day's battle, the Roman troops were hit by a terrible storm, which bogged them down completely. Many of the men were killed by lightning and mud flows poured through the Roman encampment and further demoralized the troops, who already were suffering one of the bloodiest and most severe defeats in Roman military history.

The list of battles or fortunes of war that were strongly influenced by the weather is very long. Hannibal, for example, succeeded in invading Italy thanks to the extremely favorable weather conditions. In the first half of the thirteenth century, Genghis Khan was able to cross the frozen rivers of China with his troops and cross the plains. The `sacred wind´ (*kamikaze*) protected the Japan of the Samurai in the Kamakura period in both 1274 and 1281, when typhoons destroyed the fleets of Kublai Khan, the grandson of Genghis Khan, when he tried to invade. `General Winter´ was Napoleon's main enemy in Russia. History repeated itself in the winter of 1941, the coldest of the century, even bringing the Nazis' armed panzer divisions to a standstill. The valley of Dien Bien Phu experienced twice the average rainfall at the time when the Viet Minh inflicted overwhelming defeat on the French expeditionary force in 1954. During operation Desert Storm against Saddam Hussein in 1990, strong gusty winds prevented Iraqi forces from launching some of their SCUD missiles, as they might have been blown off course and posed a threat to the Iraqi population.

Climate has had a dramatic and radical influence on many civilizations, on the economy of whole regions, on the daily life of numerous peoples – both positively and negatively. In certain instances the climate has worked in favor of development and expansion; in other cases it has been the catalyst for crisis, decline, and even ruin and devastation.

FROM THE FLOOD TO THE CATASTROPHE ON SANTORINI

In the Black Sea region, the Flood, (or perhaps one of many floods) probably occurred between 7000 and 6000 BC. It resulted from a rapid change in climate which seriously affected water levels on the land then separating the eastern Mediterranean (the Dardanelles) and the Black Sea (the Bosphorus). Water flowed into the Black Sea and overturned the life and economy of the people who were living on the fringes of what had been a lake. There remains clear evidence of former centers of habitation that have been discovered in the Black Sea itself, under 300 feet of water. Recent studies by Italian vulcanologists point to a devastating eruption of Mount Etna around 8000 BC resulting in a huge tidal wave (more than 150 feet high!) which could have raised the sea level in the eastern Mediterranean. Toward the end of the era of the Ancient Kingdom of the Nile (2700 – 2200 BC), the peaceful existence of the Egyptian people in the valley of the Nile was completely disrupted by dramatic climate change (drought and a rise in temperature), which substantially lowered the water level in the river. This engendered revolts and social instability on a large scale, thus undermining the regime, which duly fell. Around 1700 BC Egypt was invaded by large numbers of people of Semitic origin (the Hyksos), who seized power in the northern regions of the country; although it not proven, it has been suggested that these people had been forced to emigrate to escape a severe drought which occurred in the westernmost parts of the Asian continent. Historians believe that the fall of the Mycenaean civilization and the decline of Egyptian civilization in the 17th century BC were the result of the Santorini catastrophe. The explosion of this volcano in the east Aegean Sea ejected millions of tons of ash into the atmosphere and produced a tidal wave which hit coasts throughout the eastern Mediterranean.

THE COLLAPSE OF THE HAN DINASTY, THE PARTHIANS AND THE KUSHAN EMPIRE AND THE CRISIS IN ROME IN THE THIRD CENTURY AD

The climate was particularly clement during the two centuries preceding the start of the Christian era and the two subsequent ones: this epoch coincided with the rise of the Roman Empire and that of the Han dynasty in China. The Romans colonized southern England in search of tin and wool, but the region also produced wheat – and wine! But at the beginning of the third century the climate changed abruptly: Rome suffered its serious ʽthird century crisisʼ and military anarchy; and the Han dynasty collapsed (220), the Parthians were overthrown in 224, and the Kushan Empire crumbled (242). During the following centuries the climate in Europe became significantly drier, and the prices of raw materials soared, having a disastrously inflationary effect on the economy and prompting the beginnings of a proto-medieval type of society with the rise of social patronage and a class of vassals who sought protection from the rich landowners ... the first servants of the glebe. Pressure from the ʽbarbariansʼ on the Roman *limes* or frontiers can also be partially explained by their need to find additional lands, since the climate no longer permitted such regular or abundant crops. Throughout Chinese history the pattern repeated itself: drought afflicted the northern population, which then tried to find water and the means of survival in the regions further south. Indeed the Great Wall was built to protect the southern population from invasions from the north.

TANGS, MAYAS AND VIKINGS

Climatologists all agree that the climate became warmer between the 10th and 13th centuries. The impact of this change was radical and recorded worldwide. Europe enjoyed a revival of its economy and trade, with navigation throughout the Mediterranean and the setting up of trading posts, the construction of cathedrals, the steady progression of self-government, a major population increase, and the beginnings of extensive land clearance in order to increase the area under cultivation. From the military angle, there were the first attempts to contain Arab expansionism (with the Crusades and the first coalition of multi-European forces). In England, vines were once again cultivated, and in 874, Norvegians coming from Iceland settled in southern Greenland, a region which – as the name implies – was green and no longer covered by icecap. The Vikings grew highly resistant cereals (oats and rye), raised domesticated animals (except for pigs which were not hardy enough for the climate), and sailed to and traded with the eastern coasts of the North American continent in a new type of ship, known as the *knarr*. This was much wider in the beam than the smaller *drakkar*, which it replaced. From the beginning of the 14th century the climatic conditions changed again and life in Greenland was no longer viable; some Vikings abandoned the region, while those who remained died from cold (there were no trees left to provide wood for heating) and hunger (the cold prevented them from growing crops and killed off their animals).

However, at the beginning of the 10th century, conditions which were extremely favorable in Europe brought catastrophe to certain tropical regions and to the Chinese subcontinent. The Tang dynasty collapsed in 907 following serious peasant revolts provoked by starvation brought on by the drought. The dynasty was weakened initially by wars along its borders, with its first serious defeat at Talas (751) by Muslim forces, and was further undermined by a degree of corruption among the imperial bureaucrats. Power struggles between eunuchs and concubines reduced the Emperor's own power until he could no longer properly control his territories, and he withdrew into the luxury of his great capital at Xian. The dynasty considered to be China's golden age thus went into rapid decline – and recent research on core samples drilled deep into the subsoil reveals a significant drop in rainfall. The Mayan civilization which had arisen amongst the high plateaus of the Mexican and Guatemalan *cordillera* and the sedimentary lands of the Yucatan bordering the Caribbean sea also suffered a major crisis at almost the same time (probably around 909, when the Toltec people came down from the high plains of northern Mexico and seized power). Many factors contributed significantly to this collapse, but a significant rise in temperature and the consequent drought were among the most important. The Mayan civilization was based on the cultivation of squash, beans and above all maize, which requires abundant water. Famine, food shortages and the spread of disease all fuelled the rebellion against a power which was essentially preoccupied with its own interests and spent a large proportion of the wealth produced in the countryside on constructions aimed at enhancing its political and religious power.

THE VOLCANIC ERUPTION OF 1258-59

From the 13th century up until the middle of the 19th century, temperatures fell steadily and the icecap and glaciers slowly advanced. There are many documents confirming this phenomenon, in Europe and America in particular, but there are very few references to other continents. It is possible to date fairly precisely major events which had a dramatic effect on the climate. There was a particularly big volcanic eruption in 1258-59, which ejected large volume of ash and carbon dioxide into the atmosphere. Temperatures fell over a long period because the sun was obscured by the layer of gas and volcanic dust. A similar phenomenon, though on a far greater scale, brought about the extinction of the dinosaurs around 65 million years ago, although experts still disagree whether its the origin was a meteorite or a volcanic eruption.

However, geologists have confirmed that a catastrophic volcanic eruption took place in 1258-59, though they differ as to the precise volcano concerned. Many vulcanologists believe it was the Mexican volcano, El Chichon (around 3375 feet) which was responsible. At the time of its last eruption, in 1982, 3500 people were killed by the lava flow and ash, and a new crater was created, now filled by an acid lake. Other vulcanologists cite the Quilotoa volcano in Ecuador. In any case its effects in Europe are well recorded: a dry fog in France, a type of lunar eclipse in England, severe winters throughout Europe, and famine in England, Germany, France and northern Italy.

The impact of this little ice age – not caused by volcanic activity alone – was considerable: during the first half of the 14th century it resulted in famines in Europe. Around 1315 -17 between 10% and 15% of the European population starved to death; subsequently the Hundred Years War and the food shortages of 1332 prepared the way for the spread of the Black Death of 1350. At this same period in China climate problems were undermining the Mongolian Yuan Dynasty; popular discontent helped foment the peasant revolts. The final blow was provided by Zhu Yuanzhang, the founder of the Ming dynasty, who led the Red Turban Movement; under pressure from the rebels the Emperor Huizong fled and took refuge in Mongolia. The long decline of the Khmer Empire began around 1351 with the first invasions from the Thai region: water shortage was a fundamental cause of the collapse of the Khmers. Another example: the Anasazis of southwest Colorado, who along with other sedentary populations living in the Four Corners region left the region around 1300 and disappeared from history. It is likely that all these peoples abandoned their lands following major climatic change, in particular drought. The pre-Incan rich civilization of Tiwanaku (south of Lake Titikaka, Bolivia) fell apart at around the same moment. It was destroyed by a terrible drought that created very difficult conditions for the population and local power and opened the door to the Incas' invasion. Once more another pre-Incan civilization, living in the Bolivian regions of the Amazon basin, suffered severe weather disruptions at the end of the 13th century; the civilization of Moxos which had a very sophisticated irrigated agriculture, with the cultivation of 20,000

small artificial islands in the Amazon basin, disappeared and
their region was rapidly invaded by Incan populations. It seems
the fall of these three civilizations in America was largely due to
`el Niño´ that brought disastrous droughts in some regions and
dramatic rains and floods in other areas.

THE LITTLE ICE AGE BETWEEN THE 16TH AND 19TH CENTURIES

We are familiar with the great Flemish painters' many depic-
tions of frozen rivers and canals being enjoyed by skaters, gossiping
peasant women, children playing with sledges and men playing
skittles on the ice. In Holland and in England there were even ice
fairs held on the frozen surfaces. In Europe the famines of 1590,
1630, 1661, 1694 and 1709 were the direct result of poor harvests
brought on by particularly cold winters and wet summers. There
are detailed records of the advance of glaciers in the Alps, which
tell of small villages crushed or swallowed up by the advancing ice.
During the winter of 1780 the port of New York was completely
frozen and people could walk between Manhattan and Staten
Island on the ice. During the winter of 1794-95 the French General Jean-Charles Pichegru sent his hussars to capture the Dutch
fleet which was trapped by the ice – fourteen ships of the line with
850 cannons, powerless against their assailants because the angle
of the fire was too high. Behind the idyllic scenes depicted by
painters – especially the two Bruegels – and this military incident,
there lay food shortages, famine, disastrous harvests, population
migration for those seeking the means to survive and many deaths,
partly because people were unable to keep warm due to the rise in
the price of wood. In Europe there was one interval, from 1709 to
1740, when temperatures were more normal, which coincided
with an economic upturn. This was boosted by the arrival of large
quantities of gold from Brazil and the end of the great continental
wars, together with a general political thaw following the death of
Louis XIV, as has been shown by Emmanuel Le Roy Ladurie[1].

---

1. Emmanuel Le Roy Ladurie (born 1929) is a noted French historian whose work is mainly
concerned with the history of the peasantry.

However, temperatures began to fall once again, bringing food shortages and famine. One of the main catalysts of the French revolution was the terrible weather, both cold and wet, in the period preceding the fall of the Bastille. Nor should we overlook the `summerless year´ of 1816 and the serious famine of 1816-17 caused by the terrible eruption of the volcano Tambora in Indonesia; when it exploded (in April 1815) the summit lost 4100 feet. Another Indonesian volcanic explosion, Krakatoa, in August 1883 had a similar effect, with the ejection of millions of tons of ash and carbon dioxide into the atmosphere. However, if this last incident is excluded, the average temperature began steadily rising from the second half of the 19th century. Industrialization, the changes in sunspot activity and the more or less cyclical circulation of cold and warm water in the Pacific – the phenomena of El Niño and La Niña – and the interactions among them are the basis of climatic change, which will inevitably have a dramatic, or even catastrophic impact on human life.

THE RISE AND FALL OF THE MAYAN CIVILIZATION

The Mayas built perfect pyramids; they knew mathematics and were very advanced in astronomy; they invented the concept of zero (300 years before Indian mathematicians); they grew maize on the plains of the Yucatan and on the slopes of the Guatemalan volcanoes (the word *maya* comes from `maize´). They invented chocolate, which they extracted from the cocoa bean; they had a calendar that was more accurate than the Roman Julian calendar, introduced by Julius Caesar, and more sophisticated even than the Gregorian calendar introduced in the 16th century, which represented something of a revolution in Baroque Europe. Like Rome, they had public baths; and they had a highly developing trading system between the limestone regions of the Atlantic coast and the volcanic regions of the Pacific. They traded and exchanged obsidian, a substitute for metal, on a large scale and built an advanced road system.

However, in common with all meso-American civilizations, they did not have the wheel and knew little of the metallurgy of base metals, though were skilled with precious metals, which they worked with both taste and sophistication. Their society was primarily theocratic and military, with a highly well-defined and highly complex structure. Their religious rites were cruel, their ceremonies magnificent and the luxury and pomp associated with power was ostentatious. They probably invented ball games, since they used rubber ... and the captain of the winning team had the honor of being sacrificed to the gods!

AN ABRUPT AND VIOLENT END TO A CIVILIZATION

This relatively sophisticated civilization, of which traces date back to the 5th century BC (when Athens was at the height of its powers), originated in the southern regions of Mexico, Guatemala, Belize and the Yucatan. It reached its peak between the 7th and 9th centuries, with the building of towns and imposing monuments. Palenque, Copan, Quiriza, Naranjo, Uaxactum, Xultan Xamantum and their ruins are proof of their achievements, both as architects and mathematicians.

However, around the year 900, the Mayan civilization collapsed suddenly and brutally, with people abandoning the towns, especially in the south. The debate over the causes of this crisis has long been open: historians, sociologists, political scientists, climatologists and geologists have thrown themselves into the unresolved cultural and scientific dispute. The debate has, however, borne fruit, since it has increasingly encouraged an interdisciplinary approach and complex techniques of research and analysis.

DROUGHT, POLITICAL CRISIS, EPIDEMIC OR WAR?

The many hypotheses formulated by researchers are sometimes contradictory, sometimes complementary. The most common theory is that of a terrible drought which would have devastated a civilization based on agriculture – predominantly maize (Indian corn), which although high in yield, also requires a lot of water during the four to five months taken for the corn cobs, made up of 6-700 grains, to ripen. Soil bores taken by geologists in the area show that it suffered its first drought in 760 A.D.; a further decade of low rainfall occurred around 810, and in 869 there was a severe drought lasting three years. The final incidence of drought occurred around 910, and this was even more severe and lasted for six years[1]. The Mayan civilization almost certainly made mistakes in managing its resources and in storing its basic foodstuffs and water, though their knowledge of hydraulics was highly developed

---

1. The Tang dynasty (618-907AD) fell at the same period due to a sharp rise in temperatures accompanied by a very severe drought

and recalls that of the Etruscans, the people who lived in Tuscany between the 7th and 2nd centuries BC. Their mistakes probably had disastrous consequences for the starving population. The already delicate ecological balance was aggravated because they did not practice rotation or allow the soil to lie fallow, thus reducing its fertility and productivity.

Furthermore, the political structure was always very weak: it comprised a number of small kingdoms and cities – like Greece from the 5th to the 2nd centuries BC, or Renaissance Italy – engaged in constant struggle against each other and incapable of uniting in the face of a common enemy. These wars sapped the energies of the people to no purpose, because there was no convincing victory and therefore no new territories were won: it was an early and disastrous `Balkanization´ of the region. The hypothesis of revolts and total revolutions on the part of the people, against those in power who were incapable of finding economic solutions, may also be entertained; but there was no destruction of the public buildings and monuments associated with the regime, which renders the theory less likely. Some experts speak of serious epidemics such as malaria or yellow fever, which, in reality, were transmitted from Europe by the Spanish `conquistadores´ at the beginning of the 16th century.

Nevertheless, it is quite likely that infectious diseases did ravage a population already affected by a food crisis. Earthquakes may have hit the western regions (Guatemala), but certainly not the limestone regions of the Atlantic coast. An economic crisis probably sapped a great civilization which underwent a renewed upsurge with the invasion of the Toltecs; the mix of the two civilizations was to bring about the construction of towns like Chichen Itza in the Yucatan. In 1546 the power of the Mayans came to an end, their military forces crushed by the Spanish conquistadores. There was sporadic opposition from a permanent guerrilla movement which lasted until 1697, but then Martin de Ursua Tayassal took Itza-Maya, the last town to resist.

THE COWRIE SHELL: ONE OF THE FIRST INTERNATIONAL CURRENCIES

Cockles and other types of shells were long used as money in trade or as a means of storing value; they were also used to decorate clothes and sandals by both western and oriental peoples; and they can be seen still on the remains of walls or as decoration around mosaics, in villas and imperial palaces. Nero's *Domus Aurea* (Golden House) had shells encrusted on its walls.

Rather like precious stones and metals, shells were symbols of wealth, but for somewhat different reasons. Shells provided mother of pearl and pearls, which were prized for in the making of precious objects. But sea-shells were also valued for the reddish-purple dye extracted from the secretions produced by certain marine mollusks (murex). The Phoenicians employed this technique, and the difficulty of dyeing clothes red added to the symbolic value of these fabrics, which were used by priests and kings. The Assyrians even went so far as to demand red clothing as a tribute from peoples they conquered. In the mind of the common people, shells were also associated with luxury foods – oysters were served at imperial Roman banquets and at the tables of senators, wealthy landowners and merchants. In the 19th century, the well-off middle classes throughout Europe adored oysters, which were consumed with champagne – the ultimate symbol of high living.

Scallops and other shells were in use before the introduction of coins or bars of gold or other precious metals, and before the treatment of metal ores or the development of smelting techniques. But collecting shells called for skill and knowledge of the seabed. Many shells have been found in mountainous regions and areas remote from any sea, suggesting that they had a symbolic value which was used for trade and accumulating wealth.

AN ANCIENT CURRENCY IN AFRICA

Cowries are the most widely found shells throughout China, southeast Asia, Africa and the Mediterranean basin. But they originally came from the atolls of the Maldives, islands that were little known to sailors. The shells arrived in the holds of Arab cargo ships: the sailors used them as ballast. But in Africa the cowrie was a sign of wealth, a hedge against inflation and a currency that was accepted everywhere. The cowrie was the foundation of the wealth of countries such as Mali, Nigeria and Dahomey (modern Benin). For several centuries, the kings of the Mossi people (part of the population of Burkina Faso today) demanded an annual tribute of a million cowries from their vassals. In the Red Sea region, the shells were traded for goods carried by the African caravans to the coastal areas. These caravans traveled back and forth between the coast and the desert regions of North Africa, the banks of the Niger and the Atlantic coast, over distances of up to 13,000 miles, on journeys lasting as long as twelve months. In Marco Polo's time, Venetian merchants bought cowries to send on to the markets of North Africa to be traded for gold dust coming from Mali and the Sudan. Arabs, however, did not prize the cowrie. For example, the great traveler Ibn Battuta objected when he was paid in cowries in the Maldives. Nevertheless he drew up a very exact exchange rate: 1150 cowries for a *dinar* of gold. Two centuries later, you could buy a gold ducat with only 400 cowries, showing how much the cowrie had been revalued in the interim! African money-changers became specialists in the cowrie exchange rate: the most skilful used their hands to weigh them and their calculations were very precise, because we know that 16,000 cowries weighed 41 pounds. European slave-traders paid for their human merchandise in cowries and glass beads made in Venice! At the beginning of the 17th century, a slave cost 55 pounds of cowries in the markets of the Ivory Coast.

For over a thousand years the cowrie was used as an international currency. However, around the middle of the 19th century, colonial traders began to flood the markets of the Gulf of Guinea with fake cowries. These were similar in appearance to real cowries but were in fact Cypraea Annulus shells, found on the beaches of western Africa, from Zanzibar to Pemba on the coast of Kenya, and considerably less valuable – a serious blow to the stability of the currency. Further, between 1868 and 1870, around seven million cowries and other shells were poured into African markets by British merchants, largely through the port of Lagos. The value of the cowrie slumped and the colonial powers introduced their own coins, minted first in Europe, then later in the capital cities of Africa. Even today the buildings of the central banks in Bamako, Mali, Cotounou and Benin are decorated with stylized cowries. The shell is also on one face of the Ghanaian *cedi* coin. The custom of paying for goods in cowries was ended, however, only through the use of decrees and military might (especially by the French and British). The farmers of the Volta region rebelled with violence against the French authorities when the latter no longer accepted cowries in payment of taxes and Francisco de Souza, the most famous slave trader on the Slave Coast, went bankrupt when the United States decided to stop accepting the legal tender of cowries as a currency.

THE YEAR 1000: BAGHDAD
IS THE CENTER OF THE WORLD

Baghdad is a city whose very name is evocative: for centuries it conjured up the idea of mysteries, marvels, stories and legends, flying carpets and the tower of Babel. It conjures up the magic phrase `Open Sesame!´ from Ali Baba, which opened the door of the cave which hid a host of treasures; or again, the *Thief of Baghdad* and the debonair charm of Douglas Fairbanks, the Adonis of the cinema from1910 to 1920. The cradle of civilizations, the heart of Islam, the bridge between Mesopotamia and the rest of the world, the city of Baghdad was founded in 762 AD by the Abbasid dynasty (750-1050). Eleven years earlier, the Arabs had vanquished the Chinese on the banks of the River Talas, in Turkistan, and thirty years earlier, Charles Martel had halted the Moorish invasion of Gaul (Poitiers, 732). The golden political age of Baghdad coincided with the Caliphate of Haroun and his successor, Al-Mamoun (786-809). The city's success continued and it underwent impressive cultural and economic expansion: at this period Baghdad was probably the wealthiest city anywhere in the world.

BAGHDAD – `A GOD-GIVEN´ CITY

The city, whose name means `God-given´, was situated in a very fertile plain, crossed by numerous canals linking the Euphrates and the Tigris. It was officially named *Madinat al Salaam* (City of Peace) and destined to become the fortified headquarters of the

Caliph's troops – which explains its circular shape and the double concentric walls erected for protection. Around the central core, other districts sprang up, monuments were built and Baghdad became a large city with immense gardens, magnificent parks and sumptuous palaces. Under the influence of the Abbasid, Baghdad became the center of the medieval world and attracted a wide variety of peoples, traders and intellectuals. Its wealth led to the construction of mosques, schools, large private and public baths, hospitals and markets, through which there passed spices, silk and metals, including gold. The gold came from West Africa, the spices from the Indian Ocean, the silk from China and the metals from Europe. Thus European, Indian and Chinese traders were all familiar with Baghdad, the crusaders from the First Crusade (1095-1099) dreamt of the city, and other Arab caliphs tried to emulate its success.

A WORLD CULTURAL CENTER, DESTROYED BY THE MONGOLS

From the 6th to the 10th centuries the Baghdad became the world center for the study of mathematics and Arabic became the international language of science. Mathematicians translated, and thus saved, the principal Greek scientific texts, and assimilated the Indian number system (including the zero) to develop algebra, astronomy and alchemy. Arabic literature blossomed in the manner of the later European Renaissance and Muslim theology was extensively developed. This center of world culture drew scientists and men of letters from all over Europe, to a marvelous crucible of learning that benefited from the relative stability of the period on both the military and political fronts – Saladin recaptured Jerusalem in 1187 and the Muslims conquered the Ganges basin as far as Bengal in 1192. However, in the following century, the Mongol invasions of Iran (1235-1239) brought about the fall of the Baghdad caliphate. In 1258 the town was conquered and sacked by Huluga Khan, grandson of Genghis Khan and first Mongol king of Iran. It was the end of the Abbasid dynasty and thereafter Baghdad went into rapid decline.

MONKS DRIVE THE MEDIEVAL ECONOMY

As early as the 4th century Christians in the Nile Valley withdrew from society to consecrate their lives to prayer and the mortification of the flesh; these anchorites became the first monks and laid down the rules of conduct for their communities. But the real spread of monasticism took place from the beginning of the 10th century in Europe. All monasteries drew their inspiration from the precepts laid down four centuries previously by St Benedict, the founder of the monastery at Monte Cassino in central Italy. A number of different monastic communities were founded: black monks (the Cluniacs), white monks (the Cistercians, who wore habits of undyed wool and refused to wear the dyed, black habit), and other orders, each with their distinctive rules, depending on their patron saint (Benedict, Francis and others). But at their basis, they shared a single religious vocation and conjointly instigated a great cultural and economic revolution.

EUROPE OF THE DARK AGES IS SAVED BY THE MONASTIC ORDERS

Europe was going through a difficult period: the barbarian invasions in the north and east, continual attacks from Barbary Pirates, the loss of a centralized political system (following the fall of Charlemagne's Empire) all weighed heavily on its economic development. European towns and cities lived as microeconomies, centered on their local area and cut off from the rest. The growth of the abbeys helped to restart the European economy just as much as the beginnings of maritime trade between cities such as Venice, Pisa, Amalfi and Genoa and the Middle East, the most economically developed region at this time. The choice of the monks to live according to their religious ideals, in poverty and withdrawn from the world, free from all secular and feudal links obliged them to renounce the traditional sources of revenue hitherto used by the churches, such as payment for religious services, tithes, taxes on mills and bakeries, and so on. Monastic communities needed therefore to organize themselves independently and to establish rules for the `management´ of their resources.

The success of the abbeys, which was often spectacular, was based on three fundamental factors: the amassing of lands donated by the nobility, which were often inferior in quality but were improved by the monks; employment of the many 'converted' brothers who were drawn to the monasteries in large numbers; and a rational approach to planning and organizing efficiently the administration of resources. Many rich people donated money and lands to abbeys and convents as death approached (known as *donatio mortis causa*). It is estimated that between 30% and 40% of all land in the western world belonged to monasteries in the medieval period. Cluny specialized in helping the departed by offering up regular prayers for the deceased person in return for an inheritance – a spiritual activity that ensured substantial returns.

MONKS AS FARMERS, PHYSICIANS, HERBALISTS AND CULTURAL GUARDIANS

The monks started by improving poor quality land, then constructed their buildings, employing the same techniques which would later be adopted for cathedrals. They used new techniques to cultivate the less fertile soils, and built irrigation systems on the basis of know-how acquired from the Middle East and inspired by the Phoenicians, Etruscans and Romans. They stored grain in barns, selling whatever was surplus to their needs; they grew vines to produce wine for mass and again sold the surplus. Wines from Burgundy (Gevrey-Chambertin and Clos Vougeot, among others), from the Gironde, from Spanish hillside and from the Po valley were sent all over Europe. They were even exported to Scandinavia, thanks to the monks, who were both excellent winemakers and astute merchants.

In the agricultural sector, the monks began by letting land lie fallow, but soon became methodical farmers who maintained forested areas (so important for the agricultural restructuring of Europe), raised animals, rotated crops and brought organization to agriculture in general; their skills and practices were subsequently adopted by the large estate owners of the medieval period. The surplus wool produced by monks was sold and exported to various markets. Monastic herbalists developed a pharmacopeia in their gardens and became the first apothecaries; they imported many ideas from the Middle Eastern pharmacopeias and took part in the first wave of the development of western pharmacy, which had been forgotten since the time of the Greeks and Romans. Their infirmaries nursed members of their own community, as well as travellers and local peasants who asked the monks for help. Thus the monasteries became dispensaries and hospitals which took care of sick people who had no money, irrespective of their religion, political affiliation or nationality. The accommodation of travellers and passing clerics made these religious sestablishments the embodiment in embryo of today's large international hotel chains.

As the needs of the community developed the monks were obliged to learn all types of crafts and trades. Thus they became, variously, blacksmiths, masons, cobblers and carpenters; adept at all trades of the time, they not only deployed existing techniques, but developed new ones. The ironworks at Fontenay, northern Burgundy, was probably the second largest industrial building in medieval Europe after the Venice Arsenal.

The monks also received gifts of salt from salt pans, and through managing its production and, once again, selling off the surplus in the markets, became one of the major suppliers of this essential commodity in medieval times. Their knowledge of hydraulics allowed them to divert rivers and canals and have running water in monasteries. Their solitary life obliged them to create the first private bathrooms, for often each monk lived in his own cell or little house (as at the Charterhouse of Pavia, in Lombardy) and was entirely cut off from the rest of the monastic community.

TRANSCRIBERS, *INCUNABULA* AND THE RESCUE OF WESTERN CULTURE

The monks who spent all day transcribing Latin or Greek texts and translating from the Hebrew or Arabic into Latin saved mankind's cultural heritage, allowing Europe to preserve and protect that part of its culture which would otherwise have been lost in the oblivion of collective ignorance. They paved the way for the Renaissance and helped gain time ahead of the spread of printing in Europe.

Initially monks used parchment for the transcription of their writings and illuminations. For this they had to raise sheep for their skin, and then treat it using highly sophisticated techniques. Then, with the arrival in Europe of the technique of paper-making from the Arabs around 1000 AD, the monks began to produce large quantities of paper, which they used for their copying and translating. The Italian word *carta* is derived from the other Italian word *quarto*, which means a sheet of paper, folded into four; even today we talk of quarto, ottavo etc. to indicate the size of a book. The word `charthouse´ comes straight from *carta* and there are further derivations such as `charterhouse´, `chartreuse´ or `certosa´.

Thus the monasteries became major centers of parchment and paper production. But their most important role remained that of copying and illuminating books, up until the introduction of the printing press. Writing tools needed to be very accurate, and goose quills were considered to be the best – quills plucked from the left wing were used by right-handed people and vice versa. Goose husbandry became the natural choice of monasteries and the production of writing quills yet another near-monopoly which monks held outside their communities. As Vespasian said, `Money has no smell´. Moreover the monks developed the chemistry of colors in order to make their illuminations; for example, blue was obtained from lapis lazuli powder, red from lead sulfate (in Italian, called *minio*, whence `miniature´ etc.). A brief account of the techniques of illumination may be found in Orhan Pamuk's *My name is red*.

The development of color techniques and knowledge gave rise to the materials that would be used by medieval and Renaissance painters. But the monopoly of the religious transcribers and illuminators was soon threatened by lay craftsmen, who specialized in the same type of work in the towns, to supply the substantial demands of churches, princes, noblemen, universities, merchants, bankers and the newly wealthy. The price varied according to the quality of the work: for example, in 1463, the illuminator Simon Marmion received a sum of money for his work that paid for the re-roofing of his house in Valenciennes. But a professional artist of average skill had to complete sixty decorations a year to live comfortably. With the development of civil society, the competition with lay individuals caused problems for the monks. They responded by specializing in other products such as high quality wines, beer, cheeses, wool and medicinal preparations. Their prices were very competitive since they did not need to take salaries into account, and had access to sophisticated, modern techniques, since itinerant and foreign monks played a major role in transmitting knowledge and techniques.

MUCH COVETED RICHES

The monasteries therefore became centers of wealth which attracted the envy of powerful men and even of the Church itself. It was not by accident that Henry VIII decided to `secularize´ the monasteries of Great Britain. In 1530, nation's patrimony consisted of 825 monasteries with 9300 monks and nuns, whose overall revenue was 175,000 pounds, or more than twice the revenue of the English Crown at the time. In Sweden, King Gustav took the same measures: he `nationalized´ the properties of the Church and abbeys between 1500 and 1550, much to the benefit of the Crown treasury.

THE SILK ROAD: CARRIER OF GOODS, CULTURE, RELIGIONS ... AND VIRUSES

The Silk Road is probably the oldest, and certainly the longest road in the world. Its existence depended on the vicissitudes and balance of power between the principal empires which dominated the territory between the Mediterranean and China. However, it should not be thought of as a single silk road, but as two, at least; and there was also a maritime route whose use varied inversely with the fortunes of the land route. We owe the term Silk Road to the German geographer, Ferdinand von Richthofen, who in 1877 began to speak of the *Seidenstrasse* in his works about China.

SILK AND OTHER PRECIOUS MERCHANDISE

As well as silk transported from east to west along this road, there was other merchandise too, with very specific characteristics: it had to be extremely light in weight and to have a very high intrinsic value at its destination. These two fundamental characteristics were the conditions for transporting goods across thousands of miles of terrain, often highly hazardous in nature for the merchants and their camel drivers, who neither wanted nor were able to transport heavy or low value goods. Thus the caravans transported gold from the mines of Sudan, silver from the mines of central Europe, lapis-lazuli from the mines of Badakhshan and Afghanistan, jade from the Yarkand and Khotan mines in China and other precious stones. The Silk Road was also the main route for spices from India, porcelain from China, linen and woolen fabrics from Europe, amber from the Baltic, African and Indian ivory, lacquer-ware from China, coral from the Mediterranean, glass (first Roman and Middle Eastern, then Venetian), arms, medicines, plants, fruit, coins and objects of artistic value such as jewelry, statuettes, and religious items. The road was the main communication route between Europe and the Mediterranean basin, the Indian and Persian plateaus and lowland China. News, rumors and strategic information all traveled at a camel's pace.

CULTURE, TECHNIQUES AND MICROBES

As well as caravans, the road was used by soldiers, ambassadors, clerics, the occasional tourist, spies and slaves. Indeed it was Chinese slaves who took their knowledge of iron-working and later paper to the Arabs. However, it was not until 550 that the first recorded instance of espionage occurred: two monks stole some silkworm eggs and mulberry seeds from China to take them to Byzantium. The secret of silk production was thus revealed and silk production began in southern Europe. Many other technological inventions from China arrived in Europe, via Arabia, along the same route. But disease and epidemics were also carried along it; for example, after ravaging the province of Yunnan around 1330, the Black Death came to Europe this way, causing a serious pandemic. Soldiers trying to escape the disease brought it to the port of Kaffa, in the Crimea, from where ships carried the virus to Constantinople and then on to southern Italy and Marseille in Genoan ships.

En route, all these travellers crammed into the caravanserais, or inns, which were built along the road. They made journeys of varying distance, some commodities being transported for a few hundred miles and others for almost its entire length, some 4500 miles. The caravanserais served as staging-posts for the caravans. In them, men could rest, have a hot meal of fresh produce and receive medical care; animals were provided with food, water and stabling; the merchandise could be stored, sold at local markets or sent on to other destinations. Money-changers, monks and prostitutes all offered their services. With the spread of the techniques of Italian bankers, an embryonic banking system grew up, with the important participation of the Buddhist monasteries, which served as repositories for the money.

THE TRAILS BETWEEN XIAN AND ANTIOCH – AND THE MARITIME ROUTE

An axis of communication was well frequented only in peaceful periods, when men, animals and merchandise could travel without fear or hindrance. Moreover, both the importing and exporting region needed to be enjoying an era of growth. The use of the road was greatly dependent, therefore, on events in progress and on the growth of empires through which various sections of the road passed. The volume of commercial traffic was significantly affected by the economic development of such empires. Over long periods of time, only certain segments of the road were accessible, perhaps for just a few hundred miles, where they passed through a region of economic and political stability; other segments could only be taken by a few caravans.

The route was in fact a network of trails that ran from Chang'an (today known as Xian, where the Terracotta Army was discovered) to Antioch (modern Syria). It had to go around the Taklamakan Desert, one of the most arid areas of the world, as well as the mountains of Northern India, in order to reach Yarkand and Kashgar, from where it continued to Persia or India; Samarkand, Bukhara and Merv (in modern Turkmenistan) were major staging points. Then the Caspian Sea had to be by-passed in order to reach the Black Sea, the Persian Gulf and the Mediterranean. Of these various destinations, the Mediterranean was the most important, because of the markets along the Phoenician coast eager for the merchandise and the ships waiting to take the goods to other markets even further west, where there was high demand and correspondingly higher price. Alternatively, the sea route began in the ports of the China Sea – nowadays the Philippines, Brunei, Vietnam and Malacca –, transiting through Singhalese (Sri Lanka) and Indian ports, to arrive in Persia and southern Egypt; the merchandise then passed through Alexandria for western Europe and, via Venice, to northern Europe.

HOW THE ROMANS BOUGHT SILK FROM THE CHINESE EMPIRE

The life of the road was intimately linked with that of the empires through which it passed. Political expansion, economic development, flourishing trade and security on the road itself, throughout its length (or specific parts of it), all contributed to the prosperity of the Silk Road. It did not necessarily have to be operational for the whole of its length; it sufficed that a couple of thousand, or even a few hundred, miles of road were passable for the road to function.

The land route began its long existence in the middle eastern basin under the rule of the Assyrians, who wanted to control traffic through the Caucasus region. But the first real section of the road started with Cyrus (556-530 BC) and the empire which dominated the Iranian plateau, part of the Indus valley and Turkmenistan. The Royal Persian Road, built during the 5th century BC was a vast project, though it is probable that parts of it existed as long ago as 3500 BC. Clearly Alexander the Great's military and political conquests when he built his Persian-Greek Empire, reaching as far as the Indian frontier, helped extend the road. Furthermore, the creation of the Indian Empire of the Mauryan Dynasty (320-185 BC) and the beginnings of the Qin dynasty in China increased the need for a transcontinental road. Paradoxically, it was the division of Alexander's Empire between the Seleucides and the Parthians which served to demonstrate that the road had a real economic function in terms of communication, trade and culture: Greek art was exported to India and the genre of Greek-Buddhist art began to spread across central Asia. At the same time, exchanges began to take place between the Qin Empire and that of the nomads of the steppe, the *Xiongnu*, as the Chinese called them (also known as the Hun tribes), in 220 BC. Once again the road played an essential role in this cultural and commercial exchange. A period of glory and great activity was soon to follow, with the rise of the Chinese Han civilization, which, having crushed the Huns (121 BC) succeeded in creating a unified Chinese empire. Going westward, the next empire along the road was that of the Indo-European dynasty of the Kushana, which occupied the lands between China and the Parthians, who in turn controlled the territory up to the *limes* or frontiers of the Roman Empire, which was in a state of productive ferment. This period between the 1st century BC and the second century AD was an exceptional era for the Silk Road. During this time it enjoyed considerable political and military stability throughout its length, coupled with a strong demand for Asian goods (especially spices and silk) on the part of the Romans, who in turn sent gold, silver, amber, glass and coral to the East. High value goods were transported, the fiscal administrations along the route earned large sums in taxes, merchants were protected by the soldiers of powerful empires, and monks of different religions could disseminate their ideas.

The Romans tried unsuccessfully to by-pass the Parthian Empire and make direct contact with the Seric Empire another name for Chinese, from which we derive the terms `sericeous´ (silken) and `sericulture´ (silk growing). The troops of the Emperor Trajan reached as far as Ctesiphon in 116 AD, probably a day's march from the frontier with China, but there no direct contact occurred between the two empires. They also tried the maritime route: convoys left Berenice (in Egypt) and set out for Ceylon. These expeditions had some success, as the boats returned to Egypt laden with spices, silk, fabrics, sandalwood and indigo. But this trade was never more than a marginal one.

The Roman historian Florus described the visits of numerous delegations from the Middle East, India and the Seric Empire with presents of a diplomatic nature. Pliny the Elder also referred to silk arriving from the Seric Empire; he says it is a material made from a substance found in forests. Seneca criticized Roman matrons who dressed in silk – which merely veiled their nudity... The Romans were very taken with this product and also imported it by sea; the Egyptian Red Sea ports, which the Romans controlled, received Indian spices, silk and other Chinese products which were shipped mainly from Southern Chinese ports (Vietnam), though the ships were mostly Indian.

THE ROAD REACHES ITS ZENITH IN 2ND CENTURY AD

The zenith of this period, in the second century AD, was attributable to the more or less peaceful balance of power between four empires: Roman, Parthian, Kushan and Han. During the same period it is known too that both Greek culture and Buddhist religion were widely disseminated. But the equilibrium was shattered when the Han Empire in China fell due to internal weakening and incursions by the Xiongnu into the extensive Tarim basin, resulting in China breaking up into three kingdoms (220-280). The Parthians were overthrown (224), Rome underwent a crisis of military anarchy (during the 3rd century) and the Kushan Empire disintegrated. These crises in all four empires almost at the same time very badly affected trade and traffic on the Silk Road. The rise to power of the Sassanids in Iran (226-651) stabilized the situation, but in the meantime the sea route had benefited a good deal and contributed to the birth of Indian political power with the Guptas (308-535). The collapse of the western Roman Empire brought about a huge fall in the demand for the products transported along the road. It was not until the establishment of the Sogdian Empire in 558 that the volume of traffic returned to its normal level – between at one end, Constantinople and the Byzantine Empire, and at the other the Chinese Sui dynasty (581/618). However, the struggles between the Turks and the Sogdian Turks, the rise of Islam, the fall of the Sui followed by that of the Tang dynasty (which collapsed in 907) and of the Khazars (replaced by the Russians in 968) all detracted from the safety of travelers on the road, and it underwent a major decline for many years. These events, however, were a blessing for the sea route, which benefited those powers which were oriented toward the sea: the Song dynasty (960-1279), and the kingdoms of the Indochinese peninsula and southern India.

PAX MONGOLICA RESTORES THE ROAD'S FORTUNES

It was now the turn of the Mongols to take control of a large part of the road. Their 'pax mongolica' permitted travel between the Black Sea and China without the need for a military escort. It was during this time that Marco Polo traveled on the road, in what was undoubtedly its golden age. This stability also allowed Islam to make converts in eastern Asia. But the Mongol Empire collapsed in the 14th century. Once again the road was divided into different segments; and with the arrival of the Ming dynasty in China

(1368), the country became increasingly closed to the outside world over the next two centuries. Tamerlane's brief moment of glory did little to halt the slow decline of the road. There was one final attempt to create a central Asiatic empire: the Bactrian peoples, led by Baber of Samarkand (1519-1530), founded the Great Mogul empire in India. In the meantime, the circumnavigation of Africa opened a new route for trade and exploration which came into direct competition with the Silk Road. Larger ships and the creation of the East India Companies made the overland route increasingly uncompetitive, though it was still used to transport goods on a local or regional scale. The death blow was finally delivered when the first steamship came into service and, above all, with the opening of the Suez Canal in 1869, which transformed the price structure of transporting goods and passengers between Europe and Asia.

THE TEMPLARS: MYSTERIES, ECONOMIC POWER AND DECLINE

The Order of the Temple was founded in 1119 by Hugues de Payns and eight other knights, after the first crusade to the Holy Land. They approached King Baldwin II of Jerusalem with the suggestion of putting a permanent armed troop in place, in the form of an order of religious knights, who would undertake to defend the city and the holy sites, and protect pilgrims on the roads leading to Jerusalem. The order was officially recognized in 1128 by Pope Honorius II. Its rules were drawn up by Saint Bernard and drew directly on the Benedictine Rule which imposed chastity, poverty and complete obedience on the monks. In 1139 Pope Innocent II guaranteed the Templars their privileges and complete independence, apart from agreeing to be governed by ecclesiastical law.

The organization was led by the Grand Master and under him came the knights, the only combatants, recruited from amongst the nobility. Below the knights were their sergeants and squires, who were townspeople or from the artisan class, priests, who took care of religious rites and sacraments, and finally servants and various other attendants from the lowest rungs of the social ladder. The Order was a typical example of a self-governing body: every profession and role was represented, clergy and lawyers included, all coexisting within its walls.

A STATE WITHIN A STATE AND AN OUTSTANDING MILITARY FORCE

At the beginning of the 13th century, the Templars were unrivalled as a military force: they comprised 15,000 men, of whom

1500 were knights, all dressed in the famous white tunic embla-zoned with the blood-red cross. They built numerous forts (kraks) across the Holy Land. As the only organized military force in place, that is to say, with a proper system of command and a strict code of discipline, these warrior-monks brought order to the armed bands of crusaders which were as feudal as they were disorganized. Despite their military prowess, it is estimated that the Templars lost more than 20,000 men on the battlefield in the course of two centuries.

Their power was matched by their renown. In the east, they dealt directly with sultans and emirs and protected the Muslim tribes, from whom they received tribute. They were omnipresent as ambassadors and international negotiators. In 1244, they lost Jerusalem to the Islamic enemy; and with the fall of St John of Acre in 1291, the last Frankish possessions in the Holy Land finally fell into Muslim hands.

FROM MILITARY MIGHT TO ECONOMIC DOMINANCE

In 1128, the Templars organized a tour around Europe to raise funds. A second followed in 1136. Thereafter, they set up an entire communication and information network in Europe and the Middle East. They soon owned some 3000 commanderies (some say many more), of which 1200 were in France. Their financial activities should be seen in this context (also true of the two other similar orders – the Knights Hospitaller and the Teu-tonic Knights). After the loss of the Frankish possessions in the Holy Land, the soldier-monks reinvented themselves as finan-ciers and managers.

The Order became immensely rich. It drew its fortune from the donations of the wealthy (in both money and land) as well as from villeins, Church collections, and legacies of lords and knights who had joined their ranks. The Order also accumulated dues from markets and fairs, mills and forges, houses and churches, hunting grounds, wood-cutting rights, quarries, clerical stipends, tithes on its lands (at this time the Order was one of the largest landowners in Europe); they also benefited from tax exemption and special rights which had been granted them, amongst other privileges, by the Pope. Furthermore, the Templars were given the task of managing the Royal Treasury in France as early as the reign of Louis VII. Later, the Templar, Brother Aymar, treasurer to the King, was given the task of overseeing the financial incorporation of Normandy, which had recently been re-conquered.

Remarkably able as money-changers, speculators and bankers to the Church, the Order of 'the poor Knights of Christ' became one of the principal financial institutions in the West and certainly the most secure. Their skilful development of techniques for money-changing would allow their methods to go on being applied for five centuries after their disappearance. In competition with the Italian bankers, they used current accounts and letters of exchange – the precursors of checks – making up for the shortage of coinage and reassuring travelers of noble birth who were afraid to carry gold with them. These simply had to go to a Templar center and deposit their money (coins, jewelry, precious objects or deeds) in return for a receipt and then they could withdraw it at any other establishment belonging to the Order, subject to proof of identity and payment of a commission. To be able to do this, Templar commanderies and churches were designed and built as veritable fortresses, foreshadowing our banks.

Thanks to these depositories and their great wealth, the Templars became bankers to the Church and western kings (e.g. Philip the Fair, King John, nicknamed Lackland, Henry III and others), to whom they lent considerable sums to finance crusades and the royal way of life. The credit was theoretically free of interest, but was always encumbered with charges, commission and so on. They also lent money in the Holy Land and to the crusaders. In order to do this they sometimes had to borrow money themselves. Profiting from the devaluations of this era, they knew how to speculate better than anyone else of the time. They also held deposits, and carried out payment of allowances and pensions.

A BRUTAL END AND DIRE FORECASTS

As bankers for pilgrims and great men of state, the Templars amassed an immense fortune, giving them power equal to that of the Christian kings. King Philip the Fair (1285-1315) owed them colossal amounts of money – enough to put his own power at risk. Nor could he forgive them for having sided against him at the battle of Courtrai (1302) and, more than anything, for refusing to make him Grand Master. So, taking advantage of the Templars' refusal to merge with the Hospitallers, he ordered their arrest on 13th October 1307. This was an example of an early police raid, under the leadership of William of Nogaret. The Templars were imprisoned on dubious pretexts and subjected to `questioning´ (involving torture). Under threat, the Pope in Avignon, Clement V, endorsed the arrests and ordered the dissolution of the Knights Templar in 1312.

In 1310, fifty-four Templars were burned at the stake. In London the same scenario took place. In 1314, the charismatic Master Jacques DeMolay was burned alive on the Ile de la Cité in Paris, after threatening King Philip, Pope Clement V and William of Nogaret with imminent death… none of them lived to see out the year.

A LOST TREASURE

With the dissolution of the Templars, the Pope transferred their treasure to the Order of Hospitallers, with the exception of their Iberian assets, which went to local military orders. In 1313, the King asked the Hospitallers to return 200,000 *livres* to him to settle accounts. In his turn, Louis X claimed a further reimbursement and the affair was not closed until Philip V received another 50,000 *livres*.

Many of the Templars joined the Hospitallers or retired to monasteries. A few took refuge in Portugal, which refused to recognize the Pope's authority. They took the title of Christ's Militia. The ships of the Portuguese fleet were emblazoned with the red cross pattée (which closely resembles the Maltese cross).

Nonetheless the Templars' treasure was never found. Forewarned about the raid, they succeeded in hiding their valuables in different places: on the evening of 12 October 1307, twelve Knights Templar left the Temple in Paris, with three wagons covered with straw for an unknown destination. England has been suggested. The next day the coffers were empty! In view of the talents of these builders and engineers, it is possible that their treasures are still waiting to be found (echoing the legend of the Grail), though we do not even know whether they were material or spiritual in form.

THE HANSEATIC LEAGUE:
A FIRST NORTHERN EUROPEAN
COMMON MARKET

The Hanseatic League dominated trade throughout the Baltic Sea and north east Europe from the Jutland peninsula to the Gulf of Finland between the 12th and 16th centuries – the Baltic serving as a German version of the Roman *mare nostrum*. Some economic historians speak of an even greater area stretching from London to Novgorod. Around two hundred towns and cities took part in this early version of a common market that was based entirely on trade, with no written agreements and reliant on the mutual respect of rules of trade and cooperation. The Order of the Teutonic Knights, which shared certain of the League's interests, was a concomitant phenomenon to this unusual association. Nevertheless there were also substantial, often conflicting and opposing, differences between their strategies.

THE SALT ROAD IN NORTHERN EUROPE

The salt road from Hamburg to Lübeck had already existed for several centuries, bringing salt from the mines in the Lüneburg-Salzwedel region, south of Hamburg. It was used to salt fish, meat and other food products that arrived in the ports of northern Germany, or were produced in Poland and the general hinterland, so that they could be kept over a longer period. It was this trade route that gave rise, around the end of the 12th century, to the foundation of the Hanse[1], an alliance between the maritime and trading towns of the region from the western side of the Jutland peninsula, along the southern Baltic coast, to Russia and what is nowadays Finland and the far north. The aim was to create a trade area of coastal towns with duties on imports and exports reduced to a minimum, thereby boosting trade and protecting it from political interference and to provide mutual protection against attacks by pirates. The two main towns were Hamburg and Lübeck, on the west and east coasts of the Jutland peninsula respectively. Other towns further inland subsequently joined this unusual trading organization, including Cologne and many towns now in the Baltic Republics and northern Russia. These were often situated on rivers, giving them quick access to the sea and enabling them to send and receive merchandise to and from towns even further inland. In addition to the cities already mentioned, the Hanseatic League included Berlin, Rostock, Bremen, Lübeck (now in modern Germany), Gdansk, Krakow, Szczecin, Stettin (Poland), Copenhagen (Denmark), Tallinn (Estonia), Riga and Ventspils (Latvia), Kaliningrad and Novgorod (Russia), Amsterdam and Utrecht (Netherland), Liège and Dinant (Belgium).

THE USE OF THE MODERN SHIPS (KOGGE) FOR BULK TRADING

The products traded originated mostly from within Europe: Flemish fabrics, English wool and pewter, Russian hides and wood, Scandinavian iron and copper, fish from the Baltic, Polish amber, grain from Germany and Denmark, French and Spanish wines, hemp for making ropes and clothes, pitch for caulking boats, French sea salt and German mined salt. Margins on trade of this kind were low and merchants needed to increase the amount of goods traded to raise their profits. On the other hand they made more substantial profits on manufactured products from Flemish and German proto-industries (particularly textiles) and on the precious metals and spices transported by Genoese carracks to Bruges or sent from Venice across the Alps. The League merchants

---

1. The term originally meant a guild or company of merchants and then came to refer to the association of north European towns' guilds, more commonly known as the Hanseatic League.

often provided finance for farmers and craftsmen, thus effectively employing them, in that they underwrote all their basic requirements, supplying them with seed, raw materials and tools on credit. But there was no banking system of the Lombard type with its highly sophisticated practices. The merchants' businesses were organized around trading posts (*Kontore*), similar to the commercial system of the great Italian merchant cities with their trading posts in the Mediterranean and the Black Sea. There were five major *Kontore*: Bruges, London, Bergen, Novgorod and Visby on the island of Gotland. In addition, there were other less important ones in ports and other towns further inland. In 1380 a monetary union was created, based on silver coinage; the merchants had to refuse to take payment in gold, on pain of confiscation any gold they accepted.

Navigation was mainly coastal because the high seas were still dangerous and navigational instruments were still in their infancy. The ships, however, were of a new type. Following the design of the Viking drakkar and snekkar, the shipyards in the region started building the Baltic Kog. This had a far larger capacity for transporting goods, as much as 50 to 200 ‵lasts´, a measure of volume, not of displacement. One last measured roughly two nautical tons. Whereas the Viking ships had a capacity of just over twenty lasts, the much greater capacity Kog was broad in the beam, with a single mast and shallow draft. It was therefore well adapted to sailing on some canals and rivers and could enter most Flemish ports. A further technological advance was the central rudder, although of course the ships remained subject to the weather since they were still dependent on sail. Fortunately for them, there is usually plenty of wind in the northern European seas.

A MOST UNUSUAL LEGAL FORMULATION

The League was founded in 1284, subsequent to the signing of a formal treaty between the towns of Lübeck and Hamburg in 1242. It was an extremely unusual arrangement in that there were no written statutes. The Hanse's aims were to enhance and defend the privileges of the merchants belonging to guilds operating throughout the League, to protect the trade routes against pirates (who were very active on the seas of the period) and robbers (well organized on land), and to actively compete with merchants out-side the League. These aims were achieved by means of commer-cial agreements, boycotting, trade embargoes and, if necessary, military force consisting of mercenaries paid by the merchants. However the first formal meeting of the Diet (the *Hansetag*) did not take place until 1356, in Lübeck! This clearly indicated that the League at this stage was in no way political; rather it was a large trading association held together by common interests. Nonetheless, during the 14th century the Hanse began to assert itself politically and militarily as well as commercially. The Hanseatic merchants managed to inflict a military defeat on the kingdom of Denmark and on its Swedish ally and through the peace treaty of Stralsund (1370) they secured the right to free trade throughout the Baltic and to play a part in choosing future heirs to the Danish throne in Copenhagen. The war began in 1361 with the seizing, by the Danish King Valldemar IV, of Visby, in Gotland, a major Hanse trading counter. The Hanseatic mer-chants united and organized a naval fleet, which blockaded the port of Copenhagen in 1368. A year later the town surrendered to the blockade. This was probably the peak of the League's political power. There are very few instances in history when an economic organization has won a war against a political entity and signed treaties with diplomatic, commercial, economic and military con-sequences.

HANSEATIC MERCHANTS AND TEUTONIC KNIGHTS

The Teutonic Order of Knights was founded around 1130 by a handful of Knights from the German provinces. Its aim was to provide medical assistance to pilgrims traveling to Jerusalem. Dur-ing the third crusade, at the time of the siege of St John of Acre (1191), it became military Order and in 1198 was officially recog-nized by Pope Innocent III. A century later, following the seizure of Jerusalem by the Muslims, the Order returned to Germany and again changed its vocation: its purpose now was to bring Chris-tianity to the Baltic peoples and to expand the Order's influence and control throughout the region. In 1224 Conrad of Masovia, Duke of Krakow, requested military support from the Knights in taking control of the countries bordering the Baltic (later to become Prussia). From then on the Order conquered extensive territory and founded a number of towns. The League merchants provided ships for the Order for its military operations, similarly to the Italian republics' provision of ships for carrying soldiers, merchants and monks to the Holy Land during the crusades. In return, the Knights offered military protection to League ships and to the many towns that were members of the League but were under the Knights' control. In this way the interests of the Order and the League converged. However, this identity of interests did not last. Following the marriage in 1386 between the Polish Queen Jadwiga (Hedwig) and Grand Duke Jogaila of Lithuania, agreement was reached for the conversion of the new kingdom to Christianity, thereby depriving the Knights of one of their `raisons d'être´. Meanwhile a serious disagreement arose between the Hanse merchants and merchants in London.

In 1410, with the support of Lithuania, Jogaila raised an army of nearly 40,000 men and launched an invasion of territories with a view to incorporating them into Prussia. The Teutonic Knights' forces attacked the invader without waiting for reinforcements from their Livonian branch (now Estonia and Latvia), and were decisively beaten and lost many men at the battle of Tannenberg. Centuries later, in 1914, 200,000 troops of the German imperial army and 400,000 Russian imperial forces fought a two-week long battle in the same place, with the ensuing German victory enabling their army to make strategic conquests against Russia. Tannenberg marked the end of the Order's power, a body blow from which it would never recover. The decline of the Order was accelerated by the rising power of the regional states and by the Lutheran schism.

THE DECLINE OF THE HANSEATIC LEAGUE

The Order's decline had a dramatic impact on the League, which thereby lost a major ally. Elsewhere, the competition between the Flemish and London merchants was becoming increasingly intense, leading the states in the region to consolidate their political and especially their military power. Since the League was no longer in a position to confront them in purely military terms, a number of the League's free towns became subject

to tighter control by Poland and Russia. Finally, conflicts of interest and normal healthy competition between the Hanse towns
started to undermine its structure and a slow decline began. The
fall of Constantinople had major implications for trade: Russian
towns began sending their goods to Nuremburg, the League's
embargo of Bruges from 1451 to 1457 represented a pyrrhic victory
for the merchants, and the fairs at Leipzig and Frankfurt-on-Main
drew a lot of business away from the Hanse towns. The loss of the
trading post at Novgorod, which fell into the hands of the Grand
Duke of Moscow, the discovery of America and the opening up of
the spice route around the Cape of Good Hope all accelerated the
crisis and the merchants had to cope with ever diminishing
returns. The commercial center of gravity was shifting from the
Baltic Sea westward to the North Sea and the Atlantic Ocean; in
Germany they faced strong competition from the great trading
house of Fugger; and the Lombard banking system was making the
practices of the Hanseatic merchants obsolete, obliging them to go
to Bruges, Antwerp and later Amsterdam in search of precious
metals and spices. Moreover their exported products were losing
relative value and the terms of trade were increasingly unfavorable. From 1565 onwards almost four-fifths of maritime trade was
transported by Dutch vessels. The Reformation added further to
the League's difficulties: except for Cologne, all the towns followed Luther. The Flemish rebellion against Spain and the ensuing long war made trading conditions for the Hanse merchants
even more difficult. Indeed many Dutch merchants and the
English Merchant Adventurers were expelled from the region and
transferred their economic activities to Germany, especially Hamburg, but the League rules forbade trading with foreign merchants
from beyond the Hanse.

Later, Sweden's expansionist policy further destabilized the
League, which lost many towns and trading posts in the north.
The Thirty Years War (1618-48), with its disastrous impact on the
German states, ran counter to the League's interests and provided
the final blow. The subsequent peace settlement at the treaty of
Westphalia (1648) variously created and strengthened many of
the states in the region, despite the fact that it occasioned the first
official mention of the League in a document of the Holy Roman
Empire. The Diet no longer met regularly and its last assembly

took place in 1669 with only three towns represented – Lübeck, Bremen and Hamburg. This occasion was almost like a macabre burial service for the League, even though the three towns remained in contact and maintained Hanseatic traditions. But their doing so was little more than an exercise in saving face, since in practice the League no longer functioned. Although it had been flexible and had a dynamic `variable geometry´, the League was unable to adapt to the commercial revolution which overturned many of the world's economic coordinates and gave birth to the great nation states of Europe.

THE BLACK DEATH: ONE THIRD
OF THE EUROPEAN POPULATION DIES

Great pandemics have occurred throughout history: the most recent was Spanish flu, which carried off more victims than the First World War, which had only just ended. And the impact of such pandemics on the economy is always substantial and often dramatic.

A VIRUS FROM ASIA VIA THE SILK ROAD

The virus came from the high plains of the Chinese interior and Mongolia via the Silk Road and one of its main arrival points in Europe was the Crimea. In 1345, the Tartar troops of Janibek Khan, who were laying siege to the Genoan colony of Caffa (in the Crimea), were decimated by the disease, which then spread through the town. The Khan ordered the dead bodies of the soldiers to be catapulted over the ramparts – a classic case of germ warfare. The Genoan galleys, setting out from Caffa, stopped off at Constantinople and then the port of Messina in eastern Sicily. They then attempted to land at Livorno and Genoa but they were forbidden to drop anchor by the port authorities. The authorities in Marseille, thinking they might profit from the situation, permitted them entry on 1st November 1347. In this way the virus attacked Europe from the south, through Italy, Aquitaine and up the Rhone Valley. The winter was damp and cold, favoring the pulmonary variant of the plague, which was highly contagious and very often fatal. People fled the cities and towns in panic; by the end of the year they were deserting Provence and the Languedoc in southern France. The virus reached northern Europe along the Rhine, through the Milan region and from the east of the continent, through Venice and Austria. The ports of the Garonne region and Bordeaux were the stop off points for the British Isles, sea routes providing the best vectors for the virus, similarly to air travel today.

THE FAILURE OF QUACK REMEDIES

Doctors and physicians trying to halt the disease were divided into two camps. Those who subscribed to the `miasma´ theory thought that the disease was caused by particles suspended in the atmosphere; they recommended purges, bloodletting potions, the application of rabbits and toads to the abscesses in the armpit or groin, known as buboes (hence bubonic), and the consumption of other potions made with snakeskin, fish scales and goat's liver. The other camp, partisans of the `contagion´ theory, were closer to the scientific truth: they thought that the disease was passed on through human contact, and accordingly isolated those affected in lazarets – an early form of quarantine – and asked the town authorities to clean the streets and impose a degree of hygiene. The Pope exempted Irish and British pilgrims from traveling to Rome for the 1350 Jubilee, granting them dispensation as early as August 1349, so that people would not have to travel.

It would be another 500 years before the nature of the plague was understood. The bacillus – carried by rodents and transmitted to people by fleas – was discovered by the Swiss-born French doctor, Alexandre Yersin, who also identified the different human forms of the disease – bubonic, pulmonary and septicemic.

THE IMPACT ON WAGES, COMMERCE, SHIPPING, ARTISTIC STYLES, RELIGION.

More than 25 million Europeans died in five years: a third of the continent's population, already weakened from the Hundred Years War. Some trades and professions were almost wiped out: physicians, grave diggers, clergy, and bakers and butchers, who were in close contact with substances that attracted rats. Clearly the urban population suffered particularly badly due to the non existent hygiene and sanitation in towns, human proximity and frequent contact with travelers. The peasantry was better protected, and some valleys in the Pyrenees remained unaffected by the virus; strangely, the Flemish population was little affected by the disease, perhaps thanks to better hygiene.

The economy slowed as a result of population migration, the halt in production and harvesting, and an abrupt fall in trade through the ports. But afterwards wages went up due to the short-age of manpower, giving rise to several decades of growth fuelled by the increased consumption of peasants and laborers with their greater spending power. Culture was also seriously affected. Many schools and seminaries had to close through lack of teachers, and the role of Latin as the language of science and scholarship was partly reduced as a result of less well qualified people being employed to teach. These spoke the local language or dialect, causing the use of these to spread rapidly.

Artistic and literary production also suffered badly, though art-ists communicated their feelings through their works, with a new style of painting appearing – the danse macabre. In addition, so-called `flagellants´ began to travel around Europe. Coming mainly from Austria, Bohemia, Poland and Hungary, they would walk for thirty-three and a half days, flaying themselves with whips twice daily to expiate their sins and show God that humanity had sufficiently suffered. Certain religious minorities such as the Jews and heretics suffered from major pogroms, as they were blamed both for the spread of the plague and for being its cause. In the summer of 1352 the epidemic disappeared temporarily, only to strike again in 1363, 1374, 1389 and 1410, but on these occasions it was less widespread and the death toll was far lower. Other notable occurrences of plague pandemics were those in Athens in 429 BC and the terrible plague at the time of Justinian (542-543), which spread throughout the Mediterranean Basin and probably contributed to the spread of Germanic peoples and the growth of Northern Europe, which was spared by the disease. Other recorded outbreaks occurred in Nijmegen (1635), London (1664-65), Marseille (1720-22), Moscow (1771), Egypt (1799 and 1835), Yunnan (1894) and Manchuria (1910).

THE `RAGS CRISIS' AND THE PRINTING INDUSTRY

Following his victory against Persia at Pydna in 168 BC, the Roman General Lucius Aemilius Paulus stole, amongst other things, the King of Macedonia's library and sent it to Rome. After winning battles at Chaeronea and Orchomenos (86 BC), Sulla's spoils of war included Apollonius's famous library in Athens. It was said that this general and philosopher had already collected the remains of Aristotle's and Theophrastus's libraries. In 66 BC, after his defeat of Mithridates VI, King of Pontus, the *bon viveur* general Lucius Licinius Lucullus brought back to Rome an enormous number of volumes that had belonged to his adversary, placing them at the disposal of scholars in the library at Lucullus's villa in Tusculum. Charles VIII returned from his expedition to Italy with booty that included 1140 books and parchment documents from the library of the King of Naples; these works are still in the National Library in Paris and in Valence. In 1500, Louis XII seized a large number of books from the libraries of the Sforza family in Milan and the Visconti family of Pavia, and had them sent back to France. The Codex Gigas, one of the largest manuscripts in the world (3ft x 1ft7ins x 8ins, 165lbs, on vellum made from 160 donkey hides), dating from the beginning of the 13th century, first belonged to the Benedictine monastery at Podlazice in Bohemia; it then turned up in the Emperor Rodolphus II's collection in 1594; then in 1648, at the end of the Thirty Years War, it was seized by the Swedish army and taken back to Sweden. During the same war the many books in the Palatine library in Heidelberg, much coveted by the Catholic world, were viewed as part of the victor's spoils. And in the First and Second World Wars, the invaders made off with many precious books from the libraries of the occupied countries.

WHEN A BOOK COST AS MUCH AS A HORSE

This brief historical overview shows that libraries have always been thought of as part of the spoils of war – which proves that books are seen to be of great value both for what they contain and monetarily. The printer Schedel, who worked in Rome, had a catalogue dating from 1470 in which he offered for sale the *Decades* by Titus Livius, at the price of five ducats, and *Metamorphosis* by Apuleius for three; Pliny's *Natural History* was for sale at eight ducats and the Bible in two volumes cost ten. Compare these prices with others of the time: two beef cattle cost more than twelve ducats, a horse was worth about ten, a scribe's pay was roughly three carlins (1 carlin = 1/10 ducat) for twenty sides (a *quinterno*) of an average sized book and seven carlins for a *quinterno* with double columns. In 1532 the Bishop of Verona asked the scholar Gian Matteo Gilberti for no less than 2000 Venetian ducats as a deposit on John Chrysostome's *Expositio super Psalmos*, which Gilberti wanted to borrow. Gianbattista Ramusio, Secretary to the Council of Ten in Venice, asked for *argenti e pegni preciosi* (silver and a large deposit) from Maffeo Leoni, former *Avogador di comun* and later *Savio di terraferma* in Venice (respectively a senior judge and one of the high-ranking officials in charge of the administration), in return for lending him two rare codices belonging to the city's Marciana library.

PERGAMUS AND THE *PERGAMENA*

The battle to produce and possess books dates back to antiquity. Ptolemy V Epiphanes (205-182 BC), the king of Egypt of Rosetta stone fame, forbade the export of papyrus in order to prevent the Pergamos library from becoming larger and better known than the one in Alexandria. Pergamos reacted by inventing parchment (*pergamena* in Italian and Spanish, which also is the derivation of the Pergamon Press, a British publishing house that during the late

20th century belonged to the press baron Robert Maxwell). *Perga-mena* is obtained from the skins of goats and sheep through a complex process that involves treating them with human urine, collected from the town's latrines, to produce a very fine membrane. However, parchment cannot be rolled up like papyrus – the word `volume´ is derived from the Latin verb *volvere*, to roll up. Therefore the sheets had to be folded to obtain the *codex*, which could then be sewn together to form a *liber* (It. *libro*, Fr. *livre*). Parchment was very expensive because it took around twelve animals to produce a 200-page book. Nevertheless it quickly replaced papyrus, which had been in use throughout the Mediterranean region. Papyrus was made from Ciperus papyrus, a common aquatic plant found on the banks of the Nile and other rivers in the Middle East. Long, fine fibers were extracted from the center of the stem and then woven using the warp and weft method to obtain a surface that could be written on with greasy inks, which penetrated the surface and set. The ink was made from candle black and cinnabar. Once inscribed, papyrus was stored wrapped around a small stick; a second stick was then used to enable it to be unrolled on one side and progressively re-rolled on the other.

It would be a long time before parchment was replaced by paper in Europe. In China, however, paper already existed for writing and drawing purposes. According to tradition it was the eunuch Ts'ai Lun, a senior dignitary at the Han court, who first presented the Emperor with some sheets of paper produced from `old rags, fishing nets and the bark of trees´. He was greatly honored for his invention of paper, *zhi* in Chinese. Paper manufactories grew up rapidly in China for three specific reasons: the presence of clean water, an abundant supply of raw materials and a high level of demand from the imperial administration, scholars and monks. The industry used all sorts of raw materials: hemp, young bamboo, mulberry bark, rushes, moss, lichen, rice and wheat straw, silk cocoons and especially rags. The Emperor T'ai Tsong, the second of the Tang dynasty (618-907 AD), a man of great culture and an untiring promoter of learning and Buddhism, had 200,000 volumes in his library. At this time, all European libraries put together did not contain so many documents. Japan and Korea benefited from the invention of paper too, and in these two countries, as in China, newspapers were published; and they had already started recycling paper. Ink was also being studied to make it legible for longer and to reduce its cost – oils and pork fat were used. Another use of paper was to make warm clothing, and even armor to protect infantry, archers and cavalry from arrows, while giving them greater mobility than heavy metal armor.

THE SECRET OF PAPER-MAKING UNCOVERED AFTER THE BATTLE OF TALAS

The secrets of paper manufacture, closely guarded in various ways devised by the eunuchs and high officials of the Celestial Empire, were revealed following the defeat of the Chinese in 751 at Talas (in what is now Kirghizstan). The infantry of the Tang Empire, under the command of the Korean general Kao Hsie-chih, was forced back by the Muslim cavalry to the banks of the river Talas, where they were surrounded by Turkish Karluk mercenaries. Many Chinese soldiers were taken prisoner and sold as slaves, for as little as one dirham. Amongst them were workers who had been engaged in silk and paper production. The silk makers were sent to Kufa, a town on the Euphrates south of Baghdad, to develop centers of silk production in the region. Under torture, other captured soldiers revealed the secrets of paper making. Thus a major industrial secret was discovered as a result of the battle which, amongst other things, defined the western limits of the Chinese Empire – its highly efficient war machine having been literally brought to a halt – as well as the far point of Muslim expansion. Talas was a truly historic battle that remains almost wholly unknown to Europeans.

Samarkand became the leading center of paper making in the Islamic world. This great trading city was joined by Baghdad in the 793, Cairo in 900, Damascus in 985 and Fez in 1100, the know-how of Arab engineers in hydraulics having been of considerable help in setting up centers of production throughout the region, under various caliphates. Southern Spain became the first European region to introduce paper manufacturing, which started in the cities of Xàtiva (where the papal Borgias originated) and Valencia. In 1109 it was the turn of Palermo, which had remained under Arab domination until 1072; the town benefited from the cultural upsurge following the arrival of the Normans. Amalfi, one of the four large maritime republics in Italy at that time, started paper production and trade in 1220. Then came the large production center at Fabriano, near Ancona, in 1276, where the water-marking process was invented and the use of hydraulic pulping machinery was introduced for the preparation of rags. To avoid problems with mould, the workers used animal gelatin as a glue. This made the paper highly resistant to liquids, which in turn gave greater stability to the ink. Arab paper, on the other hand, still relied on vegetable gelatin, which tended to encourage mould and was too absorbent. Thanks to the semi-industrial techniques in use there, Fabriano significantly improved the quality of paper and reduced production costs. In this way Italian paper makers were able to outstrip the Arab competition. But we still do not know who imported paper-making techniques to Italy. Was it Arab soldiers captured in the Adriatic Sea, immigrants from Palermo, or Erard of Prague, an immigrant fleeing Bohemia with his family? Bologna became another important center of paper production in Europe, partly due to the demand from its great university, the first in Europe. In any case, nearly all the Renaissance artists from Italy, Holland and Germany (Dürer, for example) used paper from Fabriano for their drawings and sketches.

TWO CENTURIES OF ITALIAN MONOPOLY

For more than two centuries Italy dominated the European paper market and progressively replaced Spain and Damascus. Advanced production methods, high demand from the great cultural centers such as Rome, Bologna, Padua, Pavia, Florence and Naples, and the power of the maritime republics which dominated trade throughout almost all of the Mediterranean and on the various routes to northern Europe, all favored two centers in particular: Venice and Genoa, which were also major centers of production in their own right. Milanese paper merchants were the first to take part in the paper fair in Geneva. Paper production needed long-term and flexible financing. It took some three to six months from the purchase of the raw materials, paying wages, drying and storing the produce throughout to sale and settlement of bills. And this is without taking into account periods of drought, when there was no water for the production, or periods of heavy rainfall, when it was too wet to dry then transport the finished product.

A great paper merchant, Ludovico di Ambrogio from Fabriano, amassed a huge fortune in this sector in the first two decades of the 15th century. He became the most powerful paper merchant in Italy and had many connections with international trade. His merchandise was mainly exported to Genoa and Venice. However, around 1425 he stopped trading, and paid his debts by using his wife's dowry and selling his premises. He then moved to Foligno to help the great mercenary Braccio di Montone, to whom he became a faithful treasurer and brilliant economic adviser.

THE PRICE OF OLD RAGS ROCKETS IN EUROPE

The demand for old rags in Europe was soaring, and in many towns dealers got together to create guilds and corporations to protect the profession. Rags were available in increasing quantities due to the change in clothing styles during the 13th century: the Crusaders brought back with them the fashion for undershirts and linen and cotton underwear, which then quickly spread throughout European society. There is much evidence of this in the literature of the time (e.g. the *Decameron*, Chaucer and tales of chivalry). Nevertheless, around the end of the 13th century there was a serious shortage of rags, with a corresponding rise in the price of raw materials. It was necessary therefore to find products which could replace rags, bearing in mind that wood pulp was only used from the 19th century onwards, despite the many attempts to introduce it earlier into paper production processes. During the mid-14th century the Black Death was ravaging Europe, resulting in the deaths of a third of the population. This also contributed to the steep rise in the price of rags, because of fear of contagion. In addition the prophylactic measures taken by the authorities, such as banning the recycling of clothes and the compulsory burning of used clothing from the dead and dying, drastically reduced the amount of rags on the market. This had a major impact on their price and in turn on the price of paper. The plague of 1630-31 again greatly damaged paper production and for the same reasons. The paper workers handling the rags also died in great numbers. Only a reduction in the demand for paper, due to the slowing down of both the economy and cultural activity during and after each pandemic, helped keep the price under control.

EMBARGOES ON THE IMPORT AND EXPORT OF RAGS

Meanwhile the `Dutch cylinder´ was invented: windmills turned these cylinders which shredded and chopped the rags with their metal blades. This invention dating from the 17th century greatly reduced the need for manpower; but it was a good hundred years before it was adopted by other centers of paper production in Europe. Governments often imposed a total embargo on the export of rags, especially in wartime; they also banned imports during periods of plague. The wars of the 18th century again created difficult conditions for procuring the raw materials needed for paper. The crisis was so severe in Germany, Holland and Great Britain that paper makers began to use wood, nettles, straw, moss, leaves, cauliflowers and broom; but the quality and average life-time of the paper were considerably reduced.

It was not until 1799 that the first machine for making paper by the roll was patented by the Frenchman, Nicolas Louis Robert, an invention that greatly improved productivity. The demand for rags was such that many industrialists and engineers started to look for radical alternatives, since their price was beginning to adversely affect the production of paper that was increasingly used for making books and especially newspapers. German industry made the greatest headway in improvements and innovations. In 1844 Frederick Gottlob Keller succeeded in making wood pulp; further improvements were made by Meillier in 1852; in 1866 Tilgham, an American, introduced chemicals into the process, which was further improved by Ritte-Kellner in 1882 and Dahl in 1883.

THE ROLE OF RELIGION IN THE SPREAD OF BOOKS

Buddhism and Christianity (with the Reformation and Counter-Reformation) were probably the main drivers behind the invention and spread of the printing press with movable type, even if there were at least seven centuries separating these two religious movements. The first scroll, printed in China during the first half of the 8th century, was a collection of Buddhist prayers, and it is thought that a million copies were printed. However, the first book whose precise printing date is known was the Diamond Sutra, a wood-block scroll printed in China in 868 AD and now in the collection of the British Museum. But it was not until 1040 that the first movable type was produced, in ceramic, by Pi Cheng, a writer and blacksmith. Under the Mongol dynasty of the Yuan, Chinese printing developed strongly and the first bank notes were produced on a large scale using wood block printing. In Europe, around 1400, a few books were published using metal type – eight pages had to be engraved back to front on copper plates, which would then be used in the printing. In the meantime evidence of printing with movable metal type had been found in Korea, followed some 30 years later by the wood block. This involved the same method of working, with the plate now of wood, but the cost was enormous and production very slow.

JOHAN GENSFLEISCH: *HOFE ZUM GUTENBERG*

Movable type was invented by Johan Gensfleisch of the patrician Gutenberg family which owned the eponymous estate. In 1451 he published a Latin grammar and in 1454 the renowned Turkenkalendar (a calendar). On 30th September 1452, he and two other typographers began to set the famous Gutenberg Bible, with 42 lines, which came off the presses in 1456. Its two volumes comprised of 1282 pages with 3.8 million letters. Gutenberg's achievement was to have invented, probably with the help of other typographers and goldsmiths, movable type made from an alloy of lead, tin and antimony, and the printing press, the design of which was taken from wine and olive oil presses. His famous Bible was printed in 150 to 180 copies, of which 48 still exist today. However, Gutenberg had a financial dispute with his partner Johan Faust, who acquired all the equipment from the press after winning the lawsuit and began producing books with a new associate, Peter Schöffer.

Printing spread rapidly throughout developed Europe. Politicians, the Church, bankers, merchants and lawyers rapidly understood the importance of the new invention. In 1458, Charles VII sent Nicolas Jensac, an engraver from the Paris mint, to Germany, to learn the new technique. Other courts invited printers to set up their workshops and offered them protection. Bankers financed the printing, which was often risky and had a long repayment cycle. The printer first had to find a text, then prepare all the pages, print them, distribute the books and then finally receive payment – a complex and high risk 'marketing operation' for the financier.

Venice, the Roman Curia, and cities such as Paris, Florence, Strasburg, Cologne and Utrecht all attracted printers who were fleeing from Germany, then being ravaged by wars. In 1500 there were 236 European towns with printing shops. Many of the printers were itinerant, going from small town to small town printing documents; merchants sold small books and calendars at the town fairs, while pedlars went from village to village selling these items.

A NEW TYPE OF ENTREPRENEUR AND THE BATTLE OVER BOOKS BETWEEN REFORMATION AND COUNTER-REFORMATION

Color printing made its first appearance; Ottaviano Petrucci printed the first music in Venice in 1498; and new fonts were invented and modified or replaced gothic lettering. In Venice Francesco Griffi – later executed for killing his father-in-law – designed the stylish italic font on behalf of the great printer Aldo Manuzio. Manuzio, who counted Erasmus of Rotterdam and Pico della Mirandola among his friends, fixed the rules for punctuation and introduced the *ottavo* – a page size traditionally produced by folding a standard printing-sheet three times to form a section of eight leaves (in English `octavo´ also means `book sized´). He also produced a catalogue of the books he published. He has left his mark on European Renaissance culture through his books, which all have a frontispiece depicting an anchor and a dolphin: the anchor represents strength and the certainty of finding shelter in a friendly port, while the dolphin symbolizes speed and safety (in Greece the dolphin traditionally saved men in danger at sea). The French printer, Claude Garamond, designed the elegant font which bears his name. William Caxton – merchant, diplomat, author and publisher – was the first person to print books in England,. His books became reference texts for the English language, which was still a mixture of dialects and styles. Caxton also introduced the idea of printing a table of contents at the beginning of a book.

Printing developed at an astonishing rate. By the end of the 16th century around 200 million books had already been published in Europe, with its population of 100 million, most of them illiterate. The Reformation naturally boosted the book industry, which in turn became one of the main means for the dissemination of religion. Luther wrote 'Dass Man Kinder solle zu Schule halten' ('Children should be sent to school'), since the faithful must be able to read the Bible for themselves; both Luther and Calvin emphasized the importance of the Bible as opposed to the ritual and statues of Catholicism, which were a way of communicating with a largely illiterate population. The Counter-Reformation also promoted books as a key means of disseminating dogma and the word of Rome. European books were exported to the Americas in the galleons of the conquistadores, to the Middle East in Venetian galleys, and to Asia in Dutch and Portuguese carracks with the Jesuits who went there. The great book fairs in Lyon developed in the 16th century and were succeeded by the Leipzig fairs in the following century. From then on the great book revolution was fully under way, with its corresponding requirement for literacy.

THE MING DYNASTY:
FROM GROWTH TO ISOLATIONISM

The Ming dynasty in China was a period of great economic, political and cultural growth. It is no accident that *ming* in Mandarin means `bright´. It came between two foreign dynasties: the Mongolian Yuan dynasty (1271-1358) and the Manchurian Qing dynasty (1644-1911). In 1211 Gengis Khan conquered the Great Northern Plain; later, around the end of the 13th century, Marco Polo stayed in China, though he made no mention of the Great Wall. Around 1340, northern China was suffering from famine with no relief in prospect, in particular as a consequence of a series of disastrous floods of the Yellow River. Uprisings followed, and the chief of the Red Turbans, a minority sect, took power in Yangchow (now Yangzhou), then in Nanking (now Nanjing) in 1359. Zhu Yuanzhang succeeded in driving back the Mongols further and further north, until in 1368 he took control of Beijing. The conquest was completed in 1382. At the time, economic problems abounded and the first Ming emperor launched into investment on a Pharaonic scale. He created more than 40,000 reservoirs; regions abandoned by their populations were re-populated with migrants; and the area around Nanjing was replanted with thousands of trees.

SIX MINISTRIES IN THE HANDS OF THE EMPEROR

The Emperor took personal control of the levers of power: the Ministries of Finance, Armed Forces, Public Works, Rituals, Justice and the Civil Service. He had his senior civil servants watched by `the guards in brocade´, a very effective and powerful secret police. Hongwu – the first Emperor's original name – was succeeded by the young Huidi, who only reigned from 1398 -1402. The latter's uncle, General Zhu Di took over with a coup d'état and relaunched China's economy. He seized Nanjing and initiated huge public works. He decided first to rebuild the great canal linking Tianjin to Hangzhou via Nanjing – a vital communication route from the north to the south of the country used for the transport of grain, goods, soldiers and traders. He then took the iron and salt mines under his control, retaining the monopoly for himself, although he awarded local monopolies to private interests. He started producing money again, very important in a country that was dependent on metal imported from the west, by way of Genoa, Venice and Damascus following the Silk Road. The administration recognized the silver *liang*, weighing 36 grams, as a new monetary unit. This replaced paper money – known as the *tael*, in the language of 19th century western bankers – which underwent a sharp devaluation.

YONGLE TRANSFERS THE CAPITAL TO BEIJING

This third emperor, Yongle, had previously been a prince of Beijing, and he decided to transfer the capital from Nanjing to the north of the country. Thus Beijing became the capital of the dynasty which reigned over the New Empire. Work on the construction of the Imperial Palace began in1407. Millions of tons of quarried stone, marble from Xuzhou, wood from the provinces of Sichua, Guizhou and Yunnan (over 1200 miles away) were transported to the site by the imperial canal, linking north to south over a distance of 950 miles. Two hundred thousand laborers worked on the site, which is reminiscent of Versailles in scale, but was being built two centuries earlier; 100 million tiles and 200 million bricks from Lin Qing (in the Shandong peninsula, 310 miles from Beijing) were manufactured and sent to Beijing. The Emperor was also keen to promote China as a great naval power. A Muslim eunuch, Zheng He, was put in charge of seven naval expeditions to the seas to the east and south and to Africa. The fleets numbered 20-30,000 men and more than 200 ships. In contrast to Magellan, Columbus, da Gama and many others who wanted to discover spices and gold, their aim was to extend the Emperor's knowledge and search for curiosities such as animals, stones, plants and to find new routes and opportunities for diplomacy. Recent research suggests they may have circumnavigated the globe around 1420, although this hypothesis has been much disputed. The Emperor had already ordered the compilation of a great universal encyclopedia between 1404 and 1407 – some 350 years before Diderot's encyclopedia – to include 11,095 works of all kinds by ancient authors He also produced a penal code which caused Montesquieu to comment `China is ruled with the rod´.

EUNUCHS AND EXTERNAL THREATS SABOTAGE THESE LARGE-SCALE PROJECTS

Eunuchs enjoyed considerable freedom and power at the imperial court. They controlled the hidden policies of the empire and influenced the emperor's decisions. The creation of the Great Domestic Council, a restricted group that replaced the Mandarin advisors, altered the balance of power in the empire. Yongle's power was weakened by a number of factors: his failure to father an heir, threats arising in the south from the highly politicized peasants of Indo-China and from Japanese pirates on the seas to the east, and especially a great fire in the Imperial Palace in 1421 followed by the massacre of the opposition, who were critical of the emperor. After Yongle's death in 1424, China entered a phase of isolationism, and launched itself into building a 3000-mile extension to the Great Wall – which had been started in the 7th century BC and added to in the 2nd century BC – to protect the empire from invasion by the Mongols from the north. There would be no further expansion until the Wanli era (1573-1619).

THE BEGINNINGS OF THE PAPER ECONOMY AT MEDIEVAL FAIRS

The last few years have witnessed some very distinctive financial phenomena. Currency transactions have been centralized in London whilst the New York market is in the process of losing its near monopoly on share transactions. And on the currency markets, large centers such as Singapore, Hong Kong, Bahrain, the trio Zurich-Paris-Frankfurt and even New York, have all seen their importance diminishing in favor of London, where more than 40% of all world transactions are now concentrated.

Moreover, while still remaining `the market whose stocks influence the other international financial markets´, Wall Street is slowly hemorrhaging in favor of other markets such as those in continental Europe, Japan and other Asian countries, Latin America and even former communist bloc countries. Such phenomena are not new and the financial world has often witnessed the passing of the baton from one country to another or even from one market to another within the same country. Without going back too far in time, we can start by looking at the large medieval Champagne Fairs.

THE CHAMPAGNE REGION, THE CROSSROADS BETWEEN ITALIAN AND FLEMISH TRADE

The most obvious paradox is the fact that the Champagne Fairs came about to facilitate trade exchanges between Italian and Flemish merchants, with the local French merchants playing only a secondary role. These fairs dated from the beginning of the

12th century and were carried on throughout the year. They began with the fair at Lagny-sur-Marne between 2nd and 15th January; this was followed by the fair at Troyes from 22nd January to 5th February; then came Bar-sur-Aube, which began on the third Tuesday in Lent; the fair at Sézanne lasted the whole of Easter week. Provins held the fair of Saint-Quiriace throughout May. The `hot fair´ of mid-July returned to Troyes and was known as the fair of St John. The merchants again met at Provins during the month of September for the fair of Saint-Ayoul. Finally there was the long `cold fair´ at Troyes, which lasted from the beginning of October up until the week before Christmas. That came at the end of the cycle and mostly sold autumn produce from the harvest.

Each fair lasted about six weeks; they started with commercial transactions and finished with financial ones. It was the Troyes fair that gave its name to the Troy ounce, the measure used in the weighing of precious metals, perfume essences and other products used by chemists and pharmacists. During the last two weeks of each fair, the bankers, brokers and other intermediaries traded letters of exchange and currencies, and paid back loans and issued new ones. The many Lombard[1] bankers – in Provins they even had a lodge – Jewish bankers and the Dutch were the most widely represented; there was great freedom of actions and transactions carried out on the basis of mutual trust. During the last few days of each fair, people would offset various financial transactions, and the first clearing transactions took place then, albeit in an informal fashion.

THE FAIRS REACH THEIR PEAK IN 13TH CENTURY

Many goods – fabrics, spices, furs, wine, cereals, luxury items and precious metals – passed through these fairs bound for very diverse destinations: the Baltic and Italian ports, the Rhine valley from where they were shipped to England, Scandinavian countries, eastern Europe, the Mediterranean, the Middle East and even the Indian Ocean. The fairs reached their height in the 13th century and the Champagne region was at the center of all Euro-

---

1. Merchant bankers from Italy, not just from Lombardy, who dealt in currency exchange, gold and silver, loans and money transfers

pean trade and finance. But at the beginning of the following century they began to decline, in part due to the long war between the Count of Flanders and the French kings (1302-1310). Furthermore, itinerant trading was being replaced by the spread of fixed trading; direct shipping between the Flemish, English and Mediterranean ports was increasing rapidly. The ʿmoney merchantsʾ and the bankers no longer needed to meet each other in person because, with the rise of literacy among them, a signature on paper could be recognized by all the correspondents, who undertook to honor the accompanying financial transaction, and this was now considered sufficient. The creation of private postal services and the employment of couriers made carrying bills of exchange and the de facto transfer of money and capital much easier.

FLORINS, SEQUINS AND *GROS TOURNOIS*

The spread of freely circulating coins, accepted by everyone, led to the establishment of banks and financial markets, each one in a single fixed location. Venice minted the *matapan* (slightly more than two grams of silver); Venice and Florence began to mint the *sequin* (a gold coin) and the gold florin; Louis XI introduced *gros tournois*; Edward III started minting gold florins which were in circulation throughout England; and other countries followed the example of the Italian cities. The life of the money-changers was simplified by the standardization of coins and by the marginalization of lesser coins.

For centuries, gold had arrived in Europe from its centers of production in the Sudan and Guinea; practically all the gold possessed by the Greeks and Romans was extracted from these two regions. The case of silver was rather different since Europe possessed a few mines of its own. It was obtained mainly as a by-product of base metals (zinc, lead and tin) and from the silver mines in Germany. The discovery of America and the mining of gold and silver in Mexico, gold in Brazil and silver in Peru (at the large Potosi silver mine, now in Bolivia) radically changed the financial balance and altered the circulation of precious metals in Europe. But the Iberian peninsula was not able to cope with refining such immense quantities of precious metals and a large part was sent to Antwerp (where the Exchange was opened in

1531) and to Italy (Genoa, Livorno and Venice). Italian bankers were feeling the pinch following the shift in the economic center of gravity from the Mediterranean toward the Atlantic and the North, whilst Flemish bankers were beginning to compete seriously with the German banking family, the Fuggers.

A DRAMATIC TURN OF EVENTS

However, there came a dramatic turn of events, starting with the Low Countries' rebellion against the Spanish empire, when deliveries of precious metals to the Flemish towns dried up completely. Another factor was the growing threat from French and English privateers intercepting Spanish and Portuguese galleons in the Caribbean and at the entrance to the Channel. Much of the metal was sent therefore to Italian ports, with the Genoese bankers benefiting hugely. When the Spanish soldiers occupying Flanders demanded to be paid in gold coins, the Genovesi (Lombards and Florentines of the second rank) sent letters of exchange to their correspondents in Dutch towns, who could then hand the gold to the paymasters of the imperial Spanish army. The second bankruptcy of the Spanish state (1575), which shook the financial system of the Republic of Genoa to its foundations – their bankers had lent enormous sums to Philip II –, made the Emperor more indebted than ever to the Genoans.

THE FINANCIAL FAIRS CIRCUIT

For a long time financial fairs were held at Lyon, where the Genoese bankers exercised great power. But after their betrayal by the king of France in 1528, the Genovesi were no longer prepared to lend him money. In response the king tried to sabotage the activities of his financier enemies, but they succeeded in having the fairs transferred to Besançon in 1534. The war in the Spanish provinces of Flanders increasingly gave power to the Italian bankers, who transferred the fairs to Poligny in 1568, and then to Chambéry. Following the revolt of the Spanish troops in Flanders in 1576 – they had not been paid, as the Genoese had stopped sending letters of exchange – the power of the Genovesi over Philip became even greater. They obtained permission to hold the fairs at Piacenza, south of Milan, a situation that pertained from November 1579 until 1621. These fairs became the largest financial fairs in Europe from the end of the 16th and into the 17th century, with the whole of European finance flocking to them, including bankers from Flanders, Germany, England, France and Iberia.

PIACENZA AND THE `PAPER´ REVOLUTION

There were four fairs held each year, on 1st February, 2nd May, 1st August and 2nd November. Around 60 bankers gathered together, mainly Genoese, Milanese and Florentine. They were known as *banchieri di conto* (clearing houses) and were required to put down a deposit of 4000 crowns. It was they who fixed the exchange and interest rates on the third day of the fair. As well as the bankers, there were money-changers, who had to put down a deposit of 2000 crowns to gain authorization to present their letters of exchange and credits. Finally there was a third category: representatives of firms and brokers, known as the *Heroldi*. During the fair, everyone tried to clear all transactions in such a way that the exchange of money and coins was limited. Any outstanding amounts were settled in gold or carried forward to the next fair with interest. This was the first structured clearing system in international finance. Before 1600 the volume of transactions at each fair was worth more than 50 million crowns, a very considerable sum for the period. The arrogance and wealth of the Genoese and the development of a paper economy were important features of the early 17th century. Genoa, which also dominated the Spanish market in the Atlantic, was quicker to restructure its trading and financial network than Venice, taking account of the shift in economic development from the Mediterranean toward the Atlantic and Northern Europe. The *Genovesi* had the merit of establishing the true function of the banker as a money merchant and of separating this function from that of the merchant banker with holdings (merchandise, property and freight, etc.). Finance and wealth based only on `paper´ astonished traditional Italian bankers and those of Northern Europe, but they all had to adapt rapidly to the new reality so as not to be overtaken and swept aside by this `technological´ revolution in banking and finance.

THE SPANISH BANKRUPTCY AND THE CRISIS IN GENOESE BANKING

Another bankruptcy (1627) in the finances of the Spanish Emperor once again altered the destiny of European finances. The Genoese, who were the principle financiers of the Spanish treasury, suffered serious losses and had to concede much of their power. With the end of Spain's golden century (*el Siglo de Oro*), the financial center in Europe shifted to Amsterdam and then to London. It was not until the first half of the 18th century that other exchanges started up; the Paris Bourse was founded in 1732, Wall Street in 1792, and London in 1801, although the first transactions took place in coffee houses from 1698 onwards. Geography and politics have both had a strong influence on the location of financial centers; but the deciding element has always been their capacity to invent and use new financial techniques, and above all to create a dynamic sense of innovation. These are the two factors that will attract capital – and not vice versa.

SECRETS OF NAVIGATING THE COAST OF AFRICA AND THE END OF `PAX MONGOLICA´

After the fall of the Roman Empire, the Mediterranean was dominated by local mariners and by pirates. But with the rise of Islam, Muslim traders began shipping gold from the Sudan and black slaves to the Mediterranean, as well as silk, pepper, spices and pearls from the Far East to Europe. The rise of the Italian maritime city-republics and the crusades altered the balance to some extent, but the trading hub was still Persia, which controlled the flow of goods arriving from the Indian Ocean and Asia, by land and sea. The global warming of 1350-1400 made it increasingly difficult to cross the Sahara desert with trade caravans. Then the death of Tamerlane, in Otrar in 1405, put an end to the `Pax Mongolica´, and the routes to Central Asia became unsafe, especially the Silk Road.

NICCOLÒ CONTI'S IDEA

Niccolò Conti was a Venetian merchant who traveled in the Far East through India, Burma and Indonesia, where he faced incredible dangers. In 1437, he lost his wife and two of his children on the way back from Cairo, when an epidemic decimated the population; and he was even obliged to convert to Islam to save his own life. He was pardoned by Pope Eugene IV for his apostasy, who then insisted that he recount his adventures and reveal his geographical knowledge. Conti gave a very detailed account of the

Spice Isles – Ceylon, Java and Sumatra – and maintained that they could be reached by circumnavigating Africa.

This was not a totally new idea. Herodotus made reference to a Phoenician expedition in the service of the Pharaoh Necho around 600 BC, which having left by way of the Red Sea then returned to Egypt via the Pillars of Hercules (the Straits of Gibraltar). During the Middle Ages, there were legends telling how the 6th century Irish monk Brendan discovered fabulous islands in the Atlantic, known then as the Fortunate Isles (now the Canaries). Other legends mention the islands of Brazil and Antilla, where the Portuguese bishops were said to have taken refuge at the time of the Saracen invasion. There were many attempts to go through the Pillars of Hercules. In 1291 the Vivaldi brothers from Genoa ventured through to the Atlantic, but never returned. Dante seems to have been inspired by this for his description in the *Inferno* of Ulysses's voyages south. In 1346, a Majorcan sailor called Ferrer set off to explore the African coast, but never returned to his home port. Unofficial indications of unsuccessful voyages are readily available. For example, many portolans – sailing directions, illustrated with contemporary charts or maps – show terrible monsters engulfing boats beyond the Pillars of Hercules… it was truly *finis terrae*, land's end.

EXPEDITIONS FINANCED BY HENRY THE NAVIGATOR

The Portuguese Prince, Henry the Navigator, was aware that his country was isolated from the economic center of the world, the Mediterranean. He therefore wanted to encourage his sailors to discover other economic regions. He settled in Sagres, in the south of the country, and started a great school of astronomy and navigation techniques. The royal court was frequented by travellers, literary scholars, astronomers and mathematicians of diverse origins – Arab, Jewish, Venetian, Genoese and north European. Henry's library became one of the main collections of scientific and geographical treatises in Europe. The Portuguese court also called upon foreign captains and masters of navigation; for example, Henry took on the Venetian, Alvise Ca' da Mosto, a navigator of great experience. The engineers and ship-builders of the Sagres fleet produced the caravel, a highly maneuverable ship that could be handled by a crew of fifteen but could accommodate thirty if necessary. The caravel was ideal for expeditions in that half the crew could go ashore and the other half – in the event of the shore crew being taken prisoner or killed by the natives or failing to turn up at the agreed rendezvous point – could still return home without too much difficulty. These ships were also relatively economical to build and equip. The first caravel left Portugal in 1441 for Cap Blanc, a peninsula on the African Atlantic coast between Mauritania and the Western Sahara.

THE VOYAGE TO AFRICA: ONLY FOR THE BOLD!

Sailing through these unknown coastal waters required knowledge and expertise which did not yet exist. The prevailing winds, the geography of the coastline, any local maritime peculiarities, currents and tides – all these were unknown quantities. In addition, sailing from north to south also changes the configuration of the stars. The mariners of the period were familiar with east-west navigation (and vice versa) and stayed close to the shore when they left Mediterranean waters and sailed north along the European coast. It was the beginning of the science of navigation, using the magnetic compass and geometrical compasses, which led to new charts being drawn up. But when sailors reached the Equator, the Pole Star disappeared and other points of reference were needed. The astrolabe became an indispensable instrument for navigation, especially in regions where the sky was often covered by cloud. The experience and knowledge acquired by Lusitanian[1] sailors was much sought after by all European mariners from the mid-16th century onward. Indeed the `Atlantic´ portolanos made by the Portuguese became the targets of espionage and were worth their weight in gold. All the European courts and navies, not to mention merchants, wanted copies for their own trading expeditions. Underlying their efforts lay major economic objectives: gold from Guinea, spices, the crusade to convert African peoples to Christianity and the search for Prester John, the mythical priest who supposedly recounted in a letter much in circulation in the

---

1. A term derived from the name of the old Roman Province that included Portugal.

Middle Ages, that at the other end of the world there was a very rich and powerful Christian sovereign whose kingdom would one day be found. It was said that this king would one day come with millions of soldiers and save Christianity from the threat of Islam.

West of the Straits of Gibraltar, there are four Atlantic archipelagos: Madeira and the Canaries, with the Azores to the north and the Cap Verde islands to the south. Mainly volcanic in origin, these island groups have risen up as a consequence of the African tectonic plate pivoting to the north and sliding under the Eurasian plate in this region. Between the 8th and the 5th centuries BC, the Phoenicians, followed by the Carthaginians, sailed through the Straits in search of other lands. The Phoenicians discovered at least one of the islands of the Canaries; the Carthaginians prevented the Etruscans from conquering them in turn because they wanted to retain a place of safety in view of the aggressive Roman presence in the western Mediterranean. Plato, in his two dialogues composed in Athens after 390 BC, *Timaeus* and *Critias*, refers to the mysterious land of Atlantis, while Pliny and Ptolemy both mention the Fortunate Isles (in this instance the Canaries), which Roman sailors were familiar with.

The medieval period inherited these stories, with their vague factual basis and fantastic suggestions. Adam of Bremen, in the 11th century, speaks of an ocean covered in ice and thick fog; the Arab al-Idrisi, in the following century, describes a sea full of shadows. But in due course, in view of the crusades, the transfer of the papal seat to Avignon, the Arab advance to the canal of Otranto, and the renewal of trade by sea due to the rise of the Italian maritime republics, Europeans once again began to brave the Straits of Gibraltar and follow the coasts of Portugal and Spain to Flanders.

THE VIVALDI BROTHERS AND THE CATALAN ATLAS

In 1291 the Genoese brothers Ugolino and Vadini Vivaldi set out in search of India `per mare Oceanum´. Although they never returned, they probably landed on the Canary Isles – one of which is in fact called Alegranza (the name of the boat belonging to the unfortunate brothers). In 1313, another Genoese mariner, Lancelotto Malocello, landed on the islands and was so delighted with what he found that he remained there until his death. Indeed the name Lanzarote is derived from Lancelotto. The geographer Angelino Dalorte, who worked in Majorca, drew a *mappa mundi* on which the Canaries are clearly shown; and there is even mention of the King of Mali.

But the real masterpiece of the Majorcan school is the Catalan Atlas, compiled by the Jewish cartographer Abraham Cresques in 1375: its 12 vellum panels represent the known world in great detail, from the Fortunate Isles to China. From 1420, Abraham's son worked for Henry the Navigator, the Portuguese prince who encouraged sailors to explore the Atlantic and set off in conquest of Africa. In 1448, the Venetian Andrea Bianco, who worked in London, drew up a chart showing the Azores – discovered in 1431 and already included by the Majorcan Vallsecha's charts –, as well as the Portuguese advance as far as Cape Verde; he also sketched in an island to the west of Madeira which could be the coast of Brazil. The greatest of all the maps was produced by a Venetian monk, Fra Mauro, who worked in Murano; he received a commission from Prince Henry for a world map. This was completed before the deaths of both the geographer and the prince in 1460. It shows the African coast, the Indian Ocean (depicted for the first time as a sea that is not surrounded by land) and China, though with distances estimated well below what they are in reality. It was not, therefore, of great help to Christopher Columbus in making his calculations: he underestimated the earth's circumference by a third.

MADEIRAN SUGAR, `YELLOW METAL´ IN THE SUDAN AND THE SLAVE TRADE

The Madeira archipelago was discovered and then abandoned by the Genoese, who called it *Isole del legname* – the timber isles – as did the Portuguese, who translated this name into their own language. Wood and sugar from Madeira and produce from other islands attracted capital and financed the expeditions sent out by the king to conquer new lands, with the aim of ending Portugal's isolation in relation to the Mediterranean.

Portuguese mariners, accompanied by Genoese, Majorcans, North Africans and other experienced sailors, followed the African coast down as far as Cape Bojador in Western Sahara, 120 nautical miles southwest of the Canaries and about ten days down the coast from Gibraltar. Beyond this headland the sea became very dangerous and many boats were shipwrecked between 1424 and 1434. In 1433 Gil Eannes attempted to go further but failed; he made another attempt, and from then on all expeditions tried to conquer the next 50 leagues of land to the south. The discovery of spices, slaves and gold attracted an increasing number of expeditions, and the conquest of the African coast began on a grand scale. The combination of geographic and strategic interests (on the part of the king of Portugal), commercial and maritime trading opportunities (for slaves and goods) and religious motives (to convert to Christianity peoples who were naturally fairly peaceable) unleashed a race for `Eldorado´. The extent of the continent was of course still unknown and its size totally unsuspected. In the meantime, the political geography of Europe was changing. Some fifty years later Venice lost its monopoly of many types of spice, and the towns of Antwerp and then Amsterdam became the new centers of trade. The political power of the western Iberian peninsula was on the increase, even if Portugal was disinclined to profit from Columbus' `crazy´ project.

After 1434, when Gil Eannes made his second voyage, Portuguese sailors ventured further south along the African coast, using a mixed form of navigation – sometimes following the coast and at other times sailing out into the Atlantic Ocean. More than anything, it was the capture of slaves and the hunt for gold that were the primary goals of these voyages, the search for spices and scientific interest playing only a secondary role. Potential slaves were in plentiful supply along the West African coast, and demand was high in Europe and among Muslims, particularly as servants for the newly wealthy, who were benefiting from the economic climate created by the Italian Renaissance. At the same time the availability of gold was a lure to sea captains and their crews. The medieval western world had long dreamt of gold, calling it the `yellow metal´ of Sudan, without really knowing if it originated there or came from Senegal, Niger or Ghana. We know only that the Romans were aware of the mines in southern Egypt and that caravans crossed the Sahara to the Mediterranean transporting gold, which the Romans and later Medieval Europe needed, to buy `Indian´ spices .

THE POPE SHARES OUT THE NEW WORLD

Long before the Treaty of Tordesillas (1494), which divided up the discoveries in the New World of the Americas, the Venetian Pope Eugene IV (1431-1447) took charge of sharing out the new lands and seas. He awarded the Canaries to Castille and the other islands in the Atlantic Ocean to the Portuguese, together with any other lands in that region that might be discovered and converted to Christianity. One of the following popes, Calixtus III Borgia, granted full jurisdiction to the Portuguese king over the lands between Cape Bojador, Guinea and other lands from there to the Indian subcontinent. In 1471, the Equator was crossed, and while the Portuguese crown retained the monopoly in gold, slaves, ivory and spices, everything else was free for Portuguese mariners, merchants and adventurers, together with a few Castilians, Genoese and Venetians, to share amongst themselves. All these men were entrepreneurs who understood that the future no longer lay with the Mediterranean, but elsewhere.

In 1484, Christopher Columbus unsuccessfully canvassed the King of Portugal and then Queen Isabel of Spain to enlist their support for his plan to cross the Atlantic and to try and reach the Indies. On the other hand, two Portuguese, Dulmo and Estreito, suggested to the king that they go in search of the legendary island of Antilla in the Atlantic, with a self-financed expedition that had a clearly defined limit, namely to return if they found nothing within 48 days. Their expedition was thwarted by extremely hazardous sailing conditions. This gave Columbus his chance, though he had to wait a further eight years before he set off on his historic adventure.

THE SEARCH FOR PRESTER JOHN
AND THE CIRCUMNAVIGATION OF AFRICA

In 1487, the Portuguese King, John II, sent out two expeditions in search of the legendary priest, Prester John. The first crossed

Africa, traveling in a southeasterly direction; it was led by Pedro da Covilha, a polyglot who was familiar with the countries of Islam and who set out equipped only with a letter of exchange from a Florentine bank. He met the Negus in Ethiopia and became, like Marco Polo, his advisor, never returning to Europe. The second expedition was by sea: under the command of Bartolomeo Diaz, it sailed south in caravels, toward southern Africa. The underlying motivation of this expedition was a desire to break the Venetian, Arab and Egyptian trade cartel in spices. After many hazards – the sea was very cold and the winds unfamiliar – , the two caravels and their support boats arrived at the Cape of Storms, later renamed the Cape of Good Hope, but returned disappointed to Portugal, with nothing of any significance to show for their efforts.

A year later, in 1489, the first geographical map by Henricus Martellus showed the *finis terrae* of southern Africa. Maps had by now become strategic tools for states and indispensable aids for sailors and merchants. Later, when the Portuguese King Manuel the Fortunate obtained the monopoly in pepper, he swore everyone to absolute secrecy in regard to any knowledge of maps. The Spanish devised a complicated system, which required two keys to open the chart locker on ships – one for the senior pilot, the other for the senior cosmographer. Maps became targets for espionage in Europe and were sold for vast sums; and anyone caught stealing them could expect to be punished by death.

Backing for Vasco da Gama's expedition to conquer the Indies was provided by King Manuel. The expedition was prepared in an almost military manner: it took two years for the technical, intellectual and financial preparations to be completed before the expedition finally set out for Calicut (in northern Kerala), by way of the Cape of Good Hope, which they rounded on 22nd November 1498. They reached Calicut thanks to the maps of Ibn Majid, bought from Arab mariners who had long been navigating between the east coast of Africa and India. The convoy arrived at Calicut on 20th May 1499, with the help of a favorable monsoon wind, and returned to Lisbon in September 1499. A page in the history of Venetian and Arab power had been turned; the spice trade route changed significantly; and other products such as sugar, corn, gold and silver benefited from Christopher Columbus's discoveries and started to arrive from the `West Indies'. In less than ten years, the conditions were laid down for a progressive transfer of the world's center of gravity from the western end of the Mediterranean Basin to the Atlantic Ocean, and a global economy was born.

CLOCKS: SYMBOL OF RENAISSANCE TECHNOLOGY, BUT MERE TOYS IN ASIA

Mankind started measuring time from early in history, but the only instruments available for many centuries were the hourglass, the sundial and the graduated candle. The Egyptians were familiar with the sundial and one of these, from the era of Thutmose III (around 1500 BC), has come down to us. It is made from a graduated horizontal bar, about a foot long, ending in a small T-shaped projection which casts a shadow on the bar; in the morning the instrument was placed facing east and at midday it was turned round to the west. The Greeks' advanced knowledge of geometry allowed them to improve these instruments considerably: an example may be seen on the Tower of the Winds in Athens. In Rome the system was so widespread that the architect Vitruvius in the 1st century BC described thirteen different types.

The clepsydra or water-clock and the hourglass or sandglass are great inventions. The clepsydra of Thebes in Egypt needed 14 fingers of water on winter nights and only 12 in the summer, depending on local meteorological conditions. The Greeks used the water-clock above all to measure the time allotted to lawyers presenting cases to tribunals; and in Rome, the clepsydra – the word means 'water thief' – became a status symbol for wealthy families, just like the piano in better-off Victorian homes in later times. But it was difficult to refine the sand, and the climate-related problems of water – freezing and a difference in fluidity according to the season – were as hard to resolve as the absence of sun during the night and on cloudy days in the case of sundials.

However, it was always possible to use graduated candles, or even oil lamps that indicated the passage of time as they burnt.

The Milanese Gerolamo Cardano (1501-1576), who gave his name to the differential joint in many European languages (French *cardan*, Italian *cardano*), perfected a system which used the principle of a vacuum to steadily draw up the oil in a lamp. The Cardano lamp was in use until the end of the 18th century. In the east, the custom of burning incense helped to spread the use of time-measuring instruments. In China in 1703 – the period of the Great Drought – they even invented a `pail of incense with 100 graduations´, a relatively complex system.

THE INVENTION OF THE CLOCK IN CHINA

The first mechanical clock was probably built in China around 1090 AD, when the Emperor of the Northern Empire asked one of his scholars, Su Sung, to make an astronomical clock for him, the `son of heaven´. Built in a 30-foot high pagoda, the clock consisted of a sphere of graduated bronze rings turning on an axis with mechanical workings, and it showed the hours, days and years. But this mechanical jewel remained a symbol of power and the emperor's `toy´, the viewing of which was a privilege that he granted only with the greatest reluctance. However, in the western world the search for mechanical systems to measure time gave rise to fierce competition between craftsman and engineers from the 13th century. In 1271, Roberto Angelico described some of his plans but revealed that he had not yet found a solution. Before the end of the century there were functioning clocks on the campanile in Milan and the bell tower of Beauvais cathedral in northern France. It is most likely that the mechanical solution for measuring time was first found in northern Italy. But the first clocks were fairly crude and had to be constantly adjusted. As a result the town authorities or church canons appointed `keepers of the clock´.

A KEEN INTEREST IN MECHANICS IN EUROPE

Clocks spread throughout Europe, where interest in mechanics was growing rapidly. The taste for machines grew exponentially during the Renaissance: the most obvious evidence of this is provided by Leonardo da Vinci's drawings – at a time when oriental artists were concentrating on painting flowers, fish, landscapes and horses.

The first clocks had no face or hands because most people were illiterate and innumerate; instead they had bells and little moving figures, with which to draw the attention of the faithful. The little automaton held a hammer, called a *Jacquemart* in French (from the word `Jacques´, a pejorative term for peasants in the Middle Ages). But in 16th century Europe, the clocks installed on the church bell towers and belfries struck hours of equal length, thereby giving people a new perception of time. The first mechanical time-telling system that put more emphasis on the visual than the aural was invented by an Italian, Jacopo Dondi, whose son later built a planetarium clock in Padua. The Dondi clock, the drawings of which are today in the Smithsonian Institute in Washington, also showed eclipses, a calendar of movable holidays and a perpetual Easter calendar. Sometimes the tragic end of one of these clockmakers was recorded, for there were many towns where people were possessive about their marvelous creations; in Prague, as soon as the master clockmaker had finished his work on the facade of the belfry, the town burghers had his eyes put out to ensure that he could not replicate this technical wonder elsewhere.

Thanks to Galileo Galilei and the study of the pendulum the accuracy of clocks was considerably improved; the average error was reduced from fifteen minutes to two seconds a day, based on the precision of regular movements of the pendulum. The time in Paris, for example, had previously been different from that of another town on the same meridian, because of the imperfections of the mechanical movements of clocks.

The first clockmakers were blacksmiths, locksmiths, cannon and bell makers. A company of clockmakers was founded in Paris in 1544 and another in Geneva in 1601. England would have to wait until 1630 for one to be established in London. The main customers for clocks and watches were European royal courts, towns and cities, noblemen, the Church and rich merchants. Persecution during the wars of religion in France and southern

Germany caused many craftsmen to flee to Switzerland, England, Holland and northern Germany. The invention of the pocket watch has been attributed to Peter Henlein, the clockmaker of Augsburg, but watches long remained inaccurate. It was not until the second half of the 17th century that the spring movement was invented, probably by the Englishman, Robert Hooke. This, however, was patented by the Dutchman, Christian Huygens, who made the first spring movement watch, later used by the navy. The portable watch was revolutionary because it altered the relationship between man and time. From the end of the 17th century, the word `punctual´ started to be used amongst the well off, together with the principle of being `on time´. `O Madam, Punctuality is a species of Constancy, a very unfashionable quality in a Lady ...´ says a character in Sheridan's *School for Scandal* (1777).

JESUITS AND CLOCKS IN ASIA

There was little interest in mechanical objects in the east, and for a long time clocks were little more than curiosities. The empire of the Middle Kingdom and the Mandarins learned of the existence of these instruments from travellers arriving in Macao. Indeed the Jesuits succeeded in gaining entry to the Forbidden City thanks to two clocks which they presented to the Emperor in person. The status of the Jesuits in China was enhanced by their ability to handle and repair the clocks and the little mechanical figures. They managed to secure the position of clockmakers to the court, with responsibility for the clocks in the Imperial City – and naturally the Jesuits made sure that those of them who were sent to China those amongst were especially proficient in mechanics. The same story was repeated in Japan, where the first clock to arrive from the west was a gift from St Francis Xavier to the Governor of Yamaguchi (1555). Other missionaries offered gifts to the Japanese imperial administration in Kyoto and Edo (Tokyo). The Japanese were long fascinated by clockmakers and their mechanical know-how, but clocks were viewed as robots rather than as instruments for telling the time.

THE VENICE ARSENAL:
THE FIRST INSTANCE OF TAYLORISM

In 1570 the Venetian spies who were active throughout the eastern Mediterranean in the service of La Serenissima's *Baile* (ambassador) in Constantinople warned that the `Great Gate´ – a term derived from the Vizier's compound in Constantinople and denoting the Ottoman empire as a whole – was preparing to invade Cyprus and Venetian possessions in this strategic region where the two powers both exercised influence. Within 50 days around 150 Venetian galleys were built and launched, ready for battle. This fleet was a major factor in the victory over the Turks of Venice and Spain, supported by Pope Pius VI, at the battle of Lepanto on 7th October 1571. La Serenissima's Arsenal (from the Arabic word *dar-sina-a*, construction site) and its workers (*arsenalotti*) were the master-builders of this `industrial´ victory. The Arsenal provides a very specific example of a certain type of working organization, based on three principles: assembly line production, interchangeability of parts and vertical integration. The Venetian archives contain a report, *Il Discorso del Maneggio*, on this organization based on management principles. It was through this that the Arsenal played a vital supportive role in Venice's military strategy and the exercise of its power. In 1534 the Senate declared that `the founding principle of our power, as created by our ancestors, has always been our fleet´. The same principles used in the Venice Arsenal were applied by the American Navy during the Second World War, when US shipyards built `Liberty´ ships for transporting equipment to the European Front and later to front lines in the war against Japan. More than 2700 ships of this same type were launched between 1941 and 1945, with a peak-rate of production of more than a ship a day!

A GREAT PRE-INDUSTRIAL COMPLEX

In 1104 the Doge Ordelaffo Falier decided to build a large naval shipyard. The site was selected on the basis of two criteria: protection from attack by an enemy and the proximity to the quayside where supplies of wood from the Alpine forests of Cadore were unloaded. The first major extension took place at the beginning of the 14th century with the creation of the *Darsena Nuova* (new Arsenal) in 1325: the total surface area was 80 acres, including 9 wet docks (Venice covers an area of two and a half square miles). After the fall of Constantinople, the balance of political and maritime power in the Eastern Mediterranean shifted and Venice was obliged to prepare for permanent military conflict with the Turks. In 1473 Arsenal acquired its *Darsena Nuovissima* (newest Arsenal), a shipyard where the new triremes could be built, whilst in another area of the shipyard they built a rigging factory. This area was called the 'Tana' because the hemp for the ropes came mainly from the region of Azov, at the mouth of the River Don (*Tanai* in Russian). A century later the Arsenal covered two and a third square miles and included foundries, cannon foundries, oar-makers and rope-makers, a highly profitable enterprise for Venice. In fact, Venice was able to procure its hemp at a very reasonable price from Russia because it was the main customer and hence paid no excise duty. The material was spun and made into ropes and rigging by the many women employed by the Arsenal. These ropes were used in Venice's military and trade vessels, but were also sold to ships passing through and exported elsewhere. Because ropes were very expensive at this time, Venice reaped a huge profit from the trade, due particularly to its production method. Indeed, production was continuous and ropes were simply cut off at the required length rather than being produced to standard measurements, a system that avoided wastage.

THE TAYLORIZED ORGANIZATION OF THE ARSENAL, AS OBSERVED BY DANTE AND DA VINCI

The success of this great naval dockyard was due in large part to the organization of work. Around the end of the 16th century, the Arsenal became one of the industrial wonders of the world. The standardization of production, the interchangeability of the different parts which went into building ships, the relatively rigid hierarchy and the almost military style of work enabled ships to be constructed at a high rate. A French chronicler who accompanied the future King of France, Henry III, to Venice in 1574, wrote that a galley was built in the time it took for the prince to enjoy the meal served in his honor. The workforce consisted of carpenters, specialists in caulking, shipwrights, oar-makers and naval architects. Production lines were based on vertical integration – techniques would be adopted by the Chicago slaughterhouses at the end of the 19th century and by Henry Ford from the beginning of the following century.

When the Venetian Navy needed extra galleys, the Arsenal could build them with incredible speed (for the period) by simply sourcing pre-fabricated parts from the workshops. All the galleys were standardized, as were their components and their ordnance. This type of system is familiar to us from modern car assembly lines... with one big difference: workers in car plants are not specialists and craftsmen, and the Arsenal workers all were. Obviously there was a cost to Venice in keeping all this material in stock, but it was in any case less than that of maintaining a fully-equipped fleet in commission in peacetime. From the 17th century onwards, Venice also used English and Dutch ships, which offered their services on a mercenary basis.

The shipyard was visited in 1312 by Dante Alighieri, who describes it in the *Inferno* (XXI – V 7-8)[1]. Other celebrated visitors

---

1. As in the Arsenal of the Venetians
      Boils in the winter the tenacious pitch
To smear their unsound vessels o'er again,
      For sail they cannot; and instead thereof
         One makes his vessel new, and one recaulks
The ribs of that which many a voyage has made;
      One hammers at the prow, one at the stern,

to the Arsenal included Leonardo da Vinci in 1500, the future Henry III, Galileo (several times between 1605 and 1609), Frederik IV of Sweden in 1709 and the Emperor Franz-Joseph.

THE *ARSENALOTTI*, VENICE'S INDUSTRIAL ELITE

More than 2000 people worked in the Arsenal, sometimes rising to 3000 when mobilizing for war: one witness from 1423 even talks of 16,000 workers, but this was at a time of emergency. Venice had trouble hiring the skilled labor for the Arsenal because small private shipyards offered better wages. However, they found a solution: the workers were inscribed in a special book (*Libro delle Maestranze*) and were then guaranteed work, whereas those who worked outside had to face the serious risk of losing their jobs when times got hard. The *arsenalotti* also received medical assistance and an early form of pension; they were allowed to use personally, or sell, any discarded material; lastly, the foremen lived in houses built specially for them. On top of all this, they had the right to work elsewhere so long as they guaranteed at least 150 days' work to the Arsenal. There was near-military monitoring, with the appointment of *appontatori* and *despontadori*, responsible for registration of attendance and quality surveillance. Venice recognized how essential these *arsenalotti* were to sustaining its power. The *arsenalotti* worked alongside firemen in tackling fires, had the privilege of forming part of the Doge's guard of honor, and furnished the crew for the *Bucintoro*, the ceremonial boat in which the Doge rode once a year for the ceremony of `Venice's marriage to the Sea´. These concessions confirmed the privileged role accorded to the workers and reinforced their team spirit; they became a true industrial elite in the Republic. During the severe outbreak of plague in 1575-1577, which ravaged the population of Venice, the *arsenelotti* and their families fared better than most people due to their medical care and especially their guaranteed

---

This one makes oars, and that one cordage twists,
Another mends the mainsail and the mizzen;
   Thus, not by fire, but by the art divine,
    Was boiling down below there a dense pitch
Which upon every side the bank belimed.

Translated by Henry Wadsworth Longfellow

salaries, which gave them a higher standard of living with better food, hygiene and housing.

Many maritime states tried to attract the *arsenalotti* and their skills by offering high wages and bonuses. But Venice protected itself from this economic warfare by keeping the men and their families under police surveillance to prevent them from leaving. In the Inquisition Archives in Venice, there are records of a number of actions taken against *arsenalotti* who left the Arsenal. They were tracked down by the Venetian police, who had no scruples in the methods used to induce them to `return to the fold´. There were both gentle and not-so-gentle methods of persuasion, including poison and the infamous Venetian military stiletto – used for personal defense or, in the event of a fort or ship being abandoned, plunged in the barrels of the cannons to render them useless.

THE DECLINE OF VENICE AND ITS ARSENAL

The presence of Dutch and English galleons, hired to strengthen the fleet, changes in the mercantile and military navy – at first gradual and then rapid, as galleys gave way to galleons – and the successive loss of territories under Venice's control in the western Mediterranean, all hit the Arsenal hard. From 1718, no further military vessels were built there, and it continued only with merchant ships in small quantities. There was a brief pause in its decline during the war against Tunis in 1784, which again called briefly for the production of warships. On his arrival in Venice, Napoleon ordered the merchant ships under construction in the Arsenal to be destroyed and dismissed the 2000 *arsenalotti*. Then the Austrian government restructured the Arsenal. Betwen 1806 and 1815 it again came under French control, and was reopened with employment for 6000 people. Finally, when Venice passed into Italian control, the Arsenal became a major naval construction yard. After the Second World War it was converted into a museum.

HOW ALUM HELPED THE POPE FINANCE WARS AGAINST ISLAM

Alum is a chemical product[1] that can be found in certain volcanic soils. Some people believe it has magical properties – protection from the evil eye in North Africa and from demons in Asia. It fixes dyes in coloring textiles, clarifies certain solutions, preserves animal skins, glues paper, and is used in glass making, hardening plaster and as an astringent in medicine (men who cut themselves shaving rub it on to staunch the flow of blood). The Greeks and especially the Romans used alum to coat the skins with which they covered their siege engines for protection, because of its properties as a fire retardant.

ESSENTIAL FOR BOTH TEXTILES AND FOODSTUFFS

This `magic´ product was essential in Antiquity for the treat-ment of textiles, for food preservation and in the healing of wounds. It is recorded from 2000 BC onwards, when Egypt exported it all over the Mediterranean and to the countries of the Middle East. It was found in certain regions in the south of the country. Mention of it has been found in cuneiform script on tablets from Mesopotamia in the 8th century BC. Pliny talks about it in great detail in his books on nature; he writes particularly of the alum found in the volcanic region around Naples. The Greeks, the Romans, the Byzantine empire and Arab civilizations all

---

1. Aluminium potassium sulphate

depended on this crucial material. Caravans traveling to India and China transported large quantities of it to exchange for spices and silk.

GENOA SECURES THE NEAR MONOPOLY OF THE ALUM TRADE

The Italian maritime mercantile cities profited from trading alum and competed for its monopoly in Europe. Genoa was the most successful, managing to acquire a near monopoly of the trade in Egyptian alum throughout northern Europe. Venice merchants also obtained their supplies from Bejaia in Algeria, the destination of the caravans from Lake Chad, from the archipelago of Greek volcanic islands, from Cappadocia, from Rocca in Syria – which gives its name to `rock alum´ –, from the volcanic region near Naples, from Tuscany and from the Aeolian islands, the volcanic archipelago northeast of Sicily. The town of Siena was also able to profit from a number of alum seams from extinct volcanoes found in the nearby hills. As a result Sienese merchants grew rich fast, becoming the first Italian bankers of the time able to lend large sums of money to the Pope, emperors and princes; they also helped to finance the wool industry which was rapidly developing in the Sienese region.

A WAR LASTING 40 YEARS

Florence, which was governed by the financier family, the Medici, wanted to control the production of alum in the Volterra region. Having found a causus belli to go to war against the old Etruscan town, which until then was independent, Florentine troops attacked it in 1429, without success. Between skirmishes, betrayals and negotiations, the war lasted for the next 40 years. In 1448 the price of alum fell to an all time low of 0.375 *ducats* per 110 lbs (one *cantare*). The Genoese merchant Francesco Draperio set out on what seemed like an impossible mission: to create a cartel of all the main groups trading in alum. In this he had great success, for prices rose once again. In 1453, in a dramatic turn of events, Constanti-nople was seized by the Turks, thus making the routes to the eastern

Mediterranean and the Middle East increasingly hazardous. The price of alum rose steeply in Europe, forcing merchants to look for alternative sources to meet the high demand from the emerging textile industry. In 1461 the Republic of Venice began exploratory mining in the Tyrol; and the Republic of Genoa brought some old mines on the islands of Ischia and Pozzuoli in the kingdom of Naples back into production. Deposits were discovered in 1462 at Mazaron (Cartagena) in Spain. But the most important discovery was made in Italy in the mountains of Tolfa, a volcanic region dating from the Pliocene period, some 40 miles northwest of Rome. It was Giovanni de Castro, a Vatican functionary and naturalist who made the great discovery. He was the godson of Pope Pius II, and wrote to him as follows: `Today I can offer you victory over the Turks. They are stealing more than 300,000 *ducats* a year from the pockets of Christians through the sale of alum which we need for the textile industry... I have found seven mountains rich in this mineral which will be enough for seven worlds. I need your agreement to hire laborers, prepare the furnaces, and bake the stones... You will be able to supply the whole of Europe once more and the Turks will lose all theirs gains, and since they will be going to you, their losses will be doubly great...´. The quarries became operational in November 1462. On 7th April 1463 Pope Pius II issued a Papal Bull forbidding all Christian merchants to buy alum from the Turks or other infidels. Moreover, the Pope bought the lands at Tolfa from the wealthy feudal family, the Frangipanis, for 17,300 *ducats*. Since the Vatican administration was disinclined to manage they ceded the rights to the Genoese merchants Spinola, Centurioni and Giustiniani. But from 1466 onwards the Medici, the all-powerful Florentine bankers, obtained the management of the mines and the monopoly of alum distribution, through the founding of *Societas Aluminium*. In 1470, alum was discovered near Volterra, and the area looked set to become a major center of production. In 1472 Lorenzo de Medici sent an army to take complete control of Volterra, with 100.000 florins allocated for the operation. Thus the town became a faithful ally of Florence[1], although the mines had to be abandoned in 1483.

---

1. Volterra was freed by the Emperor Charles V, after a pact with Pope Clement VII in 1521. But Florence could not afford to lose control of the mines and in 1530 fiercely attacked the strongly fortified hilltop town, which once again fell under Florentine control.

A CRUSADE FINANCED BY PAPAL INCOME FROM ALUM?

Exploration rights from the mines at Tolfa generated some 9% of the papacy's total revenues, more than 723.000 *ducats* over the period 1462-1513. The Pope even thought of financing a crusade against the Turks and a large amount of money was paid to the Church's allies to help prepare it. The Medici bank handled the transfers. Venice, which wanted to restart importing alum from Turkey, nonetheless shared in the desire to act against a threat which threatened its position in the eastern Mediterranean. The new Pope, Sixtus IV, carried on the project against the Turks and in one year alone spent 177.000 ducats. The income from the mines at Tolfa no longer sufficed! So he had to borrow money from the Italian bankers and even proceeded to pawn items such as precious stones, ritual objects, and precious metals. Nevertheless relations between the Medici bank and the Pope became increasingly difficult. In 1476 Pope Sixtus handed over the monopoly for exploiting and trading the alum to the main competitor of the Medici bank. This bank belonged to the Pazzi family, which took part in the *congiura dei Pazzi,* an armed operation supported by the papacy and the de Montefeltro family to kill the leading members of the Medici family on Ascension Sunday 1478 as mass ended in the cathedral. Though the conspiracy went disastrously wrong, it did succeed in undermining the stability of the Medici bank.

The search for alum in Europe began to yield further results: Spanish mines started competing with the Tuscan centers of production; those in Bohemia supplied the markets in eastern Europe, even though the alum from Tolfa was of very high quality. In addition, more mines were discovered in the volcanic region of Tuscany at Massa Marittima; to prevent these from being put into production the Pope agreed to pay an annual allowance of 2000 crowns. In 1549 Bohemia banned all foreign imports of alum to protect its own production. However, the victory of Venice, Spain and the Papacy against the Turks at Lepanto in 1571 eliminated many of the dangers for shipping in the eastern Mediterranean. Venice began once more to import Turkish alum from Cappadocia. Thus the papal near-monopoly of Tolfa collapsed. Elsewhere mines had been discovered in the Tyrol, in southern Germany, in England and on the volcanic islands of the Caribbean archipelago – especially those under the dominion of France, which was seeking an independent source of its own. Demand for this product from both the textile and paper industries, which were in full expansion, remained high, whilst the physicians of the armies at war across Europe used the chemical to stop hemorrhages from superficial wounds. But with the huge increase in supply the price fell.

British naturalists visiting Solfatara – the great volcanic caldera north of Naples – began studying the properties of alum at the beginning of the 17th century. But it was Jean Etienne Guettard, Lavoisier's brilliant assistant, who described its chemistry, after an expedition in the Vosges, and in 1781 Chaptal set up an industrial alum factory at Montpellier. Alum's decline set in once manufactured dyes came into production. Although it is still used today, largely in medicine and as an ingredient in personal deodorants, alum is no longer an indispensable product in the manufacture of colored fabrics.

YELLOW CABS, TAXES, POST HORNS, AND THE STORY OF A GREAT POSTAL FAMILY

News of the victory at Lepanto, on 7th October 1571, by the coalition between Venice, the Spanish empire and the Papacy over the Turkish fleet, arrived in Venice on 18th October, and in Paris and Madrid on the 31st October. When Philip II sent orders to the governor of the Philippines, he received the reply some ten to twelve months later. To send letters at all was very expensive. For example, when on 14th July 1560, Monsieur Chatonnay, Spain's ambassador to Philip II, sent a dispatch from Chartres to Toledo, it cost him 358 *ducats* for the return journey, that is two *ducats* for each stage of the road, of which there were 179 in all. This was more than a year's salary for a professor at the University of Salamanca or Padua! Exorbitant as it was, it should be borne in mind that the content of this letter was vital, since it was a dispatch from the rebels in the Netherlands to Monsieur Montigny, who was away in Spain.

THE POSTAL SERVICE, INDICATOR OF AN EMPIRE'S POWER

Empires have always understood the importance of communication between the center and outlying regions and the need for it to be both rapid and reliable at any cost, since news plays a strategic role. Around 5000 years ago, in China, the first postal system was launched; messengers on horseback or on foot carried dispatches from the capital to the provinces and vice versa. Evidence also exists of a postal system in imperial Egypt around 2000 BC. Again in China, the Chou dynasty (1122 -720 BC) perfected a system for sending official documents and orders from the capital to the different regions, which in turn sent back information; the system was based on riders who changed horses every nine miles. Matters were improved still further under the Han dynasty (202 BC-220 AD); the empire was getting larger and the Chinese postal system brought news to the emperor, even from Rome! The Persian Empire under Cyrus (6th century BC) organized a postal system based on relays where both men and horses were changed; further, in view of the number of different languages spoken across the empire, it was decided to use a single official language, Aramaic.

With the expansion of its empire, the Roman postal system was clearly of vital importance. Rome built its road network to move its legions around and to enable dispatches to be sent rapidly. Naturally merchants and pilgrims benefited as well, with large quantities of goods being transported by road, although most cargo still went by sea. It is estimated that urgent mail could be carried at a speed of up to 150 miles in 24 hours. This top speed remained unbeaten until the appearance of railways 2000 years later! The Roman postal service was based on a system of *mutationes*, or staging posts, where horses were permanently stabled, at a distance of about three miles apart. There were in addition relay inns or hostels established especially for the couriers, where they would find still further fresh horses, located at 25 mile intervals. The *cursus publicus* was very effective: a letter from Julius Caesar dispatched in England arrived in Rome 26 days later. Herodotus and Xenophon praise the postal service, but in the letters of Seneca and Pliny are found complaints about the slowness of some deliveries. Of course maritime postal service was faster: a letter sent from Rome, via the port of Ostia, could reach Egypt in as little as ten days. Rome opened its postal service to citizens who were able to afford the cost, such as senators, wealthy landowners, and rich merchants.

The pre-Columbian empires also had postal networks, but without horses. Here it was men who ran great distances, and in the mountains too. The *chasquis* or runners were chosen according to very specific criteria and were often trained to run long distance from childhood. *Tambos* or staging posts were distributed throughout the highly developed network, as in the Roman system. The distance between Lima and Cuzco, about 500 miles, could be covered in just three days. Two hundred years after the fall of the Inca Empire, the Spanish postal couriers needed twelve to thirteen days to cover the same distance. Many empires used signaling bonfires for communicating in emergencies, such as the risk of invasion, an order for general mobilization, or the death of an emperor. Even today watchtowers still exist along the European coasts of the Mediterranean, which were used to look out for pirates and to send a warning to other watchtowers inland, that would in turn pass on the danger signal, again by means of fires.

CARRIER PIGEONS AND INNKEEPER-SCRIBES

After the fall of Rome, with the fragmentation of power in Europe, growing insecurity and the decline in demand for communication, the postal system disintegrated. However, it still remained effective in the eastern Roman empire, and partially was integrated with the Baghdad postal system which began using carrier pigeons to send important military dispatches. This same solution was used by Genghis Khan to keep in touch with his highly mobile cavalry units. The Arabs who invaded Sicily maintained and continued to use the Roman *cursus publicus*, and the Normans who later occupied the island also retained the system, placing it under the control of a high-ranking state functionary known as the *Protonotaro*. In any case, letters continued to circulate in Europe, although over shorter distances and in limited numbers: monks, students – who often went from university to university –, pilgrims, merchants and sailors all carried letters for people. Abbeys, diplomats, university professors, the Church of Rome and merchants all needed to communicate at long distance.

A new profession came into existence: that of the innkeeper who possessed sufficient skill with the quill pen to write letters for his customers and passing travellers. These letters were then carried by other customers and travellers. An embryonic postal system of this kind was thus created in parallel to the official system, thanks to the spread of literacy. The need to communicate soared with the recovery of the economy in Europe, and the growing number of fairs and the creation of a paper economy with bills and

letters of exchange. Merchants and bankers were no longer itinerant, but carried out their business in one place, even though its
geographical reach was greatly increasing. In addition, the borders
of certain states were also being extended.

THE TORRE AND TASSO FAMILIES (*THURN UND TAXIS*)

Around the mid-13th century, the Tasso family from the Bergamo region in northern Italy began transporting mail between
Bergamo and Venice. Omedeo Tasso was probably an innkeeper
and taverns were the main centers for exchanging news and
mail. Together with other families from the town he joined the
Compagnia dei Corrieri Veneti, a firm which through its reliability
had achieved a monopoly in transporting the mail from Venice
to other major destinations. Branches of the family went on to
hold a near monopoly of the postal service for the papacy,
although they lost this privilege in the mid-16th century when a
bank founded by the Tasso family in Rome went bankrupt.
Another branch of the family emigrated to the Tyrol and Styria
region of Austria, becoming responsible for Frederick III's postal
service and later working for the Hapsburgs, at a time when
Maximilian I extended his kingdom to the Low Countries
through his marriage to Mary of Burgundy. The Italian family
names were germanicized to *Thurn und Taxis*. In 1505 they were
being paid 12,000 *livres* a year to organize and manage the imperial postal system. In the contract which was signed with Philip
the Fair it was stipulated that each staging post must always have
at least one fresh horse fit to gallop. Charles V confirmed this
mandate throughout the empire, which was by now even further
extended. Giovanni Battista became `Master General of the
Mail´; his firm regularly transported mail throughout a network
which included Rome, Venice, Innsbruck, Vienna, Prague,
Regensburg, Augsburg, Lyon, Madrid, Nuremberg, Frankfurt,
Cologne and Brussels. The postal service from Rome to Brussels,
via the town of Trento, became the only regular service with a
daily departure in both directions and a timetable for arrival and
departure of the mail. Rival services never managed to achieve
the same regularity in delivery over many of the routes.

THE FAMILY IS ENNOBLED: A YELLOW COAT OF ARMS WITH A HUNTING HORN

The family was ennobled, and on its yellow coat of arms there was an animal (Tasso means badger) and a hunting horn (used by the messengers to announce their arrival). Later, the renamed `post horn´ became the international symbol for postal services in many countries; and the word taxi became an international word signifying private cars for transporting people in towns, very often painted yellow like the family coat of arms. What is more, the word `tax´ came from the same origin, since the family made customers pay a tax for the transport of letters; and it has even been suggested that the Russian news agency TASS took its name from the *Thurn und Taxis* family (though in fact it is the acronym for the Russian telegraphic agency). In 1695 there was another promotion through the ranks of the nobility: the family was elevated to princely status, the highest level amongst the Hapsburg aristocracy. The Spanish decline in Europe coincided with the Taxis postal service's loss of power; Napoleon took away their monopoly in 1806, and although the service remained in existence it had lost its main role and above all its monopoly, though it was still operational. They were even among the earliest to use stamps up until 1867 when the Prussian state nationalized the postal service.

OTHER NATIONAL SERVICES – AND THE `DARK ROOM´

Louis XI founded a royal postal service in France in 1477, Henry VIII appointed a `Postmaster´ in 1516 in England, and other smaller states created their own systems, though they were basically intended for the transmission of official messages, with concession often being granted to individuals. It was only from the 17th century onwards that states organized postal services they themselves managed, with legislation designed to protect their security. In France Mazarin always used the `dark room´, an office introduced by Louis XII with responsibility for `checking´ the mail; all letters deposited with the central post office in Paris were opened and `discreetly´ read by the secret police. Other countries used similar practices at this time. The mail distribution monopoly

was strongly protected, and Mazarin abolished the medieval privilege that allowed Paris University messengers to distribute the
post. Le Tellier, Marquess of Louvois, Superintendent of the Post,
called for competitive tenders from would-be service providers
with bids on the price to be paid to the state to win the contract.
Of course in time of war the postal service managed as best it
could, even though those responsible for carrying the post were
given something like diplomatic immunity. For example, when
relations were at a low ebb between Venice and the Ottoman
empire, the Venetian ambassador to Constantinople and other
diplomats prepared five copies of each letter, coded and numbered,
which were sent by different routes and messengers, to increase the
chances that it would reach its destination.

THE OPTICAL TELEGRAPH AND THE PONY EXPRESS

A new market naturally attracts new inventions. At the outset,
the post was `official´ only; later, merchants, monks and the
clergy were the `mass consumers´ of the communications market.
In 1691 Thomas Neale organized a correspondence service
between Europe and North America; though he tried to keep
prices low the business failed. The first American post office
opened in Boston on 5th November 1639, to great demand. The
large geographical area of the United States lent itself to a postal
service: the first route between Boston and New York was set in
1672 and it followed the `Old Boston Post Road´, now Route
One. Peter the Great's Russia became the country with the greatest consumption of postal services with an average of two letters
per inhabitant per year!

The wars which devastated Europe during the 17th century led
to the development of optical telegraph systems, with moderate
success: they were too dependent on the weather and above all did
not work at night. The Pony Express in the USA was killed by the
electric telegraph. But before that happened, for some nineteen
months the mail was distributed across a network of nearly
2000 miles with 157 staging-posts by 80 young couriers galloping
flat out on spirited horses; they earned up to $125 a month, riding
up 75 hard miles a day. As well as the telegraph, trains and
mechanically powered ships and boats played their part in putting

post riders out of a job, although they fought hard, but unsuccess-fully, to retain their monopoly. They were rapidly swept aside by new technology; and very few stagecoach companies had the foresight to invest in the railways.

THE STORY OF THE GREAT ANDEAN TRAIL: *EL CAMINO DEL INCA*

The great Inca trail was the backbone of the Inca empire. It was part of a well-organized system of roads leading from the capital, Cuzco, to Quito in the north and Santiago in the south. The network has been in existence for more than 10,000 years, since any civilization in the Andes region has required good roads to survive. The Andean civilizations of the Chavín, Mochica, Nazca, Tiwanaku, Wari, Chimu and Chachapoyas all built parts of the system. But it was the Incas who truly constructed the network and with a competence and organization reminiscent of that of modern highway engineers. The Inca Empire was very extensive: 2200 miles long, 500 miles wide, and with a population of 8 to 10 million. The geographical terrain was very varied, presenting a huge challenge to its political leaders and engineers. There were tropical rain forests in the north – modern Ecuador and Columbia – with high annual rainfall, together with wide plateaus and some high dry areas; then, between Peru and Tierra Del Fuego the vegetation becomes sparser, the mountains are arid, and there are forests and wetter areas near the coast near the coast and in Amazonia; finally there is a low-lying and very wet coastal strip. The buildings and roads had to survive great extremes of temperature and needed be constructed with special techniques to withstand them. To complicate matters further, the whole area is subject to strong seismic activity; hence any construction needed to be able to stand up to violent earthquakes and tremors.

A 15,000-MILE ROAD NETWORK

The Inca Empire exercised its power in high mountain regions for the most part and a rational and effective road system was essential They needed it for transmitting strategic news, moving troops in the event of emergencies, and transporting goods; and they needed to know that in the face of crises – mainly extreme weather conditions and external threats – the road system would remain operational. Something like a modern superhighway was built from north to south, a distance of over 3300 miles, between Tucuman (Argentina) and Quito (Ecuador). Later the conquistadores were to call it *El Camino Real*, the Royal Road: it crossed towering mountains of great height, using passes up to 16,500 feet above sea level. A second road ran along the coast over a distance of some 2500 miles, which the conquistadores called *El Camino de la Costa*. The whole road system measured around 15,000 miles in all, since as well as other north-south routes there were also east-west roads linking the Amazon basin and the Argentinean plains with the mountains of the Cordillera.

The roads were between 10 and 50 feet wide, depending on the terrain and the traffic. They were paved with highly resistant stones made from volcanic and igneous rocks such as porphyry, granite, andesite and basalt; these were often transported on logs that were either rolled or pulled along over oiled surfaces. Men in their hundreds would haul, roll and transport the stones over great distances. For the most part they relied on their muscles, using ropes made from llama hides or vegetable fibers such as cotton, linen and reeds. Local inhabitants were given the task of building the roads and subsequently maintaining them. Because of the difficult terrain, it was often necessary to construct bridges made of wood or suspended by lianas. They even used a form of cable car with large sacks to carry people across gorges. Some sections of the road consisted of stone stairways with hundreds of steps; elsewhere the builders needed to excavate short tunnels through the mountains or passages through the rock. All this work was complicated by the varied, often volcanic nature of the terrain. The various tunnels and passages were all dug with obsidian picks – pre-Columbian civilizations used metallurgy for precious metals with a poor, metallurgy for base metals. Remember too that the wheel and horses were unknown to the Incas: nearly everything had to be carried on men's backs or using pack llamas.

A HIGHLY DEVELOPED IMPERIAL MAIL SYSTEM

The imperial mail system was extremely impressive. Couriers were trained from a very young age. These messengers, who ran the mountain roads, carried news or orders for functionaries in the provinces, and the replies and messages sent to the imperial center by political and military commanders stationed throughout the empire. Since they had neither paper nor writing, all this information had to be memorized and passed on from one messenger to another. Any mistakes were severely punished – the guilty man would be thrown into a ravine! Some longer messages were transmitted through the `quipu´ system[1], a very peculiar coded assemblage of strings and knots. These messengers were running on mountain roads at great heights above sea level, which is physically extremely punishing, even though they were trained and used to it. They were required to cover a certain distance and pass the message on to the next messenger; they then would rest and wait for another message to carry in the opposite direction. There were refuges every two to four miles, in which the couriers or *chasquis* could stop and rest. Roughly every five miles there was a customs post or *pukara* responsible for monitoring the road and checking that anyone using it had the right to do so, since it was the property of the emperor. Every 13 miles there was a *tambo* or urban center, and every 30 miles or so a provincial town. There were `traffic police´ to keep an eye on movements along the roads and check travellers, though their main job was the political and social control of the population and the prevention of any protest or demonstration against the emperor. Travellers and merchants could use these staging points to obtain food, to rest, and to unload their animals and goods, but they had to have authorization to use the road as it was basically intended for the army and postal

---

1. A quipu (khipu) consists of dyed strings, woven from cotton fibres or occasionally llama or alpaca wool. It's constructed a bit like a grass skirt, with a single, long, thick cord from which dangle as many as 2,000 pendant strings. Subsidiary strings sometimes hang from the pendants. Each string typically features an array of knots. Quipu means knot in Cuzco-Quechua language.

couriers. Merchants used the roads mainly to transport food supplies destined for the towns and in turn the proto-industrial products made by craftsman in the towns for people living in the country. Very often the roads were used to transport special produce for the emperor and his court. For example, fish freshly caught in the Pacific Ocean would be quickly transported to the emperor's table in Cuzco – a hundred or so *chasquis* racing some 300 miles just to satisfy the whims of the court. Ironically, it was the roads that allowed Pizarro's conquistadores to hasten the downfall of the capital Cuzco! Once the Spanish empire seized power the road system fell rapidly into disrepair and ruin.

THIRTY-THREE POUNDS OF GOLD
FINANCE THE DISCOVERY OF AMERICA

Finding a route to the Indies was a cherished dream in the 15th century. In order to achieve it, Columbus asked for 1.6 million *maravédis* to finance his expedition.

The *maravédis* was a copper coin minted in Castille which got its name from the *morabati*, the gold coin of the Almoravids, the invaders who occupied Spain, having arrived there via Morocco at the time of the great Muslim expansionist period in the 8th century. In 1492, with 1.6 million *maravédis* it was possible to buy 33 pounds of gold – this was the cost of Columbus' expedition! At first sight this might seem an insignificant sum. But one must take into account that the total amount of gold produced from the beginning of antiquity up until 1500 would fit into a cube measuring six and a half feet in each direction (280 cubic feet), whereas the amount of gold produced up until 1905 is estimated at a cube with each side 33 feet long (36,000 cubic feet). At the time of Columbus therefore, gold was still a very rare metal.

The crown of Castille gave Columbus an advance of 1.14 million *maravédis* and Columbus provided an eighth of the costs himself, the rest being financed by merchants and bankers, the sponsors of the time. The finance was provided by the king's treasurer, Luis de Santangel – a Valencian and a convert to Catholicism from Judaism – in agreement with Coloma, a Catalan living in Valencia, and an Italian, Pinelo. A Florentine banker then presented Columbus to the Duke of Medina Sidonia. All this took place at the camp in Santa Fé, when Grenada was under siege – the city was later liberated, in the same year as America was discovered.

As for the ships and crew, the little port of Palos in southwest Spain provided two caravels – as it happened, this was the town's punishment for having engaged in privateering. But as it turned out these were the best ships and best sailors that Columbus could have hoped for for his expedition. The *Nina* and the *Pinta*, weighing 55 to 60 tons each, fared much better in the end than the *Santa Maria*, a carrack from Galicia which weighed 130 tons and was the flag ship, but which was wrecked on 24th December 1492 and never returned to Spain. Columbus set off with 87 men and letters of royal commission destined for the Great Khan, emperor of China! They were looking for a passage to the Orient, as well as gold and spices. During the second voyage he set out with seventeen boats, fourteen of them caravels, and 1500 men. The intention was to explore and colonize these lands which, in Columbus' mind, were not part of a new continent since he was as yet unaware of what he had discovered! One of history's luckiest and greatest mistakes... Columbus did say that traveling gives you a thirst for knowledge!

MERCHANTS AND BANKERS FINANCE THE GREAT DISCOVERIES

Admiral Columbus was not only a sailor but also an experienced merchant trader. Born in Genoa, as the commercial agent of the Centurioni family (Genoese merchants who were part of the oligopoly for the distribution of alum in Europe), he sailed throughout the Mediterranean, including the Levant, had been active with Catalan privateers and took his inspiration from the Florentine mathematician and cosmographer, Paolo Toscanelli. He was familiar with the African routes followed by the Portuguese sailors and their maps, the famous portolans, and from 1485 onwards he looked for a powerful sponsor capable of financing his project of discovery. Through a combination of luck and experience, he did not make the same mistakes as the Vivaldi brothers from Genoa who, two centuries before Vasco Da Gama, had tried to sail round Africa. They were lost at sea, and the Genoese merchant who financed their expedition sent men and ships to look for them. The rescuers discovered the 'Fortunate Isles' of Antiquity – the Canaries – and one of these islands still bears the Genoese name of Lanzarote – another discovery made by mistake!

Ironically, all the great discoveries which took place between 1492 and the middle of the 16th century received only minor financial support from states, kings and princes, all of whom all were somewhat nervous about risks associated with these projects. Very often they granted exploration rights, but provided little by way of finance for the explorers. Instead it was the bankers and merchants of the Mediterranean and later northern Europe who opened their purses and risked large sums. For example, between Columbus' 3rd and 4th trips, seven expeditions were organized to discover more regions of the West Indies. Peralonso Niño de Mogue left the port of Palos, early May 1499; at the end of the same month Alonso de Hojeda with Juan de la Cosa and Amerigo Vespucci (representing the Medici family of Florence) sailed from Cadiz. At the end of November from Palos another expedition left the Old Continent: it was under the command of Vicente Yáñez Pinzon and Juan Díaz de Solis. One month later Diego de Lepe voyaged from Seville. Early in 1500 a notary from Triana, Rodrigo de Bastidas, received the authorisation to sail to the northern coast of Latin America. A very large Portuguese expedition was launched in March 1500; it was commanded by Pedro Alvares Cabral and opened the `conquista´ of Brazil by Lisbon. Finally it was the turn of Alonso Vélez de Mendoza (July 1500), who was authorized by the Spanish Kings to direct his ships to the regions under control of Portugal, according to the Treaty of Tordesillas. All these expeditions had a geographical and political aim with a final target to discover new regions. The first `commercial´ voyage to the West Indies was secretly organized by the rich merchant-banker Francesco Ripparolo of Genoa and Juan Sánchez de Tesorería, a trader from Aragon. Two ships sailed to Santo Domingo, carrying several merchants – among them Francesco de' Bardi of Florence – and a lot of goods (fabrics, clothes, horses, cows and goats). Some reports showed huge profits of 300-400% from this trip! This also explains why, at a time when many ships – galleys, galleons, caravels and other ocean-going vessels – were fairly sizable (400 to 1500 tons), all the expeditions were carried out in relatively small ships, ranging from 80 to 150 tons. The aim was to keep investment in equipment to a minimum, although they called on the most experienced and skilled sailors, who had already explored the coasts of Africa, passed through the straits of Gibraltar, crossed the bay of Biscay to the English ports, and sailed in the Mediterranean in the winter when the sea is notoriously changeable. For example, Magellan's expedition cost 9 million *maravédis*, and comprised two ships of 130 tons, two others of 60 tons and a fifth of 90 tons.

CABOT IS FINANCED BY BRISTOL'S HERRING MERCHANTS

Bizarrely, the expedition of the Genoese explorer Giovanni Caboto – known as John Cabot in English – was financed for the most part by merchants who had no particular connection with the spice trade; indeed the capital came from merchants selling North Sea herrings. Many of those who produced salted fish were in difficulties due to the sudden and unexplained drop in fish stocks; it was the hope of finding other richer sources of fish in a more northwesterly region that prompted them to finance Cabot's expedition. Furthermore, Henry VII of England, who had already missed out on a significant opportunity, having rejected Columbus' proposal, agreed to Cabot's, authorizing him to sail in the name of the English crown in 1496. The merchants of Bristol put a small caravel at Cabot's disposal with a crew of eighteen men. This set sail on 2nd May 1497. Cabot, with his son Bartolomeo, discovered Nova Scotia and Labrador – and abundant stocks of fish, especially whiting. Cabot, however, was convinced that he had reached the northern coasts of China.

Such European discoveries were the result of the enterprise of merchants and bankers, but were also a response to the rise of a new power in the eastern Mediterranean: the Turkish Empire which, after the fall of Constantinople, took control of the strategic commercial routes east, both on land and at sea. The initial response was transfer sourcing of various products to the western regions of the Mediterranean and northern Europe – for example, sugar from the Algarve and Malaga, silk from Granada and Calabria, and alum from Tolfa and Mazaron. But Europe was not self-sufficient and could not count on being fully autonomous in producing these goods. It was therefore obliged to look for other routes giving access to the Indian Ocean and the Far East. The center of gravity thus moved from the Mediterranean to the Atlantic Ocean, though this was far from obvious at the time.

MAPS: STRATEGIC TOOLS, SECRETS AND ESPIONAGE

From the *tabula* of the Roman Empire to the *imago mundi* and *mappa mundi* of the early Middle Ages, people have always wanted to make representations of the world in which they live. The first geographical drawings were painted on rocks and stones – and on wood, but that has not survived – throughout the world. When talking to the Holy Roman Emperor Charles V, Hernan Cortez confided that he had asked Montezuma, the Aztec Emperor, to show him which bays would provide safe anchorage for his ships during tropical storms. Montezuma had produced a map for him of the whole Mexican coast, painted on a textile made from agave or aloe fibers. Many of the geographical documents from the New World have disappeared, victims of the iconoclastic fury of the Spanish monks, but the maps of the Tepetlaozoc Codex remain to bear witness to the geographical knowledge of the pre-Columbian peoples. Elsewhere, the maps and charts from the Marshall Islands in the Pacific reveal the extensive knowledge of these peoples, who used shells to mark the islands on large canvasses made from coconut fiber as a navigational aid for their voyages among the islands. In Mesopotamia, clay tablets dating from 2500-2300 BC clearly show the irrigated lands along the banks of the Euphrates and Tigris. The Egyptians possessed a detailed surveyors' archive used for tax purposes, since taxes were paid on cereals on the basis of the area harvested. Herodotus recounts how maps were rapidly made of the Shiite regions conquered by the Pharaoh Sesostri. He also relates that the Pharaoh Necho (c. 596-594 BC) organized an expedition to sail around Africa from the Red Sea to the Straits of Gibraltar, using Phoenician ships. The great Egyptian museum in

Turin has in its possession a map drawn on papyrus from the time of Ramses IV (1150 BC), showing roads and gold mines in the south of Egypt.

Aristotle and Pythagoras proved that the earth is a sphere. Achilles' shield is probably one of the earliest representations of the ecumene, the inhabited world, with a cartographical and cosmological interpretation of it at the time of Homer. The first descriptions of Herodotus' ecumene include a large part of Europe, all of North Africa, the Red Sea, the Persian region and Russia.

THE MILITARY MAPS OF THE ROMAN EMPIRE

Knowledge of the world was advanced both by Alexander the Great's expeditions and the scientific genius of the mathematician and librarian, Alexander Eratosthenes (even though his techniques were criticized by the Roman geographer Strabon). The Roman administration and military authorities fully understood the importance of geography and maps. Leaving discussion of such things to the philosophers, they got on with the process of describing and measuring the roads leading from Rome toward the frontiers of the empire. Augustus commissioned his friend, the valiant general Marcus Vipsanius Agrippa, to have a map made that would be at the disposal only of high-ranking officers in the Roman army. Showing all the roads of the empire in great detail, as well as the distances covered, staging-posts, major towns and military garrisons, this was a strategic document and classified as a `secret of state´. It was first exhibited publicly in summary form in the Campus Martius in 20 AD as part of a propaganda exercise which Rome carried out to demonstrate its might. A few copies of the map were sent to the nerve centers of the empire, where they were carefully guarded, being considered documents of great strategic importance. But this was only one of many maps that attempted to chart the world: there were also representations of Africa, India and China. Suetonius mentions certain maps of the empire which were completely secret; and anyone with a copy of these without authorization could expect to be punished by death – a clear indicator of the value of geographical information in the eyes of the imperial government and senior officers in the Roman army. Pliny and, later, Claudius Ptolemy, who lived in Alexandria at the time of Hadrian and Antony the Pious, were on the other hand interested in the philosophy of geography, and for the next thousand years Ptolemy's *Geographia* remained a key work of reference for a number of civilizations.

Chinese silk and spices sent to the west and the precious metals and glassware that Rome sent to the east all increased people's knowledge of the two empires, even though the ambassadors of two great powers failed to establish much contact. Gan Ying drew up a very detailed account of Western lands based on General Ban Chao's expedition in 97 AD; he speaks of the *Daquin* or Roman Empire, at a time when Roman sailors were also in the Indian Ocean, sailing in the direction of China (the first voyage was around 166 AD). Ptolemy and the Roman cartographers described China as lying beyond the `Golden Peninsula´ (Indochina). Chinese cartography was also highly advanced: under the Chin dynasty, Minister Phei Hsui had a map of China and the barbarian countries inside its borders' drawn up in 267 AD. This made use of a grid system and orthogonal projection, and showed contours, rivers and cities. It too was a state secret. Maps already existed at the time of the previous dynasty, the Han, but they were more local in nature and described the differences of the regions, their purpose being essentially military. Another very important map was produced under the Tang in 801 AD. It showed the whole empire and measured no less than 1000 square feet in area. Later, the Mongols worked rapidly on drawing maps to chart their growing conquests, but they were not very accurate due to the speed with which the empire expanded. It was not until the beginning of the Ming family's rule and the great voyages in the early years of their dynasty that there was any further development in the art of Chinese cartography. In China to possess a map was a sign of the `mandate of heaven´ entrusted to the emperor.

SAILORS, TRADERS AND PORTOLANS

For a long time traders and their goods were restricted to traveling on known land and sea routes, and people stuck to the `beaten track´ for fear of the risks involved in not doing so. Arab and Indian shipping in the Indian Ocean and the Arab-dominated part of the eastern Mediterranean between the 7th and 8th centuries benefited in particular from the development of navigation techniques. But cartography made little progress, even though the great centers of Arabic and Indian civilization exchanged Ptolemy's maps and the principles of universal geography. Moreover in Europe the theological weight of the Roman Catholic Church had an increasingly negative effect on geographical research. However, Europe came to the fore with the rise of Palermo, which replaced Baghdad from the 11th to 13th centuries as a major cultural center and looked favorably on the work of the Arab geographer Al-Idrisi dating from 1139. With the growth of the Italian maritime republics, in particular as a result of the Crusades and the development of Portuguese shipping on the Atlantic coast of Africa, *portolani* or portolans made their first appearance. These were the maps and charts on which ships' captains began to show ports and coastal outlines and indicate current and underwater hazards. These portolans were shrouded in secrecy. For example, Genoa forbade any charts to be published and only the captain of a ship was allowed to posses one – the ship's crew never knew their destination, the captain alone being privy to this information. Lawyers drawing up commercial contracts very often wrote that ships were `going wherever God willed´.

The information on roads and coastlines was gathered by merchant traders and sailors. On the other hand, geographical information about the interior of a country was collected by geographers, though they were not known as such: these were local administrators and `scientists´ who followed the armies. In both cases the information they provided was extremely useful and its production and collection was expensive and highly valued. Armed with such information, generals and admirals could familiarize themselves with territory or waters before battle started. And for the mariners and the traders who sailed in the ships, it was of vital importance to know the route, the ports and the hazards they might encounter on their voyages.

GEOGRAPHICAL INFORMATION WAS WORTH A FORTUNE

All maps, then, were very expensive and were of inestimable value, especially at the outbreak of a war or before the start of an expedition. Whoever owned a map had a semi-monopoly on information: European courts, senior army officers and merchants were avid for this type of information and used any method that they could to obtain it, legal or otherwise. When it came to marine cartography, Venetians, Pisans and Genoese had to cope with competition from the Portuguese school of cartography. The Portuguese Prince Henry the Navigator encouraged his sailors to explore the African Atlantic coast and founded a famous school of cartography in Majorca, which drew the leading experts from all European nations and religions. In Sagres, Henry the Navigator gathered all available information and bought the latest maps published in Italy and the Low Countries at any price. Scientists studied navigation techniques, winds, currents and the newest instruments. Abandoning 'TO' medieval cartography – where maps were in the form of a circle inscribed with a large T separating the three known continents of Europe, Asia and Africa, and with the Mediterranean (*Medio Terrae*) at the center – they began producing maps which reproduced reality in detail and aided navigation and trade.

The value of these maps and charts – strictly not for sale – became increasingly important. Considered as secrets that had to be protected at any cost, they were kept in strong boxes, locked with coded keys. The Portuguese imposed the *sigila* on all maps: meaning both 'sealed' and 'secret'. Secret agents of all nationalities lurked in the places where these charts and maps were produced or where they might obtain useful information: Sagres, Lisbon, Venice, Genoa, Pisa, Antwerp, Amsterdam and others, including the French center of cartography in Dieppe. In this connection, King John II of Portugal inaugurated his kingdom in 1481 by quoting a petition from the people demanding that foreigners should be forbidden from settling in Portugal and the new regions because they were looking for information on recent discoveries and spying on them all. And when an inventory was made of the deceased Henry the Navigator's effects, all his maps were confiscated by the king. In Portugal, secrets were also safeguarded by prohibiting the sale of caravels to foreigners – after 1442 this was the only type of vessel used for maritime expeditions –, and the sale or disclosure of portolans or navigational instruments. Lastly, pilots and captains of vessels were forbidden to leave the country other than on voyages for which they had obtained a specific authorization.

THE GREAT DISCOVERIES STIMULATE ESPIONAGE

With the circumnavigation of Africa, the discovery of America, Magellan's voyage and the success of merchants and European powers in reaching the Indian Ocean and the Atlantic, the search for the latest charts with the most recent discoveries and full details of the regions concerned clearly became vital for governments, the military hierarchy, merchants, the Church and diplomats. So all involved set about spying and uncovering secrets as best they could. The stakes couldn't have been higher. Francis Bacon wrote `Nam et ipsa scientia potesta est´: knowledge is power!

In 1500 Portugal founded a specialized institution to protect maps and secrets. Known as the *Padrão Real* of Lisbon. It was quickly copied by Spain, which in 1503 set up its own *Casa de la Contratation de las Indias*. But all these precautions may have been inadequate. The most striking case of espionage was the master stroke of the Italian spy, Alberto Cantino, the diplomatic representative of the Duke of Ferrara in Lisbon. King Manuel I particularly liked Cantino and took him into his confidence. In reality, Cantino was a very able and effective agent of the Duke's and managed to send him the only copy of a map, only recently completed (in 1502), showing the latest discoveries by Diaz, Columbus, Vespucci, Cabral and Coelho. The map gave details of all the newly discovered territories in the New World as far south as Brazil, the African coastline with the Mascarenas archipelago which includes Mauritius – officially discovered in 1512 –, and part of India. Cantino succeeded in buying the *Charta Del Navigare* from either its originator or one of his entourage for the very considerable sum of twelve gold ducats. The map also showed, for the first time, the demarcation line between Spanish and Portuguese possessions, agreed at the treaty of Tordesillas (1494), and officially recognized in the Papal Bull *Inter Caetera*. Under the Spanish Pope Alexander VI's arbitration, the treaty fixed the Portuguese border along an imaginary line 370 leagues west of the Cape Verde islands; to the west of this meridian, newly discovered lands and any as yet undiscovered, would belong to Spain. Another very similar map appeared in Genoa in 1504, published by the town geographer Nicola Caverio. Cantino had told the

Duke of Ferrara that `his´ map had been sent by one of his agents to Genoa for subsequent delivery to Ferrara.

The phenomenon of espionage in relation to maps and charts grew rapidly. Governments – France, England, Holland, the Vatican, and especially Venice –, bankers (see the many letters from Vespucci to the Medici bankers in Florence) and merchants were all prepared to pay very large sums of money for information, confirmation and maps of the latest discoveries. The Venice archives contain numerous reports from its ambassadors, especially in Spain and Portugal, on the latest discoveries; but the most interesting reports are those sent by Venetian spies. Nations paid a king's ransom for the experience and knowledge of pilots and navigators, who sold their services to the highest bidder. These included the likes of the Cabots (both father and son), who worked for Henry VII of England, and Amerigo Vespucci who worked for Spain, and which made him *piloto mayor* with responsibility for cartography and selecting the captains to be sent on maritime expeditions. Many of these men were financed by private capital, but other adventurers and experienced captains set out from European ports at the instigation of those in power. However, spies were able to find out about these projects by tracing the orders for food provisioning and equipment needed for the voyage which captains placed with ships' pursers. Once again, spices, precious metals and trade routes were the driving force behind this thirst for new discoveries, which was unfolding in regions of the globe which Europeans had, at best, only dreamt of.

Maps as a luxury and status symbol

Maps were not only essential tools used by ships' captains; they were also a status symbol for those in power. Pope Gregory XIII ordered 32 large maps which were hung on the walls of the 400-foot long gallery in the Vatican palace, completed in 1580. The Dutch East India Company had 180 maps of Asia, the Indian Ocean and the western regions of the Pacific drawn up. In 1507 the Duke of Lorraine commissioned the great geographer and mathematician, Martin Waldseemüller, to make a map of the world in which the `Western Indies´ were treated for the first time as a new continent: they were no longer viewed as islands en route to Japan and China. This map `invented´ the Pacific, before it was discovered by Balboa in 1513, and gave the name of America to the new continent, in honor of Amerigo Vespucci who had described its east coast on returning from his voyages.

Cartography as an economic activity grew very rapidly, helped by the spread of printing. But the number of copes made of each map was very limited no more than a hundred or so examples, which quickly became out of date as new lands were discovered. Seville, Lisbon and Venice faced strong competition from Flemish geographers and the University of Leuven. Antwerp, Leyden and especially Amsterdam became great centers of cartography. Amsterdam benefited from the wars of religion when a number of Catholic and Jewish geographers arrived there; and thanks to the increasing maritime might of the Dutch it became centrally important in map production. Its maps were sold throughout Europe, the Muslim world and even in Asia. The great publishing houses of the city – Hondius and Blaeu, among others – achieved a near monopoly in world cartography. Maps became increasingly decorative objects in the houses of wealthy aristocrats, financiers and high ranking clergy – and were the subject of envy from great universities and scholars.

THE STORY OF AN ASYMMETRIC BOAT: THE VENETIAN GONDOLA

The gondola, `queen´ of Venice, symbol of romantic moonlit nights and lovers' dalliances under the Bridge of Sighs – legend has it that couples who kiss at sunset there, when the bells of the Campanile are ringing, will love each other for the rest of their lives – is one the strangest boats in the world.

For its structure is completely asymmetric – the left side, where the gondolier stands to row, is nine and a half inches wider than the right side of the stern, where the *forcola* or rowlock, made from walnut wood, is placed to give leverage to the oar. The gondola floats on the water therefore, with a pronounced list, and it is this that allows the gondolier to control the balance of the boat better and to lean into the stroke to optimize his efforts. On the other hand the boat draws little water, allowing it to pass through the shallow waters of the lagoon and canals without difficulty. A gondola weighs about 1300 pounds and must measure 36 feet in length and 4 feet 9 inches in width; if the dimensions vary, then it is no longer a gondola but goes by another name depending on its structure and function.

A 1000-YEAR-OLD `QUEEN´

The gondola is mentioned for the first time in the history of Venice in 1094, in a decree from the doge Vitale Falier, who exempted the inhabitants of southern Venice from providing a *gondulam*. There is still a debate going on today among philologists about the origin of the word gondola: from the Latin (*cymbula* =

small boat, *cacula* = diminutive of *concha* = small shell) or from the Greek (*kundy* = little boat and *kunty-helas* = push and embark).

There remain few iconographic traces of this boat which is so important to Venice: it was only from the end of the 15th century that the Venetian painters began to put it into their pictures. Later came the famous and much admired series of twelve Venetian festivals painted by Guardi and the `photographic´ precision of Canaletto's crystal clear paintings. In the course of its history, the gondola's structure has been modified, but the Venetian authorities have always tried to regulate the construction of this boat that plays such an important role in the city's transport system.

A SOPHISTICATED TECHNIQUE UNDER THE CONTROL OF THE REPUBLIC

When Venice was at the height of its powers, many small arsenals, or shipyards (*squeri* in the local dialect) produced gondolas. Some of these specialized in repairing them, others in building them. The political leaders of La Serenissima wanted to control their production for strategic reasons, and from mid-14th century, the government began to inspect (and possibly penalize) the builders and carpenters who worked in these arsenals. Venice wanted to grant a privileged status to its skilled workers; they both worked for and were protected by the Republic and were employed in the city's great Arsenal. The city was in fact the first to apply pre-Taylorian methods to the separation of tasks, professional specialization and the rapid assembly of ships – a fleet could be built and ready to set sail in less than six months. The same principle to the regulation and protection of Venice's master craftsman and skilled glass-makers, transferred to the island of Murano to prevent the risk of fire spreading in the town as well as to facilitate control of the industry, and lace workers, brought together on the island of Burano to protect the Venetian monopoly in lace-making.

In 1607 Venice authorized the men of the *squeri* to join the *Scuola degli Squeri*, an early type of trade union, which protected their interests. Venice however maintained full control of maritime production in the city and pushed the *squeroli* into specializing in the production of small and larger boats for use on the canals of the town and in the marshy regions along the Adriatic coast.

A ROWING TECHNIQUE USED ON GALLEYS

Among the *squeroli* were joiners who made the oars. They used very hard wood which had been treated and aged over a long period; the quality of the oar is essential for the gondola as it has only one. But this very precise and sophisticated technique was also applied to making the oars which were used in Venetian galleys – the military ships long responsible for protecting convoys of commercial shipping throughout the Mediterranean. This was the reason the doges wanted to keep the *squeri* under their control.

What is more, a gondola is made from 280 different parts, using eight different types of wood – the same technique, applied on a larger scale, as in the Arsenal. Making the prow comb from metal, which has become the symbol of Venice, was also an inspired addition to the design, because apart from its aesthetic function it acts as a counterweight to the gondolier and allows great maneuverability.

PAINT IT BLACK!

Venetians liked to be ostentatious with their wealth, as is apparent from their palaces, and this preference was extended to a competition to make gondolas as elegant and brightly colored as possible. Unfortunately, in 1633 the *Provveditori alle Pompe*, the Office in charge of defining the rules of pomp, issued a decree which settled once and for all the color of gondolas: black was the color to be applied to all gondolas belonging to nobles and wealthy merchants as well as those for public hire. This decision was just one step in the Republic's gracious decline, which probably accelerated in the decades following its last great naval victory against the Turkish Empire, at Lepanto in 1571. Commercial and maritime capital progressively abandoned trade and shipping and was re-invested as agrarian capital, through large estates, and as industrial capital. This shift led to the promotion of maize production, the textile industry (especially silk), the production of luxury goods such as glassware and lace, and book publishing which, unlike the others, remained in the center of Venice. The magnificent Venetian villas in the countryside around Padua, Vicenza and Verona bear witness to changing the Venetian economic center of gravity and in particular to the nature of la Serenissima's capitalism.

IMPOVERISHED SWITZERLAND EXPORTS A MILLION MERCENARIES

It is estimated that between the 14th and the 18th centuries the various Swiss cantons `exported´ more than a million mercenaries. Switzerland was a poor country: agriculture in the mountains was difficult, the breeding of livestock and craftsmanship suffered from competition from countries possessing wide plains or easy access to the sea and trade routes. These stalwart mountain people, used to harsh living conditions, needed a new source of income during the winter months. `Making war´ on behalf of a third party was one of the solutions – even if it was dangerous. Swiss troops gained a solid reputation as resolute fighters after soldiers from the cantons crushed the Hapsburg army at Morgarten in 1315. Turning mercenary became a common pursuit. The cantons and then later the confederation imposed strict controls on recruitment, even becoming military entrepreneurs in competition with professional recruitment officers in the service of princes, kings and foreign republics.

SWISS KILL SWISS IN BATTLE

Military recruitment was not yet carried out on a national basis and many countries, when preparing for war, turned to mercenaries. Such troops cost nothing when the country was at peace, being paid only during wartime, and then often through the right to loot towns and conquered lands. The arrangement was financially advantageous to the treasuries buying this `tailor-made´ service. Though it could be expensive in times of war, it reduced their costs enormously in peacetime. It sometimes happened that these mercenary troops, made up largely of young Swiss men, would meet in battle and kill each other. The soldiers were defending neither ideals nor their native lands, but their pay was augmented by the booty they obtained from looting. Such employment also attracted many unemployed young men living in the Mediterranean countries and other poor parts of Europe. A bad harvest, a famine, a pirate raid in coastal regions or a war, could all induce young men in financial trouble to leave home and become mercenaries, swiftly learning to handle weapons and function on the battlefield.

THE *LANSQUENETS* IN COMPETITION WITH THE SWISS

The very poor peasants from southern Germany also followed the Swiss example. From the time of Maximilian I (1493-1519) the `people of the land´ (*die Landsknechte*) were recruited by agents and organized into units of 500 soldiers, commanded by a colonel (*Oberste*) who was granted the right by the king to levy troops. These troops were often depicted by artists, as they were dressed rather colorfully, almost like the *commedia dell'arte*. But the reality was quite different. These fighting men had to have suitable combat clothing which would protect them against sabers wielded by the cavalry, bullets fired by musketeers, and the long lances of pikemen, particularly the Spanish *tercios* who advanced in a line. They therefore only wore their fancy uniforms on parade. The reputation acquired by the *Lansquenets* when they and other troops pillaged Rome and the Vatican in 1527 left no doubt as to their ruthlessness.

A MERCENARY CONTRACT SIGNED IN THE PRESENCE OF A NOTARY

The ideal territory for mercenaries was in Italy. At the time of the Renaissance the country was the richest part of Europe, but political and military power was divided up among princes, dukes and republics, who despite their great wealth were unable to protect themselves and defend their frontiers. There was constant warfare between these small states, and in addition the emerging powers of northern Europe did battle indirectly, by fighting in Italy. The demand for troops was therefore very great and the Italian *condottieri* (mercenary generals) had plenty of opportunity to offer their services to the highest bidder, often being paid in advance. The *condotta* was a contract drawn up in of the presence of a notary, in which the terms of engagement were precisely stipulated and agreed upon. There were two types of *condotta*: the *condotta a soldo disteso* when the *condottiere* signed himself up together with his troops under the orders of the commanding officer of the town or state; if the *condottiere* was working for another mercenary then the contract was called *condotta a mezzo soldo*. The *condottiere* received a payment which covered his troops' expenses and a fee for himself. He in turn could sub-contract his fee to other *condottieri*, under the same conditions and rules of commercial law that applied in any business transaction. These contracts were very detailed and specified the number of men and their arms, their length of service, their objectives and their pay. Very often there was even an official observer (*il colla-terale*) whose job it was to check that the *condottiere* fulfilled the terms of their contract. Sure enough, treachery, betrayals and last-minute switches from one side to another were frequent – a rich source of inspiration for literature and opera!

MACHIAVELLI IS FIERCELY CRITICAL OF THE USE OF MERCENARIES

Machiavelli did not approve of employing *condottieri* and merce-nary troops. In the *Art of War* he maintained that an army which used a large number of mercenary troops was weakened, since they were liable to mutiny or to change sides for a few pieces of gold; and even if their military prowess and performance in the field was often impressive, there were cases when mercenaries lacked the will to fight. The great political scientist and theoretician asserted that only a national army levied on the population could guaran-tee a true defense system. In *The Prince* Machiavelli was even more detailed and virulent against mercenaries: 'Mercenaries and aux-iliaries are useless and dangerous; and if one holds his state based on these arms, he will stand neither firm nor safe; for they are disunited, ambitious and without discipline, unfaithful, valiant before friends, cowardly before enemies; they have neither the fear of God nor fidelity to men, and destruction is deferred only so long as the attack is; in peace one is robbed by them, and in war by the enemy. The fact is, they have no other attraction or reason for keeping the field than a trifle of stipend, which is not sufficient to make them willing to die for you.'[1]

Certainly, a large number of mercenary troops within an army will form an anomalous group with little loyalty and a tendency to form pillaging bands before, during and after battles. Naturally the commercial value of loyal, well-trained troops commanded by a genuine strategist was very high, and the price of such was proportional to their and their commander's professionalism. For example, Florence paid Francesco Gonzaga 33,000 florins a year to retain him and his 250 soldiers; and Francesco Maria della Rovere received 100,000 florins per year, and his company consisted of a mere 200 mercenaries.

THE SECOND OLDEST PROFESSION IN THE WORLD

History provides an abundance of stories of mercenaries and the outcomes of battles won or lost through their actions. In ancient Egypt the pharaohs had insufficient soldiers of their own and relied on foreign auxiliaries. Ramses II had four army corps, each of which included Nubian, Libyan and even Asian mercenaries. At the end of the Peloponnese wars between Sparta and Athens, when thousands of soldiers were left without employment, Persian *Satraps* (provincial governors) benefited by taking them on at a lower rate of pay. Greece always needed to use mercenaries because of its small population – a practice Aristophanes was very critical of, since he felt that it was wrong to pay more to foreign soldiers than to their own troops. In the *First Philippic* Demosthenes describes mercenaries as being like an `army on paper'. In their struggle to dominate the Mediterranean, Rome and especially Carthage relied heavily on mercenaries. Indeed in the Carthaginian army officers of minor rank were Libyan, Corsican,

---

1. From *The Prince* (Chapter XII), translated by W.K.Marriott

Sardinian, Ligurian, Berber and Greek mercenaries. In 264 BC Carthage was obliged to come to the rescue of its mercenaries from Campania in southern Italy, under siege in Messina. The war against Rome lasted thirteen years, at the end of which Carthage was no longer able to pay its 40,000 mercenaries and they rose up in revolt. Flaubert wrote of this in his book *Salambô* – it was he who described mercenaries as the second oldest profession in the world. Another example: half of Hannibal's troops were trained by mercenaries when he marched on Rome. The decline of the Roman Empire began in earnest when its citizens were no longer prepared to leave their homes and set out across the known world to fight for the glory of emperors, generals and senators. Once Rome put its military fate in the hands of `former barbarians´, it had effectively made a pact with the devil, since very often it ended up paying off, with gold, the tribes living along the *limes* to avoid being invaded.

CHRISTIAN MERCENARIES FIGHT FOR THE TURKS

A thousand years later, Joan of Arc resorted to using 400 mercenaries at Compiègne in 1430, but when she made a sortie to try and liberate the town she was captured by the Burgundians and sold to the English. Equally the Turkish artillery, whose bombardment led to the fall of Constantinople in 1453, was composed for the most part of Christian mercenaries. And for centuries after that they formed the hard core of the Ottoman army, and even used cannons produced in Germany, France, Italy and as far away as Sweden. During its wars against the Ottoman Empire, Venice called on Dutch and English armed galleons, under Dutch and English command, with mixed crews. Venice was unable to finance a permanent military fleet of any great capacity and, although the Arsenal launched several warships before the wars, they were not in sufficiently numerous to vanquish the Turkish fleet. Buccaneers and corsairs were also mercenaries: the word corsair derives from *lettre de course*, meaning `letter of marque and reprisal´, an authorization from the king (or the queen of England) to seize goods or boats belonging to enemy nations if they felt they had a grievance against them. The term buccaneer derives from one who dries and smokes flesh on a *boucan* after the manner of the Indians, a habit attributed to pirates by those who were afraid of them. Some of these `sea dogs´ received their letters of mark signed directly by Queen Elizabeth I and some of them were ennobled, like Sir Francis Drake – *el drago* as he was known by the Spanish.

THE CREATION OF NATIONAL ARMIES AND THE DECLINE OF MERCENARIES

Machiavelli's ideas were gaining ground, and enlarged and increasingly nationalistic states came to feel that mercenaries were both expensive and, above all, unreliable. Armies were becoming less feudal and more national in character, with military service introduced as a sort of `tax´ that young men owed their country. On the other hand, Louis XV's minister of war, the Duke of Choiseul, very rightly and simply said: `The acquisition of a foreign soldier is worth three men: the one you buy, the one you prevent the enemy from buying, and the Frenchman who can stay working the land´. In 1756, at the beginning of the Seven Years War, France had 80 regiments at its disposal: 32 foreign regiments (twelve German, ten Swiss, seven Irish, two Italian and one Scottish). The Irish, who came from a very poor country, gradually replaced the Swiss, and amongst their famous victories on behalf of France was the battle of Fontenoy (1745), which they won thanks to the `Wild Geese´ – the name given by the Irish to those amongst them who went abroad to fight as mercenaries – against the coalition of English, Dutch and Hanovarians. But with the French Revolution came `a new deal´. Only citizens, and not mercenaries, were now acceptable in the army. And this became the general rule throughout Europe – even the Swiss Confederation changed its constitution in 1849 and outlawed mercenaries except for the Papal guard. It was Pope Julius II who first asked the Diet to provide him with a contingent of 200 halberdiers for his protection. Indeed, when in 1527 Rome was sacked, 147 Swiss died defending the Pope. Legend has it that the distinctive uniform of the Swiss guards was designed by Michaelangelo, though in fact it was Jules Repond, commander of the guard from 1910 to 1921, who introduced their uniform.

Mercenaries still exist, mostly for armed operations in Africa and other Third World countries. Recently they have also replaced regular soldiers in paramilitary operations such as the protection of strategic sites and other `security related´ tasks, in states occupied by the US and their coalition partners. The collapse of the Soviet empire also freed up many military personnel, as well as various specialists of varying skills. Such `soldiers of fortune´ are the latter-day heirs of the Swiss mercenaries of the Renaissance period.

WHEN CANNONS WERE WORTH THEIR WEIGHT IN GOLD

When Louis XIV wanted to go to war, his Minister of War would send emissaries to Amsterdam and Sweden to buy cannons. He was not alone in this; his potential enemies made the same journey, because the great military powers of the time did not have the capacity to mobilize their arsenals at a moment's notice for the rapid production of weapons. Thus Venetian ambassadors, dotted around the various capital cities, with well-placed reliable informers – even Casanova was among them – would send lengthy reports warning of the imminence of war due to the demand for cannons rising above normal levels.

THE EFFECT OF CANNONS ON THE BALANCE OF POWER

Cannons were made from bronze or iron. Bronze is an alloy of copper and tin; copper came from Hungary, the Tyrol mountains, Saxony and Bohemia, tin mainly came from England, Spain and Germany. The production of bronze cannons was relatively simple and a good bell foundry could also produce cannons. The cannon manufacturers were based around Nuremberg, Lyon, Bolzano (near the Tyrol mountains) and Antwerp, which had easy access to the raw materials. The great bankers of the period, such as the Fugger family, even had a specialized center at Fuggerau in Carinthia. Initially cannons were mainly used to besiege citadels, but new French military techniques – thanks to Galiot de Ginouillac, the great gunner (from the Lot in southwestern France) of the Italian wars – changed everything. It is now agreed that the battles of

Ravenna (1512) and Marignan (1515) were won by the artillery. This news sparked off a sharp increase in the demand for cannons as well as for the men who knew how to produce ordnance and ammunitions and for soldiers able to transport and operate them.

GOLD, SPICES, SILK... ALL HELPED TO BUY CANNONS

Mechlin, Dinant, Namur, Antwerp, Tournai, Mons, Nuremberg, Augsberg, Marienberg, Frankfurt, Venice, Bergamo, Brescia, Genoa and Naples were all major centers of cannon production. Europe was the only region in the world to produce these weapons, which proved to be so effective in terrifying pre-Columbian peoples and against the infantry and cavalry of the Middle East and the archers of the Far East. Gold and ivory from Africa, and spices and silks from the Far East, were easy to exchange for cannons in Venice, Antwerp and Amsterdam. Philip II of Spain purchased arms with gold and silver cargo brought back by his galleons from the mines of the new American colonies. But around 1570, Spain suffered from a crisis affecting its major suppliers, Italy and Holland. So then it was the turn of England, with its iron mines and forests (wood was required for smelting) – and Sweden, which had iron deposits of even better quality because it contained less sulphur. Nevertheless England still remained dependent on the Low Countries, from which Henry VIII ordered twelve large bombards, known as the Twelve Apostles.

IRON OR BRONZE?

While the production of bronze cannons in Sussex and Kent continued to grow, iron cannons remained technically inferior – but they cost only a quarter the price. When the generals called for cannons they could be given iron ones: what did it matter if they were inferior when they were so much cheaper? Sir Walter Raleigh said that cannons were precious jewels and Elizabeth I even issued an edict prohibiting their export except to protestant countries ('friends'). But the production of and market for cannons developed most strongly in Holland, with the high demand for all types of arms, for use in the struggle against the Spanish and to equip boats sailing the high seas, attracting the most accomplished foundry men and traders to the country.

During the 17th century, Maastricht, Utrecht, Amsterdam, Rotterdam and the Hague all became major centers of production and trade. They produced bronze cannons as well as iron ones, importing copper from Sweden and (remarkably) Japan, tin from Germany and England, and high quality iron ore from Sweden. Thus Sweden too shared in the boom in military production. The Thirty Years War again boosted European production of cannons. Cologne became the main center for their trade. In the meantime the Dutch continued to play an important production role by making cannons in Tula, Russia, which were then sold in Amsterdam at very competitive prices – an early example of competition from eastern Europe.

The Wars of Religion scattered the best foundry men throughout Europe. In France, Colbert was permanently short of cannon makers and gunners, mainly for reasons of religion. Meanwhile chemists had not yet discovered the disadvantages of sulfur and the benefits of phosphorus in making iron cannons. Bronze cannons could be found on the decks of the galleons of the most powerful maritime nations; iron cannons were mostly used for defending fortresses. Small campaign cannons, all of them made from bronze, which were relatively mobile and moved around with armies, radically altered military organization and battle tactics: less armor, fewer pikemen and more light cavalry for attacking cannon batteries.

PAPAL EXCOMMUNICATIONS AND CONCENTRATION OF PRODUCTION IN EUROPE

Cannon production remained concentrated in Europe. The greatest power near Europe, the Ottoman Empire, was dependent on what its emissaries could buy at European production centers, whilst China, which had after all invented gunpowder, never got around to using it for this purpose. A major strategic error!

Although Turkish troops were all-powerful on land, this was not the case at sea; the battle of Lepanto (1571) in which Venetian, Papal and Spanish ships were victorious, was something of an anachronistic victory, in that it was a confrontation between old navies reliant on galleys armed with dated cannons. The Turkish-Muslim world possessed very few mineral deposits and forests, both of which were needed in the manufacture of cannons. It therefore depended on imports from European manufacturers who risked of papal excommunication in putting their technological know-how and capabilities at the service of the `infidel´ Muslims.

Mohammed II had a very large cannon made, the `Mahom-etta´, which proved extremely effective against the Venetian galleys – the ancestor of Germany's `Big Bertha´! In fact it made a lot of noise about (practically) nothing – but the psychological impact on the Venetian sailors was undeniable, and comparable to the terror felt by Parisians when threatened with bombardment from a special German cannon (not Big Bertha, in fact) in the spring of 1918[1]. At any rate, the Ottoman production of cannons remained small in number and of only mediocre quality.

THE CANNONS OF THE MIDDLE KINGDOM

Chinese Emperors lived in luxury, protected from the world outside their palaces. Cannons manufactured in China were of poor quality, reducing their capacity for defense against invaders. Their sole defenses lay in the Wall and their permanent control of the ports, even if the occasional Portuguese trader, Italian Jesuit or adventurer of all kinds, with their goods and their sermons, managed to gain access to the towns of the Empire.

The Japanese were also laggards in the field. They tried to obtain the `secrets´ of cannon manufacture by whatever means possible. In Asia, the exploits of Father Giacomo da Rho, an

---

1. Parisians have always claimed it was 'Big Bertha' which bombarded their capital but in reality it was a cannon designed by Dr Rausenberger of Krupp's. This cannon (project *Wilhelmgeschutz* = William's machine) weighed 750 tons, with a barrel 118 feet long and 82.5 inches in diameter (against 165 inches for Big Bertha) and fired exploding shells weighing around 400 pounds which climbed 26 miles high in their trajectory and could hit targets 78 miles away! A team of mathematicians collaborated on the project because it was necessary to take the speed of the earth's rotation and its curvature into account to calculate the trajectory. The `Paris cannon´ was hidden in the forest at Saint-Gobain near Crépy-en-Laonnais, and began firing the first shells against Paris on 23 March 1918. The first shell was launched at 7.15 a.m. and exploded in the Place de la République in Paris two minutes later. The cannon remained in operation until 19 August, when was relocated because changes at the front. In total it fired a little over 400 shells, with 351 landing on Paris, killing 256 inhabitants and wounding 620.

Italian Jesuit with a gift for mathematics, remain legendary. In 1622 the Portuguese trading post in Macao was attacked by the Dutch, but the Jesuit directed cannon fire from the town's fortress, which was similar to of the one in Lisbon. A well aimed cannon ball caused the gunpowder ships amongst the Dutch vessels to explode, thus forcing them to abandon their attack. Macao remained under Portuguese control for a further 400 years until 20th December 1999 when it passed into Chinese hands.

It has been written that Buddha arrived in China with white elephants, while Christ arrived there with cannonballs, like Baron Münchausen. The decline of China and the Far East from the 17th century onwards may well have been in large part due to the weakness of their cannon manufacturing technology. With effective cannons they would have been able better to protect their coasts and regional trade against the European colonial invasion backed up by well-armed, powerful fleets and tested trading methods ... *sic transit gloria mundi!*

THE NEW WORLD CHANGES THE OLD WORLD'S EATING HABITS

Grazie, Signor Ammiraglio! Every time you enjoy a good pizza you should thank Admiral Columbus. On 12th October 1492 Christopher Columbus landed in America. This historic mistake – he imagined he had reached China – opened the way to the New World and its great riches, including foodstuffs, soon to be exported to Europe.

Tomatoes were imported in this fashion and cultivated in southern Spain, though the dry climate did not really suit them. But Spain occupied the kingdom of Naples at the time, so they tried planting tomatoes in the volcanic and very fertile earth of the Neapolitan countryside. They grew wonderfully – the miracle of the pizza was launched, helped by the fact that the Romans had made bread closely resembling pizza 1500 years earlier.

The discovery of America led to a vast revolution in trade. Many unknown foodstuffs and other products arrived in Europe from the new continent – and the reverse.

Sweet potatoes, potatoes, tobacco, grapefruit, cocoa, maize, peanuts, cassava and turkeys were discovered by curious and hungry Europeans. Nor must we forget the tons of silver extracted in Mexico and ancient Peru and the millions of ounces of gold (Brazil) produced by labor costing virtually nothing. These precious metals financed the 'golden age' of the Iberian Peninsula, which lasted little more than a century. And the list continues with rubber, natural dyes (cochineal and others) and special woods.

So how did Europe respond? It began by exporting pigs, cattle and horses, mules and goats, vines (to South America), sugar cane, coconuts, cotton and bananas, pears, melons, onions, radishes, oranges. Later, it would be the turn of slaves, who were `hunted on the African coast´ and ended up in the coastal regions of Brazil and the Gulf of Mexico.

VIRUSES AND DISEASES CROSS THE OCEAN

All this brought about a massive ecological upheaval. In September 1493, with Columbus' second expedition, comprising seventeen ships and 1500 men (and a few women), a veritable Noah's ark came ashore: horses, cattle, pigs, wheat and rye grain, sugar cane (a reed cultivated in places in China, India, southern Spain and the Canary Islands). Diseases and viruses were also `exported´: smallpox, typhus, mumps, measles and more. These killed up to 90% of the local population, which was not immunized against these diseases and was employed in dreadful conditions in farming and mining. It was for this reason that African slaves began to be imported – because of a lack of manpower. The first contingent arrived in 1505. Over the next three centuries, some 10 million men and women crossed the Atlantic, chained together in ships, to become a workforce treated like merchandise.

The conquistadores also brought medicinal substances back to Europe, including quinine[1], used against fever and malaria – as well as diseases such as syphilis (and its antidote *guaiacum*, or lignum vitae). These medicines helped to consolidate the fortune of the Fuggers of Ausburg, who managed to obtain the European monopoly for lignum vitae. Smallpox, which had arrived in Europe with the Muslim military expansion in the 7th century, also upset the natural equilibrium of pre-Columbian populations – hundreds of thousands of Aztecs died in the two years 1519 and 1520, thus leaving the way clear for Cortez's tiny army. And in 1525, smallpox reached the Inca regions, allowing Pizarro, after an initial defeat, to take control of the Peruvian Highlands in 1532, where the Inca population was emerging from an epidemic that had weakened and decimated it.

---

1. Quinine was also called `Jesuit powder´ because the Jesuits brought back to Europe from Peru a very powerful medicine against fever and malaria. Legends claim that its name `chinchona´ comes from an ancient Countess of Chichon, whose husband cured her using the bark of this tree. Peruvian called it `quinquina´ and conquistadores called it `the fever tree´. Quinine played an essential role in the European colonialism during the 19th century, helping troops and farmers to protect themselves againts several kinds of fever.

CORN: A GOLDEN GIFT FROM AMERICA

`Give me one seed, a patch of land, water, sun and five months: I will give you 600 seeds!´ This can be found in a report sent through diplomatic channels to some Venetian financiers in 1525. It is referring to the great discovery of maize. This plant is very high in yield – today it is possible to get a return of 800-900 grains of maize for each grain sown, and sometimes double that when there are two ears!

Christopher Columbus immediately understood the significance of maize. He even brought some seeds back with him on his first voyage, and these were sown in Spain in 1493. Giovanni Verrazzano – commemorated by the bridge in New York – who worked for François I, collected some seeds from the highlands of Mexico and the Andes and brought them back for planting in the Mediterranean area, Italy in particular. Jacques Cartier, the famous navigator from St Malo, did likewise in 1535, and this maize was sown in northern Europe. Genetic analysis has shown the close links between the cultivars of southern Spain and those in the Caribbean, between the Italian cultivars and certain Argentinean and Peruvian ones, and between those in northern Europe and the North American variety Northern Flint.

NO MAIZE, NO PRE-COLUMBIAN PYRAMIDS!

Without maize and its capacity to feed whole populations, there would be no giant Mayan or Aztec pyramids, no Cyclops Walls in Cuzco or the marvel of Machu Picchu. To feed the pre-Columbian peoples, maize was planted along with manioc or cassava and intensively cultivated on the banks of lakes in Mexico and even more spectacularly, on the hillside terraces of Peru. The impressive yield of maize contributed to the growth and the power of the peoples who grew it, all the more so since the work involved in producing it is minimal. It provides a guaranteed food source, though it needs to be supplemented with meat to give a sufficiently nourishing and balanced diet. However, it was difficult to obtain enough meat, and potatoes, which originated in Peru, were insufficient to make up for the inadequacies in their diet. Chewing coca leaves blunted hunger, thirst, cold and fatigue; this, together with beer brewed from fermented maize, helped people to survive.

VENETIAN MERCHANTS GO INTO MAIZE PRODUCTION

Maize grows particularly well in regions where an abundance of water is available. Southern Spain suffered in this respect and harvests were poor. So the Spanish grew it mainly in the region around Milan – which was under Spanish control –, where there was sufficient rainfall and hot summers. The old merchant families of Venice, who realized that profits from trading with the east were not sustainable, transferred their business interests and investment to agriculture, on the plains to the west of Venice, rich in water, manpower and sunshine. It was the ideal environment for growing maize, and the lands of the eastern Po valley, under Venice's control, became the largest center of maize production in Europe. Famines were avoided thanks to *polenta*, which filled the stomachs of the peasants and those of the town dwellers in Mediterranean Europe and certain regions in the north. The by-products – stalks and leaves – were used for animal fodder and for making agricultural baskets, roofing rural dwellings and stuffing mattresses.

BOTANICAL DESCRIPTIONS OF MAIZE

Maize is described in works written by the botanists Jean Ruel (1536) and Leonhart Fuchs (1542). These reveal that the plant could be found in many European kitchen gardens, and that it was successfully grown in agriculture. After Italy, the Balkans became the second largest producer in the 17th century. Southwest France lagged a little behind other European regions, but once corn was planted there it became clear that it was ideal terrain. Its high yield saved many Europeans from famine, though too much reliance on it can result in the vitamin deficiency disease pellagra. *Polenta* in Italy, *millasse* in southern France and *mamaliga* in Romania are all words signifying `full belly´, but also have connotations of poverty. Maize was the basic foodstuff of many European peasants, though it was rarely seen on the tables of the wealthy. Flemish artists who took country fairs and festivals as their subjects – weddings, the ending of wars, saint's days and so forth – often showed large bowls of gruel made from maize in their paintings. This cereal was never depicted as food for the rich, even though ears of corn had first been painted in Europe at the feet of Mercury as part of a floral garland for the villa Farnese in Rome in a work by Giovanni da Udine in 1516. At this time it was a great novelty, and so it was included for its rarity value. Again, pineapples are sometimes depicted in paintings and carvings from Medieval times – another instance of a rare product which the painters and sculptors themselves might never have seen. Magellan's exemplary secretary, Pigafetta, wrote in 1497 that maize was not so well regarded as other cereals, and though men might eat it, so too did pigs.

MAIZE IS PLANTED IN AFRICA AND ASIA

Maize arrived in Asia via Burma in the middle of the 16th century. Chinese merchants there, who were in contact with the Portuguese, imported it to the islands of southeast Asia. Around the end of the 18th century the demographic explosion in China led to a great extension of the land under cultivation, with maize being grown even in northern regions of the country. Japan was also a major destination for maize, imported from China. Today world production has reached almost 700 million tons, which includes 280 million tons in the United States (long live popcorn!), 130 million tons in China, 35 million tons in Brazil and just over 30 million tons in Europe. More than 400 million tons are used for animal fodder.

THE PEPPER WAR BETWEEN LISBON AND VENICE LASTS 100 YEARS

In the history of spices and herbs, pepper has played a key role. Around the first millennium BC, King Solomon was visited in Jerusalem by the Queen of Sheba who presented him with gold, pepper, other spices and precious stones. Emperors, senators, matrons and rich Roman merchants were all prepared to pay large sums of money in order to procure pepper. Rome even sent an expedition – unsuccessful as it turned out – to the Arabian Peninsula in 24 BC to seize control of the pepper trade. This spice was mainly produced in India and sent to the Red Sea and Persian Gulf by ship; it was then loaded onto the long, slow camel caravans crossing the deserts, to be eventually sold in the ports of the eastern Mediterranean, for between a hundred and a thousand times its original price.

Pliny wrote that too much gold was leaving the empire to buy pepper and other spices. The high point of the Roman Empire probably coincided with the peak of the pepper trade in terms of price. Apicius, in his cookery book *De Re Coquinaria*, included pepper 349 times in his 468 recipes. In 408 AD, near the end of the Roman Empire when the Visigoths were besieging Rome, they demanded gold, silver and pepper in return for lifting the siege. The terms were accepted, but Alaric attacked the city anyway and seized all the pepper stocks! With the fall of the Roman Empire, Arab incursions into the Mediterranean and the fragmentation of power in Europe, pepper became a scarce commodity, to be found only on the tables of kings and the wealthy. The trade was completely controlled by Muslim Gujarati merchants as far as Alexandria and western Mediterranean ports, where Jewish merchants (Radhanites) bought goods which they distributed through Europe. With the general resumption of trade, the crusades and the increase in European purchasing power, the pepper trade recovered. Venice became its principle trading center, which proved highly profitable for the city and its merchants and for the Arab traders who demanded ever increasing quantities of pepper from their suppliers in the Indian Ocean.

THE CIRCUMNAVIGATION OF AFRICA ENDS THE VENETIAN AND ARAB MONOPOLY OF 'BLACK GOLD'

After the fall of Constantinople, navigation in the area became more dangerous, and the Portuguese, Spanish and other merchants looked for a different route to bring back spices from the Indian Ocean. In fact Marco Polo's voyage was specifically intended to make contact with oriental exporters of spices, silk, porcelain and other products on which Europeans were totally dependent. Columbus wanted to find a route to India but discovered the New World instead; and it was actually Vasco de Gama who arrived in the Indian Ocean having rounded the Cape of Good Hope. The new route transformed the pepper and spices trade throughout Europe. In addition, the large port of Malacca in Malaysia was conquered by the Portuguese in 1511, thereby bringing them into contact with another major source of spices.

In July 1511, Girolamo Priuli, a powerful Venetian merchant, wrote in his diary that the loss of the spice trade for Venice was as serious as the loss of milk and nourishment would be for a baby. He clearly understood the gravity of the situation. Indeed, pepper increasingly went to Lisbon, to the detriment of Venice. This situation was exacerbated by the decision taken by the king of Portugal, Dom Manuel, in 1504 to freeze the price of pepper, and his further decision two years later to appropriate the pepper monopoly for the crown. Portuguese pepper was now found everywhere in the markets and warehouses of the European Atlantic coast and the countries bordering the North Sea such as England, the Netherlands and Germany.

`Venetian´ pepper was still distributed in central Europe, north of Venice. La Serenissima closed its borders to `Portuguese´ pepper arriving through Genoa, and forced Italian territories under its control to buy pepper from the Rialto market. In 1514, Venice took further measures: it abolished customs duties on pepper coming from western Mediterranean ports and transported by Venetian galleys or indeed ships sailing under any flag. But the following year Venetian ships had to go and replenish stocks in Lisbon to ensure enough pepper was available in the Rialto market. From then on, the Venetian Republic's situation deteriorated rapidly, especially in view of the general pace of life at the time. In 1527 the Venetian senate even sent a proposal to the King John III of Portugal, suggesting he channel all the pepper arriving in Lisbon through to them. Venice was prepared to do anything to regain control of the trade. But their efforts came to nothing, and Portuguese pepper increasingly dominated the European markets. The consequences were grave for the city of the Doges. Venice was obliged to restructure its trade in favor of importing and to focus on exporting manufactured goods. Elsewhere, the Arab merchants who had dominated the pepper and spice trade between the Indian Ocean and Europe for over a thousand years – with customers ranging from Greeks, Romans and Byzantines to Germans and Russians – in parallel with the export of Islam along the spice routes, suffered an even more serious crisis than Venice, for they had very few pre-industrial products to export or negotiate with.

VENICE FIGHTS BACK: `MONEY FOLLOWS PEPPER´

Thanks to its network of trained spies, its omnipresent merchants and its highly experienced sailors, Venice tried to work on the image of `Portuguese´ pepper and produced a barrage of disinformation and negative marketing. It spread the rumor that this pepper was of poor quality and that the great circumnavigation around Africa made it lose its flavor. There was some truth in this, since several months went by between the harvesting and the arrival of the pepper, and the physical and chemical properties of the goods might well have deteriorated a little. Venetian merchants also made a point of buying only the best quality pepper in Alexandria and in the ports of the western Mediterranean; Venetian pepper was therefore of superior quality, even if the merchants had to limit their profits on this trade to around 100%! Venice exported increasing amounts of `exotic and attractive´ products – such as glassware, mirrors, jewelry and lace – to these same ports in order to obtain a good rate of exchange. Their merchants set off in galleys filled with base metals, especially copper and tin, which were much sought after in the Middle East, as well as gold and plentiful supplies of silver, which were in high demand in the Middle and Far East due to the absence of gold and silver mines in these regions. Venice also paid cash on the spot for its pepper purchases in a further effort to control the trade. In 1530, the Venetian Piero Zen remarked to the Turks in Constantinople that `money follows pepper´. The market partially recovered, especially from 1540-1550, partly because the Portuguese Empire was still young and expanding on many different fronts, thus spreading itself thin in the absence of deep commercial roots. Customs officers were unable to check all commercial transactions, young administrators were promoted, other agents were easily corruptible, and there was a high level of fraud. Moreover, transport between the Indian ports and Lisbon remained costly, with occasional shipwrecks further contributing to higher prices at its final destination. It should not be forgotten that pepper was the principal raw material in commercial transactions throughout the world during the 16th and 17th centuries.

A WORRIED LISBON OFFERS TO SUBCONTRACT ITS PEPPER TRADE TO VENICE!

Lisbon found it hard to believe Venice's reaction and the lengths it was prepared to go to in protecting its trading monopoly in `black gold´. The Portuguese authorities were highly concerned. Furthermore, a war broke out between the Turks and Portuguese in the Straits of Ormuz (1560-1563) and the Portuguese trading posts of Goa in the Indian subcontinent and Ternate in Indonesia were under siege from other powers in these regions. So in 1570 the king reorganized the spice monopoly by making it the responsibility of his ships. At the same time a new war between Venice and the Turkish Empire (1570-1573) gave Lisbon some respite, and in 1575 it decided to offer to subcontract its pepper trade to Venice. After long discussions in the senate, Venice decided not to take up the Portuguese offer, as this would in effect mean giving up the city's commercial independence. At this point the Medici family entered the fray. From 1576 to 1578 the Florentine bankers tried to negotiate the proposal, previously offered to Venice, for themselves in return for finance for the Portuguese crown. In the event a few cargoes of Portuguese pepper did arrive at the port of Livorno, and the Florentine bank lent a small sum of money to Lisbon. But the arrangement did not last.

Meanwhile in 1580, Philip II laid his heavy hands on the Portuguese kingdom and incorporated it into the Spanish Empire (on which, like the future British Empire, the sun never set). In 1585, Philip again offered Venice the monopoly of the pepper trade, and again they declined. The same offer was made to Milan, Genoa and Florence, but none of them were interested. So Philip turned to German merchants, offering them control of the trade under two separate contracts. The first of these – the Asia contract – covering the purchase and transport of pepper as far as Lisbon, was signed with the firms of Fugger and Welser and some other smaller trading houses; the second – the Europe contract – covered the distribution of pepper throughout the European continent. This was signed by the Fuggers, Welsers and some other trading firms in various countries, though the Fuggers pulled out soon after, ceding their interests to a Portuguese merchant family, the Evoras. The winner in all this was the Spanish Empire. In fact the various commercial firms involved were not very happy with the results; there were substantial losses transporting the pepper through the Indian Ocean and – after the crushing defeat of the `Invincible Armada´ – pirates infested Iberian coasts, attacking shipping with its cargoes of spices, silk and porcelain. Meanwhile pepper from the Levant was arriving regularly in Venice, which continued to distribute it through Europe; there are even records of ships from the Atlantic unloading their pepper in Venice. In any case this merchandise was by now less prized as it was more commonly available, and it lost its strategic role partly because the demand for manufactured goods was growing rapidly in Europe, in the New World and in Asia.

SUGAR: THE BATTLE BETWEEN CANE AND BEET

For a long time fruit and honey were the only means of sweetening food, and the great Roman cook Apicius very often suggested honey in the preparation of his dishes. Elsewhere in the world the cultivation of sugar cane was relatively well developed – as in New Guinea, for example. Cane was later taken to the New Hebrides, New Caledonia and the islands of Fiji; and some centuries later it was grown in the Philippines, Malaysia, India and China. Darius' Persians came across the plant in 510 BC and mention a thick, very sweet syrup. From the 3rd century BC, Indian and Persian merchants began exporting sugar to Arabia and Egypt; Indian documents dating from 400 BC mention the use of sugar in food. Nearchus, one of Alexander's generals, wrote in 325 BC that in India there was a cane with no flowers and no need for bees for pollination, from which a sweet drink could be extracted. The western physicians, Hippocrates and Galen, described a substance known as saccharose, a very rare product that was found in Greek and Roman pharmacopeias. Patrician families and rich Roman merchants used sugar cane, especially after the conquest of Egypt, but it served mainly as a status symbol.

The word sugar is Sanskrit in origin and comes from *sakara*, meaning sand; in Latin it became *saccharum*, which gave rise to several words connected with sugar.

The Arab expansion helped spread sugar cane through the Middle East and the Mediterranean basin. The Arab sugar industry learned the technique of making solid sugar from the Persians. Avicenna advocated its use in medicine. Sugar cane was cultivated in the Nile valley, Palestine and Syria, throughout North Africa, in Cyprus, Rhodes, and the Balearic archipelago, and then later in Greece and the southern parts of Italy and France. But the results were not very satisfactory because the plant is essentially subtropical and tropical. It requires a hot climate with plenty of rain, and rainfall levels in the Mediterranean region are low. The Norman king Frederick II tried growing sugar cane in Sicily, but again the results were unsatisfactory. These difficulties explain why sugar was so expensive, and its use was limited largely to apothecaries.

`ARAB SALT`, THE CRUSADES AND SAINT THOMAS AQUINAS

The crusaders brought back many products and techniques to Europe from the Arab world. Among these was sugar, which was used mainly in food for sweetening and preservation and for making candied fruit and jams. Saint Thomas even classified sugar as one of the things it was permitted to eat when fasting. Growing demand in Europe led to the cultivation of sugar cane in the islands of the Atlantic to the west of the Straits of Gibraltar. Practically everywhere it was grown, the mass use of slaves enabled production to be carried out on an industrial scale. In any case, the use of sugar as a food product continued to grow, while its application in pharmacopeias lost ground, especially after Paracelsus expressed doubts about the real virtues of saccharose.

The discovery of the New World revolutionized the sugar market and the consumption of sugar. It was first grown on San Domingo having been brought from the Canaries; the climate was extremely favorable to this type of crop and its productivity was greatly improved. Of course the colonizers used a large number of slaves, at very small cost to themselves. The first cargo of sugar produced in the region of the Caribbean was probably shipped to Spain in 1516. Cane cultivation rapidly spread throughout the Caribbean and to the Atlantic coast of Latin America. This was the beginning of the infamous triangular trade, which brought merchants and ship-owners great profits on slaves trading and led to the rapid growth of the French and English Atlantic ports. Demand for sugar grew in the various European courts, and among the wealthy bourgeoisie and the clergy; the fall in price also brought it within reach of sections of the middle class. All this was yet another blow for Venice, which long before the Crusades had been the main importer, refiner and distributor throughout Europe of `oriental´ sugar, known as `Arab salt´. Genoa, too, had profited from importing sugar from its eastern Mediterranean trading posts.

OLIVIER DE SERRES, THE CONTINENTAL BLOCKADE AND SUGAR BEET

The Greeks had long been familiar with *beta* or sugar beet, as is attested by documents dating back to 420 BC. The root was used for feeding animals, but people ate the leaves, mainly as a salad vegetable. During the 14th century the tuber (*Rapa altissima*, to give it its scientific name) came to be grown practically everywhere in Europe. In 1575, the French agronomist Olivier de Serres described certain types of beet 'recently arrived from Italy... which after cooking, produce a syrup similar to that of sugar'. But excitement over the profits made from sugar cane production made people forget about de Serres work. Between 1640 and 1750, consumption of sugar from cane increased threefold, bringing in its wake the terrible enslavement of countless men and women, mostly of African origin.

It was not until 1747 that the Prussian chemist Andreas Marggraf managed to crystallize sugar extracted from beet. His pupil Franz Karl Achard worked on selecting the variety of beet giving the maximum yield of sugar and eventually developing the Silesian White, the best beet in terms of sugar content. Achard asked King Frederick Wilhelm III of Prussia for financial help to continue his research. The king agreed because the British semi-monopoly in the sugar trade was resented in much of continental Europe. In 1796 the first sugar beet refinery was opened at Cunem in Silesia (now in Poland), but large-scale production only started in 1802. The continental blockade ordered by England against Napoleonic France gave a considerable boost to sugar beet. In 1802, Benjamin Delessert began experiments on the extraction and refining of sugar. Napoleon's decree of 25th March 1811 allocated 79,000 acres for the cultivation of sugar beet and authorized the construction of several refineries. On 2nd January 1812 Delessert was decorated with the Légion d'Honneur by Napoleon Bonaparte in person, who in turn received from the chemist the first sugarloaf made from sugar beet. The search for food independence encouraged sugar beet production throughout Europe and thus began a fierce struggle between sugar cane producers and sugar beet growers, sustained by major financial and national interests.

The abolition of slavery was a serious blow to the sugar cane market, which had to absorb a massive rise in costs. By the beginning of the 20th century, cane was supplying only two-fifths of world sugar consumption. But decolonization later followed by the agreement between the EC and the United States to reduce agricultural protectionism this time worked to the advantage of sugar cane and to the detriment of sugar beet. Today cane provides three-quarters of the world's sugar, even though the refining of beet sugar is still a large industry in Europe and the United States. But reasonably enough, the cane-producing countries are trying to take over the whole production cycle and in many cases, such as Brazil, to use cane for making ethanol.

COCOA AND CHOCOLATE,
BEVERAGE OF THE GODS

An Aztec legend tells of a princess made responsible for watching over her husband's wealth while he went to war. Enemies attacked the castle and killed the princess when she refused to tell them where to find the treasure. The cocoa tree sprang up from the princess's blood and its fruit hides within it seeds that are 'bitter as the sorrows of love, strong as virtue, and red like blood'. One day her husband, Topilzine Quetzacoatl (meaning 'feathered snake') fell ill, and was given a potion to drink by a sorcerer. Immediately losing his mind, he ran to the sea where he found a raft covered with serpents. Nonetheless he boarded, but before he left he promised to return to his kingdom in the year of the sign of Ce-acatl. In 1519, the year of this sign, when a ship full of men dressed in armor gleaming like the scales of the snake arrived on the shores of the Aztec kingdom, the emperor Montezuma welcomed them with open arms in the belief that the prophecy had been fulfilled.

We must thank Christopher Columbus for the first cocoa beans to come to Europe, which he discovered on his fourth expedition, still looking for the Indies, when he arrived at Guanaja island on 30th July 1502. A man with a noble face and a head crowned in feathers greeted him, rowing out from the shore in a boat manned by 25 oarsman. He offered Columbus some cocoa beans and poured him a bitter, highly spiced drink – xocoatl. It was not to Columbus' liking. Similarly the conquistador Hernando Cortez seventeen years later, when on tasting the same beverage, spat it out because he suspected that it was a trick to poison him. But in the course of their conquest, the Spanish soldiers got used to this drink. Cortez sent sacks of the beans to the Emperor Charles V, telling him the drink `helps relations with women… a cup of this precious drink will allow a man to march for a whole day without difficulty´. Thus cocoa came to Europe, promoted in particular by the Spanish explorer, Hernando De Soto.

MEXICO, GUATEMALA, VENEZUELA AND THE CARIBBEAN: THE FIRST PRODUCERS

Mexico, Guatemala, Venezuela and some of the Caribbean islands became the great centers of cocoa production at the time of the Spanish conquest. Spanish, Portuguese, Dutch and then French and English governors all developed the production of this crop, with the aid of the Jesuits, pirates, and adventurers. Less than 400 years later cocoa production extended throughout the tropics, in America, Asia and Africa. In 1830, production of beans reached 10,000 tons, concentrated largely in Ecuador, Venezuela, Trinidad, Haiti, Brazil and Martinique. At the end of the nineteenth century the yield had increased to 115,000 tons, with its introduction into African countries, other Caribbean islands and Oceania. A century later production had risen to 2,400,000 tons, but now it was the Ivory Coast, Ghana, Indonesia, Brazil, Nigeria, Cameroon and Malaysia which were the main producers. Production is currently concentrated in large countries, though there remain some highly prized areas of cocoa cultivation in the Venezuelan Andes, on the island of Grenada (the Spice Isle), and in Madagascar, Jamaica, Belize, Polynesia, Panama and Surinam.

IN PRAISE OF CHOCOLATE

The Aztecs and the Mayans also used cocoa beans as currency. A Spanish explorer noted that with four beans you could buy a pumpkin, with ten a rabbit, with twelve a night with a concubine and with one hundred, a slave. The Aztecs mixed cocoa with water, flour, maize, chili pepper and vanilla. The Spanish, and in particular those monks who were familiar with mixing herbs, tried to adapt this drink to the European palate by adding sugar, honey, milk, wine or beer, and a pinch of pepper. In

Tuscany they also added citrus rind, jasmine, cinnamon, vanilla, musk and milk, thus creating *cioccolatte*. Dr Henry Stubbes, a friend of the English philosopher Hobbes, himself a knowledgeable enthusiast of chocolate, wrote in praise of this product. An Austrian doctor declared that chocolate was the food of Venus. A pamphlet written in 1703 assures the reader that chocolate `will put fire in your veins´; and Casanova compared chocolate to champagne, in the art of love. In the course of his travels Goethe carried chocolate in his baggage on the advice of his friend, the geographer von Humboldt. The Swiss army, in 1870, considered chocolate to be an essential element in keeping up the morale of the troops and managing digestive problems, and provided its troops with a daily ration.

A FASHIONABLE PRODUCT DURING THE COUNTER-REFORMATION AND ENLIGHTENMENT

The Church was also interested in chocolate. Pope Clement VII (Giulio de Medici) did not manage actually to drink chocolate, because it was not yet available, but he enjoyed the mouth-watering description of it in 1523 by father Petrus de Angleria: `It is not only a delicious drink, but an excellent coinage which prevents all speculation because it cannot be kept for too long´. In 1594 Pope Clement VIII tasted a cup of cocoa given to him by the Florentine priest, Francesco Carlati, on his return from America. A debate ensued as to whether or not chocolate broke fasting. At canonization ceremonies in the Vatican during the 18th century, the participating prelates received a packet of chocolate whose weight varied according to their position in the hierarchy. The Jesuits boosted the fortunes of chocolate and helped its trade between Latin America and Europe; on the other hand, the Dominicans, who followed a very strict religious tradition, were opposed to chocolate on the grounds that it `heated the blood too much´.

Nobles, prelates, merchants and the newly wealthy all wanted to try this substance, for which some physicians claimed medicinal qualities too. Chocolate houses, along the same lines as coffee houses, opened up throughout Europe. Nevertheless, chocolate had its critics: an English doctor[1] wrote in 1706 the drink was a ruse of Satan's to weaken the spirit and reduce fertility.

The great Swedish botanist Linnaeus gave the cacao tree the scientific name *Theobroma cacao*, signifying `food of the gods´ in Greek. In 1770 The first industrial chocolate factory opened – `Chocolates and Teas, Pelletier & Co´. Then in 1815 Van Houten & Volker was founded in Amsterdam, and invented a machine for extracting cocoa butter. Cailler started a company at Vevey, and Suchard one at Neuchâtel. Meunier went into production in France in 1824. In 1875, Daniel Peter invented milk chocolate at Vevey and joined Cailler and Kohler, which merged in 1929 to form Nestlé. Cocoa started to be traded on a large scale in the London and Paris commodities markets, and later in New York. Chocolate manufacturers began competing by making ever more irresistible products.

---

1. A Treatise of All Sorts of Foods, Both Animal and Vegetable: Also of Drinkables
By Lemery, (Louis), Regent Doctor of the Faculty of Physick at Paris, and the Academy Royal of Sciences.
London: Printed for Andrew Bell at the Crois Keys and Bible in Cornhill:
1706.

THE RISE OF CHRISTIAN PAWNBROKERS FINANCED BY JEWISH BANKERS

Michele Carcano was a monk who gave give rabble-rousing sermons to the Milanese crowds at the beginning of the 15th century. On 23rd February 1462, he was invited by the Priors in Perugia, for a fee of six florins, to preach to usurers accused of committing a mortal sin and doing untold damage to the city's economic structure. Another monk, the Franciscan Barnabeo da Terni, had the idea of creating an institution similar to a bank, which would lend money to the poor against a pledge or security at a very low interest rate, or even at no interest at all.

Two weeks later a *Monte di Pietà*[1] was started in Perugia, the first in Europe. But they needed to find finance to be able to lend to those in need. The authorities first decided to target Jewish bankers, who until then had held the right to lend money in return for objects as guarantees, by threatening to withdraw this right. Then a commission was set up, made up of doctors in civil and canonical law and merchants, to draw up the statutes for the new institution. However, finance was still a problem due to the reluctance of the city's rich merchants and notables to come up with the money. So Jewish bankers were compelled to donate a large sum of money to endow the *Monte di Pietà* with capital – a decision full of contradictions, since a particular economic group was being asked to spend money to create an institution that was in direct competition with them, and could even replace them as lenders.

---

1. In French, known as the `Mont de Piété´, derived from the Italian `Monte di Pietà´ signifying `pawnbrokers´. *Translator's note*

THE POPE GIVES HIS BLESSING TO THE MONTE AND A MARKETING CAMPAIGN IS LAUNCHED

The bankers agreed to finance this setup, the Pope gave his blessing and preachers started a large scale marketing operation, explaining the function and merits of these pawnshops to the faithful. Processions of children dressed in white were organized to parade through the town, followed by the guilds and their banners, with the bishop and city authorities at their head, gathering alms and offerings of goods from the rich and well-to-do.

When the Monte di Pietà was set up in Florence, Savonarola organized a dramatic and inflammatory display: as part of it, he arranged for gangs of `naughty´ children to throw stones at the houses of the usurers and Jewish bankers. In their sermons priests stressed the novelty in economic terms of the Monte which helped the poor (and not only them) and contributed to strengthening the economy, similarly to letters of exchange and other financial tools introduced by the Tuscan and Lombard bankers. Later Pope Leon X of the Medici family, the princes of Tuscany and leading Renaissance bankers decreed that earning interest on loans with the aim of covering administrative expenses did not fall into the category of usury.

Usury had always been disliked by the Church, and Dante in his Divine Comedy populated Hell with usurers and the bankers of Cahors (in southwest France) who were known for their practice of usury. They were made to undergo punishment on burning sands at the hands of ogres and other sufferings, to expiate the sins they had committed against their fellow citizens on earth, their hands covered with the blood of the men they had killed and ruined. In Bologna, for example, the Monte Pietà was created in 1473 with the dedication: `Mons pietatis contra parvas Iudaeorum usurus erectus´ ('Built in opposition to the usury of the Jews practiced against the poor').

WHY `MONTE´?

`Monte´ recalls Mount Sinai, where God entrusted his laws for mankind to Moses, and also the Sermon on the Mount, where

Jesus preached to the faithful. It was also meant to evoke the `mount of virtue´ that the man of faith had to climb to free himself from the devil and the usurer. In the popular imagination, the Mount represented a mountain of gold, protected by towers, walls, churches and saints of the city, against outside enemies. It was the affirmation of the values of the city, which was opposed to centralized authority and wished to further establish its independence. The success of these Mounts was important, in that it enabled small businesses to be financed at lower interest rates (at the beginning of European economic recovery, particularly evident in Italy). In particular, they helped to combat poverty among people who had been hit hardest by the Italian wars – François I versus Charles V – and suffered from raids by mercenaries from Switzerland and elsewhere. The institution of the Mount or pawnbrokers then spread through central Italy, then further north and south, to the Catholic lands of Provence, to southern Germany and finally throughout Roman Catholic Europe. As of 1987 China agreed to the creation of these Mounts – there are more than 1000 of them – and in May 2002 the largest institution of this type in the whole country was opened in Shanghai.

POTOSI, CITY OF SILVER:
BETWEEN WEALTH AND MISERY

In 1544 the Indian Diego Huallpa discovered a seam of silver in the extinct volcanic complex Cerro Rico, a pyramidal mountain surging on a plateau more than 12.000 feet high, which today belongs to Bolivia. Entrepreneurs and conquistadores from Spain rushed to the area in search of silver, and founded Potosi. Luck was on their side, because in less than twenty years they found seven other extremely rich seams of silver. A century later, Potosi was the largest city in the western world with more than 160,000 inhabitants! More than 2,000,000 oz of silver were extracted during the period of Spanish colonization. This was the metal which financed Spain's golden century, paid for the heavy military expenses incurred by the army's attempts to crush the Dutch rebellion, and compensated the expense and loss of the `Invincible Armada´, launched against Elizabeth I's England. It was silver too that to a large extent financed Europe's economic renaissance, the trade between Europe and the Orient – and certainly filled the pockets of the British, Spanish and Dutch privateers and pirates who operated in the Caribbean and off the coast of South America.

EXTREMES OF WEALTH AND POVERTY

Potosi became an extraordinary city, as can be seen from the churches and the colonial-style palaces built by the newly wealthy. Cervantes has Don Quixote say `That's worth a Potosi!´, to indicate a very high price. The city also attracted a tidal wave of miners who worked in the most appalling conditions. The temperature outside the mines was what you would normally expect to find at 12,000 feet, whilst down the mine shaft it was often over 30° C and even reached 45° C in the deepest shafts. The air was thin and permeated with toxic gases, the lamps for lighting the seams burned up the oxygen, dust gave the men silicosis, hygiene was rudimentary and the climate was hard. Unsurprisingly miners died by the thousand.

It is estimated that at least a million Indians died at Potosi and some historians even talk of eight million dead. Later African slaves were transferred to the mines at Cerro Rico to replace the local labor force, which was dropping like flies. In 1638 Fray Antonio de la Calancha wrote that `each peso of silver produced cost the life of ten Indians´.

THE MITA, A SYSTEM OF FORCED LABOR

There were three types of miners: slaves, mitayos, and free men. Mountain people captured at the time of the wars against Chile were sold as slaves. Later these were augmented by black slaves brought from Africa, but the climate did not suit them and they were `uneconomic´ to use, since many of them were unable to survive at the 12,000 foot altitude. Then there were the free and independent workers, who were willing to work for the mining entrepreneurs (financed by Iberian, Florentine and English capital). Finally there were the mitayos, men requisitioned in the villages for the mita, the labor that the Indians `owed´ the Spanish state. This began in 1559 in an informal manner but the viceroy Francisco de Toledo passed a law in 1570 to enforce it; each village was obliged to designate the mitayos – men between 18 and 60 years old – to work for the state for one year. If they owned livestock, villagers could buy their mita instead of having to work it off. It was also quite common for men to abandon their villages to avoid it.

MERCURY USED IN SILVER EXTRACTION

After its enormous initial success, silver production started to slow down. The Spanish governors and the mining entrepreneurs needed to take appropriate measures. So they brought to Potosi some twenty German miners chosen for their experience, who were specialists in the use of mineral mills and fusion or smelting of the ore into bars. There was in fact strict legislation preventing foreigners from emigrating and working in the New World – but rules are made to be broken! Elsewhere, in Venice in 1540, the Italian engineer Vannoccio Biringuccio published a book entitled *La Pirotechnia* which described a method of extracting silver using mercury. From 1554 onwards, Bartolomy de Medina, a merchant from Seville, began to apply this method in the silver mines at Zacatecas, discovered in 1548, approximately 140 miles north of Mexico City. Spain produced the mercury in its mines in Almadén, the concession of which had been granted to the rich German bankers, Fugger. Mercury was transported on the Spanish galleons and then loaded onto pack donkeys, mules and llamas to be transported to Zacatecas. If the mines at Almadén could not satisfy the demand for mercury the supply was augmented from the mines near Trieste – evidence of mercury imported from China has even been found!

THE DISCOVERY OF MERCURY IN THE ANDES

In 1563 one Amador de Cabrera, a recipient of land from the king, was contacted by an Indian who told him of an old mine where the local inhabitants used to extract a product with which they painted their bodies red for ceremonies. On 1st January 1564, de Cabrera received an official document declaring him to be the `discoverer´ of the mine. Production began right away, despite the dangers involved – naturally the work was done by Indians. This mercury was not immediately sent to Potosi, but to the mines at Zacatecas. It was only in 1573 that the `master of mining´ Don Pedro Hernando de Velasco began to use the mercury method for silver extraction at Potosi. It took convoys of llamas, traveling on mountain roads, two to three months to cover the distance of nearly a thousand miles to Potosi. The costs of this operation were high, but it meant that production could be significantly increased by using lower grade ore. More mercury needed therefore to be extracted from these mines where conditions were even more atrocious than in the silver mines. Once again forced labor pro-

vided by the local villagers allowed the concessionaries of the
mercury mines at Huancavelica to meet the demand at Potosi.

In 1572, a mint was set up at Potosi to produce the new silver
coins that would travel around the world. These coins were in use
in Europe, the Middle East and the Far East; arriving there via
India or directly on the galleon which set out once or twice a year
from Acapulco for the Philippines, where they took on board
Chinese silk, spices and rare woods.

GLORY AND POVERTY

The descriptions of Potosi, in books and in the accounts of
travelers, monks and mining engineers, show us a Potosi that is
rich and glorious, the heart of the Americas, the main engine of
the State and the jewel of the Empire – but also an accursed
mountain, the scourge of the Indian nation and an abyss of iniq-
uity.

At the beginning of the 19th century mining at Potosi began to
collapse. Production suffered variously from competition from
other mines, the exhaustion of seams, the difficulty of hiring
miners, and above all the political instability due to the revolution
which to the creation of Bolivia in 1825. With falling world prices
for silver, the Potosi silver mines became unprofitable, and tin
began to be mined there instead. The population declined to fewer
than 10,000 people.

Miners' cooperatives and independent workers can still be
found there today, engaged in extracting tin, silver and other
minerals (lead, zinc, wolfram, antimony) in conditions, which are
difficult as ever. The consumption of strong alcohol and coca
leaves, anaesthetizing the throat and dulling the mind, continues,
just as in the times of Francisco de Toledo. The population is back
to 140,000 inhabitants and the town attracts a lot of tourists
visiting the mines, the Mint (the famous *Casa de la Moneda*) and
the rich baroque churches.

`PIECES OF EIGHT´ FINANCE
THE SPANISH GOLDEN CENTURY

The Athenian drachma, the Roman aureus, the Venetian ducat, the *real de a ocho* (piece of eight), the English pound and the US dollar are probably the currencies that have most dominated currency exchanges around the world. Internationally accepted even (or especially) in times of war, these currencies have had the merit of storing value over time and of transferring value in exchange for food, slaves, metals, arms, industrial and semi-industrial products and for paying soldiers' wages, ransoms and services. In particular they have played an essential role in times of crisis and political tension, when exchanges need a secure unit of currency, not only in the region they are produced but elsewhere in other, often distant, geographical zones.

VENICE MINTS THE SILVER TRON LIRA

In the second half of the 15th century particularly rich deposits of silver were found in Schwaz in Tyrol and Schneeberg in Saxony. Europe had been looking for metal with which to mint coins for a long time and now had found it in undreamt of quantities. Venice was the first state to mint a completely new currency. For a long time the coins were small disks of thin metal, susceptible to bending. In 1472, Venice decided to introduce a coin weighing 6.5 grams (6.16g of pure silver), embossed with a very detailed representation of the Doge then governing and named after him – the `Tron´ lira. Two years later Milan followed Venice's example, succeeded in turn by Turin, Genoa, the Low Countries, England, France and Florence. In

1477 Archduke Sigismund began producing the Guldiner, weighing 31.93 grams and the Halbguldiner, weighing half that amount, but these coins were mainly hoarded and not circulated very much. After the discovery of silver mines at Sankt Joachimstal, the Counts of Schlick minted a coin weighing 27 grams, which took the name of the mine – `Joachimstaler´ later shortened to `Taler´, the origin of the word `dollar´. This had a wide international distribution. Many countries then decided on monetary reform. Only Spain retained the existing system, even after the `Medina del Campo reform´ in 1497, which made provision for minting coins weighing 3.4 grams in fractional values of the peso.

SILVER FROM MEXICO AND POTOSI FLOODS THE MARKET

The abundance of silver in the New World gave Charles V the idea of creating a mint in Mexico City. Established in 1535 this was authorized to mint coins, along with the *real* itself, that were multiples of the *real*. In 1537 the viceroyalty of New Spain received the authorization to mint coins of two, four and eight *real* as well as a half *real*. This was the first appearance of the `piece of eight´ or *real de a ocho*. These coins transformed the use of money in the New Continent, because pre-Columbian civilizations did not use hard currency; they either bartered goods or exchanged cocoa beans, feathers, textiles, small pieces of tin or copper (melted and molded into the form of a T) and gold or silver dust. However, things did not initially go well for the *real*, since it was poorly minted and was easy to file it down thereby extracting a few tenths of a gram of silver. On the other hand, there were a very large number of them in circulation, because the workers in the mints which produced these coins worked hard, and earned more because they were paid as piece workers, so they had a financial incentive to produce as many coins as possible. The wide availability of silver, ever increasing, also helped fuel plentiful production.

THE MINT IN POTOSI

All the Spanish mints were supplied with silver from the mines at Potosi in old Peru and Zacatecas in Mexico, and were expected to work it up into coinage. The best solution for them was to increase coin production in Mexico City and establish another mint at Potosi (1572). The transport involved was considerable and on 16th July 1561 Philip II decided to create – like the Venetians – a highly organized system. The *Carrera de las Indias* made provision for the formation of maritime convoys consisting of trading galleons and an escort of two armed ships: the captain's ship led the convoy and the admiral's ship brought up the rear. In another decision made in 1564, it was agreed that there should be two convoys a year leaving Spain between March and September – the first would go to Vera Cruz in Mexico, the second to either Puerto Bello Panama or Cartagena, Columbia. Llamas, mules and donkeys caravans were used for transporting the merchandise to the Pacific coast where it was loaded onto ships destined for the port of Callao, Peru, from where other caravans took it on to Potosi and Lima. The same caravans were then loaded with silver and, using the same return route, arrived at the Caribbean ports. The two fleets, having spent the winter at Vera Cruz and Cartagena, then set sail for Cuba where they met and to form a large convoy that would be equipped and fitted out in March. Going via Bermuda and the Azores it would sail to Seville in Spain – weather and pirates permitting. Because all metal was taxed on import, smuggling became a national sport for sailors, ship's captains, travellers, customs officers and the men who unloaded the boats and stored the metal. Official statistics on the quantity of precious metals imported were unreliable – and there were even cases when ships officially declared only half of their cargo of precious metal.

SPAIN USES NEW WORLD SILVER TO FINANCE OTHER COUNTRIES' ECONOMIC DEVELOPMENT

Spain was living a paradoxical existence. The inexhaustible influx of silver and gold from the new colonies was largely spent in advance by the Treasury in Madrid, which had to meet the

high cost of the royal court, pay troops and functionaries stationed around the globe, and above all to staunch the serious
financial hemorrhaging caused by the wars in the Netherlands
and elsewhere. Very often the galleons arriving in Seville loaded
with silver ingots left immediately for Antwerp, Livorno and
Venice, where Flemish, Genoan and Florentine bankers and
Venetian merchants were repaid for the loans they had made to
the Spanish crown. Moreover Spain's trade balance was deeply
in the red, since its only exports were products to the new
colonies, which needed to be supplied with nearly everything.
Madrid imported many products from abroad, including metal,
fabrics, manufactured goods, arms (particularly cannons), and
luxury items such as silk, glassware, mirrors, fine sheets, lace and
books, which were in great demand amongst the newly wealthy
living in Spain and throughout the New World. This new
demand made a fortune for mining companies in central Europe,
Venetian manufacturers of glass, mirrors, lace and books,
Amsterdam book sellers and publishers, Flanders cloth manufacturers, silk producers in and around Milan (especially Como),
Swiss and English clockmakers, and the shoemakers and carpet
makers of the Middle East. But Spain also exported goods which
it acquired from the new territories, especially dyes – cochineal
for red, indigo for blue, and various coloring woods – and medicinal plants such as *gujaco*, used in the treatment of syphilis and so
sought after in Europe that the Fugger bankers tried to obtain the
monopoly. Other exports included wool from llamas, alpacas and
guanacos, spices, sugar and even Chinese silk shipped from
Manila in the Philippines.

`THAT'S THE WAY THE MONEY GOES...´

Even with all these exports, the Spanish balance of payments
remained in the red and the king's expenditure was enormous.
The gap in the balance of payments and the deficit in the State
budget was filled by silver. The Cortes (parliament) of 1588-1593
declared that Spain might well be the richest country in the world,
but all the gold and silver that arrived from the Indies was only
passing through and enriching their enemies. In 1595 the Venetian ambassador – whose role, like that of his colleagues, was

mainly that of super-commercial attaché, with responsibility for keeping an eye on trade and looking out for any economic innovations – wrote to Venice describing the influx of precious metal as being like rain falling on a roof: 'It doesn't stay there and the benefit accrues to whoever knows how to collect it'.

The Spanish silver that was disbursed throughout Europe had two specific effects on its economy. On one hand, the *moneda larga*, as the Florentine functionaries described the abundance of liquidity available, drove prices up. There was too much liquidity and too high a demand to satisfy the needs of the new continent, coupled with an overall economic climate that was very favorable throughout most of Europe. On the other hand, this huge mass of silver enabled the structural trade deficit between Europe and the Far and Middle East to be balanced. Indeed these regions did not have much use for European products apart from certain luxury goods such as complex textiles, jewelry, clocks and coral, various chemical products, surgical instruments and arms – the Ottoman Empire imported its cannons mainly from Amsterdam.

SILVER GOES EAST

However, Europe needed spices and sugar, and was eager to import Chinese, Japanese and Korean porcelain and silk. The pieces of eight therefore set out on the road to the east. The caravans traveling to the Red Sea and the Persian Gulf and the galleons sailing round Africa always carried silver, that was in such great demand in the east, where very little of it was mined. The burgeoning East India Trading Companies increasingly loaded their ships and galleons with silver to buy spices, silks, porcelains and, later, tea in response to high European demand for these. Many *reals* were in circulation in the Middle and Far East, with no requirement for them to be exchanged. Only the Mogul emperors in India prohibited their circulation, melting them down to convert into *piastras*. The *real* became the exchange currency between Persia and Russia, and it virtually became the official currency in the Ottoman Empire where civil servants began keeping the official accounts in pieces of eight.

In sum, Latin American silver financed not only the whims of European consumers but also the continent's development. It paid for imports from the Orient which, in turn, benefited from the stability this gave to its monetary system and from increased liquidity. The only big loser, apart of course from the wretched miners in the new Spanish colonies, was Spain itself, which was unable to sustain indefinitely the lifestyle of the golden century and went into gradual decline.

THE ECONOMIC ROLE OF PIRATES, PRIVATEERS AND BUCCANEERS IN THE CARIBBEAN

Carthaginian and Levantine pirates were always a threat to Roman ships in *Mare Nostrum*. During the Renaissance, Venice needed to have its merchant convoys accompanied by the naval fleet. The Ming Empire spent a fortune protecting its ships in the seas off China, which were infested with pirates. Even today, in the equatorial and tropical regions of the western Pacific Ocean, pirates make surprise attacks on merchant shipping and occasionally even cruise ships.

PIRACY AND PRIVATEERING PLAYED A PART IN THE DECLINE OF BAROQUE SPAIN

Literature and cinema have tended to celebrate piracy, depicting it as a world of liberty, open spaces, mystery, violence and adventure among the privateers and buccaneers in the Caribbean during the Baroque period. In fact, without knowing it, these men very effectively sabotaged Spain's development during its Golden Age, cutting it abruptly short. Mexican and Peruvian gold and silver were discovered in the period of the reigns of Charles V and Philip II. These two emperors and their successors organized the flow of gold and silver to Spain, where it financed the war in the Low Countries, the strictly Catholic and Baroque way of life of the Spanish court and its patronage, and the various ventures of an empire on which the sun never set. However, the precious metals had to pass through the Caribbean in order to reach the ports of

Seville, Livorno, Genoa and Venice in the Mediterranean and Dutch and other ports in northern Europe. The most effective war waged by England and France against the Spanish enemy began in the Caribbean, with the pillaging of galleons loaded with gold ingots and silver pieces of eight. Such treasures also attracted outlaws who would board the galleons commando-style and help themselves to the cargoes.

HOW BUCCANEERS AND PRIVATEERS SABOTAGED THE SPANISH DREAM

The Spanish dreamt of taking over regional trade in the Atlantic and placing all of it under Madrid's control. But the unofficial war waged by the privateers completely wrecked Charles V's and Philip II's plan of incorporating the colonies of the New World into Spanish territory by means of rapid and secure communication routes between Central America and the Atlantic and Mediterranean ports belonging to the greatest European power of the 16th and 17th centuries. The empire had at its command – at very low prices and in abundant quantities – manpower, spices, precious metals, and agricultural products, all of which were in high demand across Europe, which was generally experiencing its own economic renaissance. But Madrid was faced with ever increasing difficulties in transporting its riches.

The beginning of the war between England and Spain began with Henry VIII sending Captain John Rut to the Caribbean on two missions: to discover a route to China and above all to spy on and disrupt Spanish shipping. Queen Elizabeth I then gave the task `to fare forth and do your worst´ against the Spanish to a great sailor (but also a privateer) who would later be knighted – Sir Francis Drake. The list is long of men who received letters of royal authorization from their king or queen to attack and harass Spanish ships en route for Europe. All too often these men made little distinction between their official mission and their own enrichment. They and their companions had no qualms about appropriating the booty for themselves and lining their own pockets. Henry Morgan, John Hawkins, William `Blackbeard´ Teach, `Calico Jack´ Rackman and his two female companions Anne Bonney and Mary Read, William Kidd and Bart Roberts, were just a few of the best known of the English privateers. But there were also Dutch privateers such as Piet Hayn, who operated for the United Provinces, and French, in particular the sailors of St Malo, who obtained their `letters of marque´ from Louis XIV and Louis XV. Amongst the French there were many Huguenots, which the monarchy kept its eyes closed to at a time. In all, there were at least 6000 unofficial pirates and buccaneers.

Freebooters, pirates, and buccaneers (who attacked only Spanish ships and were so named because they smoked meat in the West Indian method over a *boucan*) remorselessly descended on any lone vessel they came across. They were violent and cruel, brave and ready for anything, their sailing vessels were swift and they were armed with long muskets which were more effective than the slow and unwieldy Spanish arquebuses. They often had the support of the local indigenous populations, through whom they were able to restock their supplies of food and water, enjoy female company, and find safe hiding places. With each attack in pursuit of booty they chanced their lives – any wound was often fatal – or risked being hung from the mast of a naval vessel. At first they were only hunted by the Spanish navy but later the English, Dutch and French navies joined in the pursuit as they too began colonizing the Caribbean islands.

THE DECLINE OF PIRACY AFTER THE TREATY OF UTRECHT

Thanks to the treaty of Utrecht, Spain became less involved from the military point of view in Europe, and could send troops to the Caribbean. Furthermore the regional economy was changing: there were fewer mineral resources available and more crops intended for export were being grown – sugar cane, fruits, alcohol, cocoa and so forth. Trading ships became less attractive prizes and the military presence of the great European powers was more important, making conditions much harder for the `professionals´ – pirates, buccaneers, freebooters and privateers were finding themselves out of a job!

`WHAT NEWS ON THE RIALTO?´ – INFORMATION IS WORTH A FORTUNE

In Shakespeare's *The Merchant of Venice*, Solanio asks Salarino: `Now, what news on the Rialto?´ Salarino replies that there are rumors that Antonio's boat has sunk on the Goodwin Sands[1]. In a couple of lines the Bard thus sums up how news got around in 16th century Europe. At the time, Venice was still the major trading center of Europe and the bridge between Europe and points east. As well as rumors, other sources of news were ambassadors, traders, sailors, travellers, and itinerant monks and clergy. Venice was a seething cauldron in which news arrived from northern Europe, Spain, Russia, Constantinople and the ports of the eastern Mediterranean where caravans peddled information coming from the Persian Gulf, the Indian Ocean and even China. Venice benefited from as much geopolitical power as London did from the end of the 19th century up to the Second World War, when it in turn would become the world center for news.

During the 15th and 16th centuries, Europe was desperate for news of the Ottoman Empire, the French and Spanish kingdoms and their struggle for European hegemony, the great ocean voyages and the recent discoveries of distant lands and new routes, novelties coming from the New World, the course of military conflicts, piracy in the Caribbean, the price of spices, industrial raw materials and precious metals. It was a period ripe for the birth of a new trade in news and information.

---

1. `The Merchant of Venice´ William Shakespeare – Act 3, Scene 1.

MERCHANTS, PAPAL DIPLOMATS, AMBASSADORS AND SPIES

From the early Middle Ages, the transmission of news in Europe was monopolized by the great merchants, the papacy – through traveling nuncios, monks and clergy –, and states with their emissaries and ambassadors. Venice's ambassadorial system was highly effective. Its diplomats were in effect mainly commercial attachés, working to promote the well-being and development of the Republic. They gathered economic information about new developments, the flow of merchandise and people, new technologies, new discoveries, epidemics, conflicts and other information which might help trade and commerce in the city of the Doges. From the 15th to the 17th centuries Venice was Europe's largest importer, and exporter, of news. For example, news of the Battle of Pavia between François I and Charles V, which took place on 24th February 1525, arrived in Constantinople on 26th March – but the Pasha did not believe it and neglected to inform the Sultan. But three days later, when a ducal letter addressed to the Venetian ambassador in Constantinople confirmed the news, the Pasha decided finally to tell the Sultan. Indeed, as the ambassador wrote, `the Pasha only trusts news coming from Venice and not much from elsewhere´. News arrived by ship, through the postal system, and with travellers stopping off in inns and taverns. The Rialto Bridge became the main center for exchanging news and rumors. Ambassadors and merchants sent agents there in large numbers, to which should be added Venice's very effective official `secret´ police, who spent their days listening in on conversations and questioning passers-by in order to compile the latest news for their employer.

A new profession was being created – that of journalist and news seller. During the decade 1470-1480 in Venice, one Benedetto Dei, edited a sheet with a selection of news from all parts of the known world. The distribution of these `notices´ grew rapidly, bringing with it fierce competition between their authors. The news sheets were of course bought by diplomats, who used them to provide information for their governments. In 1568 a papal bull from Pius V designated the profession of compiler of news sheets as `arte nova´. In Venice, it was not only Italians who practiced this new profession of *reportiste*; Germans, Flemish, French and Turks all compiled news sheets in their own languages. Later they were also called *gazzettisti* or *gazzettieri*, because the sheets very often cost one *gazzetta*, a Venetian coin in circulation from 1539. Voltaire wrote in his *Encyclopédie* under the heading of *gazette* that `at the beginning of the seventeenth century this useful tool was invented in Venice, at the time when Italy was still at the center of European trade and Venice still a haven of freedom´.

TRANSCRIBERS AND GAZETTEERS

Initially the cost of printing was very high and many gazettes were written by hand – the journalist wrote the text and then transcribers reproduced it very quickly on sheets that were delivered to customers. Naturally the best informed journalist attracted the largest clientele, and often certain customers wanted an almost personalized version, especially ambassadors and the representatives of great merchants, bankers and underwriters. For banks and underwriters in particular, news was highly valued commodity, a luxury item, and they were prepared to pay very high prices for the best information. Journalists soon began to buy gazettes published in other large European cities and would summarize them. Other major information centers included Rome, Prague, Cologne, London, Amsterdam, Madrid and Paris. Each of these cities had their own particular specialty: Madrid and London furnished news from the Americas in particular; Rome, Paris, Madrid, London and Venice all provided political, military and diplomatic news; Prague, Amsterdam and certain German cities sent news of northeast Europe; Venice was the source of information on everything happening in the eastern Mediterranean and the Orient in general. As yet there was no censorship, but the different courts and chancelleries often tried to slip in news which would shed a good light on a king, prince or leaders of the Republic, and some gazetteers became secret propagandists for their countries. Machiavelli wrote that *the Prince* should keep a watchful eye over the dissemination of news, so that it should speak well of his government and show it in a good light.

PUBLIC AND SECRET NEWS SHEETS AND THE PRINTING OF GAZETTES

Many sheets were published with the backing of those responsible for government information – such news sheets were even found in taverns and post houses. There were also `secret´ sheets that did not have to get past the censors and were sold through subscription, mostly to the courts, ambassadors, the Curia (highranking clergy in Rome) and rich merchants. All these required trustworthy, accurate information that might have an effect on the current situation. For example, in August 1499, the Venetian banker and bright diarist Girolamo Priuli learned, through letters from Alexandria, of news that was current in Cairo; this in turn had been carried by men arriving from India. The news told of three Portuguese caravels, under the command of Christopher Columbus, anchored in the port of Calicut. The merchant realized that if this information was true it could have a dramatic affect on Venice's future; but he was inclined not to believe it. Of course there had been a mistake about the commander – it was in fact Vasco De Gama. But two years later the news of Africa's circumnavigation was officially confirmed. Priuli now wrote that this was `for those capable of understanding the worst news that Venice could receive´. Rightly so, for it signaled the end of its monopoly over the Red Sea and Persian Gulf routes to Mediterranean ports, from where Venice stocked up with valuable merchandise which was then distributed throughout Europe. It was news of this kind that European powers, ambassadors, merchants and even Churchmen wanted to learn, and were ready to pay large sums of money for the privilege of getting it as early as possible. Such sheets cost between 25 and 35 gold ducats a year, while the ordinary sheets cost from five to ten ducats a year. The journalists' profits were substantial – between 350 and 450 ducats a year, it has been estimated.

With the spread of the printing press and falling production costs, many more sheets were printed, with print runs of 200 to 500 for each edition, and typographers worked for a whole day producing the copies. Very often the last minute arrival of the latest gazettes from other cities could change the whole layout. Accordingly, up until the late 20th century, typographers in the

English press used to leave a small blank space that could be filled at the last minute with news gathered on the spot or from the latest dispatch. The printing press also allowed the number of pages in these gazettes to be increased. Whereas manuscript copies contained only around 5000 characters, printed copies had between 15,000 and 20,000. Printed editions were also much more legible – a great improvement, since most of the readers were no longer young and probably had eyesight problems.

CURRENCY RATES AND COMMODITY PRICES

The oldest example of a gazette with purely economic content, giving prices of currencies and some raw materials, dates back to 14th March 1585. A broker on the currency market, Panfilo Brancacci, began regularly to publish bulletins with a listing of prices. These were highly prized, particularly by merchants, because they contained a great deal of information and especially because they came out on a regular basis. In Venice, where publication of these bulletins was even protected by a special decree, by 1647 circulation had risen to almost 300 copies a week. Similar bulletins were published in other financial and mercantile centers, and acquired an important legal status; indeed in cases of litigation between two merchants, they were used as a reference for the price of the merchandise or currency. Other gazettes specialized in military news and carried information on current wars – and once again governments, diplomatic circles and merchants were avid consumers of this type of journalism.

The first regular gazette containing all types of news was published in Strasbourg in 1605. Other cities followed suit, and such gazettes were in circulation throughout Europe. Very often these publications were known as *Corantos, Courante uyt Italien, Druytslandt* (in Holland), and *Courant d'Italie et d'Allemaigne* (in France in 1620). In Amsterdam in 1620 an English language gazette was published for the first time called *Courrant out of Italy, Germany* and the following new year it was London's turn with *Newes from Italy, Germany, Hungarie, Spaine and France*.

CHANGING PERCEPTION OF SPACE AND TIME

The regularity with which all of these publications appeared radically changed people's perception of time and of the geography of Europe. At the same time great progress was being made in cartography. Maps were now able to provide detailed representations of far-off lands. This loss of what sociologists might call `isolating space´ brought about a re-evaluation of the relationship between time and space for Europe, which was increasingly sending and receiving news to and from other, hitherto virtually unknown, continents, even if their merchandise was used in daily life. It amounted to a new understanding of the world. Even small towns on the political and economic periphery were brought into regular contact with the outside world, albeit with some delay – but this did not matter very much. A new market grew up, involving the production and dissemination of news. Many governments tried to bring it under their control or to exercise some type of censorship; but journalists always found ways around such obstacles – for example, the publication in Amsterdam or Geneva of gazettes in a type of coded or allegorical language (see Montesquieu's *Lettres Persanes*). The spread of literacy also led to a massive increase in demand for news and information.

THE GLORY AND DECLINE OF GENOA: AN INSTANCE OF STRATEGIC CAPITALISM

In Italy even today it is still said that a Genoese is a Jewish merchant, born from a marriage between a Scottish father and a mother from the Auvergne, with an Armenian uncle and a Levantine aunt, not forgetting that his grandfather was probably Chinese! The image of the Genoese remains practically unchanged, even if Genoa is no longer a financial center but has preferred to specialize in welcoming Mediterranean cruise ships and in becoming a European equivalent to those ports in Florida from which ships laden with tourists depart en route for holidays under the Caribbean sun.

GENOA'S HEYDAY – SEVENTY YEARS OF SUCCESS

Genoa's geography means that it is permanently oriented toward the outside world. It is a port without a hinterland, without any storage capacity, since there is only a 500 yard wide , densely inhabited strip between the sea and the Apennines – rather like Hong Kong. Genoa was a republic with 60,000 to 80,000 inhabitants in the city itself and around half a million people in the surrounding towns. In order to survive, it had to be very flexible, something its merchants in the 13th century understood very well: more than half the financial capital of that period was invested elsewhere. For a long time Sicily, the Greek islands, Constantinople and Odessa were Genoese trading posts for the spice trade; and Genoese carracks even sailed as far as Bruges and England.

The maritime republic lived from trade and relied on its oligarchy. However, Genoese merchants quickly became aware that their fellow citizen, Christopher Columbus, without meaning to, had done them a very bad turn: the discovery of America shifted the economic center of gravity from the Mediterranean to the Atlantic and Northern Europe. Yet it was Genoese merchants and financiers who played a determining role in the traffic between Seville and Spain and the Caribbean and Central America. Discreetly Genoa dominated Europe and its finances throughout the first half of the 16th century. Unlike its rivals the city did not exercise control through its sailors, navy, mercantile fleet or its trading capital, but through its financial capital – which was probably already `capitalist´, in the modern sense.

ANDREA DORIA SWITCHES ALLEGIANCE

When Admiral Andrea Doria, the great maritime mercenary captain, abandoned François I in 1528 and offered his services to Charles V, Genoa decided to take up the cause of the Spanish Emperor. Genoese capital was beginning to be attracted to the court in Madrid, whilst Genoese merchants were financing and trading with the New Indies. With the decision by Charles V and Philip II to borrow more and more from Genoese financiers and the dramatic Spanish bankruptcy of 1557, the era of the north German bankers, especially the Fuggers, came to an end. The Genoese stepped in and immediately filled the vacuum. They offered a steady flow of revenue to the Spanish emperor, in return for fiscal resources and the rather less regular imports of `American´ silver. This financial arrangement was very advantageous to them and allowed them to be less involved in financing Spanish-American trade and even Iberian mining operations. The loans provided to Charles V and later to his son Philip II, brought in a return of 10%, even after late repayments and expenses had been deducted. Genoa had a semi-monopoly in trading silver, which arrived in Spanish galleons from Mexico and the mines of Potosi (old Peru). The Middle East and Asia were eager to obtain silver, which was not readily available in these regions. The crates of silver ingots arriving in Genoa from 1570 allowed the city to dominate Europe. Genoese bankers issued letters of exchange against the silver in their coffers, enabling them to pay out any sum of money anywhere in Europe – fine example of the mobilization of credit.

SUCCESSFUL SPECULATION: GOLD VS. SILVER

Until 1550, silver was relatively rare in comparison with more readily available African gold. Genoa was therefore able to profit greatly from this revaluation of silver. But from the second half of the 16th century Genoese financiers began putting their money into gold, using silver only for making payments especially for conversion into gold, because they realized that silver was going to be in increasingly abundant supply in Europe and that gold would be revalued accordingly. Genoa exported silver to Italian towns that traded with Aleppo, Cairo and Middle Eastern ports. When Philip II understood that the monopoly of Spanish silver lay in the hands of the Genoese, he decided to dispense with their services and chose to pay only in gold, which had a negative effect on the price of silver. But the Genoese succeeded in preventing the circulation of gold. The Spanish troops, who had not been paid for a long time, mutinied, and in November 1576 sacked Antwerp. The Emperor had to accept the Genoese conditions. In return for American silver, Genoa then paid the Spanish troops in the Low Countries in gold by letter of exchange. Such is finance!

GOLD, SILVER AND LETTERS OF EXCHANGE

Genoa's success was based on three things: control of gold from Africa; control of silver from the mines of Mexico and Peru; and letters of exchange enabling the Spanish troops fighting in the Low Countries to be paid in gold. Silver was refined once it arrived in Genoa and then sent on to the Italian trading cities and to the Middle East. The fairs in Piacenza – in the middle of the Po valley, between Milan and Bologna – became the equivalent of the trade fairs in Champagne in the Middle Ages. However, in Piacenza it was essentially letters of exchange and contracts for interest rates throughout Europe that were negotiated – the largest clearing house ever seen prior to the creation of the London Clearing

House in the 20th century. Genoese bankers were great patrons of these fairs, by means of which they could extensively dominate the distribution of credit in Europe.

THE WIND CHANGES

The Genoese grip on Spanish and European finances lasted for a little over 70 years. After that a series of events conspired to militate against the Genoese Republic. The peace treaty signed between the England of Charles I and imperial Spain in 1630, stipulated, amongst other things, that silver from the Spanish colonies in the Americas, destined for Dutch ports, must be transported on English ships. The English were the main privateers, together with the French, who plundered the Spanish galleons in the Caribbean. Part of the money that Genoa transferred to Holland by letter of exchange now became unnecessary, since silver itself was delivered there directly. In financial terms this was a retrograde step, but Genoa could do nothing in the face of this treaty. Genoese merchants and bankers still dominated the Spanish silver trade through their presence in Cadiz, Seville and throughout Andalusia, where much of the traffic was based on contraband. Then in 1627 the second Spanish bankruptcy occurred – the king refused to honor his commitments. This had a major impact on European bankers, especially the Genoese, who decided to withdraw increasingly from financing the Spanish crown and to get involved in other financial operations instead.

GENOA AND BLUE JEANS

Genoa began a massive, radical reorganization of its commitments and its financial deployment in Europe. Its merchants invested in Venetian funds, they flirted with papal finances, and they financed imperial, princely and ducal courts, as well as trade in Austria, Bavaria, Sweden and Milan (then occupied by the Spanish). Furthermore, they financed textile production, including that of `bleu de Gênes´, a type of fustian used to make sailors' trousers (from which `blue jeans´ is derived) – in competition with the city of Nîmes in France (*de Nîmes* = denim) – as well as silk brocades and paper for use in cigarettes (which were replacing raw pipe tobacco in India). But the financial center of gravity, together with that of international trade and economic power, were all moving progressively to the north, first passing to Antwerp, then Amsterdam in the 18th century (Holland's Golden Age) and finally to London.

Thus Genoa became a city of only secondary importance in economic terms. Nevertheless, it financed the unification of Italy in the 19th century and remained the principal Italian financial center until World War I, ahead of Milan, which overtook its rival after the war, thanks to the rise of industrial independence encouraged by Mussolini's government.

TECHNICAL PROGRESS IN EUROPE AND THE MYSTERIES OF PRODUCTIVITY

Alan Greenspan is said to have remarked in the course of a meeting of the Monetary Policy Committee of the Federal Reserve Board that it would be easier to formulate a theory about events in Ancient Rome based on the length of Cleopatra's nose than to calculate exactly the rate of increase of productivity. True or false, the anecdote does seem to be well founded – for in practice, economists today scratch their heads over the fact that all the equations resulting from their macro-econometric models give results that differ widely from reality. The development of the service industry sector, computer technology and the internet economy are in the process of radically changing the structure and fundamental equilibrium of the economy. It lacks, therefore, a standard measure with which to evaluate accurately the growth of productivity. The acceleration of productivity is not a recent phenomenon. Fire, the wheel, progress in agricultural methods, in mineral extraction and in metallurgy, all date back several thousand years. But the truly great revolution dates back to the medieval period and the Renaissance.

THE LIMITED PROGRESS MADE BY THE GREEKS AND ROMANS

If the pyramids were built thanks to miracles of engineering, just like the Etruscan aqueducts, the Greek temples and theatres, the Roman roads and circuses, we must not forget that the progress of productivity in ancient civilizations was relatively limited. Indeed the fact of slavery testifies to the choices made by these civilizations, since slavery is by definition the most obvious example of a choice made in favor of anti-productivity.

Progress made in productivity levels in Europe began, ironically, with the rise of the Muslim world. European nations made very few discoveries or inventions, but were adept at assimilating the applied techniques of other civilizations.

From the 5th century the water wheel – known to but little used by the Romans – became increasingly common. From the 7th century onward the heavy plough, probably of Slav origin, came into general use in northern Europe. Crop rotation on a three-yearly basis spread from the 8th century onwards, whilst from the 9th century, horses began to be shod with iron throughout Europe (although the Celts were already familiar with this technique before the Roman Conquest). It was around then too that pack-saddles for horses made their first appearance – a practice originating in China – as did the double yoke for harnessing animals to carts and ploughs.

EARLY INDUSTRIALIZATION IN EUROPE

Amongst these various innovations, the most important was the water wheel, since this new source of energy gave rise to primitive industrialization in Europe, along with economies of scale. The watermill or wheel was used in sawmills, metallurgy, textile and paper production. In the 13th century, the mariners of the Republic of Amalfi began using the compass – it was of Chinese origin – which greatly facilitated navigation. Equally radical in its effects on land was the introduction of the windmill with a horizontal axis. Already in use in certain regions of Persia – though probably with a vertical axis – this technique was brought back by the Crusaders. Navigation in the Mediterranean underwent a real technological revolution with the perfecting of the gyroscopic compass, the adoption of the water-clock or clepsydra to measure the distance traveled by a ship, the systematic production of charts (portolans), the compilation of trigonometric navigation tables (known as the *tavolate di marteloio* by sailors throughout the Mediterranean), and the adoption of the stern rudder along the median line of the ship. These various instruments and techniques allowed ships to sail during the winter season, thereby greatly increasing their overall use and productivity.

In the 14th century, clock manufacture saw major improvements, as too did marine construction methods, enabling ships to navigate without hugging the coast. In 1434, the Portuguese managed to sail round Cape Bojador on the west coast of Africa, thanks to their knowledge of sailing, in particular their experience of winds and their ability to calculate latitude with great accuracy. By 1480, the year Gutenberg invented his printing press, there was already talk of astrolabes, and spectacles were also coming into general use as techniques for making optical lenses became more widely known.

EUROPE COPIED AND THEN INVENTED

Europeans showed themselves adept at assimilating, copying and using certain technical procedures and techniques which had arrived from other countries, in a similar manner to the Japanese after the end of the Second World War. Gunpowder was invented by the Chinese who only employed it themselves to make fireworks, whilst in Europe it was used in artillery and firearms – a truly European invention. The Chinese were fascinated by the European galleons which spat fire in their seas from the 16th century onwards. Paper was also invented in China and arrived in Europe via the Byzantine empire. Byzantium itself did not promote the production, so it fell to the Spanish paper manufactories of Xativa (1056), the Sicilians (from 1102), and the Italians at Fabriano (1276) to produce all the paper for Europe and the Ottoman Empire.

Europe alone, of all the regions of the world, acquired a passion for all things mechanical. This enthusiasm led to the invention of many instruments and tools of a technologically advanced nature – resulting in enormous gains in productivity. Studies show that productivity in iron production in Britain increased by a factor of eight between 1350 and 1550. In shipping, the ratio of cargo to crew rose from 5 or 6 tons per sailor in 1400 to 8 tons per sailor around the turn of the 16th century. In Milan, the administration of the *Fabbrica del Duomo* – responsible for technical aspects of constructing the cathedral – investigated a machine, powered by a single horse, that could replace four men in cutting stone.

THE CONTROL OF KNOW-HOW THROUGH THE DEATH PENALTY, AND VENETIAN LEGISLATION ON PATENTS

In 1554, Wolfgang Lauschner built a system of pumps to empty the water from a mine in the southern Tyrol. This machine required six workers to man it and in eight hours could pump out around 26.500 US gallons of water, equivalent to the labor of 630 men! There are also many obvious examples of increased productivity in the agricultural sector, resulting in improved yields in crops, milk and meat production. Thanks to the development of the printing press, explanatory manuals in various spheres – mechanical, maritime, agriculture, stock rearing and so on – began to appear everywhere. Many governments tried to limit the spread of this know-how that was the basis of their growing wealth, even threatening their workers with the death penalty if they went to work abroad. Venice was the first State to draw up legislation on patents, in 1474. Known as the *Parte Veneziana*, this historic document laid down for the first time the four basic principles underlying all patent law: encouragement to inventors, compensation for the inventor's costs, the inventor's rights over his invention, and above all, the social utility of invention. However, many states tried to attract industries and their skilled workers through the enticement of tax benefits and other inducements to make such a transfer attractive and adequately to compensate the risks.

The wars of religion contributed to these migrations: French Protestant clockmakers emigrating to Switzerland and England, German defectors who introduced ship-building techniques in Norwich, the French glassmakers who left for Germany, and so forth. Military campaigns, wars of religion and revolutions all fuelled the transfer of technology and increased productivity through population migration. Three examples are particularly worthy of note. The secret of paper production was known only to the Chinese and Japanese until the 8th century, but at the battle of Talas in 751 the victorious Arabs took many Chinese prisoners and thus acquired the know-how. They quickly realized the importance of this new means of spreading Islam – and Samarkand became the first center of paper production in the Muslim world. The revocation of the Edict of Nantes drove Huguenot clockmakers and printers to Switzerland, northern Germany, Holland and England. And the French Revolution resulted in artillery officers fleeing, this had a bad impact on the French Navy, that during the battle of Trafalgar was shown in a lack of artillery is mentioned elsewhere in the book; experience and accuracy in dismasting against Nelson's cannons whose rate of fire was tree times greater than the French ones. There were many other examples. German printers fled the war in their country and settled in Italy (particularly Venice and Rome), other specialists – foundry workers, textile workers, mechanics, specialists in metallurgy and mining – migrated to various countries during the Thirty Years War, as did a large number of Flemish at the time of the revolt by the Netherlands against Spanish domination. These illegal movements, driven by political, military and religious events, were paradoxically very beneficial to the European economy, because they accelerated – despite all the human dramas involved – the circulation of ideas and in particular the transfer of technical know-how, the key element of development.

CHINA MISSES OUT ON THE TECHNO-LOGICAL REVOLUTION, DESPITE ITS INVENTIVENESS

Until the 15th century, Europe and the Indian and Arab worlds owed much of their technical capability to the Chinese. Evidence of ploughshares dating back to 5000 BC have been found in China – they had ploughshares made of bronze in the 15th century BC and of iron in the 5th century BC. It would be a long time before Europe copied these inventions.

Another Chinese invention was the wheelbarrow. It was first used for transport in the 1st century under the Han dynasty, whilst in Europe it only appeared from the 11th century onwards – having been imported by Middle Eastern merchants. The drive belt was already present in Chinese silk-producing workshops from the 1st century BC; this particular application of technology was only known in Europe around a thousand years later. Suspension bridges also have their origins in China; in his *Records of the Grand Historian* (circa 90 BC), Sima Quian mentions the existence of several suspension bridges used to cross rivers and ravines.

The Chinese were also the first to invent pig iron and to discover steel-producing methods, even before the 2nd century BC, using fairly sophisticated techniques. From the 1st century BC their ships were equipped with rudders, and compasses appeared a century later. In Europe the compass arrived via the Arabs during the 11th century, where the first record of it being used was by the sailors from Amalfi, one of the four great Italian maritime republics. Problems of navigation between canals at different heights were solved by the introduction in the 10th century BC in China of inclined levels. Fishing reels began being used in the 2nd century AD – contemporary writings make reference to them, and later they can be seen in graphic works, one of which dates from 1195. But the greatest Chinese intellectual advance is probably decimal calculation, dating from the 15th century BC, and the use of the zero in calculation tables. Of course, this system of calculation and the concept of zero came to Europe via India and then the Arab world, arriving several centuries after they first appeared in China – and the Catholic Church at the time opposed its introduction on the grounds that the zero represented nothingness, which it saw as evil.

CHINESE TECHNOLOGY TRAVELS ALONG THE SILK ROAD

The first mechanical clocks were also Chinese. The largest clock in ancient China was Su Song's Astronomical Clock Tower, built around 1092; the 40-foot-tall wooden tower was topped by a power-driven bronze armillary sphere that reproduced the movements of the sun, moon, and specific stars important in Chinese astrology.

However, one question in particular springs to mind: if China was so advanced in all these different technologies, why did it not succeed in extending its influence and power throughout the world (bearing in mind that gunpowder, paper, silk and many other `miracles´ of technology were all invented there)? Historians think that the country, particularly during the Ming era, was stifled by the sterile attitudes of the court to technology; nearly all inventions were sent to the Emperor, who very often merely considered them as marvelous toys for his amusement. So much so, that the spread of these techniques and their economic use and export were sabotaged by the imperial system, with its scholars and eunuchs working only to serve the emperor with blind devotion or, on occasion, for their own interests The example of clocks produced in Europe, initially in Italy to start with, then by Protestants in France and Switzerland, serves to make the point. Jesuits arrived at the imperial Chinese court and managed to ingratiate themselves by presenting some clocks to the Emperor, who thought they were marvelous and something quite extraordinary.

He authorized the Jesuits to remain and preach their religion (see the memoirs of the Italian Jesuit Matteo Ricci), making them responsible, amongst other things, for keeping the clocks working. Anyone who has visited the Forbidden City in Beijing will certainly have admired the wonderful collection of about 200 clocks still on display in of the palace rooms.

EXPULSIONS OF MORISCOS, JEWS, HUGUENOTS... AND THEIR ECONOMIC IMPACT

The economic consequences of political decisions essentially motivated by religious considerations are often disastrous, quite apart from the cost of such decisions from the moral, human and political standpoint. Two examples make this very clear: the end of the *reconquista* in the Arab regions of Spain and the revocation of the Edict of Nantes.

SPAIN EXPELS THE JEWS AND THE MORISCOS

The military weakness of the Caliphate of Cordoba and its ultimate collapse are the underlying causes of the *reconquista* (reconquest) of territories that had been occupied since the Moorish invasion of 711-714. After the Fall of Toledo in 1085, only the Caliphate of Grenada remained under Muslim control. Isabel I of Castille married Fernand II of Aragon in 1469; Spain was now stronger and able to step up the fight against Grenada, which fell at almost the same time as Columbus discovered America. In 1494, kings of Spain were given the additional title of `Catholic Kings´ by Pope Alexander VI after their `Western Crusade´. However, from 1492 onward there was increasing animosity toward Muslims and Jews, with specific decrees against them combined with a deliberate and ferocious policy on the part of the Inquisition. At the end of the 15th century the Jewish population in Spain was estimated at between 200,000 and 300,000 and these were all threatened with expulsion if they refused to convert to

Catholicism; the same happened again in regard to the Muslim population from 1502 onwards. When they were able to, these minorities left. Many Jews – probably around 120,000 – fled to Portugal, but they were expelled from there by King Manuel I in 1497; others went to the Low Countries, Italy and elsewhere. Muslims who did not convert to Catholicism left for North Africa and other Mediterranean countries. A second Christianization campaign began early in the 17th century, but it was not successful. In 1609 Philip III decreed the definitive expulsion of the Muslim population, who left for North Africa: 150,000 from the Grenada region, 90,000 from Andalusia, 64,000 from Aragon, 50,000 from Catalonia and more than 100,000 from Castille.

SPAIN'S STRUCTURAL ECONOMIC CRISIS MASKED BY THE DISCOVERY OF THE NEW WORLD

The economic structure of Spain suffered badly from this sudden exodus. The Arabs were above all traders, farmers specializing in certain types of cultivation – oranges, cotton, sugar cane, and rice, for example, called for knowledge of hydraulics – and craftsmen working in leather, fabrics and ceramics. They also included a number of intellectuals, scientists and translators, who had made a substantial contribution to the spread of the Arab and Indian cultures in Europe. Indeed in the late 12th century, Toledo was a center that attracted intellectuals and academics from all over Europe, who went there to find translations of Greek, Arabic and Indian texts, very often translated from the original Latin. Amongst these scholars were Gerard of Cremona, Plato of Tivoli, Adelard of Bath and William of Moerbeke. The departure of the Jews entailed a loss of traders, merchants with international connections, bankers, physicians and other intellectuals and scientists. As a result the economy suffered a terrible reversal, but this was partially masked by the discovery of America and by the wealth – gold, silver, spices and other exotic products new to Europe – arriving in the Atlantic ports and in Seville. The Iberian Empire was increasingly living on the credit extended to it by the international bankers – Fugger, Florentine banks, Genoese and Jews – and, above all, the import of goods that the country either did not or could not produce because of its low level of pre-industrial development.

Spain did have the merit of being the financer of the scientific revolution in other European countries. It imported fabrics and silks from Northern Italy, glassware, books and lace from Venice; nails, cannons and books from Holland, and watches from France, Switzerland and England. There was an additional irony in the fact that the Arabs had exported the technique of paper making, from rags and paper pulp, to Spain, around the 12th century; this technique was widely copied and developed in Italy (in Fabriano) and Spain began to import paper from Italy, having formerly been a major producer and exporter itself. Spain also had to bring in `foreign´ engineers, especially from Italy and the Low Countries – specialists in mechanics, hydraulics and theoretical scientific matters. In the library of the royal palace, the Escurial, there were a mere hundred or so mathematical volumes, only eleven of which had been written by Spaniards and printed in Spain, and two more written by Spaniards, but published in Antwerp and Messina. What is more, in 1557 Philip II forbade his subjects to travel abroad for purposes of study; the decree was only annulled in 1718 by Philip V. Cervantes and Quevedo bore ironic witness to the cultural decline of the country which undermined the `Golden Century´ and its glories.

THE REVOCATION OF THE EDICT OF NANTES AND THE STAGNATION OF THE FRENCH ECONOMY BETWEEN 1684 AND 1717

The Edict of Nantes, signed by Henry IV in 1598, affirmed the religious freedom for a sizeable minority of the French population – around 10% between 1561-1562 – and also confirmed the powerful influence that they had over the economy and public administration: the Prince of Condé, Admiral Coligny and Sully were all Protestants. The Revocation of the Edict of Nantes in October 1685 led to a rapid exodus of around 1% of the French population, some 200,000 men and women who played an important role in the life of the country, most of them concentrated in specific regions. In purely economic terms, this had relatively serious consequences for France; on the other hand, it had a very positive

effect on the countries which received and welcomed this influx of
new citizens, often with open arms. Indeed, the Protestants, or
Huguenots as they were called, had a relatively elevated level of
culture and education because they had to read the Bible for
themselves and worked in economically sensitive sectors. Almost
all the clockmakers, cannon smiths, a large number of book sellers
and printers, many officers, medium-sized bankers and scholars
with scientific interests, left the country. Clockmakers and clock
sellers went to the Swiss canton of Geneva and to England, where
they had a great influence on the organization of their profession.
Calvin obliged Swiss goldsmiths to alter their trade in favor of
watch-making, by forbidding them to make `crosses, chalices or
any other material used in the service of the papacy and idolatry´.
Swiss clock and watch-makers also managed to infiltrate the trade
in Constantinople and Isaac Rousseau, the father of the philosopher Jean-Jacques Rousseau, worked as official clock maker to the
Sultan, in charge of all the clocks in the Topkapi palace. Many
booksellers, librarians and printers went, yet again, to Amsterdam,
London and Switzerland : Henri Justel, who used to invite his
friends Leibnitz and Locke to his house in Paris, went to live in
London; Paul Colomiez from La Rochelle also went to England;
Elie Bouhéreau left for Dublin; Louis Compiègne de Veil, a former
Jew who had first been baptized as a Catholic, converted to Cal-
vinism and went to England, like Michel Mattaire...to mention
but a few.

FRANCE GIVES ITS KNOW-HOW TO PROTESTANT COUNTRIES

Medium-sized banks which had been located in Lyon, Paris,
Bordeaux and Nantes ceased trading and set up again in French
Switzerland (the Mallet bank, for example) or in Holland and
northern Germany. On the other hand, certain Swiss banks
remained in France, but they limited most of their business to cash
transactions and reduced their financing commitments. In certain
specific manufacturing sectors – paper production, hat-making,
foundries for cannons, textile, and especially silk production –
emigration was particularly high, with the host countries benefiting from this influx of free *savoir-faire*. In Frankfurt many of the

Huguenots settling there were entrepreneurs or skilled craftsman in advanced sectors such as textiles and the formulation of medicines. Some analysts estimate that Prussia's economic development was brought forward by as much as half a century thanks to the arrival of these French emigrants. In this way, Germany was able to make up much of the time lost through the Thirty Years War. The French retail trade also suffered from the loss of small shopkeepers and of merchants working in international commerce, especially with countries that were largely Protestant. In a manuscript written in 1701 by those responsible for trade and commerce in the French administration (*Mémoire sur le commerce de France*) it is noted that the country's commerce had begun to decline after the Revocation of the Edict of Nantes. Sailors also took part in the exodus, especially the Atlantic navigators based around La Rochelle and in Brittany, particularly St Malo. Some even became privateers working for other nations, for the most part joining crews of ships attacking Spanish galleons in the Caribbean. Some army officers, especially engineers and artillery officers, left the army, resulting in a shortage of manpower in certain specialized fields. With the French Revolution, history would repeat itself, as many artillery and naval officers, so important to the Battle of Trafalgar and some of Napoleon's early battles, left the services and fled the country.

The revocation of Nantes was not the sole cause of stagnation in France's economy, which was to last at least thirty years. But it substantially contributed to it, especially by provoking the crisis which ensued in certain pre-industrial crafts in specific geographical regions and in the level of exports to Protestant countries. These were benefiting from increased economic growth compared to the countries of the Mediterranean, which were undergoing a major crisis, among them the Iberian Peninsula, now entering its period of decline. In any case, various industrial sectors outside France grew apace thanks to Huguenot emigration, while the loss to France due to this unfortunate episode is hard to quantify.

THE COURTESANS OF BAROQUE VENICE: A SIGNIFICANT SOURCE OF TAX REVENUES

The population census of 1509 reveals that the city had 11,164 prostitutes out of a total of 130,000 inhabitants. This is likely to be an underestimate, since many people used to pass through Venice – merchants, artists, politicians, ambassadors, spies, monks, clergy and scholars. The population was therefore larger in reality. But the ratio between women practicing the oldest profession in the world and men, even those in transit, was still very high, in this city where commerce in spice and silk from the Orient, salt and works of art, books and lace was inextricably mingled with the commerce of seduction.

Around the middle of the 14th century, courtesans were required to live in an area of the city close to the Rialto Bridge (where there were large markets), and in the evening, once the bells tolled nightfall, they had to return home. If they were found in the street after this `professional curfew´, punishment was severe – ten lashes of the whip, or even fifteen if they tried to attract the attention of men before Christmas, Easter or other holy days.

TWO GRADES OF COURTESANS

There were lower grade courtesans who offered their favors to the general male population and to passing seamen, and those of a higher rank, more like Japanese geishas, in that they were skilled in matters of culture, conversation, music and good manners. The latter enjoyed considerable freedom, lived in beautiful houses and organized parties, philosophical debates and concerts. They were protected by the noblemen and rich merchants who were their main clients. For example, Veronica Franco, born in Venice at the beginning of the 16th century, was the most sought after courtesan of the period, due to her grace, beauty and intelligence. She would receive musicians, painters, men of letters and noblemen at her house. She was even known abroad, and when a large banquet was organized in honor of the future king of France, Henry III, she appeared reclining in a revealing gown on a large dish placed on the table.

PROSTITUTION AND THE POLICE

The more the city developed, the more rapidly money passed from one person to another, attracting merchants and visitors of all kinds. The secret services of various European nations and especially of the Republic itself frequently used the charms of these women to gather pillow talk and secrets – 18th century Venice was a real crossroads for European spying. The powerful and omnipresent Venetian secret police often called on the `services´ of courtesans of all ranks to obtain restricted information from visitors, captains of ships anchored in the port, ambassadors and their secretaries, merchants and traders of strategic materials such as arms, luxury products, rare spices and books, and *gazzettieri*, the early journalists who published newsletters for their clients. All of this information was gathered, examined and sent by the police – both secret and conventional – to the Doge and other high officials. The police were also very much aware that some of these women might be gathering information on behalf of diplomats posted to Venice or foreign spies – information that might well be used against la Serenissima. Genoa too had an old tradition of `debriefing´ ship's captains arriving in the port, to obtain information.

Visitors making the famous `tour of Italy´ wrote that Venice had the greatest concentration of *filles de joie* of anywhere in the western world, `twice the number to be found in Paris,´ wrote de Brosses, `the largest European city of the time, which had a population four or five times greater than that of Venice´. In addition there were a certain number of women who offered their favors only at Carnival time, which nonetheless lasted for over a month.

There were also male intermediaries or procurers who promoted these women's services. Montaigne, Montesquieu and Rousseau were all greatly impressed by the quality of life the women enjoyed, earning large sums and able to live in as much luxury as princesses. In 1574 a `social directory´ – *Il Catalogo* – appeared, listing all the courtesans in the city, with their professional `qualities´ and their tariffs.

THE AUTHORITIES TAKE STEPS TO REGULATE THE PROFESSION AND COLLECT TAXES

The *Procuratori*, officials of the city, were well aware that this sector of the population was a major source of revenue, and accordingly tried to regulate its activities. The women were required to wear a yellow scarf around their neck, to respect a certain timetable, and to submit themselves to medical examinations – the `French disease´ (syphilis) was rife. To exclude the presence of transvestite men, it was even stipulated that their breasts must be exposed – and the `the Bridge of Breasts´ (*il Ponte delle Tette*) may still be seen in today's Venice, where prospective customers could admire the feminine attributes of these professionals, who would show themselves at the windows of the houses facing the bridge, like in the red light district of modern Amsterdam.

In regard to homosexuality, Venice was uncompromising: many documents from the archives refer to the arrest and sentencing of certain `gentlemen´, who were beheaded or even burnt alive for `unnatural´ acts. During the 16th century, women prostitutes found themselves facing by a wave of competition from homosexuals and formally requested the Doge Antonio Contarini to `do something to protect them´ – whence the origin of the *Ponte delle Tette*. They also paid taxes – a substantial contribution to the Venetian budget. Once the city started going downhill economically, its large numbers of prostitutes helped attract foreign currency, a major factor in slowing its decline. The growth of gaming houses and casinos in la Serenissima also favored the recreational activities of these women, becoming an important source of revenue for the city as a whole, not just the tax authorities. Montesquieu noted the economic significance of the courtesans: `they are the only ones to earn and distribute money´. The richest amongst them, desirous of saving their souls before departing this world, left substantial sums of money to the Church, and in some cases even had convents built to take in abandoned girls. Money proves after all to be more useful than its absence – and not only in matters of finance!

LOUIS XIV – THE PRECURSOR OF ROOSEVELT?

The Tennessee Valley Authority (the large hydroelectric project), massive public works programs, public assistance for the least well off... were all part of the economic plan of a president who had to confront one of the greatest economic crises in America's history. Roosevelt's solution was known as the New Deal, in which the ideas of a British professor of economics were applied to the letter. Thus Keynes became the uncrowned king of political economy for the next few decades.

Less well known is the fact that Roosevelt had a predecessor in Keynesian policy: Louis XIV, who had already applied Keynes's policies, without knowing it, just for his own enjoyment.

VERSAILLES: *LA FOLIE DES GRANDEURS*

Invited by Fouquet, his Minister of Finance, to the Chateau of Vaux le Vicomte, Louis XIV was overcome with envy for the marvelous new residence his minister had built. Convinced that Fouquet had been filling his pockets from the state coffers, Louis had him arrested by d'Artagnan and, in a rigged trial, sentenced to prison in perpetuity. Fouquet was transferred to Pinerolo[1], a fortified town in the Piedmont region – under French domination at the time – where he died fifteen years later. Unable to stop at this, Louis XIV launched into the construction of his own chateau.

---

1. The impressive dungeon of the large fortress hosted some important men of the `Louis XIV history´; among them the unknown but famous `Iron Mask´, the prisoner who spend 12 years in Pinerolo and died in the prison of la Bastille in Paris (1703).

It took 54 years, from 1661 to 1715, to build one of the greatest royal palaces in the world. The total cost of this 'folly' is estimated at around 1.23 billion euros! To put this into perspective, when Louis XIV died in 1715, the state deficit was estimated at 1.25 billion euros. Such is the scale of the economics lying behind an extraordinary project that was a mixture of aesthetics, grandiose ideas, technical innovation, economics and the symbolism of power. To maintain Versailles still costs around 3 million euros a year. Some 36,000 workers – 22,000 of them soldiers – worked on the construction of the buildings, the terraces and the hydraulic schemes. Simply to divert the River Eure, the largest single component of the overall project, required between 10,000 and 30,000 workers for three years, with somewhat fewer in winter. The initial project envisaged diverting the Loire River, but Charles Perrault, the author of *Sleeping Beauty*, helped to prevent this costly mistake; the writer was a high official in the administration and played a key role in organizing the construction site, together with his brother Claude, who designed the Allée d'Eau. Many learned members of the Academy were brought together to study and work as consultants on the hydraulics, building techniques and architecture of the chateau and its grounds. The whole was to be a showcase for French technology, using the latest techniques in construction and structure.

MILLIONS OF ÉCUS, THOUSANDS OF WORKERS – ALL FOR GLORY

Between 1664 and 1690 more than 28,000 cubic yards of marble (75 million euros worth) were transported to Versailles, many million cubic yards of earth were moved for the terraces and to fill in the marshy land, and dozens of miles of cast iron pipes were buried throughout the parklands to provide water. In addition there was the work involved in sculpting the statues, creating the stucco work, manufacturing of mirrors – which were at the leading edge of contemporary technology – and building the foundry for the bronze and other metal statues inside the palace and in the gardens. Even the scholars of the Academy were in permanent demand. Mansart, Vauban, Le Nôtre, the Francine family (Italian in origin, for the hydraulic works) and an army of artists, were all mobilized for these Herculean works, reminiscent of the pyramids, the great Roman amphitheatres, the Great Wall of China, the pre-columbian pyramids and, indeed, the vast dams on the Tennessee River or on Lake Powell, the source of Las Vegas's water.

LITTLE DID HE KNOW ...

Of course, Louis had no idea that his dreams of grandeur were fuelling the economy through the extraordinary sums involved – not to mention the artistic aspect and the impact on French culture and its influence throughout the western world at the time. Throughout a difficult period from an economic standpoint – several wars were under way, especially during the summer months, that were costly both in terms of lives and financially – the `peaceful´ expenses of building Versailles were an important factor in relaunching of the economy.

Of course such astronomical sums of money could have been spent on building roads, bridges, schools and houses, with an even more direct and immediate effect on the country's economy and infrastructure. At the time, however, those in power felt it necessary to make a greater display of their position than nowadays. Various libraries, arches and other great monuments still recall the projects of Roman times, intended to confirm and legitimize the power of the emperors; the great cathedrals still celebrate the power of the Church; the chateaux of the Loire and the castles of the Rhine valley – rich in legends (the Nibelungen, Siegfried and Rheingold) – and of Tuscany, bear witness to the grandeur of kings and princes, just as the sumptuous palaces lining the Grand Canal testify to the wealth and power of Venetian merchants.

THE DECLINE OF VENICE AND THE DUTCH GOLDEN AGE

In 1453 Constantinople fell into the hands of the Turks. An empire more than a thousand years old succumbed to the battering of the invaders' artillery, which began by bombarding the city from Theodoseus' wall. Ironically, the artillery was both commanded and manned by European Christian mercenaries. The Turks were attracted partly by the vulnerability of what remained of the powerful Byzantine Empire, but mostly by the prospect of controlling the spice trade between the Indian Ocean and the eastern Mediterranean, which was dominated by the Venetian merchants and naval fleets. The merchants of the La Serenissima had an important power in all trade between the eastern Mediterranean, northern Europe and the Iberian Peninsula. Combined with the instability already created by the fall of Tamerlane's empire, making the Silk Road more dangerous, this change in the ˋstatus quoˊ made trading conditions difficult and the transport of merchandise coming from the Indian Ocean, the Middle and the Far East unreliable. This silent revolution impelled the kingdoms of Portugal and Spain and the city states of Genoa and Florence to start looking for alternative routes to the Indian Ocean. The great geographical discoveries, including in particular the unthimkable and dramatic discovery of America, encouraged the great powers to take to the oceans and radically altered trade routes.

With its secure income and substantial industrial base – textiles, glass, metallurgy and precious metalwork, pharmaceutical products, the new printing industry, luxury goods and the slave trade – Venice immediately took up a defensive stance to protect its interests and maintain its dominance in as many sectors as possible. Slowly, however, mercantile and marine capital abandoned Venice and shifted into the industrial and agrarian sectors. With the great geographical discoveries, the process accelerated and the financial and commercial centers of gravity transferred from the Mediterranean to northern Europe and toward the Atlantic Ocean. Other factors also came into play: the Thirty Years War, which hit overland trade between Venice and central northern Europe; constant raids by English privateers on the Venetian fleet in the Mediterranean; the technical revolution in mercantile and naval ships which made the Turkish and Venetian galleys obsolete; the corporatism of the working classes and the loss of dynamism among a large part of the Venetian ruling classes – all this caused far greater damage to Venice than the cannons of the Turkish fleet ever did. The decline of Venice was long and golden … but, alas, inevitable! Its commercial and military power became steadily weaker despite occasional brief moments of revival. Much of its decline was disguised by the cultural influence of the city, which long remained one of the great European centers and certainly the most liberal city in the whole of the Italian peninsula. The powerful administrative structure, a discreet but very effective network of ambassadors, a powerful trade policy, `modern´ industry, its geographical position (Venice remained the main port in the Mediterranean until the 17th century), its agricultural dynamism (maize, rice, mulberries, raw silk and stock rearing), all helped to slow its decline.[1] But from now on, it was largely a matter of keeping up appearances for `The Lion of St Mark´, until such time as its independence came to an end with the arrival of the first Napoleonic troops.

A CARGO OF PEPPER CHANGES ANTWERP'S DESTINY

Bruges was one of the largest north European ports, trading with the towns of the Hanseatic League, England, North Germany, France, and the Iberian Peninsula. Many Genoese carracks also

---

1. Venice maintained its cultural position for a long time and became an important port of call for young men on their educational Grand Tour. It was Europe's leading center for opera, with 17 theatres for a population of only 140,000.

arrived there regularly, to unload spices and take on board metals and textiles. The Portuguese sent spices, imported from western Africa. However, the town's political life was often in turmoil with frequent insurrections by the poorest classes. Then in 1482 the death of Mary of Burgundy sparked off a revolt against her husband, Maximilian of Austria. For ten years or more the city suffered political instability and military intervention. Eventually, the Burgundian court left the city and its traders began to move to Antwerp. From 1499 Antwerp became a Portuguese trading post for spices, initiated when the Portuguese King's *feitor* – a combination of diplomat and commercial agent – moved there temporarily to escape the troubles in Bruges, then, on Maximilian's advice, stayed on indefinitely. The pepper trade was a state monopoly and the *feitor* took charge of it. The first cargo of spices, consisting of pepper and nutmeg, arrived in August 1501, and the first spice distribution contracts drawn up with local merchants – they agreed to receive the cargo and transport it inland by means of barges on the Scheldt and its canals – date from 1504. Increasingly the town exported base metals such as lead and tin coming from Germany and England, as well as fabrics and cereals. These products were destined for the Iberian Peninsula and the new colonies. Silver from Germany was also loaded in Antwerp. The town had the advantage of possessing a large network of rivers and canals in its hinterland; medium-sized boats could call at the port and unload part of their cargo, thereby reducing their draft, and then continue their voyage up river. The city soon became a financial center as well a trading center. It attracted capital and the representatives of large trading houses such as Fugger, Welser, Hochstatter and Tucker, and many bankers from southern Europe, notably the Italians and Portuguese, set up branches to finance trade with their regions. The English, especially after the founding of the 'Merchant Adventurers Company' in 1407, a guild or livery company for overseas merchants, mainly traded in wool and metals. Antwerp, however, had no international traders or large local banks of its own, remaining a major trading post that gradually began specializing in processing imported products, mostly textiles – Italian merchants became the principle suppliers of alum, the volcanic chemical product needed to fix dyes –, Spanish leather, French and Spanish wines and Scandinavian wood. The town also developed fish salting, the processing of cereals, the refining of Indian and Madeira sugar and soap manufacture. The port traded in many products used for dying materials, such as pastel, indigo, Brazilwood and cochineal.

`ONE OF THE WONDERS OF THE WORLD´

The English diplomat, Richard Sampson, described the town as `one of the wonders of the world´. And Ludovico Guicciardini, nephew of Francesco Guicciardini, one of the masters of political science and great friend of the older Machiavelli, wrote a long account in praise of the town after his visit there. He described four large annual fairs, among them the *Sinksenmarkt* which started in June, at Whitsun, and finished at the end of August, and the *Bamismarkt* which started in September and finished in mid-November. The stock exchange was founded in 1531, the name of which in Flemish and French (*Bourse*) comes from the Van der Buerse family, who owned the two inns in Bruges where the first trading of stock took place in 1453. The family coat of arms showed three purses or *bourses*, and merchants would talk about `meeting at the purses´ when they went to negotiate merchandise or money. Thanks to its flourishing economy, the town became an important cultural center for northern Europe, with writers, painters, poets, musicians and scientists all coming to live there. At the height of its success the number of inhabitants reached 100,000. Antwerp even attempted to break up the Portuguese spice monopoly to disrupt the growing protectionism of the English, and to control Hanseatic trade. But in 1549 Portugal revoked its royal spice agency and the town's social and economic position declined, with conditions for unskilled labor becoming particularly hard. Finally, in 1557 came the public finance bankruptcy of the Spanish and French with serious consequences for Antwerp's bankers, since the whole money circuit was disrupted. These three elements contributed to the end of the city's period of success, and thereafter it went into rapid decline, although its industrial activities compensated for some of the worst effects of the collapse in trade. In 1576 Spanish infantry troops, Philip II's famous *tercios*, not having been paid for some considerable time, rebelled and sacked Antwerp. This resulted in the death of more than

8000 people and caused extensive destruction. Genoese bankers finally paid the Spanish soldiers through letters of exchange, imposing their own terms on the Spanish Emperor. By this point Antwerp was bled white and on its last legs. The River Scheldt was closed to traffic following the Treaty of Munster in 1648, which put an end to the Eighty Years War between Spain and Holland and which virtually closed down the port of Antwerp, the only rival to Amsterdam on the North Sea coast.

AMSTERDAM DIRECTLY BENEFITS FROM ANTWERP'S COLLAPSE

From 1585 onwards, under pressure from the Spanish, about half the population of Antwerp moved to Amsterdam, a city that was well situated, well protected, and had direct and easy access to the sea. The surrounding area provided cheap labor and soldiers. The canals leading from the town were a well organized and economical transportation network. The climate was maritime and moderate with plenty of wind to turn the windmills, which were often run by retired sailors with much experience with sails. The easy availability and low cost of energy helped the city's development, which not only benefited from windmills to grind cereals and drive sawmills and other proto-industrial activities, but also had a large available supply of peat, transported by barges on the canals. All Amsterdam needed was capital, negotiating experience, commercial activity and peaceful political conditions. The population rose from 50,000 in 1600 to 200,000 in 1700. In this hive of activity lived a mixture of Flemish, Walloons, Germans, Portuguese, Italians, Jews, French Huguenots and English. The city became the largest commercial center in northern Europe. The adjoining port welcomed whaling fleets from the northern seas (whale oil was used in making soap and for domestic lighting) and was known for salting fish, its naval shipyards (building ocean-going vessels), its ship resale market (the second largest in Europe), and a large market in cannons and firearms. Amsterdam fishermen had two specialties: they kept live fish in submerged baskets, which then arrived fresh in the port, and they used to salt the fish when they were still at sea, a process facilitated by the large Dutch ships (which had made Mediterranean galleys obsolete when they began commercial operations in the Mediterranean for the first time, either under the Dutch flag or leased by merchants of other nationalities). Vessels from Amsterdam transported cereals from northern Europe to the Mediterranean, returning with wheat from Sicily and Egypt. Even Venice used Dutch galleons as mercenaries in its struggles with the Ottoman Empire.

`WEALTH BRINGS FREEDOM, FREEDOM BRINGS WEALTH´

After the Spanish Empire took control of Portugal in 1581, Madrid decided to prohibit Dutch boats from entering the port of Lisbon. This move encouraged the Dutch to set up the East Indies Company, followed by the West Indies Company. By doing this they were able to consolidate their semi-monopoly of the spice routes from the Indian Ocean and the islands of the western Pacific. As in Venice and Genoa, the politicians who governed Amsterdam were essentially merchants, and like all mercantile oligarchies their first concern was to protect their own interests and indirectly those of the town. With the blessing of the ruling house of Orange the naval fleet, of considerable size after 1645, became a means of watching over and defending Dutch maritime trading routes. Taxation laws were very much to the advantage of the rich merchants, whereas the poor were heavily taxed with the *Heere Geld* levy, imposed on all servants and people of modest means. Indirect taxation was the mainstay of fiscal policy. Dutch financiers were slowly replacing Genoese bankers. For instance, during the War of Spanish Succession, French troops fighting in Italy were paid through the intermediary of Amsterdam, much to the annoyance of the English (according to Fernand Braudel), who were allies of the Dutch against the French. Trade was completely free, or as the French diplomat Gaspard de Coignet de la Thuillerie put it in a letter (dated 31st March 1648) to Mazarin: `le gain est la seule et unique boussole qui conduit les gens cy´ (`profit is these people's sole motivation´). Religious freedom and freedom of expression were an essential part of the cultural life of the city, a state of affairs that attracted many printers, freethinkers, philosophers, writers, painters, musicians and architects. These last were responsible for building the great houses on the circular canals, intended to demonstrate the success of merchants, bankers and politicians. The city's philosophy could thus be summed up as: `wealth brings freedom and freedom brings wealth´.

Success in Asia, problems in the New World

The sailors and merchants of Amsterdam were active throughout the Far East, where they were slowly replacing the Portuguese. They increasingly dominated the spice trade, in particular in mace, nutmeg, cinnamon and cloves; they bought silver and gold, often in the form of Japanese *koban*, a gold coin from the Edo era, as well as Japanese copper; they transported Indonesian fabrics to India and porcelain from Japan, Korea and China to Europe; and they exported gold mined in Sumatra and Malacca to India, Persia and the port of Mokha, today in the Yemen. But their commercial successes in the Orient were not repeated in the New World. They experienced all sorts of problems in Brazil: their large ships were insufficiently maneuverable in the shallow waters off the Brazilian coast and they were unable to dislodge the Portuguese as they had done in the western Pacific. On the other hand, Amsterdam became one of the main players in the triangular Atlantic trade in slaves and the first port of call for slaves destined for the European market.

The second half of the 17th century, a period of wars and upheavals, did not go well for the city, which had to absorb the serious economic crisis caused by the huge speculation in tulips. The speculative bubble ended in a financial bloodbath in 1637 and the consequences were felt for more than twenty years. From 1650, William II Prince of Orange sought to set up a monarchy in the United Provinces, as they were known, with the tacit support of France. He viewed Amsterdam as an enemy of the Princes of Orange, because its rich and independent burghers of the city had never offered allegiance to them. Attempting to take it by surprise, he mustered his troops in secrecy and marched swiftly on the city. However, his plans were foiled by the vigilance of the town council, which opened the flood gates, forcing the Count of Nassau, the leader of the expedition, to retreat. A compromise was reached: certain councilors who were opposed to William were removed, while William paid for the burghers' companies to be expanded from 20 to 54 men, soldiers to be enlisted and new fortifications to be built. The French ambassador, Brasset, wrote `Ces messieurs de Hollande ont plié sans être terrassés´ (`These Dutch gentlemen have given ground but not been floored´). When William II died on 6th November 1650, Amsterdam had an allegorical medallion struck in honor of having defended its freedom: it showed a spirited horse galloping toward the sun which was rising over the city; on the reverse it showed Phaeton falling from the sky, having flown too close to the sun, with the caption `Magnis excidit ausis´ (`His great ambition was his downfall´ Ovid's *Metamorphosis*, Book II, line 328.)

AMSTERDAM'S DECLINE, LONDON'S RISE

In the face of conflicts with the English, who were trying to extend their colonial empire and enhance their power on the high seas, and further confrontations with Louis XIV, who wished to acquire Flanders' rich economy for himself, Amsterdam's power was gradually undermined, bringing in its train a steady decline. In 1672, during the war against France, in spite of opposition from part of the town council, Amsterdam flooded the countryside by breaching the dikes, thereby halting the advance of Louis XIV's hitherto victorious armies. On 28th June of the same year, when peace negotiations were under way, Amsterdam protested against the harsh demands made by the French King. But the city agreed to confer greater powers on William III and on 4th July 1672 passed the resolution of the States General that the prince should be proclaimed *Stadtholder* (roughly corresponding to the position of governor), captain and high Admiral of Holland.

After the Revocation of the Edict of Nantes, the city once again began to prosper. 160,000 florins were raised in Holland for the refugees, of which 80,000 were contributed by Amsterdam. The city also welcomed large numbers of printers and booksellers, metallurgists and cannon makers, apothecaries with deep knowledge of pharmacopeias and chemistry, clockmakers and other specialized mechanics, opticians – who invented binoculars, a great aid to navigation –, shopkeepers and traders with wide international experience. But the semi-permanent war between Holland and Louis XIV hindered Amsterdam's development and drew heavily on its wealth. On top of this, constant friction with England further weakened the city. As a consequence, its merchants began to invest their capital where they felt it would be safer, often in the form of loans to foreign governments; London was steadily taking over Amsterdam's financial and mercantile role; and Hamburg was poised to become the great northern European trading port. In 1781-1782, war once again broke out between Holland and England, and Amsterdam suffered further losses. From this moment on the city went into decline and its importance diminished significantly. In 1787 the Prussian army, which was sponsoring the restoration of William V, entered the city without difficulty. The Napoleonic occupation of Holland signaled the end of Amsterdam's greatness – though evidence of the Dutch Golden Age now graces the walls of art museums throughout the world.

THE `WAR OF MIRRORS´ BETWEEN FRANCE AND VENICE

The first records of glass date back to the third millennium BC in Mesopotamia; and it is known that Assyrians and Babylonians used it for making phials containing cosmetics, precious oils and medicines. The Egyptians developed glass-making and the technique was transmitted to Asia after the Persian conquest of Egypt, although the glass workshops at Aleppo and Damascus were the two leading centers of production in the Middle East. Before they created their own glass industry, the Romans imported it from Egypt. It was also part of Egypt's tribute to Caesar. Roman glass and its improved techniques spread throughout the Mediterranean and the Middle East, with production on larger scale bringing significantly lower prices. Trade in glass reached as far as China, Japan and Korea, through merchants using the Silk Road. The demand from oriental buyers was comparable to that of western clients for silk. With the fall of Rome the major glass-making centers were relocated to the region around Constantinople and in particular to the Arab world. During the 10th and 11th centuries Venice developed the art of decorative glass, initially through Jewish artisans from Byzantium, and thereafter became the main supplier of glassware to Europe and the eastern Mediterranean.

GLASS-MAKING MOVES TO MURANO FOR FEAR OF FIRE AND ESPIONAGE

In 1279 the guild of glass workers was founded in Venice, and the city authorities quickly understood that they needed to protect their monopoly. The industry and the organization of its production was strictly regulated by means of the *mariegola* (= *mater regulae*), a type of log book of the glass workers guild listing master craftsmen. The Council of State, the Senate and the Council of Ten took many legal and administrative decisions in relation to the industry. A decree issued in 1285 by the Grand Council prohibited the export of the raw materials used in glassmaking, its techniques and even broken glassware. Ironically, Venice imported sand from Dalmatia, wood for the ovens from Carinthia and workers from Turkey and Greece! In 1291 the Council took the further major protective measure of transferring all production to the small island of Murano on the grounds of fire risk. This decision had two objectives: first and foremost it was a precaution against the real and permanent risk of fire spreading from the furnaces, which sometimes caused serious damage. But the measure also served to localize the workers and techniques in one place, where it was easy for the police to keep them under surveillance. Venice made a similar decision in regard to the lace-making industry: the *merlettaie* were confined to the island of Burano and threatened with having their eyes put out if they left the island and took their skills to another country.

POLICE AND HIRED ASSASSINS GUARD THE SECRETS OF MANUFACTURE

Venice was ready to go to any lengths to protect the secrets of glass manufacture, as it represented a major source of revenue for the city, employing a large number of artisans as well as merchants involved in exporting the products. Highly placed Venetian officials were determined to maintain their monopoly at all costs. But some of the workers were tempted by the large inducements offered by other towns to set up alternative centers of production. Treviso, Padua, Vicenza, Mantua, Ravenna, Ferrara, Bologna and Florence all succeeded in attracting a few Venetian glass workers, and Florence and Altare (in Liguria) opened small production units. Venice unsheathed its claws, making it very clear to fugitive glass workers that they would be punished. Article 26 of the statutes stated: `If any worker or craftsmen goes elsewhere, he will be ordered to return. If he fails to do so, his relatives will be imprisoned. If, despite the imprisonment of his family, he continues to remain abroad, an emissary will be sent to kill him.´ The Venetian archives contain many instances of this legislation being put into practice. Some glassmakers' wives spent days or weeks locked up in the *camerotti* or lead-roofed cells of Piombi prison, emissaries were sent abroad – especially to Rome, where the Curia attracted many craftsmen to work on articles intended for the rich prelates and churches – to bring the fugitives back to Murano, and hired assassins were dispatched to kill them by means of the notorious Venetian stiletto or poison.

COLBERT ENTICES FOUR VENETIAN GLASS WORKERS

In the 16th century the Murano glass workers began making crystal – an extremely fine, colorless glass – and glass mirrors. From time immemorial people have tried to find ways of looking at their reflections. In early times they used obsidian highly polished with goat's milk; later mirrors were made from polished silver. But the reflected image was rarely perfect, and the invention of the glass mirror was the ideal solution to the myth of Narcissus! As well as for looking at oneself, mirrors were also used for decorating houses, and soon became a status symbol. With the women in European courts, courtesans, powerful men and barbers all wanting mirrors, Venice profited immeasurably. The glassmakers of Venice exploited this invention – attributed to the Gallo brothers in Murano – to the maximum. The process involved producing a very thin layer of glass behind which was applied a fine leaf of tin amalgamated with mercury (obtained from Mount Amiata in Tuscany or from Spain). The whole of Europe wanted Murano's mirrors, and France – one of the richest countries at the time, with an aristocracy that loved to show off and spend money –- was the perfect customer. In this way the `war of mirrors´ began between Colbert[1], who wished to obtain the secret production techniques at any cost, and a Venice determined to protect the secret and retain its monopoly, using any means necessary (even state sanctioned murder!).

---

1. French minister of finance from 1665 to 1683 under the rule of King Louis XIV.

In the autumn of 1664, Colbert ordered the French ambassador in Venice, Pierre Bonzi, Bishop of Béziers, to offer money to a group of Murano glass workers to entice them to Paris. Accordingly Antonio Cimegotto, Gerolamo Barbini, Giovanni Civran and Domenico Morasso left their island in secret and went to Paris, where they found Pietro Mazzolao – who called himself De La Motte –, a highly skilled craftsman who had already worked in several European countries. They set up a factory on the outskirts of Paris, directed by Nicolas Du Noyer. Production benefited from the arrival of further craftsmen from Venice, and Colbert added further incentives by paying them all substantial wages, helping their wives move to France, and offering the bachelors Barbini and Morasso young women as brides along with dowries of 25,000 écus. Louis XIV visited the factory in the Faubourg Saint Antoine, giving the craftsmen very generous gifts. In 1665 a second factory, at Tourlaville in Normandy, was granted the royal seal for making mirrors. One of the partners, a Monsieur Poquelin (a cousin of Molière), having once been one of the largest importers of mirrors from Venice, was able to use his connections to attract more Venetian craftsmen and started up the Saint-Gobain factory.

VENICE'S COUNTEROFFENSIVE

Emissaries from the *Inquisitori di Stato* – the magistrates responsible for Venice's security – put as much pressure as possible on the craftsmen who had moved abroad, but in vain. On 14th August 1666, Marc'Antonio Giustinian, the Venetian ambassador in Paris, received the order to `liquidate´ Antonio della Rivetta, who was considered to be the leader of the expatriates; his death was intended to frighten the other craftsmen into returning to Venice. Giustinian contrived to create ill-feeling between Mazzolao and della Rivetta, who was wounded in the course of a fight. A few days later another craftsman died in suspicious circumstances. On 25th February the following year Domenico Morasso also died. Colbert ordered an autopsy, which left no doubt that poison was responsible for his death. A Venetian emissary offered 4000 or 5000 ducats to any craftsman willing to return to the Murano. In 1669 the two glass workers Civran and Barbini contacted the French ambassador in Venice to make known their wish to return to France, but they received no reply. French production was by now fully operational and had all the necessary know-how. In 1672 France even took protectionist measures to ban the import of mirrors from Venice and the export of sand from Creil and Dieppe, which was used in glass-making. Then in 1682 the factory was given the very substantial order for the Hall of Mirrors in Versailles. In 1692 it perfected the technique of making large-scale mirrors; and the following year it moved to Saint-Gobain in Picardy. Venice had lost the war of mirrors with France.

BUT VENETIAN GLASS PRODUCTION DOUBLES WITHIN TWO CENTURIES!

Ironically, it turned out that this defeat for La Serenissima was not so serious after all. For some considerable time, Murano had been making small, multicolored glass beads, known as *perline*, that could be threaded together to make necklaces. These were in high demand from slave-traders, who exchanged them on the African coast for cargoes of slaves, and from women throughout Europe and the Middle East who, though unable to afford gold and silver jewelry, found these sparkling bracelets and necklaces made a very good substitute. Venice also specialized in making small personal mirrors, that required a large, highly skilled workforce. And Venetian entrepreneurs even started producing glass wine bottles, using technology that had been `copied´ from England. But the use of wood in the furnaces due to the absence of coal handicapped this type of manufacture, which requires very high temperatures. In any case, glass production in Venice in the 18th century was twice as great as during the two previous centuries. The guild system had been abandoned and product innovation was now the long-term strategic aim.

FRANCE STEALS THE SECRETS OF LACE-MAKING FROM FLEMISH TOWNS AND VENICE

Legend has it that Dolfina – young, beautiful, blonde, but poor –, who lived on the Venetian island of Burano, and Polo, a young fisherman, wanted to get married. Polo had just enough for himself to live on, but not enough for two; nonetheless, he wanted to give his beloved a present to show his love for her. He found work on a boat that took him far from Venice in an attempt to earn enough money to get married. One day, Polo found some seaweed in his net that had been calcified by the salt water – `Mermaid's Lace´ (*Halimeda opuntia* or *Cactus algae*). When he got home he gave it to Dolfina, who did not know how to keep it from spoiling. So she decided to copy the design with thread and was so skilled with her hands that she made a masterpiece – thus *merletto* or lace-making began! The Venetian island became one of the main centers of production in Europe. In fact, evidence of this weaving technique has been found in Egyptian and Etruscan tombs. The Romans referred to it as *laqueus*, from which the words *lacis* and *lacet* in French, lace in English, *laccio* in Italian and *lazo* in Spanish all derive. Nobody knows quite where it started. In any case, it was rediscovered by the crusaders and trade developed with the Middle East. It is even said that there was a Chinese method for making lace from silk.

VENICE AND FLANDERS

Many towns in Flanders and Brabant (Bruges, Ghent, Antwerp, Brussels and Malines) specialized in producing lace with bobbins.

Venice and other Italian towns (Milan, Genoa, Offida, Cantú and L'Aquila) specialized in particular in lace making with needles, though there is evidence that the Flemish method was directly imported from Venice. At the time fashion travelled fast, though in an unusual way: merchants used dolls dressed in the latest fashions to display their wares. Students going from one center of learning to another, as well as clerics, monks and nuns moving between monasteries and convents also helped spread changing fashion.

In 1300 Joan of Navarre visited Bruges and on her return she told her husband, Philip IV of France, that she was particularly impressed by the quality of the clothes worn by the women she saw, even in the street. Indeed they were better dressed than she was herself. As a result, taxes on the inhabitants of Bruges were increased; and in response they rose up and killed the French soldiers stationed in the town. The king sent more troops, under the command of Robert d'Artois, to punish the Flemish; but they met with defeat at the battle of the Golden Spurs in 1302, a date that subsequently became a national holiday in Flanders.

Kings and princes used great quantities of lace – a symbol of wealth and refined taste – in their ceremonial robes. Listed among the possessions belonging to Anne of France, there is mention of a lace ruff ordered specially from Venice for the King's coronation ceremony of 1480: this cost 250 pieces of gold and was two and a half years in the making. When Richard III of England was crowned he wore lace and ribbons made in Venice. In 1516, Henry VIII gave permission to two Florentine merchants to import lace into England on condition that they sold it to the court. When she died in 1603, Queen Elizabeth I left a wardrobe of 3000 gowns, many of which were decorated with Flemish and Venetian lace. In the accounts of King William III of England there are many entries for buying lace; one of the bills mentioned is for payment of £158 for buying six lace cravats. Charles II spent 20 pounds 12 shillings on a single cravat to wear for his brother's birthday; James II ordered the cravat for his coronation from Venice, which cost 36 pounds 12 shillings. The French King Henry II wore a large lace ruff to hide a scar, and in 1545 the sister of François I, Marguerite of Angoulême, wrote of *dantale de Florence*, Florentine lace, that she used as a kerchief for her neck. Louis XIV is reputed to have worn a lace ruff at his coronation, made from white human hair. Certainly Louis XVI wore a cravat at his coronation made from *point tresse* (human hair). In France the liking for lace was made all the greater by the arrival of Catherine De Medici, who started the fashion for wearing it at court.

VENETIAN LACE, COURTESANS AND PUNISHMENT FOR DEFECTING LACEMAKERS

Ironically, the lace industry in Venice developed as a result of a decision by the *Provveditori alle Pompe*, the magistrates whose job was to rein in the conspicuous excesses of the nobles and rich merchants. These classes used fashion, jewels and gondolas (which had to be painted black) to show off their wealth. During the 15th century, the magistrates forbade dressing ostentatiously with the display of jewelry. So lace became fashionable for ornamenting clothes, women's especially, which had padded sleeves and lace to set off low-cut bodices, shoulders and hair. Lace was also much used to decorate women's underwear, especially as worn by rich courtesans, such as the renowned Veronica Franco. Venice tried to concentrate the production of lace on the island of Burano, much as it had done for glass production on the island of Murano. This was motivated entirely by economic reasons. The lace industry was one of the city's most profitable exports and brought in substantial revenue which had to be protected at all costs. Legislation for the lace industry was very clear: any *merlettaia* who emigrated would be punished by having her entire family imprisoned; furthermore, if she failed to return to Venice, the hired assassins equipped with stiletto blades who worked for the secret police would find the girls and put out their eyes or even kill them.

Glass workers made their contribution to the lace-making industry. They blew rounded bowls (rather like those used for goldfish), which the lace workers filled with water and used as magnifying lenses to help them with their work. Venice also published more books on lace-making techniques and designs than any other city. Probably the first (undated) work on embroidery was written by Alex Paganino; this was followed in 1528 by a book by the Venetian Giovanni Antonio Tagliente on *punto in aria* (literally *stitch in the air*, an early form of needle lace). Then came

Matia Pagan's *Giardinetto novo di punti tagliati et gropposi per eser-
citio et ornamento delle donne* (The new small garden of lace stitches
and cutwork for practice and embellishment of ladies), published
in 1542. Another anonymous book, titled *Le Pompe* (*Pomp*) was
published in Venice in 1557, and Federico Vincioli dedicated the
book he published, in Paris in 1587, to Catherine De Medici. This
work on women's underwear – *Les singuliers et nouveaux pourtraicts
du seigneur Fédéric de Vinciolo venitien, pour tout sortes d'ouvrages de
lingerie* (*Remarkable new images of all kinds of lingerie*) – was so
popular in Europe that it ran to fourteen editions, the last being
published in 1658. There were at least 22 works on lace produced
in the 16th and 17th centuries, two of them written by women:
Isabella Catania Parasole (1600) and Lucrezia Romana (1620).
Even Titian's nephew, Cesare Vecellio, created designs for lace,
and one of these works is still preserved in the archives of the
Ducal Palace in Venice, dated 1591 and dedicated to the illustri-
ous lady Viena Vendramin.

THE GREAT LACE MARKETS AND A STATUS SYMBOL
FOR THE NEWLY WEALTHY

European lace production was boosted by the improvement in
living standards and high demand from the newly wealthy. These
nouveaux riches included many people eager to attract the favors
of kings and princes as well as the merchant middle classes wanting to display their wealth and business success. There was also the
wealthy clergy of the Roman Curia and the Counter-Reformation,
who not only liked highly decorated churches but appreciated
sumptuous vestments for bishops and cardinals.

Many artists painted women and men in elaborate clothing,
showing finely made, and very expensive, embroidery and lace (as,
for example, the lady's head-dress in Van Eyck's painting of the
Arnolfinis). Clothing was an even more ostentatious way of dis-
playing one's wealth than wearing jewels and gold. Many paintings from the Spanish *siglo de oro*, the Italian Baroque Counter-
Reformation and from the Flemish golden age, show lace and ruffs
in abundance on wealthy men, women and children of the upper
classes, children of royal families, senior officers, political leaders

from the larger towns, academics from great universities, canons, diocesan prelates and high-ranking bishops.

Purchasers could find lace in the cities where it was produced, as well as in markets specializing in luxury and costly fabrics, as could be found in Lyon, Beaucaire, Marseille, Leipzig, Frankfurt, Milan and Bolzano. The extent of these markets and the value of the merchandise may be judged from a contract dated 1476, drawn up in Milan, which lists in detail the merchandise that the supplier will deliver, namely a band worked with bobbins (*striscia lavorata con i fusi*) to decorate linen for a rich young woman's trousseau. As a result, the producing regions enjoyed a period of great wealth and prosperity. Many women worked as lace-makers at home, organizing their time according to their household and maternal tasks. Very often the same merchant-businessman would provide the materials, place an order and collect the finished product. However, the women who made the lace – including nuns and young novices in the convents, working for little more than their daily bread and the glory of God – often suffered from occupational illnesses such as the progressive loss of eyesight and gastric problems caused by the position in which they spent long hours bent over their work.

THE SPANISH WARS IN FLANDERS AND THE CRAVAT AT THE BATTLE OF STEENKERQUE

Venice and the other Italian cities were able to take advantage of the situation in Flanders with the war against the Spanish Empire, since this created problems for both work in the region and the export of lace (amongst other commodities). Burano's moment of glory came in the 16th and 17th centuries, thanks to the general demand for lace and its protection by the wives of the Doges (*Dogaresse*) Giovanna Duodo and Morosina Morosini. In 1664, the French ambassador to Venice wrote that the export of lace from the city was worth 400,000 ducats each year, and that the labors of the thousands of lacemakers provided a living for many families and convents. In the meantime `lace wars´ were being waged. Before engaging in bloody combat, the lace-wearing officers of opposed armies would exchange affable remarks and courtesies. They would then take their places at the head of their regiments and throw themselves into battle against their enemies, to the sound of fifes and drums. During the Thirty Years War, so taken were the French officers by the Croatian officers' cravats – this is the origin of the word – that they too began wearing a knotted lace scarf. Their men followed their example, except that in their case it was a leather strip, not lace, which served to protect their necks from the saber blows of the enemy cavalry. During the battle of Steenkerque (3rd August 1692), the French officers in their encampments were hurriedly mobilized. They did not have the time to dress themselves according to etiquette; so instead of knotting the lace, they simply crossed the ends over and tucked one end into their jacket buttonhole. The battle was won by the Marshal of Luxembourg against the Prince of Orange, and the `Steenkerque´ – the tie tucked into the sixth buttonhole – became a highly fashionable mode of dress for French men and women, soon imitated by the English and other courts that followed French fashions.

LACE SMUGGLERS USE DOGS, AND COLBERT LAUNCHES YET ANOTHER ECONOMIC WAR

France wanted to take measures against the lace imports from Flanders and Italy. Accordingly the parliament passed laws banning imports, in order to protect local production mainly intended for the royal court, despite being of inferior quality to that produced abroad. As a result, lace smuggling developed, with dogs used to carry the contraband across the border. Between 1620 and 1635 no fewer than 40,278 dogs were killed by customs officers and private citizens as they crossed the border; a reward of three francs per dog encouraged hunting them down. However, Colbert, Louis XIV's Finance Minister, understood that it was difficult to stand in the way of fashion. For example in 1635 in England, Charles I also banned the import of foreign lace, but Cromwell and other aristocrats defied the King's decree. In 1662 an English newspaper wrote that the English demand for foreign lace accounted for an outgoing of more than £2 million a year. Colbert realized that the French balance of trade was being very adversely affected by the high level of imports, among them lace, glass, mirrors and tapestries. He applied the same solution to the problem that he had already used for the glass industry, and he stated in particular that, `La mode devrait être pour la France l'équivalent des mines du Pérou pour l'Espagne´ (`Fashion should be to France what the mines of Peru were to Spain´). So he tried by every means available to hire lace workers from Venice and Flanders. In 1665, with the help of the French ambassadors to Venice and Flanders and secret agents, he managed to convince some young women – with an eye to long-term production – and a handful of older women – with experience that could be passed on – to move to France and work in a specialized lace workshop. About 30 women came from Burano, in many instances disguised as nuns, as well as another 22 – a figure that later rose to 200 – from Ypres, Malines and Brussels. The Venetian senate was quick to respond, threatening any women who betrayed their country with the most severe punishment. In 1671 the Venetian ambassador in Paris wrote `Vaillement le Ministre Colbert porte les lavori d'aria à la perfection´ (`Minister Colbert is valiantly trying to bring lace production to perfection´); but six years later, his successor Domenico Contarini wrote that `the French are now perfectly well able to make their own *punto in aria*´ (literally, `stitch in the air´).

FRANCE PRODUCES LACE, BUT OF INFERIOR QUALITY

Saint-Denis, Villiers-le-Bel, Caen and Aurillac were already lace-making centers, though the quality was not nearly as high as that of Venice and the Flemish towns. Ursuline nuns settled in Caen in 1624 and began producing lace with bobbins. It was known as Nanking lace, because they used Chinese silk. At Aurillac – formerly occupied by the Romans and named after the gold found in the region – lace was made from gold or silver thread. Lace using precious metal threads was also made in Lyon, Paris and Cluny; in Italy it came from Milan, Venice, Lucca, Genoa and Sicily; in Germany, Nuremberg was the main center, since the town already specialized in metal work, making high quality and ornamental armor; in Spain, it came from Barcelona, Talavera, Valencia and Seville (the term `Spanish stitch´ referred to lace made with precious metal thread and silk). In England a major scandal occurred in regard to gold thread lace. The monopoly for its production was granted to George Villiers, Duke of Buckingham; but the gold thread was mixed with copper, which had a corrosive effect on the hands of the workers and on the skin of people wearing it. Anyone daring to protest was imprisoned, but finally the House of Commons intervened and the monopoly was abolished. In Holland they managed to produce 'silver' thread which was actually copper coated in silver (using the wiredrawing technique) – though it was still sold at the same price as silver!

COLBERT WANTS A FRENCH LACE INDUSTRY

On 5th August 1665, Colbert decreed that lace factories should be set up in the towns of Quesnoy, Arras, Reims, Sedan, Château-Thierry, Loudun, Alençon and Aurillac. The first two factories to be properly established were in the Château Royal de Madrid in the Bois de Boulogne, near Paris, and at Alençon. There were several hundred women already making a living from lace in this town. Colbert appointed an agent for the new company – Jacques Prevost, a local man. Unfortunately, because of his wife, he had already had problems with the local lace makers, who were angry about the arrival of Venetian and Flemish women who were threatening their livelihood. Colbert replaced the manager with a woman with great experience of lace, one Madame La Perrière (Marthe Barbot). Around 1650, this lady of good family and the widow of a surgeon, imitated and perfected the Venetian stitch; and around 1660, she invented the 'Alençon stitch'. Colbert's plans clearly much helped the work of this lace-maker with a gift for management. The legislation he introduced granted ten years' monopoly, prohibited individual enterprises and obliged lace workers to work for the factory. Madame La Perrière organized the work along almost Taylorist lines, with each lace-maker specializing in a specific part of the work. Not only did she perfect her own technique, but she continued to make lace secretly in her own workshops. She did not become rich, however. Having handed over the management of the factory to her son, she died in 1677 at the age of 72. Although in 1675 the monopoly was not renewed, more than 8000 people continued working in this trade in the town and the surrounding villages. Further workshops and factories were set up elsewhere in France, and the country even began to export lace – some from Alençon was even imported by Venice.

In France almost all centers of production were set up in areas far from the borders in order to avoid a repetition of Colbert's maneuver in the opposite direction. But when Louis XIV issued the Revocation of the Edict of Nantes in 1685, many Huguenot lace workers left France for Flanders, Protestant Germany and Switzerland, taking their skills with them. This emigration put the French industry in crisis; but the most serious aspect was the loss of know-how and experience, which went to the competition with no compensation for Paris. Prussia benefited to such an extent from the Revocation, since many skilled workers fled there from France, that Frederick William of Prussia quipped that if France wanted to give him a present then it should revoke the Edict again!

Naturally the French RevolutionS with its uncompromising new ideology swept aside all lace-making, but Napoleon resuscitated it with his requirement for lace in his robes of state. But in 1768, in Hammond near Nottingham, lace began to be made by machines. Thenceforth lace-making by machine had serious consequences for lace-makers working in traditional factories or, for greater flexibility in raising families, at home. In the late 19th century handmade lace began to be again produced in Venice and in a few Flemish and French towns; the aim was both economic and social, in that it provided work for many women who had to stay at home. These days handmade lace comes to us from Asia and other regions with cheap labor, nearly all European production has ceased, and Japanese collectors have become the main purchasers of old European lace.

EAST INDIA COMPANIES: EUROPEAN GROWTH AND THE START OF GLOBALIZATION

The British East India Company was founded in 1600. In 1602 came the Dutch East India Company, followed in 1664 by the French Company. Other smaller companies included the Danish, Swedish and Prussian Companies, as well as the Antwerp, Trieste and Livorno Companies, which played a largely marginal role in trade with the East Indies. All of these enterprises resulted from the reactions of different states and trading cities to the near-monopoly of the Portuguese in oriental trade (especially spices), after the route around the Cape of Good Hope was opened up by Vasco Da Gama in 1498. In contrast to Venice's furious reaction, the English aimed to outflank Portugal by setting up the English Levant Company in 1581 and opening up an overland route across Russia and the Caspian region – they even managed to obtain a concession from the Ottoman government. But the real solution to finding a route to the Indian Ocean and the spice trade was to travel by sea. The first English ship arrived in the East Indies in 1591, followed in 1595 by four Dutch ships sent by the Far Lands Company, set up in 1594 by nine Amsterdam merchants. The trading philosophy of the English and the Dutch was totally different from that of the Portuguese: for London and Amsterdam, `the worst type of peace is much better than the best type of war´. There were therefore few military engagements, no demonstrations of force, and above all trade and exchange.

A MAJOR TRADING REVOLUTION

These two companies were based on a new type of organization and financing. Firstly, there was a clear separation between those putting up the capital and the commercial organization of the company, which was managed by salaried administrators. Indeed this is one of the fundamental characteristics of the functioning of capitalism. Moreover, expeditions were not organized directly by the government, in contrast to Spain and Portugal where all such expeditions were the result of a political or strategic decision made by the king or emperor. The companies' strategies were essentially motivated by profit. In practice, these companies had an only marginal effect on the geopolitical power of the regions in which they operated – at least to start with. There is only one instance to the contrary, in the Spice Isles (the Banda and Molucca archipelagos) in southeast Asia, where the Dutch East India Company exercised much more power than was justified by commercial needs and which became increasingly political in nature. On the other hand, the English and Dutch companies initiated and perfected the interdependence of trade between the west (the Red Sea and the Persian Gulf), the center (the Indian Ocean) and the east (the Philippines and Indonesia). For example, the purchase of cotton on the coast of Coromandel served to pay for spices bought in the Indian Ocean – an important and revolutionary development for trade in this region. Very often the VOC (Verenigde Oostindische Compagnie – Dutch East India Company) would export silver to China, where it then bought silk that was sold in Japan for gold or copper which in turn was exported to India, where it paid for the textiles that were so popular in Moluka, Indonesia.

Planning these voyages was mostly carried out in London and Amsterdam, enabling each of them to be extended into a series of linked, planned stages. Whereas Arab, Indian and even Chinese trade continued to be organized on the basis of one voyage at a time, the centralization employed by the Dutch and English allowed for more efficient use of capital and for a more global vision of risks and their management.

A STRATEGIC MISTAKE: THE MANHATTAN TRANSFER

The VOC was a Dutch chartered trading company, founded by a small number of merchant family companies, eight in all, to which the state granted a trade monopoly with the East Indies – the region Christopher Columbus had been aiming for, and which de Gama and Magellan finally succeeded in reaching. These Dutch merchants were hoping to find gold and spices, and they were able to take advantage of Portugal's weakness, even though the Portuguese had arrived there a century earlier. In addition, Portugal refused to let Dutch boats enter the port of Lisbon.

The initial capital of the company was six and a half million florins, divided into small shareholdings. The management was put in the hands of 'seventeen gentlemen' (*Heeren XVII*), the directors chosen from amongst sixty members of the assembly representing the shareholders. The VOC moved in and formed special relationships with sultans and other rulers in the great Indonesian archipelago. In 1619 the town of Batavia was built on the island of Java, with canals reminiscent of Amsterdam. It was a special kind of colonial conquest in that the primary aim was not to occupy territory. The VOC created entrepots and markets and defended them against the interests of other colonial empires, initially Spain and Portugal, later the rising powers England and France. Twelve senior officials of the VOC were the only foreign traders to be accepted by Japan, though they were compelled to live on the small island of Deshima, in the port of Nagasaki, where VOC ships could load and unload their merchandise.

The VOC did not hesitate to use force and armed men; they imposed restrictions on producers in the Asian region, directly controlled production and cruelly repressed any signs of native rebellion; some VOC ships behaved like pirates against Portuguese ships, attacking them without compunction. By the end of the 17th century the VOC had 12,000 employees and its profits amounted to about 30% of its capital. But the VOC made a strategic mistake: in the struggle with the English to keep control of the island of Run in Indonesia – a major production center for nutmeg –, it pushed the Dutch government into ceding the peninsula of Manhattan (bought from the Lenape Indians in 1626 for 24 dollars) and the town of New Amsterdam (now New York, in honor of the Duke of York) through the treaty of Breda (1667). But the price of nutmeg fell, while the economic role of America soared. The VOC originated a commercial empire on a vast scale, especially in comparison with the relatively small size of the Republic of the United Provinces. The company contributed substantially to the Dutch Renaissance after the long war against the Spanish. In the 17th and 18th centuries Amsterdam became the world economic center, enjoying a period of economic and cultural expansion generally known as the Dutch Golden Age. But the VOC did not survive the events of the French Revolution and the rise of the Napoleonic Empire. The company was nationalized and lost strategic outposts such as the Cape and Molucca to the English in 1795. The Dutch East Indies became a crown colony, the old company was forgotten – though its silver coins may still be found in Jakarta flea market – and its merchants and traders were replaced by planters and settlers.

THE EAST INDIA COMPANY BRINGS TEA TO EUROPE

Created in London before the end of the 16th century as a company of London merchants, the East India Company obtained its first charter of incorporation from Queen Elizabeth I on 31st December 1600, though its final designation only came in 1711. Its charter gave it a monopoly, initially for fifteen years, over English trade in a region stretching from the Cape of Good Hope to the Magellan Straits, in practice the whole of the Indian and Pacific Oceans. The initial capital of £72,000 was divided into 125 shares; from 1612 onwards, these were transferable. The assembly of shareholders elected a governor, a vice governor and a board of 24 directors. In 1657 Cromwell increased the share capital to £740,000. In 1612 the company established its first trading center at Surat in India, and in 1616 it obtained the authorization from the Grand Mogul to set up trading posts under the same conditions applying to those of the Mogul Empire. This was the period of building fortified trading posts – Fort Saint George (Madras) in 1639, Bombay in 1668, Fort William (Calcutta) in 1696. In China the company chose Canton as the hub for its activities.

The EIC (East India Company) had a different strategy from that of the VOC: it preferred to rent ships rather than buy them and, although its wealth was based on spices, to trade in tea and industrial products such as cotton and other fabrics. But the company's role changed under King Charles II, when he decided to use it as a tool for developing British political and military power in the Indian Ocean. The English victory in the Seven Years War put paid to all competition from the French, whilst the victories of Plessey (1757) and Buxar (1774) by EIC troops against the Nabob of Bengal brought the region under the political and military control of London. Britain decided to extend its possessions in India by using the Company as a civilian branch of the state, and up until 1858 the EIC did indeed act as a real government in the occupied regions. It was only after the mutiny of the Indian troops in 1858 that London took control of India and, after the Sepoy Rebellion, Queen Victoria was named Empress of India.

COLBERT DECIDES ON A FRENCH EAST INDIA COMPANY

The brainchild of Colbert, the *Compagnie Française pour les Indes Orientales* (French East Indies Company) was founded on 27 August 1664. Treated similarly to a royal factory, the company paid no taxes and had a total monopoly over trade in the eastern hemisphere, with a capital of 8.8 million pounds . Its motto was `florebo quocunque ferar´ (I will flourish wherever I am taken). It was clearly Louis XIV's response to the great English and Dutch East India Companies. The license specified the company's aims, variously commercial, political and cultural. Although it did not succeed in founding a colony in Madagascar, it managed to create trading posts on the islands of La Réunion and Mauritius (Ile Maurice). In 1719 it established itself in India. But by then it was on the verge of bankruptcy, and John Law decided to merge it with other French trading companies (*Compagnie de l'Occident, Compagnie du Sénégal, Compagnie de Chine, Compagnie de Barbarie* and *Compagnie de la Mer du Sud*) to create the *Compagnie Perpétuelle des Indes*. But the original company found new vigor and restored independence with substantial help from Indian political figures trying to prevail against the British East India Company.

One of its directors, Joseph François Dupleix, was even nominated a nabob by the Mogul Emperor in 1750. With the treaty of Paris, France lost its colonial empire and retained only five trading posts in India: Pondichery, Karikal, Yanaon, Mahe and Chandernagor. The Company was entering a period of slow decline and in 1769 it lost the monopoly, subsequently shared out among several private ship-owners. In 1785 Louis XVI created a new Indian Company, on the advice of his minister, Calonne. At this point then there were two Indian companies: the *Compagnie Perpétuelle*, still in the process of being wound up (completed in 1794) and the new one. But this company lost its privileges in 1790 and the *Convention* (the post-Revolutionary government) pronounced its dissolution in 1794 – although it was not finally wound up until 1875.

THE ORIGINS OF WESTERN INDUSTRIAL CAPITALISM

West Indian Companies were of course also created. Among the most important were the British, Dutch, French (set up by Colbert in 1664) and the Danish. The products traded here were totally different: furs from North America, sugar from South America and the Caribbean, cocoa and cereals from Central America and gold, ivory, cotton and slaves from Africa. The VIC (the Dutch company) was very active in piracy, particularly against Spanish galleons with cargoes of precious metals. These companies started producing large amounts of food products, and were also very active in the slave trade.

In any case, the various India companies (both east and west) were of great importance in that they prepared the way for the rise of western industrial capitalism, which was very different from the merchant and banking capitalism of the Italian trading cities (Venice, Florence and Genoa), the Champagne Fairs, the towns of Hanseatic Germany and the Low Countries (Antwerp and Amsterdam) and latterly London. For it was the profits from these companies that allowed the new wealthy dynastic families to finance the businesses of the industrial revolution. In their plantations the principles of Taylorism were put into practice long before they had been defined as such, for managing slave-based production in the factories. The western commercial model won out over the equivalent Chinese and Arab models, which were more adventurous but less organized. Europe's great expansion and development occurred at the turn of the 17th and 18th centuries, easily surpassing the Ottoman Empire and the Empire of the Middle Kingdom.

LOTTERIES FINANCE WARS, THE GREAT WALL OF CHINA AND LEADING AMERICAN UNIVERSITIES

`A qui le tour?´ (`Whose turn next?´) and `Tous les gagnants ont tenté leur chance´ (`Every winner has chanced their luck´): the celebrated slogans of the French lottery `Loto´ have nourished a million dreams of fortune. Games of chance go a long way back in human history. The Bible tells how Moses used a method not unlike a lottery to share out the lands on the banks of the Jordan to the faithful (*Book of Numbers*, Chapter 26). At the time of Julius Caesar, lotteries were organized every December to honor the god Saturn, and a winning number was drawn from amongst the tablets bought by participants. Keno was invented by General Cheng Lung of the Chinese Han dynasty as a way of avoiding further tax increases; and revenues from it were used to help finance the construction of the Great Wall. The result of the draws (among first 120 Chinese ideograms, later reduced to 90) in the large cities was sent by pigeon post to the countryside and small villages – hence the name White Pigeon Game. Chinese immigrants exported it to the United States when they crossed the Pacific to help build the American railroads. Mohammed forbade Muslims to play games of chance – an indication that they existed in the Arab world as well.

One of the first records of a lottery in northern Europe dates from 1446, when the widow of the great Flemish painter Jan van Eyck put some of her husband's canvasses up for sale by lot. At the beginning of the sixteenth century, at Amerfort near Utrecht in Holland, property owners used a lottery to sell real estate assets, which were not easily divisible. Tickets were offered at low prices to take enough money to cover the value of the property being sold – and whoever drew the winning ticket acquired the property.

Known as 'Dutch auction or lottery', this system was soon copied by Venice. The *Consiglio dei Pregadi* – a body which would be replaced by the Senate in Venice – sold properties (mainly shops) in the Rialto neighborhood. This process became known as 'the Rialto bridge lotto'.

THE ORIGIN OF THE WORD 'LOTTO'

Lotto (*loto* in French) may come from the French word *lot* ('prize' or 'share'), derived from an old Frankish term originally meaning either 'inheritance' or 'luck'. Other philologists talk of the Teutonic word *Hleut* signifying a sacred object, disk or stone thrown in mystical rites and used to resolve quarrels about the division of property. In Dutch the word *loten* means 'drawn out of the hat'. On the other hand certain Italian writers suggest the number eight, '*l'otto*', when anyone drawing that number would win the prize. In English the archaic verb 'to lot' is similar to the verb 'allot' or 'to portion out in lots'. Overall, the Teutonic origin would seem to be the most probable.

GENOAN LOTTO AND THE FIRST BOOKMAKERS

As early as 1448, the game of 'Purse of Fortune' was played in Milan, involving seven purses containing 300, 100, 75, 50, 30, 25 and 20 ducats. The players bought the right to place a piece of paper with their name written on it in a basket (they were free to buy as many as they wished). Pieces of paper representing the seven purses were placed in a second basket. Drawing lots from the two baskets then decided the winners of the various purses. In 1465 a number of Flemish towns raised capital through lotteries, using it to build chapels, warehouses, canals and ports. In 1539 François I, who spent time in Italy during the wars against Charles V, introduced a similar system in France, known as *Blanque*, with the aim of raising money to cover the state budget deficit.

But the real game of lotto was invented in Genoa. From 1515, the citizens placed bets on the names of the people standing for election to public office. In 1576 Admiral Gian Andrea Doria laid down a new constitution for the Genoan Republic. 120 members were chosen (later it was 90 – and the current Italian lotto is based on drawing five numbers out of 90) from the wealthiest of the city's aristocratic families. From these, five names were drawn from a hat to replace three members of the Senate and two members of the Council of Prosecutors. The process was repeated every two years. The baskets in which names of the candidates were placed were called the *seminario* and a bet placed on the winners' names was called `the game of *seminario*´. Although placing bets in this way was illegal – the authorities thought it disrespectful – rich merchants and speculators were happy to play the role of bank and pocket the profits.

In 1588, Genoa even passed a law banning betting on the lives of the Pope, the Emperor, kings and cardinals, the outcome of a battle or war, marriages, the election of magistrates and even the plague! But the passion for gaming attracted many professional players to Genoa and money was passed rapidly from pocket to pocket. A new variant was introduced: it was called the *lotto della zitella*, `the lottery of the girl to be married´. The numbers represented poor girls; if they were lucky enough to see their number drawn from the basket then they would receive money for their trousseau. The game of lotto was finally legalized in 1644. The city then introduced a tax on the profits, placing the organization and management of the game in the hands of private interests, who naturally had to pay a substantial sum of money to the city treasury.

CASANOVA AND THE LOTTERY

Many towns in Italy and in other European countries organized similar games along the lines of game of *seminario* in Genoa. By legalizing such practices, large amounts of money could be raised from the players and the organizers of the game, a role later assigned to public auctioneers. Italian adventurers were largely responsible for suggesting these games to various European courts and financial authorities – Casanova exported the game to France. On the other hand Rome considered gambling to be immoral, and in 1728 Pope Benedict XIII banned it, threatening any practitioners with excommunication. Three years later, the new Pope Clement XII restored it on condition that the profits went to the aid of poor young girls. Then in 1785, Pope Pius VI decided to make over the profits to `pious´ causes, i.e. the finances of the Roman clergy and papal court. Lotto also enabled the drainage work on the marshy lands (*paludi pontine*) around Rome to be financed.

The politicians who founded the United States of America also followed these practices in the early days, in order to raise money. Benjamin Franklin financed the purchase of cannons for the American Revolution through the lottery, and John Hancock paid for the reopening of Faneuil Hall in Boston in the same way. Money for the construction of Mountain Road, which opened up the West from Virginia, was raised by George Washington through lottery. Even Thomas Jefferson, who was $80,000 in debt toward the end of his life, was able to pay it off by raising money by lottery with his property as prizes.

In England a lottery provided financing for the British Museum (1753). Across the Channel, in 1757 Louis XV created the Royal Lottery to finance the Military Academy, later know as Saint-Cyr. And in the United States, between 1790 and the Civil War, lotteries financed the construction of 300 schools, 200 churches and 50 universities – Harvard, Yale, Princeton and Columbia among them.

LOTTO AND THE ECONOMIC SITUATION

Wherever lotto and various kinds of lottery have been introduced, they have nearly always been a success. The theory of probabilities has been used to create other types of lottery, in which the state or the organizers (who paid a tax to obtain authorization) earn substantial sums of money through one or other of two systems. Either the prizes paid to the winners are lower than their chances of winning according to probability, or the value of the prizes paid out is reduced from the start, so that public finances may `help themselves en route´. Furthermore it is apparent everywhere that the sums involved are often correlated with the economic state of the country, since lotto remains a formula for getting rich or merely for `getting some money to live a little better, by risking a small amount´ ...many poor can make a few rich!

HOW STATES BECAME CROUPIERS

In England, for example, 28% of the money paid in by those playing the National Lottery is used to finance charitable and cultural good causes. A painting by Raphael in the National Gallery, which was about to be bought by an American museum, remained in England thanks to the intervention of the National Lottery, which financed its purchase with a check for £16 million. British cinema also benefits from the lottery, to the tune of £30 million a year. London was chosen by the Olympic Games Committee to stage the games in 2012; the British lottery has already committed to spending a billion pounds on financing the necessary infrastructure for this massive sporting, media and political event.

A lottery on a European scale has been launched. The French, British and Spanish organizations holding the respective monopolies have started a three-nation game which should attract around 160 million players, with winnings worth 40 million euros. The prize is a rolling one, in which if there is no winner that week's prize are added to the following week's prize. Called Euro Millions or the European Lottery, it has been at least ten years in the preparation. It should have been started at that same time as the single currency but came a little later. If the game is successful in the three start-up countries then it will rapidly be promoted elsewhere, to increase the amount of money paid and the number of winners.

HOW REMBRANDT HELPED LAUNCH THE ART MARKET IN AMSTERDAM

Rembrandt was an innovator not only in painting but in terms of commerce as well. Indeed he actively participated in setting up the free art market in Amsterdam and worked hard to substantially reduce the role of patronage. The same idea would be taken up by composers and musicians and in other arts.

MERCHANT WEALTH HELPS CREATE A TRUE ART MARKET

Rembrandt's artistic training coincided with a moment in history when ideas were in ferment and money was flowing freely, thanks to the Dutch golden era, helped by the end of the war against the Spanish occupation and the independence and unification of the Low Countries. Painting was inspired by Italian art and the Antwerp School, dominated by Rubens. But the Flemish style was developing a taste for smaller, finely wrought canvasses destined for the houses of the wealthy merchants and powerful politicians, rather than for churches and the chateaux of the aristocracy. The Calvinist religion and the presence of a large Jewish community fuelled artistic reflection on Biblical themes. In 1627 Rembrandt completed his apprenticeship in Amsterdam and returned to his native town of Leyden, where he opened a studio with another young painter, Jean Lievens. The following year he personally sold his first painting in Amsterdam; tradition has it that he carried it on foot to the big city and that he concluded the transaction himself like a businessman.

The two associates met Constantijn Huygens, secretary to Prince Frederick Hendrick of Orange, a well-known diplomat, poet and artist and very much someone who was able to appreciate art. Following this meeting he became the agent for the two painters, offering their pictures to international collectors. The high quality of the two painters' work enabled Huygens to sell their pictures throughout Europe. In 1630, Rembrandt came into contact with the art seller Hendrick van Uylemburch, who offered to become his dealer; in exchange Rembrandt would get a studio in Amsterdam and a percentage of the prices of the works sold.

REMBRANDT IS STRONGLY OPPOSED TO PATRONAGE AND ADVOCATES A FREE ART MARKET

In 1632, Rembrandt left Leyden and went to live in Amsterdam. There he helped create a genuine art market, for which the artists produced works without receiving a prior order on the part of their patrons who automatically became their owners. Rembrandt managed to convince other artists that freedom of creation was well worth the risk of a work remaining unsold.

Before this, artists were not free to create as they wished, but dependent on rich and powerful patrons. Rembrandt also made sure that he got the highest possible prices for his works in a competitive market that offered him far more artistic autonomy than when dependent on a small number of patrons. Clearly, it was easier to achieve this revolution in a wealthy city such as Amsterdam with its permanent and transient population of merchants, bankers, businessmen, lawyers, diplomats and foreigners. Furthermore, Amsterdam was in the process of becoming the hub of European business, with ever closer ties to America and the East Indies. Rembrant's success allowed him to rent large premises, where his pupils could work and have at their disposal a large collection of theatrical costumes to help them when painting historical subjects. However, his wife's death and various love affairs with complex legal consequences brought ruin to the artist. In 1656, he sold his personal collection, which included some of his own pictures, together with Italian works of art he had bought during his period of success, followed by his house. He died in poverty in 1669.

HIS CONCEPT OF A FREE MARKET BENEFITS THE WORK OF MUSICIANS SUCH AS MOZART

The concept of a market in art spread to the world of music. A little under 100 years later, Telemann, Bach and Handel expressed their strong dissatisfaction with having to work `to order´ for their patrons. Handel is perhaps the most striking instance. In the course of his life, he became bankrupt no less than five times and occasionally had to write operas for his theatre, which he managed in London, in just a few short weeks. Mozart was probably the first musician who was truly free to compose on his own account. He wrote works which he sold to music publishers; he gave lessons and was paid for public performances. He earned his living as a true orchestra director. Howard Gardner, the cognitive psychologist, has written that Mozart laid down the basis of independence and voluntary creation. But Mozart too ended his life in poverty – art and business do not always make the best bedfellows.

JAPANESE PORCELAIN PRODUCTION IS BOOSTED BY THE MING CRISIS AND EUROPEAN DEMAND

The early decades of the 17th century were an exceptional period in the production of porcelain[1] in Asia. Kaolin (from the Chinese town of Kao-Ling) or China clay had not yet been discovered at Meissen or elsewhere in Europe and this new technique for producing tableware and other objects generated great enthusiasm at courts, in the houses of wealthy merchants and the aristocracy and amongst upper echelons of the clergy. A complete service of porcelain cost as much as equipping an entire company of infantry for battle! The court of the Ottoman Empire (see the Topkapi museum in Istanbul), the grand European royal courts, and rich Italian and Dutch merchants all wanted these porcelain services, the status symbols of the period. Dining from silver or gold plates was all very well and quite fashionable, but it was always possible that one might receive a royal command to donate these precious metals to one's country's cause... china dinner services, on the other hand, cannot be melted down to make ingots or coins.

---

1. The word porcelain comes from the Italian *porcella* (little sow), a shell reminiscent of the animal's vulva. But there is also another explanation: the translucent porcelain might have been given this name by Westerners because they thought that it was produced by crushing shells. Marco Polo was the first to describe porcelain ware.

THE CRISIS IN THE MING DYNASTY AND JAPANESE EXPANSIONISM

The Azuchi-Momoyama period (1573-1598) consolidated the Japanese archipelago's great transformation, which moved from the era of the samurai, constantly quarrelling amongst themselves, to the unification of the country under the military dynasty of the Tokugawa (1603-1868). In the meantime, the power of the Ming dynasty (1368 -1644) in China was being dissipated under attacks from the Manchu and due to the immobility of the emperor, imprisoned in his `golden cage´ surrounded by eunuch-counselors, a few powerful concubines and senior officials who were brilliant scholars but knew little about effective administration. Portuguese merchants were beginning to set themselves up in Japan, after the initial peaceful invasion by Jesuits and other western monks. Commercial ties between Japan and Europe were strengthening; artistic and cultural exchanges followed. The production of Japanese porcelain and ceramics benefited from exceptional circumstances. Following the invasion of Korea by the Japanese General Nabeshima, a number of Chinese craftsman, in particular the ceramicists who had worked at the imperial kilns in Jingdezhen, emigrated to Japan and settled. This took place mainly from 1615 onwards, at Karatsu and Hizen, on the outskirts of Arita on the island of Kyushu, where a Korean, Risampei, discovered deposits of kaolin in 1616. The great ceramics school of Raku was at its height during this period and the production of Japanese porcelain grew by leaps and bounds. Japanese craftsmen were familiar with Chinese porcelain and its techniques, but did not make it themselves. On the other hand the Korean ceramicists were also very familiar with it, having made it from as early as 1125, and had their own deposits of kaolin, according to accounts by Chinese travelers.

HIGH VOLUME EXPORT BY THE EAST INDIA COMPANIES

This period coincided with the fall of the Ming dynasty and a structural crisis in China, which for several centuries had held the monopoly for porcelain production intended for export to Europe. The crisis had a strong adverse impact on Chinese trade, leaving the market open for other Asian countries to step in and export large amounts of products to Europe.

Initially *Jiki* or Japanese porcelain was fairly simple in style and similar to Korean porcelain. None of it was exported, and there are very few examples in Europe of *shoki Imari* (first Imari). But from 1620 onwards, Japanese producers began to copy and reproduce the Chinese style (*Tianqi*). At first they made only small pieces, mainly tea sets, owing to the limited size of Japanese kilns at this period. These products began to be exported, passing through the port of Nagasaki, the only commercial point of contact between Japan and international – mostly Dutch and Chinese – merchants. The Chinese exported pieces to Canton, Amoy, Chousan and Taiwan, where they were bought by the British East India Company; the Dutch, confined to the little island of Deshima, shipped the products to China on the galleons of their East India Company. In 1659, for example, this purchased 64,858 pieces, according to the company archives. The Dutch also started providing Japanese potters with wooden models to work from, in line with European tastes. Naturally this increased demand led to new kilns being brought into service; Imari-Arita was no longer the only center; other kilns were set up in Mikawachi and their wares were exported through the port of Hirado.

THE MAJOR CUSTOMERS: SHOGUNS AND EUROPEANS

Production was mainly destined for three types of clients: the emperor, the shoguns, the political and military governors in Japan, and rich Europeans – royal courts, merchants, high-ranking clergy and the aristocracy – who were satisfied with products of a shade poorer quality. Production for the former two categories was in Arita and known as *Arita-Nabeshima* (the name of the local feudal lord). This used large amounts of cobalt applied under a coating of glaze, in accordance with the Chinese technique from Quinbai. Arita also had kilns specializing in production for export. This was known as *Kakiemon*, from the name of the red ferrous glaze used (hence the name of a family of artists who worked in the town, and are still there today). The influence of European and Portuguese Baroque introduced a greater variety of forms and the idea of polychromatic pieces for the European market. Ships filled with Japanese porcelain now replaced the Portuguese, Dutch and Spanish galleons which some decades earlier used to leave the port of Canton and the trading post of Macao loaded with Chinese porcelain and pottery. But Chinese production was facing a new crisis following the arrival of the Manchu Qing dynasty, which only began restructuring the pottery industry from 1683. In Europe, this porcelain was known as 'Holland', since most of it was carried in Dutch ships.

THE RISE OF EUROPEAN PORCELAIN

The high cost of these products and their transportation stimulated European chemists to look for deposits of kaolin and to perfect techniques that would enable porcelain to be made in Europe. The Elector of Saxony, Augustus the Strong, determined to find a European solution, handed the task to Count Tschirnhaus. The count had some scientific knowledge and set up a laboratory in the fortress of Koenigstein, where it so happened that the alchemist Johann Friedrich Bottger (1682-1719) was imprisoned. Bottger advised Tschirnhaus on how to research porcelain manufacturing techniques. The Elector had Bottger transferred to the fortress of Alberstein in Dresden, and it was there that the first porcelain factory was founded. On the pediment over its entrance was inscribed the eloquent motto: 'Secret to the grave'. In 1708 a factory was built at Meissen in Saxony, and large deposits of kaolin were discovered at Aue. Soon other major production centers began springing up, among them Chelsea, Worcester, Sèvres and Capidomonte. Once again, the secrets of production had been uncovered by industrial espionage and by using large sums of money to attract craftsmen. The competition from these factories steadily replaced imports from Japan and from China (where production had restarted with the stabilization of the economy under the Qing dynasty). Nevertheless, oriental designs continued to feature prominently on European porcelain.

COLOR WARS: EPIC BATTLES OF THE DYES FUELLED BY GEOGRAPHIC DISCOVERIES

Alexander the Great spoke of the purple fabrics found in the royal treasury of Susa, the capital of the Persian Empire which he had just conquered, and later, of wonderfully colored cotton worn by wealthy Indian families. The Roman Emperor Aurelius refused to allow his wife to buy clothes colored purple because they cost as much as their weight in gold. The reddish purple dye came from `Brazilwood´, which grew in Malaysia, India and Sri Lanka and which gave its name to Brazil – and not vice versa – when it was found growing there too by the Portuguese navigator Pedro Alvarez Cabral. The battle of the red dyes, between madder and cochineal, created huge economic waves, as did a trial of strength between indigo and woad for blue dyes.

As always, Venice was the great European bazaar for the products used by dyers and the colors sought after by artists; other towns such as Florence, Pisa, Genoa and a few towns in northern France, Amsterdam, Southampton, Basle and Frankfurt, were all part of the distribution network. In the second half of the 19th century the German chemicals industry developed around the production of artificial dyes, drawing on applied scientific research of great value. And first civil disobedience of the Indians against the British Empire gained its impetus from the decision in London to replace indigo with the artificial blue coloring that British industry was producing. The economic history of colors combines aesthetics with the employment of thousands of farmers growing plants and thousands of dyers working in stinking conditions – a history that ranges from the economic interests of nations to the search for the color to secure the researcher's individual reputation. There was also the mordant, the substance required for fixing the dyes. Alum, human and animal urine, copper, lead, aluminum and other metal salts were all used to stabilize dyes, which in turn were made from a host of materials obtained from mines, the land and the sea.

THE INDIAN OCEAN: A WHOLE PALETTE OF COLORS

The lands around the Indian Ocean first and foremost, then Europe, and later the Americas, were the largest producers of dyes. With the industrial revolution, the search to create artificial dyes moved to Europe and demonstrated the primacy of the German chemical industry, which was staffed by highly trained scientists. In this multi-colored palette, politics was mixed with espionage in the constant quest for new products and methods, while capital was provided by the bankers and merchants who financed expeditions in search of new dyes (as well as gold and spices) and who invested in mines, agriculture and the manufacture of the finished product. Political movements and population migration also influenced the production of dyes, as did fashion and religion, which in the days before mass literacy, communicated by putting across their messages in semantically coded colors recognized by the faithful.

PURPLE FOR ROMAN EMPERORS AND CARDINALS

Red is the first color that newly born infants learn to recognize, since red light has the longest wavelength and has a stimulating effect. Red is the symbol of authority, pride, dignity and recognition, passion and of love, as well as being the color of blood and revolution. It is much favored by royalty, since red clothes – military uniforms, the red dresses of *femmes fatales*, red of emperors' robes and religious leaders – attract the attention of those watching. The red carpet, the red riband or ribbon, the thin red line, red letter, to be in the red – all these are familiar expressions in which red indicates privilege, urgency or importance. Today many well-known brands use red, such as Coca-Cola (which was the first to make Santa Claus's costume red instead of its traditional green), Campbell's, Ferrari and others, and feature it prominently in their packaging.

In antiquity the color purple (or reddish-purple) was made by crushing mollusk shells (especially *Murex trunculus* and *Murex brandaris*) found in the eastern Mediterranean. According to legend this color was discovered by a dog owned by the Phoenician god of colors, Melkhart. One morning his dog picked up a shell between its teeth and this dyed its mouth a splendid color; the nymph Tyros greatly admired it and asked the god for a tunic of the same shade. The Phoenicians were great sailors and merchants, but also great producers of coloring materials; and the capital of their country, Tyre, and the town of Sidon, became rich by selling these products. The Greeks learned the technique from the Phoenicians. The Roman Republic reserved this color for the use of people in high office, especially victorious generals, and imperial Rome chose it as an official color conveying prestige and rank. Much later, in 1464, Pope Paul II introduced the purple robe into ecclesiastical protocol as the garment for cardinals, a distinctive mark of their power.

It takes around 10,000 shells to obtain a single gram of the coloring matter – which accounts for its price! This is why Roman emperors dressed in purple, and why they forbade other Roman citizens to dress in the same manner, on pain of death if they did so. With Alexander Severus the production of all purple dye came under imperial monopoly (*officinae purpurarie*). Dye workshops elsewhere in the empire were authorized and regulated by the emperor; a special guard unit was created to protect and keep an eye on them. In the ninth book of his *Natural History*, Pliny carefully describes the techniques used to make this very precious substance. Evidence of these products has been found in Chinese history too. The Mayas and the Aztecs used similar shells to produce red, though they had a different technique for removing the mollusk inside, blowing into the shell whereas in the Mediterranean they crushed it. The Romans also made a less expensive red with other substances. For example, Pompeii red, which still today decorates the walls of rich villas in Pompeii, was obtained from cinnabar (mercury sulfide), which is ground to a powder to produce the famous vermilion color. The mercury came from the mines of Almadén in Spain. But this red was still very expensive, and was therefore only used in the dwellings of the well-to-do. On the other hand, an ordinary red color can be obtained from the roots of madder, a plant belonging to the large rubiaciae family (like coffee, quinquina – used to produce alcoholic bitters – and the expectorant ipecac). Madder is found in many parts of Europe, including Provence, northern France, Holland and central Italy.

SPIES, PIRATES AND PROTECTIONISM

With the discovery of America, the Spanish began sending cochineal red to Europe. This was obtained by crushing the female of an insect parasite of the nopal cactus, found in particular in the Oaxaca region of Mexico. The price for this high quality product was extremely competitive compared to madder, and as a result the European dyes industry was restructured after 1570 to work mainly with cochineal red. The Spanish Empire had a monopoly of production, and in 1587 its galleons imported 65 tons of this precious substance to Europe. But the monopoly gave rise to espionage on the part of other countries and certain merchants who wanted to discover the secret of its production – in Europe no-one knew if it came from an animal, a fruit or a plant. A raid was organized to attack the Spanish galleons, and under the command of the Earl of Essex, the English pillaged a convoy of Spanish galleons, returning with 27 tons of red cochineal. But European nations were reluctant to be so dependent on the Spanish monopoly. For example, Colbert published 'Instructions for the cultivation and use of madder' to promote its production in France. At this time in Europe, the Dutch led the way in madder cultivation, the soil of the polders being well suited to the plant.

A century later another battle over red dye began. The Turks exported a magnificent red cotton dyed with 'Turkish Red', a compound of lead chromate and lead oxide. The city of Andrinopolis (now Edirne), founded by Hadrian in 125 AD, located on the western coast of Turkey, was the main producer and exporter. Eager to discover the secret of this red, French and English dye manufacturers sent agents to try and bribe the workers. French manufacturers in Normandy succeeded in attracting some of the workers to their factories around 1746, and the British in turn managed to obtain the secret in 1784. France, however, like other nations, continued to prefer to use madder and their soldiers wore trousers dyed with madder up until 1914. On the other hand, cochineal was the preferred choice for dyeing the jackets of the Guards on duty outside Buckingham Palace and elsewhere – an ancient contract, still in operation, specifies the use of this coloring agent. But all these battles over markets, through which masses of workers could find themselves out of work from one day to the next, were halted at a stroke by the invention in 1869 of artificial alizarin by German chemists at BASF (Badische Anilin und Soda Fabrik).

EGYPTIAN BLUE, WOAD AND INDIGO

Blue, the color of the sky and the sea, produces a calming effect and for the Chinese is the color of immortality. The Greeks and the Romans on the other hand disliked blue, and in Rome blue eyes were considered to be almost unlucky. The Church adopted it from the 12th century and painters always depicted the Virgin Mary dressed in blue; Louis XIV had a particular liking for it; and it is used for the blue helmets of United Nations forces, by the Food and Agriculture Organization and UNESCO, and in the European Union flag.

The Egyptians obtained a deep blue color by grinding lapis-lazuli (*lapis* = stone in Latin, *lazhward* = blue in Persian), but it was very expensive. They also had a cheaper alternative: in potters' kilns they baked a mixture of silicon, limestone derivatives, copper and native hydrous sodium carbonate, a residue found on dried-out lake beds. This was the first synthetic dye made by man, around 4500 years ago. Known as Egyptian blue, it was used for sarcophagi, for decorating walls and in precious textiles. However, this blue was not very popular elsewhere in the Mediterranean, and it was the Orient that adopted it in particular, using mainly indigo. The people of the Middle East are very partial to blue, and most words for different blues are of Arabic and not Latin origin – `azure´, for example, comes from the Arabic *al-lazward.*

Certain barbarians, living at the limits of the Roman empire, used woad to paint their bodies blue in order to intimidate their enemies in battle: `pugnaces Pictis´ (`aggressive enemies, who are painted´), as Caesar described them in his *De Bello Gallico*. In any case, Indian indigo could already be found in Rome at a price of twenty denarii the pound, as related by Pliny who also mentions its origin – *ex India venit* – and says it is obtained from plants and not marine rocks, as many people believed.

THE LAND OF PLENTY IN CRISIS

With the Crusades the color blue became popular once more in Europe, getting a boost from the Church and the royal and princely courts which adopted it. The cultivation of woad spread across various regions on the continent and made the fortune of many farmers and master dyers and the guilds which protected them in the main European cities. The industry linked to this production was so wealthy that it financed stained glass windows in Gothic churches in towns throughout the continent, windows in which the color blue was often featured. Local feudal lords and kings imposed heavy taxes on the industry – but the profits were so large that the taxes were not resented. The region around Toulouse in particular benefited from a burst of development thanks to the cultivation of woad or pastel (from the Latin *pasta* or `paste´, because originally the leaves were ground up by mills into a paste which was then fermented and dried). The Toulouse region was even called `the land of Cockaigne´ as a result of the wealth created by this cultivation and production. Trade with the Middle East also benefited from Indian exports of the blue obtained from indigo, from which the plant got its name; this product was of a better quality, with a higher concentration of pigment. Small quantities of indigo blue were soon found in Venice and in the principal markets of the continent. The main center for its supply was the city of Baghdad, from which derived the Italian word *baccadeo*, used by the Italian artist Cennino Cennini in his study *The Book of Art*, a key work on color from the early 15th century.

The fortunes of woad began to wane once Diaz opened the maritime route around Africa in 1498. At this point competition from indigo became overwhelming, and the entire European trade collapsed rapidly as a result of supplies from India. In 1598 indigo was banned in France and certain regions of Germany; the penalties for those contravening the ban went as far as capital punishment. Competition was further increased by production in America, where the Spanish began to develop the cultivation of indigo, *Isatis tinctoria*, on the slopes of the Central American hills. Aztecs and Toltecs already knew this plant, called Mayan blue, which is found in the Temple of the Warriors at Chichen. The French colony of San Domingo and the British colony of Jamaica became major production centers in the West Indies.

ONCE AGAIN BASF ENRICHES THE COLOR SPECTRUM

The East India Companies, especially the British company, became the principal buyers of Indian indigo (mostly produced in the Bengal region), and from 1837 production exploded following the decision to give the farmers ownership of previously expropriated land. But once again, scientific research produced a synthetic replacement for blue dye. In 1880, BASF acquired the patent for a dye: 18 million gold marks were spent on research and putting the dye into production. It was finally marketed in 1897. In the same year, Britain distributed 10,000 tons of natural Indian indigo, whilst Germany produced nearly 600 tons of synthetic dye. But by 1911 these figures were reversed: 870 tons of indigo for Britain and 22,000 tons for the powerful German dye industry. In India the first incident of civil disobedience began with demonstrations against the British when they decided to replace natural indigo with synthetic production, thereby provoking a deep crisis in the Indian dye industry.

FROM THE PRODUCTION OF COLORS TO THE CREATION OF THE NEED FOR COLOR

Other synthetic products providing a spectrum of colors were researched, patented and launched onto the world market by the chemicals industry, through large international companies, particularly American and European, which were able to invest large amounts of capital in research. The first half of the 20th century was particularly fruitful in this respect, and the industry even benefited from the two World Wars. During the final decades of the last century, the emphasis was more on the marketing of dyes and coloring agents in order to attract consumers to new colors, to orient them toward the need for an ever extending palette, and to encourage them to give up white in favor of other colors, particularly in household linens and lingerie. The battle has moved on from the creation of colors to the creation of a need for color. In the words of Luciano Benetton: `I wanted to color the world and I succeeded!´

THE FIRST ENERGY CRISIS:
WOOD IN 17TH CENTURY EUROPE

In 1973 there was a major energy crisis: the price of oil (Saudi Arabian Light) shot up from $2.59 per barrel to $11.65 a barrel between September 1973 and March 1974, when the embargo ended. The price rise occurred for both economic reasons (OPEC succeeded in imposing its power as an oligopoly) and political reasons (the Arab embargo against the West). This crisis overturned many aspects of the way people lived, above all the structure of relative prices in the industrial world, and had a major impact on energy markets and alternative energies, and even on daily habits (the hour change for summertime was reintroduced for economic reasons in 1976). Yet a similar crisis occurred in Europe in the 17th century, creating the ideal conditions for triggering the industrial revolution, in Britain first of all, and then on the European continent.

A HOTTER EUROPE

There are many indicators showing that the temperature in Europe at the end of the first millennium was relatively high. Southern Greenland was covered in trees, with barley and winter cereals being grown there (they were sown in winter and harvested in the summer). According to the Vatican archives, which contain many letters sent to Rome by missionaries in the region, Greenland was well populated and traded with northern Canada.

Large tracts of Europe were covered in forest, which were able to grow because of the changing climate and, ironically, the continent's backwardness. Economic growth in Europe increased between 1000 and 1350, at which point the plague took its terrible toll: out of 100 million Europeans, 30 million died in horrible suffering, swept away by the pandemic known as the Black Death. The consumption of wood was suddenly reduced by at least 20%, and prices dropped. For the next two centuries the European population slowly recovered, but the amount of wood consumed remained relatively small.

The economic development following upon the discovery of America altered the status quo and gave rise to increased consumption of wood. This was used for building houses and especially ships, for domestic heating (temperatures were falling at this time and with people generally better off than before they heated their homes more) and for the making charcoal for use in industry (following a strong recovery of mining in central Europe and increased cannon manufacture, especially of those made from iron, as a result of the wars of the 17th and 18th centuries).

THE ROCKETING PRICE OF WOOD

In 1631 the English vicar Edmund Howes wrote that in the memory of man, wood had never been so scarce. He went on to add that the demand for wood for building ships and houses, making furniture, barrels and carts, and for heating houses and providing energy for factories, had recently become very high and that prices had risen accordingly. In England the price of wood rose 300% between 1560 and 1670, and that of charcoal increased fourfold, against a general increase in prices estimated at around 200%. The same phenomenon was evident throughout Europe, and wood arriving from the New World failed to fully meet the demand. In fact the cost of transporting wood was too high, and it was preferable to load the galleons with precious metals and spices in the New World and luxury products such as textiles, arms and passengers in the Old, destined for the West Indies. With the exception of rare and prized species, the transport of wood, much like that of sand and cement today, was simply unprofitable. The resulting energy crisis extended from the early 17th century well into the next.

HOUSES BUILT FROM BRICK AND MARBLE

Gradually wood was replaced as a building material. All over Europe houses were now being constructed from brick for the less well off, stone for the middle classes and marble for the wealthy and aristocratic ... a process that is clearly visible in the history of architecture. The demand for wood nevertheless continued to grow, together with its price. As a result people switched to coal in regions where it was available. But what was needed was high quality coal, since lignite and peat had an insufficiently high calorific value. Coal was used in homes in Britain, Belgium, the Ruhr region and in northern France, even by the wealthiest, but this led to high levels of pollution. Coal was also used to produce the heat required for the furnaces of the iron and steel industries and for certain chemical processes. However, wood still had to be used in ship-building, for roof supports, some agricultural implements and barrels.

INDUSTRY RELOCATES IN COAL-BEARING REGIONS

Wood was replaced by coal, particularly in the metallurgical industries, because it produces more heat. As a result the balance of economic power once again shifted among European countries. Those with coal-bearing areas were at a clear advantage and could make much more rapid progress, on condition that the new middle classes and businessmen provided financial backing. Thus Europe graduated to another stage in its development. The industrial revolution could begin.

THE HOPE BANK AND SPECULATION
IN THE COCHINEAL MARKET

The Hope Bank was a large financial institution operating in Amsterdam in 1787, mainly concerned with placing Russian and other loans on the Dutch market, which was in strong competition with London. The bank's directors believed there was an excellent opportunity in the cochineal market[1], one of the principle raw materials used in dyeing textiles. The price had gone down since 1784, at the end of the fourth war against England. The trade in this product, which came from Mexico, notably the region of Oaxaca, had been overlooked by the large trading houses and banks. For a long time it provided a lucrative business for the merchants from Seville, supported by Genoan bankers who understood that cochineal was important in the manufacture of luxury goods. According to information obtained by Henry Hope, the harvest had been bad and existing stocks in Europe were low, even

---

1. Cochineal is a parasitic louse of the nopal cactus, from which people in Central America obtained a red dye, known as 'cactus blood'. The insects, which feed off the cactus sap, were ground up some five months after they hatched and mixed with stannous chloride to obtain a bright red powder. After the conquest of Mexico by Hernan Cortez, the Spanish imported specimens of cochineal into the south of the country, but production was difficult and it remained concentrated around Oaxaca. From 1540, the weavers of Antwerp used this product in large quantities. In 1630 the governor of Yucatan had 3 million cactuses intended for cochineal production, with a harvest three times a year. There was strong demand from Europe and production spread to the countries south of Mexico: Honduras, Guatemala, San Salvador and Nicaragua. The French botanist Thierry de Menouville was sent to Oaxaca in 1777 to study the insect and in 1787 published a book on the cultivation of the nopal and the cochineal. Trials to try and set up production elsewhere in the world had limited success: only the Dutch succeeded in starting production in Java. From 1850 production declined with the introduction of synthetic colorants and dyes. Since the discovery that certain chemical colorants are carcinogenic, the carmine from cochineal is once again being used in the food and cosmetics industries, for products such as lipstick, make-up, taramasalata, mortadella, and cake decorations.

though the price had been falling for some years. The stock amounted to 1750 bales, mainly located in Cadiz, London and Amsterdam.

AN ATTEMPT TO CORNER THE MARKET

Hope's idea was to quickly buy up a large quantity of cochineal at low prices and then to cause the price to rise as a result of the shortage and to resell what they had bought. He predicted that the investment would cost between 1.5 and 2 million florins, a substantial sum of money, from which he expected to reap even greater returns. Henry Hope thought that there was very little of risk making a loss, even if prices did not rise much. Furthermore, the complicity of Baring's bank was assured in all the markets since the English bank was taking a quarter share in the speculation. It was a total fiasco! The slowness of the postal service resulted in late delivery of the order, which in turn undermined the whole operation. In addition the information that the bank was acting upon was inaccurate: stocks were much higher than estimated. Hope dug himself in the even deeper, buying up cochineal stocks in Marseille, Rouen, Hamburg, Italy and St Petersburg, but to no avail. Even though he had twice as much stock as originally planned, the price remained unchanged and the Russo-Turkish war in the Levant was creating problems for selling the merchandise. It was another attempt to create a monopoly, which the merchants of Amsterdam had been such brilliant forerunners.

ENORMOUS LOSSES

The end result of the operation was that substantial losses were incurred. Fortunately for the Dutch banking house this did not result in its destabilization because it was making large profits issuing and placing national loans with European high finance. But the image of the Hope Bank suffered badly. Everybody knew about their failed speculation and although the losses were absorbed without difficulty, the name of the great Dutch banking house appeared in the gazettes and was much discussed by financiers, who traditionally always forget successes and long remember failures, especially of their competitors.

THE ROYAL NAVY 'PROMOTES' PORT, MADEIRA AND MARSALA

Following an ancient tradition the British Navy always passes the port around the table from right to left at the end of the meal. This practice conforms to a very well-defined etiquette: the person who has the bottle of port must serve his neighbor on his right and then pass the bottle to his neighbor on his left, who in turn serves him, and so on round the table. If one of the diners wishes to have some more port, he must catch the attention of the person with the bottle in front of him. If he fails to understand what is wanted, then the first will ask him: 'Do you know the Bishop of Gloucester?' This cryptic message having been understood, port will be poured; if not, the person wishing to be served will continue, saying, 'The Bishop is a splendid fellow, but he always forgets to pass the port.' The Navy was and still is one of the largest consumers of port, Madeira and Marsala – and in the past was probably the most active marketing agent for these wines! Indeed what wine should one serve to the officers of Her Majesty's Royal Navy, given that English wine has not been renowned for its quality in the past? And that the water taken on board the old sailing ships soon deteriorated, with serious risk to the health of the sailors.

ALCOHOL ON BOARD TO COMBAT ALCOHOLISM!

Navy rules drawn up to eradicate alcoholism were very precise. The senior purser, or in certain cases a young commissioned officer, was put in charge of the stores, and it was his job to 'serve each mariner with a pint of wine, or half a pint of brandy, rum or arrack, or a gallon of beer´. (The next rule specified the exact menu for the various meals). Wine, however, did not travel well on board ship and from 1703, following the treaty of Methuen, port became one of the alcoholic drinks served in the Royal Navy. The treaty made Portugal an ally of the English and Dutch against the Catholic League; Lisbon gained fiscal advantages for its exports, but lost a certain degree of political and military freedom. At the same time, French wine was heavily penalized by a high import duty into England, greatly reducing the trade. English wine merchants went to the region of Oporto and settled there, soon establishing themselves and their businesses hading to the creation of the great port houses, among them Croft, Taylor, Dow, Graham, Symington, Offley, Sandeman and Smith-Woodhouse. To its surprise, the Royal Navy discovered that the more these wines traveled in the barrels in the ships' holds, the better they were. There was little risk then of the quality deteriorating as had so frequently happened with wines with a lower alcohol content. The navy ordered large quantities from British merchants, some of whom themselves became producers of high quality port.

LOADED ON BOARD IN `PIPES´ AS BALLAST

Madeira wine is made mainly from the malvasia grape from Crete (this is also the derivation of `malmsey wine´), along with which some Riesling is added and another grape from Tuscany. All these Madeira vineyards were planted at the time when transatlantic navigation was growing strongly in the 16th century. East India Company ships would often stop at Funchal when heading westward to take on provisions, especially fruit and water, but they would also load barrels of Madeira wine, which functioned as ballast for the voyage. These barrels, containing 100-120 gallons of wine, were known as `pipes´. The ships carried little cargo out to the Indies, but came back heavily laden. And once again it was found that the wine was better on the return trip, especially if it had crossed the equator twice and in the heat of the tropics! When it arrived on English and to a lesser extent Dutch tables, this *vinho da roda* (`return journey wine´) was much appreciated. The earthquake which devastated Lisbon in 1755 created serious problems for Portugal; the country lost much its political and economic power, enabling yet more British merchants to settle on the island of Madeira. To the houses already mentioned were added the names of Cossart-Gordon, Leacock-Madeira, Gould-Campbell, and Blandy. There were also some French – Rozès and Gilberts – and German companies – Burmenster, from south of Lübeck – as well as old Portuguese or Madeiran families such as Ferreira (their Quinta do Vesuvio port was produced as early as 1565). The Royal Navy bought these wines from English merchants for its crews and in particular for the Officers' Mess on board ship and for staff officers based in London and other ports of the British Empire.

NELSON, TRAFALGAR AND MARSALA

An English merchant, John Woodhouse, discovered another wine similar to port by mistake, namely Marsala, produced from the vines grown on the western extremity of Sicily. The word Marsala comes from *Mars Allah*, the port of Allah. In 1773 Woodhouse was heading for a Sicilian port further to the south to load up with caustic soda, when a storm obliged him to anchor in the port of Marsala, where he drank some of the local wine. As a result he altered his route, loading 5000 gallons of the wine on board, to which he added some extra alcohol to stabilize it during the voyage. The wine was an immediate success in London and Woodhouse returned to Sicily, where he bought an old tuna factory and converted it into a wine warehouse. He encouraged the growers to increase production, helping them with finance, and began exporting the wine, destined for the Navy once again, the wealthy middle classes and aristocracy. The Navy alone got through 500 barrels a year. After Nelson's victory against Napoleon's fleet, the great courage shown by the English sailors was attributed to the Marsala they had consumed, and it was accordingly referred to as Victory Wine.

Other English merchants were drawn by the success of their competitor. Benjamin Ingham arrived in Sicily in 1806 and suggested rules covering the production of the wine and quality criteria. With his nephew Joseph Whitaker, he became one of the main wine producers of the region. Other English wine merchants, such as the Hopps and Pyne families, were eager to join this new market. In 1833 Vicenzo Florio, the son of a Calabrian spice merchant who built up considerable international experience from his travels, built a *baglio* or wine warehouse between the two factories belonging to the English producers Woodhouse and Ingham, and with an investment of 200,000 ducats, started exporting the wine throughout the world. Beginning with his existing ships, he had others built until his fleet totaled 99 vessels. At this point the Italian government issued a decree forbidding him to build any more, in order to prevent his fleet becoming larger than the Italian Navy. But Florio savored a small revenge by establishing the famous *Targa Florio* motor race in 1906, a year earlier than the Indianapolis motor race was first held.

A UNIVERSAL RAILWAY GAUGE, THANKS TO THE ROMAN EMPIRE

Today there are four main railway gauges in the world: the standard international gauge, the reduced gauge, the metric gauge and a few specially adapted gauges such as those found in Russia and countries formerly belonging to the Soviet system, as well as those of Spain, Portugal and Ireland. In Ireland, there were three types of gauge before a commission chose the intermediate one (5ft. 3in. = 1600mm), thus eliminating the one created by Stephenson; the Irish gauge was introduced into certain Australian states by Irish engineers as well as Brazil and Argentina. In the United States the various lines were initially built with different gauges, generally wider than those of Europe, extending up to 7 feet 6 inches. However, by the end of the 19th century the 84 different gauges had been replaced by the international standard gauge. This is the most frequently used railway gauge in the world: 4 feet 8 1/2 inches. Why was this particular width chosen?

THE ROMAN EMPIRE: THE GREATEST ROAD BUILDERS IN EUROPE AND THE MEDITERRANEAN REGION

The Roman Empire was based on a vast military machine able to conquer and hold territory – a significant part of Rome's revenues came from the proceeds of conquest and pillage – but its success also derived from its ability rapidly to integrate many diverse geographical regions into a great commercial empire. Rome therefore needed a well organized, well maintained and well protected network of roads in addition to a common currency, common administrative language and common legislation.

Roman roads were used by the army to get from one place to another, by messengers – the postal service was one of the best in antiquity – and by merchants transporting goods (although considerable amounts of merchandise traveled by sea and river). The administrators of this great Empire decided that there should be standard rules for building roads and managing them. They therefore established a fixed distance between the wheels of chariots, in fact determined by the width needed between the shafts for two horses to gallop as fast as possible side by side. Such is the origin of the 4 feet 8 1/2 inches gauge! Logically enough, this measure was chosen by default to be the width for all commercial vehicles using the roads and city streets of the empire. It was one of the first examples of geographical standardization over a wide area, and was applied throughout the Roman Empire, including a large part of Eastern Europe and regions bordering the Mediterranean – Egypt, Turkey and part of the Balkans.

THE INSPIRATION FOR ROLLING STOCK ON THE RAILWAYS

Almost 2000 years later, when British engineers began to build the railways, the main producers of carriages and engines were already established as makers of horse-drawn carriages and of carts pulled by horses and oxen. The traditional distance between the wheels of these vehicles remained unchanged, since many European roads still followed the Roman imperial routes with their traces of chariot wheels. The English gauge of the first trains was therefore applied to the rest of Europe and then spread automatically around the world. From the start of the spread of railways the locomotives were British made, and so engineers building new networks throughout the world applied the same rules. Once again this is an instance of standardization on a global basis.

THE NAPOLEONIC INVASIONS AND THEIR EFFECT ON GAUGES

Obviously, for technical reasons, other gauges were created. This was often the case for tram networks (especially those built with Belgian finance). Such networks allowed for a system that could extend beyond the city center, and was much lighter and less expensive to build. Trams were much used at the end of the 19th century in particular, in Europe and in other countries that were beginning to develop industrially, such as the United States and Russia. Trams used a narrower gauge, but again of a standardized width. Other gauges were used by mountain railways, as found in the Alps and the Rockies. Metric gauges were in widespread use, but only locally. Finally, a number of European countries opted for wider gauges simply for historical reasons. For example, Spain and Portugal, following Napoleon's invasion, decided to take measures to protect themselves in future against further invasion and chose a different gauge from the European norm. Russia, another country invaded by Napoleon, also chose a different gauge for its rail network and for the same reason. In the First World War, Germany was slowed down in its march eastwards in part because of the difference in gauge on the Russian railway network. The High Command of the Third Reich learned from this and organized Operation Barbarossa – the invasion of the USSR in 1941 – on the basis of rapidly refitting the Soviet rail network, carried out by the Wehrmacht's dedicated, and extremely efficient, military rail battalions. These specialists followed a few days behind the frontline troops with instructions to modify the gauge and repair the network, so as to enable the increasingly extended supply lines to the troops to function efficiently over great distances and bring arms, munitions, fresh troops, spare parts, medical aid and food supplies to the front.

THE POTATO FAMINE CHANGES
THE HISTORY OF IRELAND

Martin Scorsese's film *Gangs of New York* depicts the hard life of the Irish who fled their poverty-stricken land to seek a new life in another country where they might have a brighter future. The ˋnatives´ did not always appreciate this influx of hands hoping to earn a crust.

Between 1846 and 1849, 945,000 Irish left their country: most of them for America and England, but some for Canada and Australia. Over this terrible period, the population of Ireland fell from 8 million to less than 6 million – about one million emigrated, and more than a million died. It was the time of the Great Famine which completely changed the structure of Irish society and the fate of the Gaelic language – the number of Irish speakers fell from about 3 million to only 600,000 and English became the predominant language.

There were many causes of this disaster, but the principle one was mildew (a parasitic fungus), which destroyed the potato harvest from 1846 onwards, a scourge which stalked the country for four years. During this period potato stocks dwindled away to nothing; and the climate remained very wet, limiting the harvests. The diet of the population was based on cereals and the potato (its cultivation having been introduced on a massive scale from the 18th century onwards), and the people no longer had enough to eat. Famine, malnourishment, dysentery and typhus decimated both the young and the old, whilst those of working age were desperately weakened. There are records of little children who were deprived of food so as to give any available food to sustain their older brothers who were capable of working in the fields.

The British government under Robert Peel imported American maize to feed the people, and voted for the abolition of taxes on wheat to reduce prices. Charitable organizations, both Catholic and Anglican, distributed free food, and the government, rather belatedly, followed their lead and organized free soup kitchens. However, these measures soon became inadequate due to the lack of compassion shown by many of the wealthy landowners and their land-agents who, as a rule, expelled farmers who were incapable of paying their rent. Certain landlords were more humane but could not compete with their more unscrupulous neighbors and had to sell their lands to speculators, who were mainly English. A contributing factor was the Corn Laws, which had been in force in Great Britain since 1815 and whose purpose was to protect the country's cereal production. This legislation encouraged local production and intensive farming practices and above all kept the price of land high. Under pressure from the Anti-Corn Laws League, who were in favor of a free market in both production and trade, the British parliament repealed the Corn Laws and after 1847 the price of cereals fell. The price of land also dropped considerably in a climate of economic difficulties brought on by the Bank Act, which raised interest rates and impeded growth. Irish landlords were hit hard by these measures and often had to lay off farmers and leave their land fallow.

THE POTATO: RICH IN NUTRITION AND HISTORY

This plant tuber, of which traces have been found in the Andes and in Bolivia dating as far back as 5000 years BC, belongs to the family of *Solanaceae*, as does the tomato. The Incas used it under the name of *papa*, and together with maize, it was an essential part of pre-Columbian peoples' diet.

The Spanish conquistadores imported the potato to Spain around 1532 and its first scientific description came from Charles de Lécluse, the Keeper of the gardens for the Emperor Maximilian in Vienna. Sailors liked the potato a great deal because it helped keep scurvy at bay during voyages. In 1565 the Emperor Philip II of Spain presented some potatoes to Pope Pius IV, assuring him that it was a very effective cure for rheumatism. It subsequently became popular in Italy, where it was called the *tartufulo* or little truffle. Sir Walter Raleigh introduced the potato to Ireland in 1585, changing the eating habits of the inhabitants, whose diet had been based mainly on boiled oats. The damp local climate and the cold were favorable to the growth of the potato and protected it from viral damage. It requires little care, is rich in carbohydrates, minerals and vitamins and will grow in all soil types: a true miracle! In the 18th century Frederick II commanded the Prussians to cultivate and eat the potato – or else they would have their ears chopped off! Parmentier, who had been a prisoner in Prussia, introduced it to France, where Louis XVI named it the `apple of the earth´ (*pomme de terre*), whilst to improve its image, Marie-Antoinette wore potato flowers as a corsage. This is how, for a long period, the potato came to replace bread, which was too expensive for many peasants.

KARL MARX, THE FAMINE AND IRISH EMIGRATION

In one of his articles on the British economic crisis (*Die Presse*, 6th November 1861), Karl Marx clearly sums up the impossible choice facing millions of Irish during the potato crisis – emigrate or die. There was great demand for passages between British, and later Irish ports, and America (initially £5 for a single journey from Liverpool to New York). Many emigrants died from illness or hunger on ships which were tramp steamers meant for carrying goods and totally unsuited to the transport of passengers. They were called 'coffin ships' because of the high death rate on board during these very long voyages.

Those Irish who did make it to the American continent (more than one third of all immigrants during the 1850s) were prepared to work at anything, whether legal or illegal, no matter how difficult or humiliating, including prostitution and other such activities. Gangs were organized to protect their people from attacks by other groups of immigrants and the locals. Following a very difficult period, they became integrated into American society. It was then the turn of other groups to suffer the traumas of settling in a foreign land, including Italian, Polish and particularly Chinese immigrants, whose labor played such a large part in the construction of the railways.

FROM SUEZ TO PANAMA:
SUCCESS AND SCANDAL

The Suez Canal is one of the world's principal maritime arteries. Nowadays ships drawing 50 feet of water can use it; oil tankers weighing 260,000 tons are able to navigate through it and even overtake or pass each other going in opposite directions – its navigation takes between eleven and fifteen hours. More than 15,000 ships go through it each year and about 14% of world shipping uses the canal, whose increase in size and depth is currently being planned and worked on. Egypt charges ever-increasing duty on each passage; this duty comprises one of its three main sources of income.

The history of the canal goes back a long way. The pharaoh Sesostri first asked his engineers to plan a link between the Mediterranean and the Red Sea around 4000 years ago; the Egyptians estimated that it would be possible to open a waterway between the eastern branch of the Nile and the Great Amer Lake and from there navigate to the Red Sea. Other studies were launched by the pharaoh Necho (600 BC), and Herodotus described the canal thus: it took four days to navigate it, and two triremes could pass each other; it was a massive project and 120,000 workers died during its construction. Darius I, King of Persia (522 – 486 BC), took over the project, and it became known as the Canal of the Pharaohs. Ptolemy II increased the canal's capacities and developed trade, creating maritime routes which went as far as the Horn of Africa. The canal then fell into disuse until the Roman invasion of Egypt. In 106 AD, the Emperor Trajan had the canal (*Amnis Trajanus*) rebuilt and this allowed Rome to locate a fleet in the Red

Sea and to partially control the spice trade. The Byzantines ignored this great construction until it came to life once again under Arabic expansionism in the 7th century; the naval ship-yards were opened and trade benefited a great deal from this route. But the canal was finally closed in 842 by the Abbasid Caliph of Baghdad, Abu Jafar, who wanted to protect and develop the spice route overland.

VENICE AND POPE SIXTUS V AND LATER LOUIS XV CONSIDER REOPENING THE CANAL

In 1574 the possibility of constructing a canal was submitted to the Council of Ten in the Venetian Republic; its ships would be able to sail through to the Red Sea, then on to the Indian Ocean. This might make it possible for them to avoid transporting merchandise by caravan across the deserts and above all to buy spices and other products direct from their place of production, without going via Arab merchants and caravaneers. In 1671, the mathematician Leibnitz presented Louis XIV was with a plan to construct a canal; but this was generally considered to be madness. Pope Sixtus V (the only pope from Croatia) lent his support, but the project was abandoned because of the exorbitant costs involved. Louis XV and Louis XVI showed some interest in similar projects, but it was the shippers and merchants from Marseille who addressed the Constituent Assembly in 1790 to ask for the Canal to be built. Talleyrand claimed that the Suez route would have as fatal an effect on Britain as the discovery of the Cape of Good Hope had had on Genoa and Venice during the 16th century. One of Napoleon's missions in Egypt was to study the possibility of building this canal. The engineer Charles le Père was sent by the Directory in 1799 to Egypt to study the problem but in his report he wrote that the project was impossible because of the difference of height in sea level between the two seas, estimated at 33 feet.

Half a century later this incorrect analysis was amended by another French engineer, M.L. Linant de Bellefonds, who maintained that the two seas were almost the same level. Luigi Negrelli de Mondelba, an engineer born in Trentino under Austrian domination, dedicated twenty years of his life (1838 – 1858) to a mission given to him by the Austrian Chancellor, prince Metternich, which was the study of a project for the canal. Meanwhile another engineer, Prosper Enfantin, made a presentation in 1845 to the French, Austrian, Italian, British and German Chambers of Commerce in which he proposed that an international company should be set up to study the project of building a canal. The Company for the Study of the Suez Canal was created in 1846. Negrelli joined the company, representing an Italian-Austrian-German alliance which had been formed between the Venetian and Trieste chambers of commerce together with the mayoralty of Trieste and Lloyds of Trieste.

ENGLAND AND FRANCE VIE FOR THE PROJECT

The Company for the Study of the Suez Canal was in competition with a British group led by Stephenson, the son of the railway engineer, and the French group led by the engineer Paulin Talabot. The English government feared that their presence in the Indian Ocean would be threatened by the canal and proposed an alternative: the construction of a railway between the two seas. The technical debates over the corresponding sea levels delayed this project and the political events of 1848 in Europe created other problems.

The following year the Egyptian viceroy, who was strongly in favor of the canal, died. He was replaced by Abbas who had close links to British interests, and therefore preferred Stephenson's project to build a railway line between Alexandria and Cairo. But in 1854 Abbas was replaced by the Viceroy Said Pasha, who in turn was well disposed toward France and a great friend of Ferdinand de Lesseps (the former French consul in Alexandria) and Enfantin. The decree to grant Ferdinand de Lesseps the concession to build the canal was signed by Ali Pasha on 30th November 1854. The technical project was drawn up by the French engineers Linant de Bellefonds and Mougel; and after some modification, the plan was approved by an international commission. The British opposition from Lord Palmerston remained firm and British `experts´ predicted an inevitable silting up of the canal. De Lesseps quickly found 200 million francs to underwrite half of the capital for the new *Compagnie Internationale du Canal Maritime de*

Suez (Suez Maritime Canal International Company), thanks to the support of the Emperor Napoleon III and the Empress Eugenie who had family ties to De Lesseps on his Spanish mother's side. Thanks to 25,000 underwriters, De Lesseps did not need to go to the banks, and especially not the Rothschild bank; the banking world was not in favour of the project. The Egyptian government shared in the capital, contributing the sum of 18 million francs.

FROM PICKS AND SHOVELS TO EARTH-MOVING MACHINES

Work began on 25th April 1859 and, following many technical and political difficulties, was completed on 17th November 1869. It is estimated that one and a half million Egyptians worked on digging the canal, many of them as forced labor until 1864, and that around 125,000 died, mostly from cholera. The work began with picks and shovels and ended by using large dredging machines powered by coal and steam. The day of the inauguration, 48 ships traversed the length of the canal; on board there were many members of royal and imperial families, politicians, financiers and top European businessmen. The Cairo opera, built by the Khedive Ishmael Pasha, was opened on 1st November 1869 with a performance of *Rigoletto*. The Khedive asked his friend Camille du Locle, the director of the Comic Opera in Paris, to commission Giuseppe Verdi to write an opera about Egypt; after much hesitation, Verdi agreed. After a considerable number of delays caused by the outbreak of the Franco-German war, which held up the scenery, the costumes and the singers, the first performance of *Aïda* was given, to a standing ovation, in the opera in Cairo on 24th December 1871.

The benefits to world trade from this new communication route quickly became apparent; the cost of transport dropped considerably, as did the time needed to travel between Europe and Asia. It saved, on average, 5000 miles of navigation and the canal also facilitated colonial conquests on the Old Continent.

In 1875, Egypt had to face up to its economic problems and sold its share in the canal to the United Kingdom for 100 million francs. The Prime Minister, Disraeli, with the help of the Rothschild bank, seized the opportunity to buy into a project which was essential for the British Navy and British trade, and in 1882 Great Britain sent troops to protect the canal. In 1956 Egypt seized control of the canal; France, Britain and Israel sent troops to `liberate´ the canal, which remained closed for several months. The United Nations declared that Egypt was the rightful owner of the canal, and it was reopened. However after the Six Day War in 1967, the canal was once again closed until 5th June 1975. As OBO ships (oil, bulk and ore), which transported oil, dry goods in bulk and minerals, were now obliged to go round the Cape, there was a significant increase in their production and size. In the early 1970s ships of this type were built to reduce transport costs.

SUCCESS ENCOURAGES DE LESSEPS TO BUILD THE PANAMA CANAL

Ferdinand de Lesseps was on the crest of a wave after the technical and financial success of the Suez Canal. So he decided to act on another pharaonic idea that had already been much talked of – building a canal in Panama. Pre-Columbian routes linked the Pacific Ocean and the Caribbean Sea and were used by the Waunana and Ngobe peoples, who were the inhabitants of the Panama isthmus. The conquistadores used these routes to get around in the equatorial region where movement was difficult. In 1513 Vasco Nuñez de Balboa was the first European explorer to discover the Pacific; he built a road about 45 miles long between Santa Maria del Darien, on the Caribbean, and the bay of San Miguel, on the Pacific. The following year, Antonio Tello de Guzman found a track from Panama to Puerto Bello which the local population used; this route was passable and they improved and paved it. It became known as *El Camino Real,* along which the precious metals destined for export to Spain were transported.

In 1523 the Emperor Charles V realized that a canal crossing the isthmus could greatly speed up the export of precious metals, spices and other `American´ products and would above all greatly reduce the time needed to sail to his burgeoning Empire in Asia. At this time, a letter with orders from the Emperor sent from Madrid to Manila was answered between ten and twelve months later on average! Charles ordered a feasibility study to be made on the subject of building a canal. The first plan was prepared in 1529, but the risk of investing large sums of money, and then encountering complicated technical problems, was too great for the political and economic conditions of Spain in Europe. Men and merchandise coming from Spain and Europe made their way to the high plateaus of the Andes by *El Camino Real*, after a short voyage in the Pacific; other merchandise left these plateaus destined for Spain and Europe, following the same route in reverse. This route became clogged with the sheer numbers of soldiers, merchants, priests and monks, investors, royal administrators, clerks and merchandise. The traffic was often delayed by the hostile climate.

EL CAMINO DE CRUCES

In 1533 Gaspar de Espinosa suggested to the king that a new road should be constructed, leaving from the town of Panama on the Pacific and leading to the (later fortified) town of Cruces. Here ships would be able to load up with men and merchandise en route for Puerto Bello, a large town with royal warehouses on the Caribbean Sea. The road became known as *El Camino de Cruces* and was used for over four centuries. In the mid-nineteenth century, gold diggers on their way to California during the Gold Rush (1848-55) used it to avoid having to sail around South America or cross the whole of North America to reach the West, as the transcontinental railway had not yet been built (it came into service in 1869).

In 1698 five ships left Scotland carrying pioneers intending to found the colony of Darien and build a road which would develop trade with Japan and China. The project was a total failure, and many pioneers died in the process. Trade relations between the American Atlantic coast, the Caribbean region and the countries of the western Pacific basin were developing more and more, but there was still no quick and easy way to cross the American continent.

The German geographer Alexander Von Humboldt came up with the idea of the canal which would cross the Panama isthmus, and in 1819 the Spanish government authorized its construction, but the plans never came to fruition. In 1826 the American Atlantic and Pacific Ship Canal Company was created, with the aim of constructing the Nicaragua canal, and in 1850 the United States and Great Britain signed the Clayton-Bulwer treaty concerning control of the canal. The annexation of California by the United States (2nd February 1848) and the discovery of gold in the north of the state made the construction of a canal and/or a railway line across the isthmus essential. The construction of this railway line, built between 1851 and 1855: proved very difficult; the climatic conditions were terrible, and more than 12,000 workers died in accidents or from illness (cholera and malaria). Eventually, however, the trains began to run regularly and transported large quantities of passengers and goods between the two oceans. The line was used a great deal by gold prospectors who were on their way to California, as well as for carrying the precious metal to the financial market in New York.

De Lesseps' exploits and miserable failure

In 1876 the American Commission was set up to choose between the different routes (the isthmuses of Tehuantepec, Nicaragua, Panama, Darien and Atrato). The Nicaraguan plan was chosen. In Paris, Ferdinand de Lesseps had been basking in the glow of his success with the Suez Canal and confirmed that he wished to participate in the project. On 15th May 1879 an International Committee for Geographical Studies was set up, naturally under Lesseps' chairmanship. He presented a paper on his plan which was a copy of his' Suez Canal project. This was approved by the Committee who envisaged a canal 46 miles long, 26 feet deep, 72 feet wide, without locks. It would take twelve years to dig and the estimated cost was 1178 million francs: 612 million for the construction work, 153 million for over-budget costs, 134 million for maintenance, 38 million for administrative and banking costs and 241 million to repay anticipated interest and capital on the loans. During the month of August 1879, de Lesseps launched the first subscription to cover initial expenses. It was a fiasco. He only managed to raise 30 million francs, 5 million of which were used to buy the Colombian concession for the construction from its owner, an Italian general. He also promised the Colombian government that they would receive shares to the value of 5 million francs.

On 10th January one of his daughters officially inaugurated the construction work. During the month of October, de Lesseps founded the *Compagnie Universelle du Canal Interocéanique et la Compagnie Nouvelle du Canal de Panama*, to take over the activities of the previous company involved. It had a capital of 1335 million francs. He launched another subscription, expecting to raise 300 million francs. In fact, he obtained 600 million between 7th and 9th December 1880. It was an incredible success and de Lesseps was more and more confident.

The work started in early January of the following year but soon became a Sisyphean odyssey. The climate was very difficult with torrential rains, it was necessary to cross the Andean cordillera, there was a significant difference in sea level between the two oceans and, lastly, tropical diseases sapped the morale of the workers and the engineers and took a terrible toll on them. Up to 40 deaths in one single day were recorded and it is estimated that more than 22,000 men died between 1881 and 1889. The main obstacle was presented by the Culebra Range a more than 1.000 foot-tall mountain; it was clearly essential to use locks but for two long years de Lesseps failed to make this decision. Further capital was raised on the markets, which remained very confident: seven share issues between 1882 and 1888. Already in 1886, the government had asked Armand Rousseau (an engineer and Councillor of State) to start an enquiry which came to a single conclusion: the project was flawed and the company could not be saved; the project must be changed to include locks.

A CANAL WITHOUT LOCKS? EIFFEL IS SUMMONED

As early as 1887 the company had already sunk 1400 million francs into the project but only half of the canal had been dug. Toward the end of 1887, de Lesseps finally asked Gustave Eiffel to help, and he agreed: he restructured the plans completely and included locks. There would be additional costs and delays. This meant that de Lesseps needed still more capital and it was vital not to alarm the investors. Those in charge of the Company decided to use their influence on politicians and the public. Four million francs were 'distributed' to a group of politicians and journalists to help sway public opinion. This manipulation was organized by Cornelius Herz, and the events inspired Emile Zola to write his novel *Money*. Emile de Girardin, a well-known journalist, joined the Company board, despite the fact that he had written highly critical articles in the newspaper *La Presse* on the project and the Company's strategy. The `chequards´ (the people who cashed the checks paid out as bribes) as they were thereafter known, received further money for promoting the project and supporting it.

On 9th June 1888 de Lesseps obtained authorization from the Chamber of Deputies to launch a final issue of 2 million bonds, but it was too late. On 4th February 1889, the Company was put into liquidation. The result was a serious Parisian, French and international scandal. It has been estimated that around a million small bond and shareholders were swindled: some lost everything and the portfolios of others were badly hit. Faced with this débâcle, Loubet's government began by trying to cover up the affair. Despite their efforts, the scandal broke, however, and became public knowledge, damaging the reputation of many politicians. All work on the project was stopped. In 1891 an official inquiry was opened on the company's administrators. The following year Edouard Drumont's newspaper, *La Libre Parole*, openly denounced the liberal spending of de Lesseps' son Charles, and the administrators were prosecuted. Baron Jacques Reinach died in suspicious circumstances and Cornelius Herz fled to London. Loubet's government refused to open an inquest into Reinach's death and was ousted from office. The new Minister of Finance in Alexander Ribot's cabinet, Maurice Rouvier, was forced to resign as Reinach's check stubs were soon traced to him amongst many others. On 16th December 1892 Charles de Lesseps was arrested and within days there were calls for his parliamentary immunity to be lifted. During the month of September 1893, Ferdinand de Lesseps and his son Charles were sentenced to five months in prison and given heavy fines, Gustave Eiffel to two years in prison and a fine of 20,000 francs, and two of the Company officials were also fined and imprisoned. But the decision of the court was overturned and the end result was that only a minister and one accomplice were sent to prison; Charles de Lesseps received one year's sentence but was released in September 1893. His father, who had become senile, died the following year. The legal investigations continued up until the end of the century.

THE INAUGURATION OF THE CANAL TWO DAYS AFTER THE START OF THE FIRST WORLD WAR

Nonetheless, the need to build the canal was becoming more and more urgent as international trade was continuing to develop in the *Belle Epoque,* and in 1893 the project was relaunched. Columbia signed a new contract with France to restart construction. A New Canal Company was created and work began again in 1894; but it was difficult to raise the necessary funds, especially after the terrible scandal which had shaken the French stock exchange. The American government was convinced that a canal linking the oceans could play a strategic role for the country. Theodore Roosevelt's administration renegotiated the Clayton-Bulwer treaty, and replaced it with the Hay-Pauncefote agreement of November 1901 and in December, the French government and shareholders of the New Company authorized the sale of shares to the United States. On 29th June 1902, the American Congress authorized the purchase of the shares for $40 million, instead of the $109 million asked; the transaction took place on 22th April 1904. However there was strong opposition on the part of Colombian politicians who wanted Columbia to own the canal, and a very powerful lobby mobilized in parliament in favour of this position. Finally on 22th January 1903, under the Hay-Héran treaty, the New Canal Company transferred all its rights to the United States, and ceded its construction and management rights to Washington together with a strip of land extending three miles on either side of the canal. The Colombian parliament viewed this as territorial infringement. The United States put maximum pressure on Columbia: two American naval vessels were sent into Colombian territorial waters and a `spontaneous rebellion´ in the Panama region was triggered by a declaration of Panamanian independence. This new Republic was immediately recognized by the United States and it became a protectorate but, most importantly, the sovereignty of the canal zone belonged to them. In fact, the Republic of Panama was `excluded from exercising such sovereign rights, powers or authority′ according to the Hay-Bunau-Varilla treaty signed in New York on 18th November, 1903. The press dubbed it `a treaty sealed with ignominy′.

The work started anew, but with a very strict health protocol for the personnel and with the use of much heavy machinery. The total cost was $387 million, mainly financed by the American government: this was three times the amount estimated in 1880. On 10th October 1913, from nearly 2000 miles away, the American President Thomas Woodrow Wilson pressed a button and exploded twenty tons of dynamite thus destroying the last dam at Gamboa which separated the waters of the two oceans. The official inauguration date, 3rd August 1914, came two days after Europe had been thrown into the turmoil of total war which according to the politicians, generals and ambassadors would be of brief duration.

ANOTHER CANAL?

In 1977, the Torrijos-Carter treaty created the Panama Canal Commission to replace the old Company and in 1999 the United States ceded the canal back to the Republic of Panama. Meanwhile millions of miles of ocean navigation have been avoided: for example a ship leaving San Francisco and going through the straits of Magellan to get to New York covers nearly 14,000 miles; if it passes through the canal the voyage is reduced to 6,000 miles. Almost a million ships have used the canal and paid the toll ($2.50/ ton for a cargo ship and a little more than $2/ton for a ship without cargo). But the competition for transport between the Asia-Indian Ocean, India-Europe and Asia-Panama-Europe routes, is fierce – the Pacific crossing and in particular the increasing size of the ships is adversely affecting the Panama canal which was only designed to take vessels of up to 300,000 tons of merchandise and under 980 feet in length. Early September 2007, some big works for the construction of another canal were launched; this would speed up the passage of very large ships by 2014. The current canal only takes nine hours to navigate in theory but from sixteen to twenty hours in practice, taking the wait for access into account.

LEVI STRAUSS, `BLEU DE GÊNES`, JEANS AND DENIM

In 2003 the Levi Strauss Company in San Francisco announced the closure of its last four factories located on the North American continent – one in Texas, the other three in Canada. The last four factories in Europe were hit by the same news – one in France and three in Belgium. The American company had laid off more than 20,000 employees in America and Europe since 1997. In an ironic twist of fate, the last announcement coincided with the 150th anniversary of the business, which had started at the time of the conquest of the American West, and gone on to clothe everyone from the workers of great industrial enterprises to weekend do-it-yourself fans, demonstrating students and casual chic fashionistas: a legend!

LEOB STRAUSS, AND `BLEU DE GÊNES`

Leob Strauss was born in Bavaria in 1829. In 1847, he left Germany with his mother and two sisters to join a half brother who was managing a small unbranded clothing shop in New York. As soon as he turned eighteen, he decided to change his name to Levi Strauss and in 1853 he became an American citizen. At the age of 24 he left for San Francisco to open a subsidiary of the small New York shop and to take advantage of gold fever. Legend has it that on his arrival a gold seeker suggested that he should not sell material for tents, as he had intended, but use the fabric to make very hard-wearing trousers, which were much in demand from the miners. The technical name for this fabric at the time was `serge de

Nîmes´, because originally it was made in France, but later it was produced in Britain.

This is the origin of the `denim´, which was known in France before the 17th century, but at that time it was made from silk and only later from cotton. In fact it goes back even further: sailors from Genoa had for a long time been wearing trousers that were blue in color, very hard-wearing, and had flaired bottoms so they would dry more quickly when wet. Later these were adopted by many of the merchant marines and navies in Europe. From the 16th century, this material was also produced in Lancashire, but kept the name of `bleu de Gênes´ (blue of Genoa), from where the term `blue jeans´ later came. The true difference between denim and jeans is that the color of the thread used in their production differs: blue and white for denim, for jeans a single color.

THE IDEA OF STUDS AND METAL BUTTONS

Levi Strauss' trousers were a great success and were worn by the adventurers, farmers, miners and cowboys who all took part in the conquest of the West. But he wanted to make the trousers even more hard-wearing. In Reno, the tailor Jacob Davis, one of the company's clients, employed a man who had the idea of putting studs on the trousers to reinforce them. Jacob Davis wrote to Strauss to suggest the idea to him and especially to obtain the patent, which he did in May 1873. Production began on this new type of clothing the same year, but the exact date is uncertain because all the early records of Levi Strauss & Co were lost during the San Francisco earthquake and fire of 1906. Nearly all the denim was supplied by the Amoskea factory in Manchester, New Hampshire. In 1890 the `501´ line was invented, to reinforce their identity.

In 1891, the patent expired and numerous other producers began to copy the style. This created problems for the business, so they tried to diversify into other types of clothing. Levi Strauss died in 1902 at the age of 73, but his four nephews, Jacob, Louis, Abraham and Sigmund Stern continued to manage the large business with care, and in particular to rebuild it after the events of 1906 in San Francisco. The next year Jacob Davis sold his share of the capital.

WESTERNS, THE WAR AND YOUNG PEOPLE POPULARIZE JEANS

From 1930 onwards many Western films portrayed honest cowboys, hardworking and in love with their wives and girlfriends, all dressed in jeans; John Wayne and Gary Cooper are amongst the best known actors of this genre. And it was Hollywood too which created the « stone wash » process to make new jeans look old. Western Wear consultant Nudie Cohen invented the process in 1960: new jeans are washed with pumice stones to abrade the fabric and give it a worn, lived in look. More recently, because stone washing is time consuming and therefore expensive, the same results have been achieved using increased amounts of enzymes in the washing process. During the Second World War, GIs all carried their own blue jeans in their personal luggage when they were sent to the different military fronts to fight. From the 1950s the company began to distribute its products throughout America. With the boom in American society, jeans became not only work clothing, but also casual wear, as illustrated by James Dean in *Rebel without a Cause*. The jeans market was expanding rapidly: in 1971 Levi Strauss & Co turnover was a billion dollars, and this was doubled by 1979. The company started making large acquisitions at the end of the 1970s, but with only a small degree of success. In 1984 they took a strategic decision to concentrate on their traditional core business. International competition and rising production costs in the western world compared with those of developing countries obliged LS&Co to adapt and transfer their production abroad. This was their most recent decision, followed shortly by the opening of Levi's shops aimed solely at women.

THE ROCKEFELLER SAGA:
THE ARCHETYPE OF WASP CAPITALISM

John D. Rockefeller was the founder of a dynasty that bears his name and perfectly embodies unbridled capitalism at the end of the 19th century. Although the name of Rockefeller was synonymous with the rapaciousness of trusts in Theodore Roosevelt's era (not to be confused with Franklin Delano Roosevelt, the creator of the New Deal and US President during the Second World War), it has lost some of its more negative connotations with time, thanks to the organization of charitable foundations, activities in the property sector in the center of New York and businesses which are increasingly rarely connected with the world of oil. The biography of this renowned capitalist is closely linked with the story of American economic history for the greater part of a century.

THE CREATION OF STANDARD OIL

John was the son of a traveling salesman. He settled in Cleveland, became the accountant in a grocery firm, and then managed a food wholesalers. He decided to go into the oil refinery business in 1865, and within fifteen years had built the Standard Oil empire, which in 1879 controlled 90% of American refineries. His strength lay in his ability to negotiate extremely advantageous transport contracts with small rail companies in exchange for large volumes of freight; his competitors, on the other hand, were offered prohibitive tariffs, a practice suggestive of collusion. Furthermore, Standard Oil carried out dumping campaigns in order to

326 / THE ROCKEFELLER SAGA: THE ARCHETYPE OF WASP CAPITALISM

wipe out competition and practiced systematic commercial espionage. In 1882 Rockefeller united all his companies under one trust; this was a merger in disguise, a practice forbidden by law because the companies were operating in different states. In truth he created a complete monopoly. This move was universally and loudly criticized, and hostility to the trust became increasingly strong – Standard Oil was forced to move its headquarters from Ohio to New Jersey, a more flexible state that was more welcoming to large companies. A furious campaign was launched against Rockefeller by Ida Tarbell, the daughter of a small oil producer who had been ruined. Compelled by the strength of public opinion, the State was obliged to apply Sherman's Law of 1890, and forbid the monopoly. But it was only in 1911 that the Supreme Court backed the order to dissolve Standard Oil, which was divided into several small, regional companies.

A PERSONAL FORTUNE WORTH A BILLION DOLLARS

Sometime later, Rockefeller left the stage, and his son and authorized representatives took over management of the companies. He retired with a personal fortune of more than a billion dollars – one of the most hated and admired men in the United States. However he was also a profoundly religious man of the Baptist faith; for a long time he had been donating 10% of his revenue to charitable and philanthropic works. He increased these activities from the end of the century up until his death and in 1934 the total of his gifts reached the enormous sum of $540 million. The principal beneficiaries were the Rockefeller Institute for Medical Research (which was founded in 1901 and became a university in 1965), the Rockefeller Foundation, the University of Chicago and the Laura Spellman Rockefeller Memorial Fund, created in memory of his wife. With his great rival, Andrew Carnegie, he created the truly American tradition for philanthropy amongst rich businessmen: the fruits of pure and simple capitalism.

His son, John D. Rockefeller junior, found it difficult to step into his father's shoes. He got off to a bad start with a notorious incident: in Colorado the armed guards employed by the numerous companies he controlled attacked a camp of striking miners with a machine gun, killing 30 people including women and children. He kept up a fierce struggle against trade unions, but, discouraged by his experiences in industry, he turned to philanthropy and even built an interdenominational church in Riverside, near Columbia University in New York. He financed the building of the Cloisters in northern Manhattan (made from stones of a real cloister transported from France); he financed the construction of the Rockefeller Center in New York, but refused to support Roosevelt's reforms under the New Deal, without directly opposing them. A patron who was more and more isolated in the worlds of business and politics (despite the fact his sympathies were Republican), he took advantage of his fortune to make his dreams of being one of the world's greatest philanthropists come true.

THE CHICAGO SLAUGHTERHOUSES INSPIRE HENRY FORD

It is a general assumption that Henry Ford invented the assembly line for the manufacture of his cars – yet another of his myriad ideas. In fact, he applied (as he himself said and wrote on several occasions) the work methods that he had observed in the slaughterhouses on a visit to Chicago. Except that in Chicago they took the animal's carcass apart, whilst in the Ford factories they put the car together.

THE RAILWAYS AND WIRE HELPED CREATE THE GREAT ABATTOIRS

At the end of the American War of Independence, European capital flooded into the United States, attracted by the perspective of economic development and above all by the rail network, of which Chicago became the main hub. Between 1868 and 1873, 28,000 miles of new lines were built and, after the financial crisis of 1873, in the course of the next decade the railway companies added a further 70,000 miles of line to the 93,000 already in existence. The price of transport dropped sharply, which allowed cereals and animals to be transported over long distances. The Chicago Union Stockyard was created around 1865, specializing in raising stock (particularly cattle and pigs) in high density, in large stockyards. They were raised *in situ* in warm weather and then sent to the slaughter houses, where their carcasses were prepared for storage during the cold weather. A large number of employees were needed to handle the thousands of animals. The first workers were Irish immigrants who had finished building the Illinois & Michigan Canal; they were followed by German immigrants, and later, during the 1890s, by men from Eastern Europe and by Italians.

GREAT ADVANCES IN TECHNIQUE

Around 1872 refrigerated rooms came into existence, then metal binder was invented in 1873 by Locke and the twine binder in 1879 by Appleby. The construction of refrigerated ships also allowed for the export of meat and, in 1873, 55,000 tons of meat arrived in the French port of Le Havre, transported in the refrigerated ship the *Paraguay*. In 1882 the railways began carrying refrigerated rolling stock.

All these inventions helped to centralize stock raising and its slaughter on an industrial scale. Chicago became the largest center of meat production in the country; the city and its region produced 82% of the national total. The introduction of the refrigerated line removed the limitations on numbers slaughtered and the carcasses were able to circulate on large production lines, where workers specialized in particular cuts or butchery techniques (dissecting the carcass, skinning and so on). It was this principle of working in a factory line that Ford applied 30 years later, a technological innovation which was called Fordism. More than 25,000 workers were employed in the reception and sorting of the animals arriving from the great prairies, another 25,000 worked on the lines, the whole process imparting a strong smell which only the northern winds blowing through Chicago (the 'windy city') could disperse. During the most prosperous era of the slaughterhouses, the industry occupied 475 acres, with more than 50 miles of roads and 130 miles of railways on site and an average of more than 16 million carcasses leaving the abattoirs every year.

The area attracted writers: Upton Sinclair wrote his novel *The Jungle*, the poet Carl Sandburg described the site in his poem, *Chicago*, which he called `The Hog Butcher for the world´, Brecht wrote *Saint Joan of the Stockyards* and the Edison Manufacturing Company even had James White make a short film there, in July 1897, to show the arrival of the sheep in the railway wagons and the techniques of the stockyards.

ROADS AND REFRIGERATED TRUCKS CONTRIBUTE TO THE DECLINE OF THE CHICAGO STOCKYARDS

After the Second World War, the improvement of the road network in the United States and a large availability of refrigerated trucks began to make a dent in the supremacy of Chicago, a great metropolis which was becoming more and more urbanized. There was a move toward raising stock near the large centers of cereal production, setting up slaughterhouses of smaller dimensions and transporting the final product by refrigerated truck. In 1955 Wilson and Company were the first to leave Chicago, followed by many others. The last to close was the old company of Chicago Union, which folded on 31st July 1971, about 100 years after it was created – one of the greatest American companies in the food sector, which processed more than a billion animals in the course of its existence.

THE GREAT DEPRESSION OF 1873-96:
THE FIRST GLOBAL CRISIS

Many economic historians have compared the international crisis that began in Asia in 1997 with the first worldwide crisis which began in 1873 and had well documented consequences: a period of depression that lasted 23 years, up until the beginning of the *Belle Epoque* or Edwardian era.

The crash began with the stock exchange in Vienna plunging, and rapidly spread to other continental financial centers, hitting the New York Stock Exchange and forcing it to close down for ten days. It destabilized vulnerable financial sectors and currencies throughout almost all Asia, particularly those tied to silver. For 23 years the price of raw materials and manufactured products fell and stock exchanges everywhere remained depressed.

THE CAUSE: FRENCH GOLD?

In 1870, Prussian troops inflicted a serious defeat on France; the treaty of Frankfurt obliged Paris to pay 5 billion francs, or 23% of the gross domestic product of the country. These heavy reparations started a period of deflation in France and a period of exceptional growth in Germany and Austria, which benefited from the monetary effect of the damages, from the fall in competitiveness from French exports and from the inflationary effect fuelled by the dropping of bimetallism, even though this in fact failed.

Plentiful liquidity encouraged speculation on the stock exchange, in property and in agricultural land. This gave rise to a new social class known as the *Milliarden-Bauern* - peasant farmers who sold their lands at exorbitant prices. Large amounts of capital were exported also, to finance the development of railways and developing industries in Europe and the United States, which was enjoying a period of rapid growth. But at this point, Germany made a fatal mistake: now that it held French gold, it decided to abandon bimetallism. However, the government failed to withdraw all the silver thalers immediately. There was too much liquidity and this fuelled speculation; the effect of this choice on the price of silver was catastrophic: parity of 15.5oz of silver against 1oz of gold was destroyed at a stroke and the price of silver plunged.

In February 1873 a serious scandal broke out in Vienna: the government was accused of giving preference to certain railway concessions. Speculators became seriously worried, but there remained a glimmer of hope: the Viennese Universal Exhibition, which it was hoped would relaunch the real economy. But the exhibition was a great disappointment and stock prices plummeted between 5th and 6th May; the Stock Exchange placed a moratorium on all settlements until 15th May, the National Bank and merchant banks created a guarantee fund. Nonetheless, the crash spread rapidly and affected German, Italian, Dutch and Belgian stock exchanges.

THE CRISIS CROSSES THE ATLANTIC

Finance, industry and the railway companies in the New World were mostly financed by European investors and speculators, who were now hard hit by the crisis on the Old World stock exchanges. They were obliged to close their purchasing positions on the American stock exchanges and sources of finance dried up. The collapse of the Crédit Mobilier de Paris in 1871, a French joint-stock bank, had already left serious scars and made international financiers everywhere more cautious.

The finance house Jay Cooke of Philadelphia was the first to fall on 18th September. Prices plummeted on the New York Stock Exchange; it was forced to close its doors for ten days – 5000 business firms and 57 brokerage firms closed permanently. The New Orleans and Pittsburgh Exchanges closed for two months! Cooke

had been the main buyer and distributor (with much sharp practice) of the Northern Pacific Rail Road Company's bonds, the
latter was looking for fresh capital. The early harvest on the
prairies meant that banks had to find enough liquidity to finance
the payments to farmers; credit conditions were very tight and the
New York banks were heavily committed to financing the small
Midwest agricultural banks.

The stock exchange crash cost investors and European speculators at least $600 million, despite the fact that the New York banks
tried to stabilize the situation by pooling part of their reserves. For
the first time a crisis on one continent quickly spread to others. It
was the beginning of the Great Depression which lasted over
twenty years and had repercussions throughout the world.

BIMETALLISM ABANDONED IN THE WESTERN WORLD

The Scandinavian countries and Holland rapidly followed in
Germany's footsteps; in 1878 the members of the Latin Union
(France, Belgium, Switzerland , Italy and Greece) abandoned
bimetallism. The price of gold rose due to demand and consequent
scarcity; indeed, after the discovery of gold in California in 1848,
there were no further major discoveries until 1886 in South
Africa. On the other hand the price of silver plunged – in twenty
years it fell from five shillings an ounce to less than three. This
crisis hit the Asian economies especially hard, as their monetary
systems were based on the silver standard. China, Hong Kong,
Japan, India and the other large countries of the region (except for
the Philippines and Batavia, which were linked to the gold standard), all experienced steady devaluation. This, however, allowed
them to export more and more raw materials and to lower their
prices (another factor causing deflation). A growing number of
countries abandoned silver as a standard and switched to gold
before the end of the century.

BUT DEFLATION IS ALSO FUELLED BY TECHNOLOGICAL PROGRESS

The opening up of the great cereal plains in the United States,
thanks to investment in railroads and higher seed yields, brought

down the price of cereals on world markets. Moreover, the progress in the building of bulk carrier vessels (with new motors which were more powerful and much faster) considerably reduced the costs of freight. The opening of the Suez Canal in 1869, brought down the cost of transport between Asia and Europe, because it saved 4,000 miles of navigation.

The invention of wire (Locke's metal binder in 1873) made it possible to centralize stock, which was less expensive, and to sort them into a limited geographical area, thus encouraging stock raising. With the introduction of refrigerated ships, the amount of meat destined for Europe rose steadily, and prices dropped accordingly. Europe needed cheap protein. Furthermore, great progress was being made in the iron and steel industries; until 1879 Bessemer converters and the Siemens-Martin process could only use non-phosphorus minerals (available mainly in Sweden and Spain). However, with the introduction of the Thomas process, it was possible to use any type of mineral and so the expansion of the German metal industry was launched. The cost of basic goods and manufactured items fell, because demand was weak and supply was increasing dramatically.

PROTECTIONISM AGAIN AND THE BIRTH OF TRUSTS

When prices fall, governments attempt to protect their production and manufacturers seek to avoid further price declines. After a period when many countries signed bilateral agreements to limit and above all reduce customs duties, a backlash was triggered by deflation. This started in 1877 when Austria withdrew from nearly all international trading treaties. The United States also wanted to protect their customs' revenue, at a time when income tax was plunging. Furthermore, businesses were trying to defend their margins: as a result, trusts were formed and alliances made (more or less secretly) to maintain prices artificially. Some companies tried to create true monopolies (either in production and/or distribution), whilst certain sectors were hit hard by the dumping practiced by some producers and exporting countries. Sugar producers in Asia (Java especially), were hit by competition from European sugar beet producers who had abandoned the production of cereals in the face of American competition; coffee plantations in Indonesia were ruined by the new Brazilian competition; the crash of the Oriental Bank Corporation was the result of all these reversals in the new geographical distribution of production.

THE US ECONOMIC CRISIS OF 1893 FUELS INDUSTRIAL STRIFE AT PULLMAN'S

The history of American railroads has often been marked by strikes and violent demonstrations, the first of which took place in 1877 and stopped all trains between the nerve center of Chicago and the east and the west of the country for several weeks. But the biggest strike – the Pullman Strike – took place in 1894. Its origins are well known: in 1893 the serious international economic crisis turned into a generalized panic on all stock markets and the price of raw materials dropped through the floor, with catastrophic results for the economic situation. Small investors queued in front of banks to withdraw their dollar holdings and buy gold, seen as the last refuge in terms of security. Unemployment soared, and the flow of commerce dried up, with a corresponding reduction in the number of rail passengers and freight.

THE SILVER CRASH AND BLACK FRIDAY

In 1890 the President of the United States, Benjamin Harrison, signed the Sherman Silver Purchase Act, which had been passed by Congress. The Treasury was therefore obliged to buy 4.5 million ounces of silver each month (roughly the country's monthly production) and exchange it for gold. The aim of this law was to help American silver mines, which could not compete with the international mining industry. In addition many European countries had abandoned bimetallism and chosen gold as their monetary standard. The price of silver in the United States went from 0.84¢ to $1.50 an ounce and fuelled a certain amount of speculation. But opposition continued to mount against the Sherman Act: international investors feared a large fall in value of the dollar. The international financial situation was also very fragile, but it was the situation on the American financial markets which was the most worrying. On 20th February 1893 a large railroad company, the Philadelphia and Reading Railroad was declared bankrupt: the liabilities amounted to $18 million against $100,000 of realizable assets. The money crisis had other victims – most companies wanted to pay their employees with silver certificates, but the workers refused and went on strike. On 5th May (Black Friday), the shares of the large National Cordage Trust plummeted on Wall Street and this triggered sales in other shares – the most serious panic the United States had experienced up until then. Later, of course, in the twentieth century, there would be even greater moments of panic.

Most of the selling was done by international investors who no longer had confidence in the dollar, which was too closely linked to silver. Furthermore, the gold reserves of the Treasury were beginning to fall because of foreign and national investors cashing in silver in order to buy gold. In July, Grover Cleveland, the new President of the United States who had moved into the White House at the beginning of March, asked Congress to suspend the Sherman Act, which took place on 28th August. The effect on the price of silver was dramatic: already down to 83¢, it fell further to 62¢ an ounce. Obviously many mines, particularly those in Colorado, and refineries, had to go into liquidation. The repercussions of the industrial and financial crises were catastrophic – a huge drop in prices on Wall Street and in the price of many industrial and agricultural raw materials. At the end of 1893 there were more than 15,000 bankruptcies, 642 banks had shut down, around 20% of American workers had lost their jobs and the international economic situation had seriously deteriorated. This was the crisis behind the bitter strike in the Pullman factories.

GEORGE PULLMAN, PULLMAN TOWN AND THE GREAT STRIKE OF 1894

George Pullman[1] was the man behind a new type of wagon for the railroads – the Pullman sleeper wagon, intended for overnight journeys and long distance travel in great comfort. In the suburbs of Chicago, he even built a town which bore his name; but he was no philanthropist – the housing was rented to the workers, as were the shops, the theaters and even the church.

The crisis which hit America had serious consequences for the Pullman Palace Car Works – the railroad companies suspended all investment. Pullman decided to reduce the number of workers from 5500 to 3300 and those who managed to keep their job suffered a 25% reduction in wages. However, there was no reciprocal lowering of price in food and rents in the town which lodged the workers. These conditions were considered unacceptable and a meeting took place between Pullman and his employees, but without a satisfactory result. The next day three of the workers who had participated in the negotiations were fired. The following day (11th May), a general strike was declared at Pullman's. During April the workers had joined a powerful trades' union called the American Railway Union (ARU). The union asked for further meetings with Pullman to negotiate five compromise propositions but met with refusal. On 21st June the ARU delegates decided to boycott all rail trains which included Pullman cars from 26th June onwards. The strike was well supported: 50,000 participants paralyzed the transport system throughout the whole network. 27 states were affected and the strikers seemed to be winning,

---

1. George Pullman (1831 – 1897) left school at fourteen. When he arrived in Chicago he noticed that the streets were in a very bad state and suggested a technique which his father had already developed during the widening of the Eire canal. It consisted of raising and consolidating each block of houses, and with two associates he applied the method to one block. Then between 1860 and 1863 he worked as a gold merchant in Colorado. He invested profits in developing the Pullman sleeper wagon which cost five times as much as those of his competitors. It was then that he had a marketing stroke of genius – he offered to transport the remains of President Abraham Lincoln from Washington to Springfield. He then started producing his wagons in a factory he built on Lake Calumet, in the Chicago suburbs. He built a town for his workers, where he rented out all the buildings (hotels, libraries and churches included). The rent was deducted directly from his employees' wages, as well as food purchases. After the dramatic outcome of the strike, the workers' hatred of Pullman lasted a long time. The remains of the entrepreneur lie in the cemetery at Graceland, in a vault buried under several tons of reinforced concrete to protect it from attempts at vandalism.

especially in the Chicago region, which was the heart of the American railway system. However on 29th June, after a visit from Eugene Debs, the president of the ARU, to the town of Blue Island in Illinois, an incident broke out and the strikers derailed a locomotive and destroyed the rails. This gave Judge Onley, the Attorney General, the ideal opportunity to take legal action against the strike. An injunction was signed on 2nd July and troops were called in. Their presence was deemed unacceptable by the strikers and it transformed a peaceful strike into violent demonstrations. Union officials were unable to intervene due to the injunction. The Governor of Illinois and the Mayor of Chicago called for the troops to be withdrawn, but the President of the United States, Grover Cleveland, authorized the sending of further Federal troops. On 6th July, the violence reached its peak: 6000 demonstrators destroyed 700 wagons and caused damage totaling $340,000 to the South Chicago Panhandle Company. The following day, after attacks on National Guard troops, the soldiers fired on the crowd, killing and wounding people. On 7th July, Union president Debs and other union officials were arrested. On 12th July, the American Federation of Labor decided that it could not support the ARU's actions, and finally on 2nd August the Pullman factories were reopened. Those held largely responsible for the union's action were not rehired and those who went back to work had to sign 'yellow dog contracts', in which they undertook not to join a union on pain of losing their job.

Thus the strike which had gone down in the economic, social and trade unions' history of the United States came to an end, but it had raised questions about strikes on the national railroads and transport in general and on the use of Federal troops against strikers. Meanwhile the economic situation remained very unstable for the following two years, and it was only after 1897 that the economy once again took off.

THE MYSTERY OF DIAMONDS: FROM ALEXANDER THE GREAT TO THE DE BEERS LEGEND

Diamonds have always been surrounded with a halo of mystery and charm and have the privilege of being `a girl's best friend´ (as Marilyn Monroe famously sang in *Gentlemen Prefer Blondes*). Legend has it that Alexander the Great, when marching to India, heard talk of a great pit filled with diamonds in a place protected by snakes, which struck down any intruder who dared to look at them. The Macedonian suggested to his soldiers that they use mirrors to avoid these evil guardians. Then he had the men throw sheep into the pit whilst carefully avoiding the snakes' gaze; the diamonds stuck to the sheep's wool and vultures devoured their bodies. The soldiers then simply had to shoot the vultures with their arrows in order to recover the precious stones.

Of course the legend of Alexander is a metaphor which reminds us of the difficulty, and the occasional unexpected ease, with which diamonds can be found: it takes a ton of rock to produce 0.5 to 2 carats of raw diamond and on average 50% is lost in cutting and cleaning to obtain the final product. These gems have always stirred desires and passions, and provoked battles and even wars between adventurers and political regimes, over the control of an industry with a turnover of $55 to $60 billion a year.

CANADA: A NEW ELDORADO

When one thinks of the diamond extracting industry, Botswana, South Africa and more recently Russia spring to mind.

Canada is the latest addition to this list. Over the last ten years the discovery of huge mines in Canada has provoked a major upset in the structure of the world market. Diamond fever in the northern regions of the country has attracted hoards of prospectors, geologists and mining engineers and a great deal of international capital. Between ten fruitless explorations and many successes, in very difficult climatic conditions, these investments have managed to raise Canadian production to the level of the main traditional producing countries. It is following the same pattern as West Africa at the end of the 19th century, when diamonds were prospected for in the alluvial deposits of rivers.

THE STORY OF DE BEERS AND THE *KAFFIRS*

In 1866, diamond-mining began in the region of Kimberly, South Africa, when the De Beers brothers, owners of a very large farm, decided to sell their land for £6300 to some prospectors who, by an enormous stroke of luck, came upon very rich deposits. Helped by the Rothschild Bank, Cecil John Rhodes, who had already participated in financing the railway between the Cape and Kimberly, succeeded in merging his company with that of his competitor Barney Barnato, forming the large group of De Beers Consolidated Mines. The black miners who worked in the mines were called *kaffirs* (Arabic for 'infidel'). They lived in camps surrounded by fences to stop the precious stones being smuggled out and their wages were around double what they could have earned as laborers and field workers on the farms. The word *kaffir* is also used on the London Stock Exchange for South African mining shares.

The Boer War (between the British Empire and the South African Boers) stabilized the diamond situation in South Africa. This was the beginning of a golden era for the De Beers' company which, for over a century, would retain the monopoly in producing and commercializing diamonds in the country, with singular success. Through 'on sight' sales, the company distributed its production and also that of other large producers which it had bought out. Every five weeks, these sales are organized at Charter House, in London, where 125 hand-picked diamond dealers are invited. They are shown boxes with a selection of diamonds with a sale price fixed in advance. The selling technique of `take it or leave it´ is applied, but the diamond dealer who refuses will never be invited to the next sale. From London, the rough diamonds are sent to the large cutting centers: Antwerp (which deals with about three quarters of world volume), India, Israel, New York and, in recent years, China. After that they are distributed amongst the commercial centers – Antwerp once again, Amsterdam, London, New York, Tokyo, Hong Kong and lately Dubai, which has even set up an exchange for rough diamonds.

However, for several years now, the diamond trade has been disrupted by the supply coming from countries which are victims of civil war: more than 5% of rough diamonds are placed on the market illegally. The smugglers export stones mainly from Botswana ($1.8 billion exported, of which a large proportion is illegal), from Angola ($600 million over 27 years of war), from the Democratic Republic of the Congo ($120 million over four years of war), from Sierra Leone ($50 million during nineteen years of war) – and the list goes on.

DE BEERS MANAGES TO STABILIZE THE MARKET

The Russian agency Alrosa which produces and markets 99% of Russian diamonds, most of which come from the Republic of Sakha (Yakutia, eastern Siberia), signed an agreement with De Beers to sell them $800 million worth of rough diamonds a year, a fifth of its total production. The agreement involves the renewal of the previous contract which expired 31 December 2001 and which had been preceded by very sensitive negotiations. In January 2001, De Beers together with LVMH, created a company whose aim was to market the gems under the De Beers label. But there were signs that the market was changing and finding a new equilibrium, reminiscent of the situation at the beginning of the 16th century. Before this period, Venice held the European monopoly for diamonds, which mainly came from India. These were sent on to be cut in Bruges, then some were returned to Venice to be distributed. But the steady silting up of the port of Bruges, combined with the possibility of sailing to the Indian Ocean around the Cape changed the situation. Antwerp became the new center for cutting and distribution; the diamond dealers changed their cutting techniques considerably and created new shapes and forms. From the 18th century Amsterdam became the center of delivery and distribution for rough diamonds. Cutting was divided between Antwerp and Amsterdam. The latter city was taking full advantage of the end of the war against Spain and the Wars of Religion, which brought an influx of Jews, cutters and small diamond merchants. In practice, the diamonds cut in Antwerp were of a lesser quality; the best quality merchandise was cut in Amsterdam. Obviously the Second World War had a disastrous impact on the diamond business in the two ports: a large percentage of the Jewish population had to flee to London and New York, others died in Nazi concentration camps. After the war Antwerp recovered its position and specialized in cutting gems of a lower value, which was now possible through technological progress, and it also carries out research on and analysis of gemstones.

THE PANIC OF 1907 AND THE BIRTH
OF THE FED

The world was enjoying a golden period. It was the start of a new century, the Belle Epoque, and with investment booming and international stock exchanges registering record levels the champagne was flowing at the tables of financiers and the rich. In Paris the comfortably-off middle classes were flirting with the can-can, in Vienna were feasting in the heady decadence of what, unknown to them, would prove to be the final years of the Austro-Hungarian Empire, in Berlin were cashing in the profits from the triumphal march of German industry and in London were basking in the glory of an empire that covered a third of the earth's surface, while in the casinos of all Europe Russian *rentiers* were squandering their fortunes at the roulette tables. Even the economic and social conditions of the working class were becoming more tolerable with the general improvement in diet, housing and hygiene. America attracted millions of Italian and Polish immigrants and once again the Irish flocked there in steady numbers, in search of fortune. Furthermore there were not too many political tensions worldwide. But could it last?

THE SAN FRANCISCO EARTHQUAKE OF 1906

The American financial market was running like clockwork; throughout the year the New York markets had sufficient liquidity. Traditionally at the beginning of Autumn, this cash was transferred to banks in the mid-West to finance the grain companies which had to pay for the farmers' harvests. After that the cash would return to the banks and large financial markets on the east coast. It was also a general tendency for interest rates to undergo a certain amount of strain during the autumn.

However, the great San Francisco earthquake and consequent fire of 8th April 1906 created flow problems on the gold market. This was due to the fact that it was British insurance companies which largely paid for the damage; they represented about 40% of the insurance market in San Francisco. Companies paid the heavy bills in gold and around 14% of British gold reserves were sent to the United States. Moreover, the US Treasury Secretary considered liquidity on the gold market to be insufficient, and took steps to attract gold into the country. The British pound was under very heavy pressure and the Bank of England tried by every possible means to rebuild the stocks of gold in the London banking vaults. It raised its discount rate from 3.5% to 6% between the months of September and October 1906. Gold returned to Britain (a sum equivalent to the exchange value of $30 million at the time), but the exchange rate discouraged British and European banks from financing the operations of American banks, which had to face a situation of squeezed liquidity. Between February and November 1907, the Dow Jones lost 40% of its value.

HEAVY SPECULATION ON THE COPPER MARKET

Around mid-August 1907, the American economic situation was particularly precarious: the business climate was in recession, share prices were suffering and liquidity on the monetary market was very low, with interest rates under pressure to rise. However, in October, Augustus Heinz, president of the Mercantile National Bank of New York, started speculating heavily on shares in the United Copper Company. His intention was to create a squeeze on the mining company's stock; in fact, he believed that a number of speculators had sold stock short. He bought a substantial amount, even buying on credit, because he hoped to force the shorts to buy back at a much higher price. On 14th October, the UCC stock price rose from $39 to $60 in just a few minutes, before the opening of the stock exchange. Two days later the price fell to $10 because the sellers had not sold short and held shares they had agreed to deliver! The brokerage house belonging to Heinz's brother was forced to cease trading and rumors about a major financial disaster for the Heinz brothers spread rapidly. This operation would not have had such serious consequences if the crisis had not already been brewing on the stock exchange, which, since the beginning of summer, had been experiencing a deep-seated sense of unease. The Mercantile Bank's clients rushed to withdraw their money. Heinz resigned from the presidency of the bank, under pressure from the market. The New York Clearing House supported the Mercantile, as the situation there seemed quite healthy. But the Clearing House began to examine the accounts of other banks and discovered problems with the financier C.F. Morse, who was a director of seven banks in the New York market. He had taken part in Heinz's stock operation, and was also obliged to resign; the Clearing House tried to calm things down by offering guarantees for depositors.

A GROUP OF BANKERS ACT AS A CENTRAL BANK

Bankers J.P. Morgan, James Stillman (National City Bank) and George Baker (First National Bank) organized an informal committee to keep track of the crisis. On Monday 21st October, the National Bank of Commerce announced that it was no longer accepting checks drawn on the Knickerbocker Trust Company. Depositors once more rushed to the bank to withdraw their money: $8 million were withdrawn during the morning and by the afternoon the counters were closed. The much hoped for help from J.P. Morgan did not materialize. On 23rd October, it was the turn of the Trust Company (which had to pay out $13 million to its clients) and of the Lincoln Trust. J.P. Morgan deemed the Trust Company creditworthy and refloated it with an injection of $3 million; banker J.D. Rockefeller deposited $10 million. The New York bankers held a top level meeting, and the Secretary of the Treasury gave the order to the Treasury to deposit $25 million with the New York banks. In the meantime, on 24th October on the New York Stock Exchange, the margin interest rate rose from 6% to 60% and finally reached 100%. The president of the New York Stock Exchange (NYSE), Ranson H. Thomas, contacted Stillman to ask for assistance. In a highly publicized move, the trio of Morgan-Stillman-Baker put $25 million at the disposal of the Exchange. On 25th October, another cash injection was arranged, but the interest rate operating on the exchange remained around 50%. Finally a solution was found: the New York Clearing House decided to issue loan certificates, an operation which might be compared to mere monetary production. Certificates worth more than $500 million were issued in an attempt to allay panic – nothing less than an enormous cash injection into the system. And it was the same trio of bankers which saved New York City Hall. City Hall had to take a loan of $30 million to refloat its finances, but clearly the conditions were unfavorable. So on 29th October, the three bankers subscribed the entire bond issue for $30 million. Obviously the aim of this operation was to stabilize the markets which were panic-stricken. The Trust Company of America and the Lincoln Trust were again in need of a cash injection; J.P. Morgan managed to convince the other banks to deposit a further $25 million. The financial situation seemed to be improving in New York, but in Europe panic was rife.

THE BANK OF FRANCE COMES TO THE AID OF THE BANK OF ENGLAND!

From the very first signs of problems on the New York Stock Exchange, the European exchanges were also gripped by panic, with heavy losses on stocks. Cash was in such short supply that the Bank of France had to physically send gold bars (400 troy ounces) and ingots (32.15 troy ounces) to the Bank of England, to help it deal with its liquidity problems and avoid a major crisis on the London financial market. To calm speculation and panic, the principal central European banks raised their discount and intervention rates without realizing that they were aggravating the situation and making conditions for refinancing stock operations more difficult. A treatment of `serious bloodletting´ was the only solution that the central banks knew for solving the problem. But the damage done to the economies was considerable.

The financial crisis was slowly absorbed at high cost to the real economy: growth and exchanges world-wide suffered the consequences throughout the year 1908. This crisis was the first time that the Belle Epoque, or Edwardian era, faltered in its glittering progression, at least until the outbreak of the First World War. It also coincided with the end of the cycle of investment in railways and the beginning of investment in the production of electric power. But this crisis also indicated which path to take when the financial markets succumbed to panic (i.e. a massive injection of cash) and prepared the terrain for the creation of a Central Bank in the United States. The Federal Reserve Bank was set up in 1913 with two clear objectives guiding its monetary policy: to fight inflation and optimize growth. However in 1929 the central banks would repeat the same erroneous policy of `blood-letting´, with terrible consequences for the world economy.

THE FIRST WORLD WAR:
A MAJOR LESSON IN ECONOMICS

An analysis of the First World War from a purely economic standpoint leads to one very clear conclusion – it was absolutely essential for the Central Powers (Germany, Austro-Hungary and the Ottoman Empires) to win the war in as short a period as possible, otherwise the conflict would become a long and punishing war and defeat would be inevitable. 1564 days of warfare directly or indirectly affected one billion one hundred million citizens in 33 warring countries. It is estimated that 70 million men were mobilized in fourteen theatres of war: 20 million were injured, 15 million were left permanent invalids, and 20 million died, approximately half of whom were soldiers and half of whom were civilians who died mainly from disease and hunger. It was the first real human disaster on a global scale; but this depressing record would be outstripped by far by the Second World War, which lasted 2194 days. 62 nations with 1.7 billion citizens were embroiled in this second hellish cauldron, which mobilized 110 million men and women. The death toll was around 55 million, to which should be added 35 million wounded and 25 million invalids.

MISPLACED OPTIMISM

Generals, politicians and ambassadors on both sides were nearly all unanimous: it would be a short war. Propaganda stirred up the general public. Soldiers marched for glory and to the fronts with a song on their lips, the band playing, the people applauding them, girls throwing flowers and politicians' rhetoric thundering in their ears. It was not long before the soldiers' and the generals' dreams of glory were obliterated and the situation was transformed into one of the worst butcheries that humanity had ever seen or even been capable of imagining.

The complete lack of preparation by the aggressors for a long and punishing war was quickly apparent, as was the economic incapacity of the Central Powers to win the war. In fact these countries had a population of 152.7 million, a gross national product of $374.2 million (according to League of Nations data and the calculations of Professors Broadberry and Harrison), with a per capita product of $2,450. On the other hand, the Allied Powers had a combined population of 1271.7 million citizens; this figure takes the Russian population into account (173 million) which abandoned the fight from the end of 1917, but it was replaced by the arrival of the United States with 96.5 million citizens. The gross national product of this group was $1760.6 million (roughly 64% of world GNP), but the per capita product was $1,384, significantly lower than that of their enemies.

The first consequence of this wealth and level of culture in the countries comprising the Central Powers was revealed in their capacity for troop mobilization. Initially their armies benefited from better military preparation and Prussian discipline, which gave them a significant advantage. Moreover, they were better placed to mobilize the railway network for transporting troops, arms, animals, food and medical aid. Since 1905 the German High Command had required the various German railway companies to keep a specific number of wagons in each region in the event of such a mobilization. Clearly the German economic fabric, with its strong industrialization and well organized social structure, facilitated the implementation of the military command hierarchy. Many of the junior and lower ranking officers had formerly been in charge of workshops and assembly lines in industrial companies and were therefore used to organizing, directing and commanding men, and taking responsibility. The late industrialization of certain of the warring countries (for example Italy, the Austro-Hungarian Empire and especially Russia) had a very negative effect on the chain of command in their armies, which had to organize regiments mainly composed of peasants, who were less accustomed to a collective life and a hierarchical system.

PROBLEMS OF THE HARVESTS AND FACTORIES AFTER MOBILIZATION

The two camps mobilized their troops rapidly, but very serious and hard-to-resolve economic problems were immediately apparent. The most obvious of these were that many factories had to close because their workers, employees and management were mobilized and it was impossible find other men or even women capable of carrying out certain specialized tasks to replace them. On the other hand, some factories could employ unqualified labor, but the workers had to be hired and then transferred to where they were needed. Elsewhere, in the countryside, there was a shortage of manpower for the harvests (such as cereals, fruits, and grapes, as it was summer), to look after the farm animals and, later, to prepare the fields and sow crops. Muscles and knowledge were required; but muscles were needed elsewhere for handling weapons, and only women and the elderly remained with the technical know-how. The elderly, women and children had to take care of the farming as well as they could; but some harvests were lost and a lot of land was not replanted.

Furthermore, the railways, roads, postal and public health systems, hospitals, schools, governmental and local administrations, communications and transport of goods, were all completely disorganized by overall disruption of the economic structures of the warring countries, and steps had to be taken to re-establish a minimum of organization. It is clear than that the participants in this conflict were not well enough prepared and were obliged to find new solutions to the problems, while very often citizens had to fend for themselves on an *ad hoc* basis. Meanwhile the stock exchanges were closed and in all the countries at war currency conversion to gold was suspended.

THE CENTRAL POWERS' DIFFICULTY IN OBTAINING SUFFICIENT SUPPLIES

The geographical situation of the Central Powers was not particularly favorable to obtaining supplies and the blockade of the German coast by the British Navy increased these difficulties, even if at the outset Britain continued to export products to Holland (a neutral country) which served as a platform for supplying Germany. The blockade explains the maneuvers of the Kriegsmarine to try and break through the net which was preventing the import of all food products, raw materials and energy supplies.[1] France had a similar problem in terms of supplies, because nine departments located in the north and east of the country were occupied by the German army. These regions were vital for their coal and mineral industries, with many industrial centers specialized in manufacturing. The loss of these seriously impeded industrial production and the process of mobilization. France and Britain could obtain supplies of some raw materials from their colonies, although the submarine war waged by the Kriegsmarine from February 1915 onwards severely affected these imports and supplies could not be guaranteed. The Allies tried to anticipate the purchase of raw materials made by the Central Powers from non-aligned countries, such as Holland and Switzerland or Italy, which only entered the war in May 1915. Many exports were prohibited because the products were essential for military needs; these included salt, minerals, metals, food products, alcohol, textiles, leather, chemical products and energy supplies (petrol, coal, oil and so on).

Furthermore, France had to cope with the serious problem of internal migration due to people fleeing the theatres of war. This mass of people had to be channeled along roads that had also become strategic for the army, and then they had to be sheltered and provided for. A similar problem arose in relation to prisoners: they had to be removed from the front, housed, fed and kept under controlled conditions in some form of incarceration, since they

---

1. During the last two years of the war the supply problems for Germany became extremely serious. The country had to make enormous efforts to provide enough essential products, needed to continue the war and to feed the population and the masses of prisoners. The situation was the same during the Second World War, when those in charge of supplies were prepared to do anything to obtain certain products such as platinum. This precious metal is used in the petro-chemical industry and in many strategic items, but the producing countries were mainly Germany's enemies (Russia, the United States, Canada and South Africa); German submarines were therefore sent to the Rio de la Plata estuary to link up with fishing boats transporting ingots of platinum extracted as a subproduct from the silver mines of the Andean Cordillera. These ingots were exchanged for one, two or even more gold ingots (conversation with Dr. Otto Böss from the Degussa Corporation). Hitler's decision to give up the occupation of Moscow and send the majority of his troops to the oil fields of the Caucasus was motivated by the urgent need to gain control of essential energy resources in order to continue the war.

remained enemies. This was not an entirely new problem because in the course of previous wars senior military officers had also been obliged to organize the management of prisoners. This time, how-ever, the numbers were enormous and respect for international conventions was much greater than in the past, when few agree-ments or rules had yet been laid down. Once more the warring parties showed that they were totally unprepared for all these problems and very often makeshift common sense solutions had to be found.

TOTAL WAR: THE NEED FOR MEN, EQUIPMENT...

The longer the war dragged on and became bogged down in the trenches with its terrible and unimaginable toll on men and mili-tary equipment, the greater the need to find new recruits to send to the different fronts, and fresh capital to pay for army orders for fresh supplies from the different nations' industries as well as from international industry, which played a vital role. At the time of the Musketeers a soldier could fire three rounds a minute, the strength of the two opposing armies rarely exceeded 50,000 men, and whilst infantry and cavalry attacks were supported by artillery and the death toll was high, the battles lasted for only a few hours. In 1914, a foot soldier could fire fifteen rounds a minute and a machine gunner 600 rounds a minute – without taking into account the firepower of an artillery battery. Once the attack was launched a battalion of 1000 soldiers could be wiped out in a few minutes. The destructive power of artillery bombardments against companies of infantry was truly terrible and the artillery of the different navies was capable of hitting an enemy ship nearly twenty miles away.

The populations of the Central Powers began to be inadequate for all the human effort needed, even including the population of around 11 million of the German colonies. Their enemies could count on much greater numbers of people from the colonies, but geographically they were distant and did not have an adequate military standard. At the end of the conflict France had enlisted only 60,800 colonial troops and throughout the war the Allies had been underpowered due to an insufficient number of able-bodied men. On the other hand fresh troops arrived from the United

States from the end of June, 1917. Their first engagement against the Germans was on 21st October and Russia rapidly abandoned the conflict (their armistice with Germany was signed on 15th December 1917). The United States had a population of 96.5 million; but above all, the country possessed enormous stocks of raw materials and could count on military industrial production that was essential to the war effort and most probably played a strategic role in the eventual outcome of the war.

... AND CAPITAL

The capital markets and national savings also played an essential role in the conduct of the war. The national treasuries needed to pay hard cash for the purchase of military supplies and imports. Resorting to a steep rise in direct or indirect taxation is always difficult and, in the former case, there is a time lag before the treasury actually gets the money. The remaining alternative is voluntary and/or forced subscription loans to find the increasingly necessary capital as quickly as possible. Governments may play the patriotism card, but it is essential to have markets capable of mobilizing savings and it is only in the wealthiest countries that this is a reliable option. The financial markets which were the most efficient in loan subscriptions were those in Germany, France and England – the markets of the other participants were mobilized, but to less obvious effect. Therefore it was necessary to have recourse to further financial markets to obtain loans, and above all to their banking systems to obtain credit. The United States favored the Allied camp, even at the time of its neutrality, whereas Switzerland and Holland were more susceptible to German diplomatic pressure. Once again `no money, no war´, and much military effort was sustained by financial manipulations, which allowed for supplies to be bought abroad on a strictly cash basis. In certain cases, national industries gave priority to international demand (naturally from allied countries) over internal demand, making purely financial and economic choices. The `free´ pricing of supplies from abroad was always higher when compared to the prices negotiated with those in charge of the national armies.

Inflation also dominated the scenario of war – on average, prices quadrupled between 1914 and 1918 in Europe and the situation was considerably worse in the countries which had lost the war. An entire generation of *rentiers* were ruined by the inflation fuelled by a war and in the decade following the end of the conflict, inflation created conditions particularly favorable to the birth of authoritarian regimes in Europe.

FALLING GROWTH AND THE ENORMOUS COST OF THE WAR

During the war years the gross domestic product of the countries where fighting took place suffered disastrously. French GDP shrank the most, going from 100 (base 1913) to only 63.9 in 1918, with a large part of its mining and manufacturing production lost in the northern and eastern regions. German GDP fell from 100 to 81.8 at the end of the war. Austrian GDP fell from 100 to 73.3, due to the same causes as in Germany, but their industrial development was less advanced. Russia registered huge negative growth: GDP went from 100 to 67.7 in 1917. Russia was a largely agricultural country and paid the price for political instability with the revolution of 1917. Italy experienced a slight fall in growth (from 100 to 94.3). The regions affected by the military operations were restricted to the northeast (mountains and farming), while the industrial triangle of Milan-Turin-Genoa remained outside the area of conflict and even managed to increase its potential, limited only by the difficulty of obtaining supplies of raw materials. Elsewhere, countries like Great Britain and the United States benefited from an increase in growth because their territories were only marginally affected by military events, as in the case of Britain, or completely spared, as in the case of the United States, where GDP rose from 100 to 113.2. The GDP of the British Empire did even better, going from 100 to 114.8.

Calculations have also been made on the costs of the war. Taking into consideration only direct costs which figured in the states' budgets, it is notable that the Central Powers financed their expenses for a sum which was around half that paid out by their enemies: $60.1 billion against $145.3 billion. The statistics on the indirect costs (dead and wounded, destruction of property, infrastructures and ships) show the same proportions, with $22.5 billion for the Allies and $11 billion for the Central Powers. Naturally these calculations are only economic and do not take into account the human suffering, and the sacrifice of an entire generation of men.

SOME POSITIVE CONSEQUENCES OF WAR

Wars will always transform the economic and social structures of a country. Compared to all previous wars, the First World War was the first conflict to have a determining and massive impact on civilian society, on economies and on technology. Millions of women joined the ranks of those employed in the industrial economic sector through their work in factories; assembly line methods of production developed enormously; technological progress transformed economic structures (the airplane, communications, machines and chemistry) and many countries were propelled into an extremely rapid industrialization. Social mobility accelerated, as the distinctive demarcation between the different classes diminished; women hoped for and came to expect the right to be considered on an equal level with men, social institutions were called into question, social relations moved toward a greater degree of democracy. The war accelerated the fall of four European empires: Russian, Austro-Hungarian, German and Ottoman. But it also sowed the seeds for conditions which favored the rise of nationalism, the dictatorships of the 1930s and 1940s, and racial hatred, all of which were significant contributing factors to the outbreak of the Second World War.

ROUTE 66: FROM ECONOMICS TO LEGEND

Route 66: the name is both legendary and redolent of a pitiless world. It evokes rock and roll, Harley Davidsons, Kerouac's Beat Generation, vacations, the boom years of the American economy, and teamsters in long distance trucks. It is also the road men took when setting out for the Asian front in the Second World War, and the road which guided the odyssey of the poor Oakies, whose plight was immortalized in Steinbeck's *Grapes of Wrath*, when whole families were destroyed by the Great Depression and the dust bowl. It is also the road which features in the dramatic and intense photos of Dorothy Lange.

Until the end of the 19th century the roads connecting the east to the west of America were essentially trails made by American Indians, which were later taken by the pioneers heading to the far West, despite the fact the intercontinental train linked the two extremities of the country from 1869 onwards. Nonetheless, right up to the 1920s the comfortable Pullman cars took two days and three nights to cover the distance between Chicago and Los Angeles. The first legislation concerning the major road system came out in 1916; but the construction program could not be launched until a new version was signed by Congress. The fathers of Route 66 were two businessmen, Cyrus Avery, from Tulsa, and John Woodruff, from Springfield, who supported the project to the hilt. The latter became the first president of the association for the promotion of Route 66 – one of his ideas was a running race between Los Angeles and New York in 1928 called the Bunion Derby to publicize the road.

A STRATEGIC AXIS BETWEEN THE GREAT LAKES AND THE PACIFIC

In 1925 the plans for the road's route were approved. The aim was to facilitate travel between the region of the Great Lakes and the Pacific and to link a large number of small towns in Illinois, Kansas, Arizona and Missouri with the large cities of Chicago, Santa Fe and Los Angeles. It was a project of strategic importance for the USA, which was in the middle of a large-scale industrial revolution post-First World War; but the country's road network was not well developed. More than 2500 miles long, Route 66 would cross three time zones and eight states. The official starting date was 1926; work began promptly using large numbers of workers and unskilled labor, reminiscent of the construction of the railroads which were built by battalions of Chinese workers in the US prairies and mountains. By 1929 there was a ribbon of tarmac through Illinois and Kansas, the rest being still little more than a dusty trail, barely passable in bad weather. Nonetheless, the midwest was less and less isolated. Facilities for welcoming and helping teamsters and other travellers sprang up like mushrooms along the road – gas stations, motels and restaurants offering travellers a degree of comfort – and Route 66 began to compete with the powerful railroad network.

BETWEEN THE GRAPES OF WRATH ERA AND WW2

It was unfortunate for Route 66 that the 1929 crash came so suddenly. America found itself in the middle of a traumatic crisis which shook it to its very foundations, the volume of merchandise to be transported collapsed and many Americans could no longer afford to travel down `the Main Street of America´. The road was the backdrop to a dramatic crisis which hit many families, who headed west to try their luck and escape the economic disaster back east. On top of this, the great drought and the terrible sandstorms of the 1930s which swept through the midwest forced more than 200,000 farmers to leave their land and go in search of work in California, fleeing poverty for a more worthwhile life on the coasts of the Pacific. Some gave up even before they reached the Rockies.

Between 1933 and 1938 thousands of unemployed workers were hired to tarmac sections of the road. But soon Route 66 was needed for a different purpose: with the entry of the United States into the war, it was necessary to transport men and supplies in the biggest military mobilization in the history of the country. Those who were called up took the road on their way to the large training camps in the western states, then took the `66´ again to the embarkation points in the Pacific heading for the front in the Far East. Others set out for Chicago, the Atlantic ports and the European front. The road also had to cope with heavy traffic – trucks transporting large guns, tanks and other military vehicles, mainly manufactured in the factories of the industrial region of the Great Lakes. This entailed a massive amount of organization and the military high command greatly appreciated the functionality of Route 66 which linked the centers of production to the points of embarkation and allowed for the rapid transportation of men and equipment. In this context, the government invested around $70 billion, mostly in California and in particular on the San Diego-Los Angeles axis, between 1941 and 1945. Many new factories destined for military production were located near Route 66, to take advantage of the road network.

A SYMBOL OF THE CHANGES IN SOCIETY

At the end of the war, many soldiers originally from the large urban regions of the east or the industrial area around the Great Lakes, decided to settle further west, and Route 66 was instrumental in this transfer. In the course of the 1950s the mobility of the American people altered the structure of society; this was helped by a rise in incomes and by the rapid spread of the car. Route 66 benefited fully from this new state of affairs. The `66´ attracted a lot of investment from chains offering highway service – gas stations and technical assistance to cars and trucks, motels and especially fast food restaurants proliferated along the road. Many improvements were made in the road structure: several towns built by-passes to allow drivers to skirt them, thus avoiding the small town roads.

However the success of Route 66 came at a high price in human terms – the heavy traffic caused many fatal accidents, and the road was even nicknamed `the bloody 66´. For at least fifteen years it was the principal axis carrying holiday-makers from the east and north to the large amusement and wildlife parks in the west and the beaches of the Pacific. It was a major symbol of the changes in American society, from the development of tourism and mobility to the spread of commercial transport and the huge rise in the use of trucks to transport merchandise. Furthermore the road represented key aspects of American optimism – the dream of progress and the conquest of territory. The population movements of the 1930s and 1950s were essential to assure better redistribution of manpower with regard to the location of resources. However, competition from the railroads remained strong and this combined with the extraordinary development of civil aviation led to Route 66's slow decline. The death-blow came in 1956 with the government's decision to launch massive developments of the road network and a major program of interstate highway construction. President Eisenhower, re-elected for his second term, had been very impressed by the German *Autobahnen* network built by Hitler, and had understood the strategic importance of these axes whose economic function was essential but which could also play a decisive role in the case of military mobilization (this was at the height of the Cold War). Sections of four-lane highway gradually replaced the `66´ and at the beginning of the 1970s it was entirely replaced by the interstates 55-44-40-15-10. A few sections were still used; but in 1985 the Transport Commission decreed the death of Route 66.

THE `ROUTE´ BECOMES A LEGEND: FILMS, SONGS AND MARKETING PRODUCTS

However, Route 66 remains alive in the American subconscious and unconscious. The `Mother Road´, the `Great Diagonal Way´, the `Main Street of America´, the `Will Rogers Highway´ is still present in the name `Phillip 66´, the gas distribution network created by two chemical engineers in Tulsa. At the end of the 1920s they drove down a stretch of the road in Oklahoma at the speed of 66 miles an hour, and got the idea for the gas's brand-name. A very popular TV show was launched on CBS at the beginning of the 1960s with the name `Route 66´ and the

Tulsa basket ball team is known as the 'Tulsa 66'; the chain of shops, K-Mart, has a jeans label called 'Route 66'. The road features in many movies including *Stargate SG-1*, *Thelma and Louise*, *A Goofy Movie* by Walt Disney, *Baghdad Café* and *Easy Rider*. Many Americans' fond memories are bound up in this road with its rock 'n' roll museums, old motels and dilapidated service stations: *Get your kicks on Route 66!*

FRONT WHEEL DRIVE:
A GREAT SUCCESS STEMMING
FROM THE COLLAPSE OF CITROËN

From time to time success and failure coincide. The concept of the front wheel drive, launched in 1934 with Citroën's *Traction Avant* model, known as the TA, was almost immediately followed by the Citroën group's bankruptcy, although it was saved from the brink by Michelin in 1935. André Citroën was the son of a Dutch diamond merchant, and graduated from the prestigious French higher education institute for engineering and management, the *Ecole Polytechnique*, at the age of 22. He was constantly in search of innovation and this helped make him a great industrialist. During a visit to Poland in 1900 he observed an extremely significant process in use: a herring-bone, double helical type gear and took out the patent on what was to become the symbol or logo of his firm. He joined Jacques and Paul Hinstin's company, who were already making gears and he invested a large part of his inheritance to found the company Citroën, Hinstin & Co, which expanded and opened branches abroad, where Skoda was using its patents.

In 1908, André Citroën joined the company Mors Bros, which specialized in electric railway signals as well as manufacturing cars, and subsequently became the managing director. In 1912 he visited the Ford factory in Detroit and learned about Taylorism. His experience as an officer in the artillery during the war, prompted him to suggest to the director of artillery that a factory should be built in Paris to produce 75mm shells. The experiment began badly, but eventually was a success when the factory became a top supplier to the Allied armies. The war ended, and Citroën decided to reconvert the arms factory to automobile manufacture; in September 1919, the first Type A car left the factory followed by Type B and Type C. Citroën managed to supply 30% of the automobile market in France; he started making taxi cars, utility vehicles, lorries, fire trucks and cars with caterpillar tracks which became famous with the `Black Trek´ (1924-1925) and the `Yellow Trek´ (1931-1932). He also began distributing signposts for the road system, and provided the illumination of the Place de la Concorde and the Arc de Triomphe – the Eiffel Tower displayed the factory name spelt vertically over 300 feet or so.

FRONT WHEEL DRIVE: A GERMAN IDEA

At the suggestion of Gustave Baehr (a large car distributor in France), Lucien Rosengart, a producer of small cars, went to Germany to meet the engineer Rohr, founder of the Adler car company, and who was pioneering front wheel drive in his country. At the time only a handful of enthusiasts were in favour of the idea of front wheel drive – Grégoire and Fenaille in France, Miller and Ruxton in the United States. Rosengart was fascinated by the idea and returned to France with all the rights to the front wheel drive system, on condition that he manufactured and sold at least 2000 vehicles a year. Rosengart presented the project to André Citroën who accepted it immediately – the model would be called `Super-Traction´, and both the design and the building of the cars were to be organized in Rosengart's factory; Citroën became involved only at the last minute.

However Citroën's engineers had the brilliant idea of building a monocoque, or monohull, which was much more economical. The Italian sculptor Flaminio Bertoni designed the bodywork (he also designed the 2CV and the DS, both of them legendary Citroën cars), and the decision to produce the new model was taken by André Citroën, with the help of his wife who had an aptitude for design. In November 1933, Bertoni and the Citroën engineers traveled to the United States to arrange for the machine tools to be made at Budd's. Rosengart's Super-Traction was presented to the public at the motor show in Paris in 1933, but Citroën launched it officially on 24th March 1934, to the group's dealers.

On 18th April, it was presented to the press and on 3rd May the first car was sold: the venture had begun! A great idea that was undermined by global crisis. The American Depression in the 1930s threatened the very existence of Ford, General Motors and Chrysler, and helped bring about the downfall of Citroën, at the time the largest producer of cars in France and Europe. The crisis was the price André Citroën paid for his counter-cyclical strategy: he continued to invest massively at a point when the market was shrinking dangerously, with the complete rebuilding of the factory on the Quai de Javel on the outskirts of Paris, the launching of the revolutionary model (with a long and difficult period fine-tuning and perfecting the car) and was forced to ask for a large amount of credit to finance the project. The constructor, which since 1919 had enjoyed repeated success and met with very few problems, and had introduced American-style methods to the world of automobile production and distribution in Europe, collapsed in the face of this recession and the mass of debts accumulated as a consequence of it.

In the spring of 1934, when the front wheel drive model was launched, the company's excessive debts almost destroyed it – the main banks backing the group (Crédit Lyonnais and the Union Parisienne) withdrew their support. The state refused to intervene, in the name of the free market. Citroën was compelled to ask its main suppliers for help – some extended their credit, others brought cash injections. Michelin, one of the main suppliers, agreed to help the group: with 60 million in loans it became their principle creditor. However, Michelin remained discreetly in the background, so other car makers would not fear that a huge Citroën-Michelin industrial conglomerate was being formed and withdraw their custom from Michelin.

THE COMPULSORY LIQUIDATION
OF THE ANDRÉ CITROËN LTD

Michelin put forward a four-year restructuring plan, based on cost cutting, reduced spending, the reduction of surplus stocks and the reorganization of production. This plan came up against the powerful banks, Lazard's and Paribas, which insisted that the founder of the company should stand down and major restructuring take place. Michelin therefore decided on drastic measures: the sale of the service companies (taxis, transport and insurance) and a complete reorganization of the industrial tooling. In six months the number of workers went from 25,000 to 18,000 and by June 1936 stood at 11,500 – the company had to improve productivity at all costs. Furthermore the production of the 'TA' front wheel drive car was still encountering serious difficulties, especially in terms of quality, and the reliability of assembly line. Michelin and his chief engineer Pierre Boulanger worked to improve the production of the model, gave it a separate management and started up a marketing department to analyze consumers' needs and adapt the production of the cars and the range of models, with a certain amount of success. But André Citroën did not live to see the results: he died on 3rd July 1935.

THE PENALTY FOR COUNTER-CYCLICAL STRATEGY

The drastic reduction in car production by the Citroën Company was the price paid for a counter-cyclical development policy at a time when the economic situation in general was very difficult. It dealt the French and European economy a hard blow in the aftermath of the 1929 American crisis. In June 1934 it took 955 hours of work to make the bodywork of the new TA front-wheel drive model. This was too high; the aim was to reduce it to 580 hours or 10% less than the time needed to manufacture the 'Rosalie', Citroën's previous model. American machine tools were brought in, and only eight months later the time was reduced to 535 hours, then to 440 hours the following year. These were very substantial productivity improvements, even if the workforce still had to be cut drastically. Moreover, the project for another car – the Traction 22 – a front-wheel drive model to compete with the Ford V-8 or the top-of-the-range Chrysler was abandoned. A factory in Forest, Belgium, and one in Slough, England, carried out the assembly of the TA from 1934 to 1935; assembly line production was more or less well developed and was also being used in Germany, Denmark, Poland, Italy and even Australia. The company concentrated on the 7 and 11 models with two different engines; from 1938 the 15 model was launched: this had a six cylinder engine and was destined for the top of the market.

PRODUCTION RUINED BY WAR

In 1940, the production lines were making 25,200 cars. In 1941 the figure fell to 7,400 after the factory on the Quai de Javel was bombed. And since only 96 cars were manufactured in 1942, production was stopped in 1943-1944. The French army considered there was no point requisitioning TAs because of the chassis, but this proved to be a serious mistake. In fact, TAs were to be found in Russia, the Balkans and North Africa, being driven by the men of the Wehrmacht and the Gestapo. In France it became the car of the *maquisards*, the members of the Resistance.

After the war, production began again and the last TA came off the assembly line in July 1957. The car had some remarkable qualities both in terms of its appearance and its reliability. Many small garages began limited productions of these cars in France, Switzerland, Britain and Belgium. Police and thieves alike discovered its qualities of speed and handling, despite the fact its wind resistance was too high. This made it less competitive in the medium term, especially with the introduction of more aerodynamic cars after the war, such as the Dyna Panhard, the Peugeot 203 and the Renault 4CV. But its purchase price, the ease with which spare parts could be found, and its rather Spartan finish, were all big plus points. In the first post-war rallies the TA car featured on all the podiums.

A LEGENDARY CAR WHICH WAS A TECHNOLOGICAL REVOLUTION

A revolutionary pre-war car, it became the car favored by the less well off in the 1960s, when it could be found, modified and rebuilt as a van at markets and at fairs, or already in junkyards. But collectors' passion for this car puts it amongst other legends, like certain models produced by Cadillac, Mustang and Mercedes and the Fiat 500, the Volkswagen `Beetle´ and the Mini. Throughout the world, enthusiast clubs organize meetings simply to show off their TAs, and certain garages specialize in the repair and rebuilding of the Tractions (such as the one near Paris which is world-famous, even as far as Japan). Film producers like to use TAs, and they can often be seen on the screen, particularly in historical reconstructions. The story of the TA is also that of the misadventures of André Citroën (who went bankrupt launching an exceptional car), as well as being the test bed for the great industrial restructuring in the pre-war French and European automobile sector. It also represented the Popular Front's negotiations on wages and conditions, but most of all was an example of the rapid esthetic ageing of a product launched before the war and produced afterwards, when tastes, techniques and economic conditions were changing.

THE US `SYNTHETIC RUBBER PLAN´ CONTRIBUTES TO VICTORY

On the 27th June 1942 the President of the United States, F.D. Roosevelt sent out an urgent appeal to the nation by radio: could everyone please take everything they had made from rubber, from old tires to children's toys, along to their local gas station, 40,000 of which were scattered across the country. The appeal raised 457,000 tons of rubber, half of which was possible to recycle; during the year there were further deposits and 1.1 million tons were collected. Unfortunately this was nowhere near enough to meet the army's needs. The President of the Rubber Commission, who was also part of the War Manpower Commission, Bernard Baruch stated clearly: `Of all critical and strategic materials, rubber is the one which presents the greatest threat to the safety of our nation and the success of the Allied cause. If we fail to secure a large new rubber supply immediately, our war effort and our domestic economy will collapse... the rubber situation gives rise to our most critical problem.´

THE LOSS OF RUBBER SUPPLIERS

It was the fall of France and certain British Colonies in the Far East, and above all the Japanese military occupation of western regions of the Pacific basin, which cut supplies of natural rubber coming from the Dutch East Indies, Papua New Guinea and Indochina and caused the crisis. Ceylon and India remained under British control but these regions, together with Latin America, were only able to provide 10% of military needs, or 130-150,000 tons of rubber. Therefore, the sooner the country could begin to produce 800,000 tons of synthetic rubber, whilst maintaining production of the other raw materials necessary for the war, the better.

THE CRISIS OF 1939 TO 1941

Toward the end of the 1930s, with geopolitical tensions increasing, various American industrialists suggested setting up pilot production schemes in five experimental factories. At the end of 1941 the United States was producing 8338 tons of Government Rubber-Styrene (GR-S) per year, which represented only 0.8% of national peacetime requirements.

But after the military defeat of France, during the month of June 1940, certain high officials in the American administration suggested a plan for the production of synthetic rubber, whose purpose was to guarantee the availability of 100,000 tons a year, manufactured in twelve factories, financed by a federal program of $100 million. The program was rapidly downsized to 40,000 tons, because the government could not allocate more than $25 million. The plan needed 18 to 30 months before it would be operational and it involved two companies in the sector: Standard Oil and Union Carbide. A government paper of 20th February 1941 clearly indicated that the United States, even whilst entirely cut off from all supply sources, had some reserves of rubber. Following this memorandum, production was reduced to four factories, with a unit capacity of 2500 tons per year. The experts did not expect the conflict to spread very far, and certainly not to include a German invasion of Russia or that of the Japanese Empire against American interests in the Pacific. It is important to note, at this point, that Germany had developed synthetic rubber production during the First World War, with a moderate degree of success. Production was abandoned between the two wars only to be suddenly revived, in an improved form, before the invasion of Poland in 1939.

REACTION TO PEARL HARBOR

After the attack on Peal Harbor, the American people were in a state of shock, and unable to evaluate the situation immediately.

The country was cut off from natural rubber supplies; it faced a serious potential crisis within its internal transport system and difficulties in mobilization both in terms of military transport within the country and on the military fronts. There was still hope for the Anglo-American navies' mobilization plan, but the country rapidly had to face harsh reality there as well. The war machine went into motion, and rubber production was immediately increased – on 20th December 1941 it went from 40,000 to 120,000 tons a year and at the beginning of 1942 it had risen to 400,000 tons per year. After the invasion of Singapore, production climbed to 600,000 tons per year (3rd April 1942) and further to 800,000 tons from 21st April. Restrictions on domestic consumption were particularly drastic – the maximum speed limit for cars was reduced to 35 miles an hour, with systematic checks on the state of the tires, and the management of rubber reserves was taken over by the government.

The Synthetic Rubber scheme was launched to satisfy domestic demand and primarily to facilitate the war effort. Public opinion was strongly antagonistic toward the group of industrialists who got together to produce synthetic rubber, relying on the antitrust law. President Roosevelt was obliged to intervene personally in March 1942, to explain that this production had been put in the hands of the chemical industry trusts as a part of the strategic decision to avoid the country's collapse on an industrial or military level.

Later, the press launched an even more virulent attack on Standard Oil, which was accused of creating a cartel with the German company IG Farben to gain a monopoly over synthetic rubber production, and in doing so, to have undermined American strategy from the beginning of the hostilities, as no other American company was ready to produce synthetic rubber. An article in the journal *Industrial & Engineering Chemistry* directly accused the politico-economic world of strategic myopia and urged them to make up for lost time and overcome their differences so that synthetic rubber production could proceed as speedily as possible and no more time be lost in unproductive debates.

WHY NOT USE SURPLUS WHEAT?

At the same time, it became impossible to export wheat, and the cereal market was suffering from a sharp fall in prices. It was suggested therefore that excess production of wheat should be transformed into ethyl alcohol through fermentation, which could then be used in the production of the gas butadiene, a key component in synthetic rubber production. On 22rd July 1942 Congress passed a law decreeing that butadiene and GR-S were to be produced in factories located in the large agricultural regions; these production centers were placed under the direct control of the President of the United States. But Roosevelt vetoed the law and nominated a three-man commission comprising the Director, Bernard Baruch (formerly responsible for industrial mobilization in the First World War), J. Conant (a great chemist and president of Harvard University) and Karl T. Compton (president of MIT). In less than a month, during which 25 experts testified (the most prominent industrialists, economists and academics in the country), this commission produced the Baruch Report, on 10th September. It gave an extremely detailed summary of the situation and made concrete proposals for the production of synthetic rubber. The document details how after Pearl Harbor the United States lost 90% of its supplies and that they had to be replaced as rapidly as possible in order to avoid losing the war. It proposed that the project should be given to industrialists under the control of the federal administration. The GR-S project came under government ownership which then financed the factories, the research and the patents ($700 million).

SUCCESS DESPITE DIFFICULTIES

At the beginning of 1943 production was still relatively small; 65 large companies were working for the project. Pentagon officials were becoming impatient, as many of their offensives were being delayed due to the limited availability of rubber – it was only in the second half of the year that the supply of the new product began to stabilize. Many whisky distilleries were converted to produce ethyl alcohol, an important component of rubber. Around 18 months later, the army could count on a regular supply of rubber to prepare the D-day landings and guarantee military operations in the Pacific, North Africa and the Mediterranean. Without the spur provided by war it would have taken a dozen or so years to obtain the same results!

It is important to note that the main enemies of the Allies (especially Germany under Hitler and Italy under Mussolini) were able to sustain the war for a longer period thanks to their production of synthetic rubber. The strategic decision taken by Hitler in the war against the USSR, to stop concentrating his military efforts on the capture of Moscow, and to launch a major attack in the southern USSR to obtain control of the oil fields, which were so important to the German military industry, is another example of the economic constraints which sometimes influence military choices. The fiasco of Stalingrad was a strategic defeat for Hitler, proving that wars can only be won with the right economic support.

VESPA: FROM AIRCRAFT MANUFACTURE TO THE LAUNCH OF A LEGEND

The Vespa was created during the winter of 1944-45 in Biella, a large textile center in Piedmont, where the Piaggio workshops and research department were moved after the destruction of their aircraft factory in Pontedera (Pisa). They were studying designs for a motor scooter to be used by parachutists. Enrico Piaggio understood that he would no longer be required to build fast motor launches, patrol boats, and small bombers. So he decided to take a chance on the fact that at the end of the war the Italians would have great need of mobility in a country where the roads and railways had suffered terrible damage. Amongst the engineers at Biella was Corradino d'Ascanio: the man who had designed the first piloted helicopter, had worked with Piaggio on aircraft design and had achieved several records between 1937 and 1939, including that of height (56,047ft). In Biella they made the first prototype, which the workforce dubbed *Paperino* (duckling). It was not the first scooter in the world – that was produced in 1902 – but it was the scooter that was going to be the most famous in the world. Piaggio did not like the look of the `Duckling´ so D'Ascanio redesigned it. The aircraft engineer's touch is easily recognizable. The Vespa (wasp) looks a little like the insect that it was named after: a zippy front end, a narrow waist and a large, rounded body. It was Piaggio himself who exclaimed when he saw the second prototype: `It looks like a wasp!´ D'Ascanio disliked motorbikes and the Vespa differed mechanically in several ways: it has a weight bearing shell, the gear change is on the handlebars, there is no longer a transmission chain, the wheels are very small, the driver does not sit astride it, but instead with his legs protected by the front shield, and the rear fork is reminiscent of an aircraft's landing gear and allows for rapid wheel change.

AN IMMEDIATE SUCCESS IN ITALY AND ELSEWHERE IN EUROPE

In April, 1946, the first fifteen Vespas left the factory at Pontedera. The first models were presented at the prestigious Golf Circle in Rome, but the press gave them a cold reception. Experts and technicians were divided into two camps. On the one hand cynics criticized the design and technique; on the other enthusiasts admired its futuristic aspects and above all the marketing concept which provided new answers to new needs. Faced with early difficulties, Piaggio offered the Vespa distribution to his friend and competitor, Count Parodi of Genoa, owner of the famous Guzzi motorbike company (another Italian icon), but the count declined. So Piaggio had to carry on alone and this time asked the Turin motor car producer, Lancia, who had a top-of-the-range distribution network which embodied the charm and charisma of quality cars in Italy. At the end of 1949 they had produced 35,000 scooters altogether and their success was quite clear. From 1951 Vespa began to enter the American market through the Sears, Roebuck Company. The publicity slogan was `Power–Safety–Economy´. The American weekly *Time* magazine wrote: `Not since the Roman chariot, have the Italians made a vehicle so peculiarly and proudly their own´. Piaggio then had a brilliant idea: he created Vespa Clubs for owners and fans, and thus promoted the image of the name and made it famous throughout the world. From 1955 Vespa had its own distribution network in the U.S.A. In April 1959, *Fortune* magazine included the Vespa amongst the hundred products which were `best designed in the world´. In the middle of the 1950s the Vespa was also produced in Germany (Hoffmann-Werke in Lintorf), Great Britain (Douglas in Bristol), France (ACMA in Paris), Spain (Moto Vespa S.A.) and Belgium (in Jette on the outskirts of Brussels). Production soon followed in South Africa (where the model was christened `Bromponie´), Iran and China.

THE BIG SCREEN HELPS PROMOTE THE VESPA

The cinema gave a great boost to the Vespa. In the 1953 film *Roman Holiday,* William Wyler had Audrey Hepburn and Gregory Peck ride a Vespa amongst the monuments of Rome and the surrounding countryside, resplendent under the sun and filled with history. It was the best possible publicity; and there are more than 200 films in which the actors drive Vespas. The Vespa is symbolic of the *Dolce Vita* and warm Roman nights. Marcello Mastroianni, Charlton Heston, John Wayne, Henry Fonda, Nanni Moretti, Sting, Antonio Banderas, Matt Damon, Gérard Depardieu have all driven Vespas. And Audrey Hepburn is far from being the only woman who has ridden one – others include Ursula Andress, Geraldine Chaplin, Joan Collins, Jane Mansfield, Virna Lisi, Marina Vlady and Mireille Darc. The Vespa is driven without having to sit astride it, which makes it ideal for women. There are even science fiction films in which the Vespa-Alpha became the protagonist in a 007-style spy adventure. This particular model is fast on the road, can fly and even float in water! The French and Italian armies ordered models to be used by parachutists and special assault units.

With its legendary status and easy mobility the Vespa has become a socio-cultural and economic phenomenon throughout Europe, the USA and developing countries which are becoming increasingly dependent on motorized transport, abandoning their bicycles for small cylinder cars, and driving scooters as a means of familiarizing themselves with motors, speed and the highway code. The Vespa is made in thirteen countries and sold in 114 throughout the world. But it is also copied: on 9th June 1957 Izvestia announced that production was being started in Kirov of the Viatka 150cc, a clone of the Vespa.

A 49CC VESPA: THE VESPINO

From 1963 in Italy and many other European countries economic problems created difficult conditions for the motor market. Piaggio launched the Vespino, or `little Vespa´: it had a 49 cc engine and was aimed at the youth, women and urban transport markets. It had a significant advantage – no need for a driving license because its cubic capacity was under 50cc! From that time onwards engineers, designers and marketing people all competed in producing a vast range of products aimed at satisfying existing needs and even creating new needs in urban and close range transport. However they were overtaken by the Vespa fans, launching themselves into even more extraordinary adventures. The Frenchman, Georges Monneret, built an amphibious Vespa and crossed the Channel with it in 1952, just after the world speed record for a 125 cc engine had been recorded at 106 miles an hour. The Vespas took part successfully in many world rallies: an Italian student Giuseppe Tironi drove to the North Pole, an Argentinean Carlos Velez crossed the Andes, the Italian Roberto Patrignani drove from Milan to Tokyo. The American James Owen rode from the north of USA all the way to Tierra del Fuego, and the Australian Geoff Dean drove around the world for the first time ... on a Vespa!

CHI VESPA, MANGIA LA MELA! ... NEW VERBS INVENTED BY A COMMERCIAL

Of course the Vespa phenomenon was sustained by aggressive advertising and marketing designed to appeal to people's unbridled fantasies, with a cultural content to tease consumers' subconscious and unconscious. In 1969 Italy was plastered with large pictures of apples, sometimes covering whole sides of houses. The media fanned the flames of public interest inquiring what the meaning of this advertising might be, and a few weeks later a slogan appeared which became very famous: `Chi Vespa, mangia la mela´ meaning, `Those who Vespa, eat apples´. The mysterious message became clear – the apple has strong connotations of both sex and freedom, so whoever drives the Vespa also bites into the apple ... of freedom, youth, the forbidden, and sex! The slogan thus created the verb `vespare´, to vespa, in the same way as we now say `to google´ when talking about looking something up on a search engine. Advertising was one of the strengths of Vespa throughout Europe and also in the USA where the slogans `Be different. Go Vespa´ and `Maybe your second car shouldn't be a car´ were extremely successful for their imagination and direct message. In Europe the advertisements spoke of `a paradise for two´ or `Vespa makes you want to do it´ and very often alluded to *la dolce vita.*

FROM CRISIS TO MP3: A REVOLUTIONARY TRICYCLE!

Piaggio, a company based in Sestri Ponente (Genoa) was created in 1884 to produce inboard equipment for boats and ferries; rapidly moving into the railway sector, in order to keep up with the fashions of industry. Rinaldo Piaggio soon realized that aviation was the future; he employed the best engineers from Italian aviation and produced civil and military aircraft which beat many international records before the Second World War. The P108 model used very advanced techniques: the same structure was used for small passenger planes and for bombers. The Vespa was the final stroke of genius by this great manager who dared to take risks, who understood and anticipated markets' evolution and had the courage to seize opportunities. In 1964 Enrico bought out his brother Armando's shares, who then went on to found IAM, a company specializing in producing civil aircraft, which had great success in the luxury and business aircraft sector for short haul flights.

Enrico Piaggio died in 1965, at a crucial moment of social unrest in his factories. The Agnelli family bought a large number of shares in the company. Umberto Agnelli was married to Antonella Bechi Piaggio and the press dubbed the marriage `the six wheel wedding´ (four from Fiat and two from Piaggio). In 1969 the company was bought by the Italian motorbike producer Gilera. But it went into decline in the face of tough Japanese and French competition in the scooter sector. The deaths of Giovannino Agnelli in 1997, and of his mother Antonella Bechi the following year, pushed the heirs into selling their shares to Morgan Grenfell in 1999 for 1350 billion lire (nearly $1 billion). Toward the end of 2000, businessman Roberto Colaninno (following the Olivetti takeover of Telecom Italia) started putting capital into Piaggio and relaunched the brand with new models; in 2004 he bought the Italian motorbike producer Aprilia, a major player in international competitions. Recently Piaggio has taken a big gamble in launching in a blaze of publicity the MP3, the revolutionary tricycle with two wheels in front!

THE VIETNAM WAR BOOSTS THE CONTAINER INDUSTRY

Malcom[1] McLean lived in the North Carolina countryside. For a small wage, he sold his mother's hen eggs and during the Great Depression he managed to get a job in a gas station. He worked hard and saved hard to buy an old truck, with which he began transporting goods for farmers. By 1940 his company had 30 or so trucks. By 1955 his company managed 1776 trucks – he then sold it for $6 million to buy the Pan Atlantic Tank Company which owned a few old ships used in transporting oil. He changed the name of the company to Sea-Land Co. and acted upon an idea that he had had since 1937 – the transport of containers. At that time he was still driving trucks, and one day he became impatient with the time it took for the dockers to unload the merchandise (in this case cotton balls) from his truck and he was unable to do anything to help speed things up. All his other teamsters were also losing a lot of time during the loading and unloading of their trucks. So he had the idea of `packaging´ the goods to speed up the operation, which would require fewer dockers and reduce accidents and losses between the quayside and the boat. The first experiments were inconclusive. Some rail companies began to transport the truck bodies without tractor cabs; when they reached their destination, new cabs were employed to haul them to their ultimate destination. But these railroad solutions were mainly a strategic choice by the railway companies to try and compete with the large truck transport network, where more trucks were becom-

---

1. Born `Malcolm´ he later changed his name to the traditional Scots spelling

ing available as a result of military demobilization with a significant impact on prices.

McLean, the Father of Containers

McLean used his small maritime company to fulfill his dreams: `packaging´ the goods in large boxes and transporting them on ships which had loading beds like those of trucks. Special cranes were needed for this operation and enough room on the quayside to store the containers, which also had to be standardized. On 26th April 1956, he experimented with an old ship (the *Ideal X*) which had been converted at deck level to be able to transport 58 containers from the port of Newark to Florida and Houston. The harbor fees for loading the boat were $5.86 per ton and with McLean's method they came down to 16¢! It must be taken into account that at the time loading systems which were almost automatic, with conveyor belts and pallets, were coming into use. McLean opened up international transport lines, departing from New Jersey, where he bought docks and adapted them for stocking containers, loading and unloading them onto the ships with special cranes. To raise new capital McLean sold his company to R.J. Reynolds Tobacco Co., which cashed in many of their investments and even bought a specialist oil company (energy was the main cost element in the company's transport budget). In 1978 McLean bought United States Lines and attempted to repeat the operation by creating an even larger business with transport lines throughout the world; but in 1987 USL went bankrupt because its system was too dependent on energy, the cost of which was rising steeply. In 1992, McLean, at 78 years old, created the Trailer Bridge Company which mainly operated between Florida and Puerto Rico.

When Malcom McLean died in 2001 at the age of 87, the Secretary of Transport in the United States said: `A true giant, Malcom revolutionized the maritime industry in the 20th century.´ An article in the famous *Harvard Business Review* also called McLean `the truck driver who reinvented shipping´ and said that `by the end of the [20th] century, container shipping was transporting approximately 90 percent of the world's trade cargo´.

THE US ARMY IS THE FIRST CUSTOMER

But the launch and development of the container were also in part due to the support of the American Army, whose involvement in the war in Vietnam was mounting. They needed to transport goods and arms which were relatively standardized and could be `packaged´ in containers, to be then taken on to wet, hot regions with very bad roads. Containers provided the best solution, which, in addition, limited material losses. The American Army became the industry's main client and played an essential role in its development – the industry needed investment in harbor structures, in ships (with a new structure also) and in the creation of a fleet of standardized containers. The American Army's logistics experts increasingly used containers to send arms, spare parts, medicines and foodstuffs to supply the 540,000 GIs in the Vietnamese jungle. Furthermore, meeting their needs helped to develop containers capable of transporting refrigerated goods at a constant guaranteed temperature; containers which could be parachuted; still others which could be lived in and/or be used as campaign hospitals; tank containers; and both open-top and side-opening ones. The Pentagon was committed to providing troops with a maximum of military, medical and food supplies; rapidity of response and facility of transport were therefore of primary importance. In 1965, the Pentagon signed a contract with the Sea-Land Co. to transport 1200 containers a month between the ports of California and the port of Cam Ranh Bay in Vietnam. The volume of material transported soared as American military involvement in the region increased.

STANDARDIZATION

The container was standardized by the International Organization of Standardization, which fixed the dimensions at 8 feet high by 8 feet 6 inches wide, by either 20 or 40 feet long. For a guaranteed fixed temperature the size was standardized at 20 feet in length. This considerably reduced the cost of shipping and gave a boost to international trade, which was already expanding rapidly. Furthermore, some port authorities had the foresight to become equipped to receive these ships, load and unload them, accommodate the trucks and trains transporting the containers, organize storage space and manage the container traffic. All of this was helped a great deal by growing use of computers and instant communications systems. Other ports followed suit but they had fallen behind, and lost valuable time. However, all the ports were confronted with the anger of the dockers who were being put out of work.

Many Asian ports, developed or built recently to deal with the explosion in exports from their countries, have been directly designed as container ports, while older ports in other continents have had to deal with serious difficulties in restructuring and changing from their original use. Merchant fleets (and in certain cases navies) have had to modify their ships and to increase their container fleet. At the moment the largest ship (the *Pamela*, 1050 feet in length) can transport 9000 containers. Certain important routes – the Panama Canal in particular – can no longer accommodate ships of this size, and are being forced to consider rapidly restructuring. The container system has also had a significant impact on rail and road transport, which have been obliged to adapt to the new structures. Containers too have transformed air transport, which has adopted smaller containers, still standardized however, to transport goods and especially passenger luggage.

THE PIRELLI CALENDAR: AN `EYE-OPENING´ PRODUCT AND TEXTBOOK MARKETING

It is dubbed *Il Calendario*: the name `Pirelli´ has become super-fluous. 40,000 copies were distributed amongst a very particular elite in 50 countries. It was started in 1964 and is therefore over 40 years old, but one would never guess... it is still as young and attractive as ever. But this calendar is not intended simply for truckers or garage mechanics: it is the complete antithesis of a Playboy-style calendar.

The Sunday Times regularly publishes the price of the calendars (which never falls). Between 1975 and 1983 publication was suspended not only because of the oil crisis, austerity, the recession, terrorism in Italy, but also because of militant feminist opposition, although these same feminists ended up admiring its aesthetic content. But *fluctuat nec mergitur* (tossed by the waves, she does not sink – the motto of the city of Paris), production was relaunched in 1984. Umberto Eco has written about it, page upon page has been published about it by anthropologists, sociologists, sexologists, semiologists, and communications and marketing experts. The best photographers in the world compete to be invited to photograph the women judged currently to be among the most beautiful on the planet. It is a cult object which began with the modesty of the early 1960s and continued through to scandalous shots, seduction, the artistic interpretation of sensuality, and the aesthetics of the artistic nude.

WHERE? FIFTEEN IN EUROPE, NINE IN THE UNITED STATES

It cannot be said that the calendar is Italian and partisan: there have been very few Italian women featured in it, the photographs have been taken in Italy only twice (in the Naples area), and very few of the photographers have been Italian.

The criteria for selection are quality and novelty. For example, even women photographers have accepted the challenge. It was only after 1968 that the first outline of a breast was seen – the idea of the photographer Harri Peccinotti, who was inspired by the poems of Ronsard and Allen Ginsberg. But it was a female photographer who showed the whole breast for the first time – Sarah Moon chose a `fluid and calligraphic´ framework for its unveiling.

The long awaited renewal of publication took place in 1984, and came with a huge barrage of publicity and media exposure. It was also a commercial success, because it showed parts of women's bodies covered with tire marks… buttocks, breasts and torsos!

The 1987 issue marked another controversial innovation – it featured only black women, including a young sixteen-year-old called Naomi Campbell. In 1988 another change took place: face-less men wearing tights featured amongst the women all in dance poses. The 1999 calendar focused on the Olympics – entirely in black and white, it was a homage to photographers Arthur Elgort and Leni Reifenstahl, and their dramatic photographs of the 1936 Olympics and of the `grandeur´ of the Reich and Hitler. Many felt it to be in poor taste, but esthetics triumphed.

From 1994, the Pirelli calendar started choosing fashionable women who appeared in the big glamour magazines, and were the target of paparazzi in St Tropez, Rome and Hollywood. In 2002 two VIP nieces featured amongst the women photographed: Lauren Bush and Kiera Chaplin.

AN EXTRAORDINARY MARKETING OPERATION

The calendar is an extraordinary marketing operation, easy to imitate but difficult to produce. It has the monopoly on this combination of the picture, the idea, the selection of the theme and the type of women. It is like the silk craved by the Roman matrons in the time of the Caesars, the pepper so sought after by European courts in medieval times, the salt in the western regions of China under the Ming, and the coffee and cocoa which European nobility became so keen on in the 17th century. To be selected as the photographer is a little like receiving the Nobel prize for photography, and to appear in `the Cal´ is a great honor for a woman, who is considered not merely beautiful, but alluring enough to display her nudity artistically. Of course it is a celebration of youth. But the 2007 calendar broke with tradition; homage was paid to beauty of all ages (an `ageless´ Sophia Loren was an example). A heady mix of provocation and legend, this *calendario* throws down the gauntlet with its anti-ageist stance. It deserves the epithet in a newspaper review of the retrospective exhibition of Pirelli calendar photographs in Germany (Berlinische Galerie, March 2006): `an old success story of photographs, which combine eroticism and irony, Zeitgeist and advertising, and which have gained fame all over the world´.

CONCLUSIONS: M.E.S.R.C.!

There is not much new under the sun or indeed in the hearts and minds of mankind! Books about the methods and activities of the secret services reveal the mix of rational and irrational factors that motivate men and women to work – and risk their lives – as informers for their own or enemy countries' secret services. Such motives may be summed up in the acronym MES. M stands for `money´. Throughout history many people have worked very hard for meager returns – barely enough to live on or perhaps sometimes enough to indulge their whims. How many people tied to the land have worked hard throughout their lives to earn their daily bread? How many millions of men have endured the unendurable under the yoke of slavery? How many Venetian merchants worked and took risks in order to display their wealth by means of a mansion on the Grand Canal? And how many hedge fund managers buy Porsches or Ferraris, the ostensive proof of their success in the markets and of bonuses received?

E stands for `ego´. This too has played its role in history – and still does – the prime motivator, driving action and behavior: Alexander the Great, Roman and Mongolian generals, the Conquistadores and Napoleon all threw themselves into unimaginable adventures. Sailors took insane risks going off in search of new lands or simply to load up with spices for delivery to Venice or Amsterdam. Numerous financiers, giddy with success, have forgotten the fundamental rules of their profession in order to obtain even more power for themselves.

This infernal trio is completed by S for `sex´. How many rash or courageous decisions have been taken to win a lady's (or a man's) heart, with unforeseen consequences for the destiny of a kingdom, an industrial giant or even the papacy? In many instances eunuchs manipulated the levers of power behind the throne in the Chinese and Ottoman Empires, ensconced behind the fortified walls of the Forbidden City and the Great Gate of the Topkapi, and astonishing sums have been spent to listen to the crystal-clear voice of a castrato.

But this magic cypher, this great engine turning the wheel of history, lacks two further initials. First and foremost, we must add the letter R for 'religion'. The course of economics and history has frequently been altered by religion; every idolatrous or over-zealous religious act, every exercise of dogmatism has had a marked effect on society. The exodus of the Jews from Canaan to Egypt, the expulsion of the Moriscos and Jews by the ultra-pious Queen Isabel of Spain, the Revocation of the Edict of Nantes, all had adverse effects on the economies of the countries which banished these minorities and highly beneficial effects on those countries offering them shelter. The Reformation and Counter-Reformation overturned political boundaries, markets and industries, as did the spread of Buddhism in Asia or the triumphant march of Islam (which set out to conquer the world militarily but which in many countries fosters a humanist culture). How many wars of religion have or have had an underlying economic rationale? In all of these instances 'chance' (C, the final letter of the acronym) has also played its nefarious, fundamental and occasionally hackneyed role. How many sailors passed through the Straits of Gibraltar in search of Atlantis, but failed? Christopher Columbus 'twiddled his thumbs' for over a decade before finding a backer for his completely madcap scheme, but he completely changed the balance of the world – without realizing it! Yet nobody remembers the names of the sailors who first discovered trade winds or of the men who understood the functioning of the Monsoons.

The flow of money financing Spain's Golden Age and the development of Renaissance and Baroque Europe foreshadows the way in which Asian capital currently finances the trade and budget deficits of the USA. International investment banks engaged in speculation and the mobilization of capital are latter days versions the merchants and bankers of the Italian Renaissance and the Dutch Golden Age and of Levantine, Jewish and Chinese traders. The East India Companies which developed economic globalization were not so different from the multinationals of today with their global strategies. It is true that they are no longer national companies (American, Japanese, European and Chinese and so forth) – they are global, even if their headquarters are physically, fiscally and legally based in New York, a European capital, Tokyo or Shanghai. Hedge funds transfer billions of dollars from one place to another at the click of a button or by sending orders via direct intercontinental telephone calls, just as letters of exchange once transferred large quantities of florins or thalers and silver pieces of eight from Florence, Venice or Genoa to Antwerp or Amsterdam. The trade routes for silk, obsidian, amber, salt and spices are echoed today in the transport of oil and transfer of energy, along with all the concomitant rivalry and greed in political, economic and military terms.

Modern industrial espionage reminds us of the desperate pursuit of the production secrets of silk, paper, porcelain, glass, mirrors, lace and maps. Wealthy Roman matrons swathed themselves in silk to show off in imperial Rome, medieval kings wanted spices on their tables, the prelates of Catholic church adored chocolate, princes and nouveaux riches were festooned with lace and had their portraits painted by the Dutch and Italian masters, clocks adorned the palaces of the Chinese and Japanese Emperors in the 17th century, coffee was a luxury indulged in by the wealthy and intellectuals of Europe – and today the newly wealthy and the powerful wear Ermenegildo Zegna and Hugo Boss, drive around in Maseratis and Aston Martins with Hermès luggage in the back, holiday in Tibet, visit Tierra del Fuego and buy Ming statuettes and paintings by Andy Warhol from Christie's. Information equals power, as the Venetian gazetteers, who were the first to work with information and the power it brings, well knew.

Does all this mean that the present inevitably reproduces the past? Gianbattista Vico, the historical philosopher, would have said so! Many historical events, especially in economic terms, repeat themselves even today – but Penelope no longer weaves her tapestry at the same pace! It took ten months for Philip II to receive replies to the letters he sent from Madrid to the Spanish administration in Manila. Now the news of a volcanic eruption in the Philippines, an earthquake in Japan, a *coup d'état* in Africa, the price of shares on the world's stock exchanges or the contents of a speech by the governor of the FED all reach us in `real time´. The earth is flat! The `domino theory´ now rules world events. The real challenge facing the 21st century is to assess the relative value of events and accord them their true importance in the gigantic jigsaw puzzle whose constituent parts change even as we look at it.

SELECTED BIBLIOGRAPHY

Acot, Pascal, *Histoire du climat*, Perrin, Paris, 2003

Alberi, Eugenio, *Relazioni degli Ambasciatori Veneti al Senato*, Firenze 1840

Anderson, Mary, *Hidden Power : the Palace Eunuchs of imperial China*, Prometheus Books, Buffalo, 1990

Appriou, Daniel, *Ruses et stratagèmes de l'histoire*, Acropole, Paris, 2007

Asselain, Jean-Charles, *De la révolution industrielle à la première guerre mondiale*, Presse de la FNSP/Dalloz, Paris 1991

Ball, Philip, *Histoire vivante des couleur*, Hazan, Paris 2005

Banco Central de Reserva del Peru, *Museo Numismatico del Peru*, ED BCRP, Lima 2003

Barbier, Frédéric, *L'Europe de Gutemberg*, Belin, Paris, 2006

Beltrami, Daniele, *Storia della popolazione di Venezia dalla fine del secolo XVI alla caduta della Repubblica* Cedam, Padua 1954

Bernstein, Peter, *Against the Gods – The Remarkable Story of Risk*, John Wiley & Son, Inc., New York 1998

Bernstein, Peter, *The Power of Gold*, John Wiley & Sons, Inc., New York 2000

Bonelli, Franco, *La crisi del 1907*, Fondazione Einaudi, Turin 1971

Bonnant, G., `The introduction of Western Horology in China´ in *La Suisse Horlogère* I, 1960, Geneva

Boorstin, Daniel, *Les découvreurs*, Robert Laffont, Paris 1986

Boudet, Jacques, *Les mots de l'histoire*, R. Laffont, Paris 1990

Braudel, Fernand, *Autour de la Méditerranée*, Ed. De Falois, Paris 1996

Braudel, Fernand, *History of Civilizations*, Penguin Books, London 1993

Braudel, Fernand, *La Méditerranée et le monde méditerranéen*, Armand Colin, Paris 1979

Braudel, Fernand, *Civilisation matérielle, économie et capitalisme*, Colin, Paris 1989

Broadberry, Stephen & Harrison, Mark, *Economics WW1*, Cambridge University Press, Cambridge 2005

Brooks, John, *Once in Golconda – The True Drama of Wall Street 1920-1938*, J. Wiley & Sons, New York 1999

Bruckner, Gene Adam, *Firenze, l'impero del fiorino*, Mondadori – Milano, 1983

Bruner, Robert and Carr, Sean, *The Panic of 1907 : Lessons learned from the Market's perfect Storm*, Wiley, New York, 2007

Bureau of Mines *Mineral Yearbook US*, GPO, Washington, 1980

Butler Greenfield, Amy, *A Perfect Red*, Harper Collins, London, 2005

Caceres Macedo, Justo *Culturas prehispanicas del Peru*, Ed. Lovation, Lima 2005

Caceres Macedo, Justo *El ùltimo dia de Francisco Pizarro*, Alberto Massa Murazzi Ed. Lima 2003

Camusso, Lorenzo, *Guide du voyageur dans l'Europe de 1492*, Ed. Liana Levi, Milan 1991

Cardini, Franco, *1492 – l'Europe au temps de la découverte de l'Amérique*, Solar, Paris 1989

Carus-Wilson, E., *The Merchants Adventures of Bristol in the XVth century*, Bristol 1962

Charle, Christophe, *La crise des sociétés impériales*, Seuil, Paris 2001

Chanu, Pierre, *Histoire et décadence*, Perrin, Paris 1981

Chanu, Pierre, *Le temps des Réformes*, Hachette, Paris 1996

Chernow, Ron, *The House of Morgan*, Touchstone Books, New York 1990

Chevallier, Jean et Gheerbrant, Alain, *Dictionnaire des symbols*, Laffont, Paris 1982

Chown, John F., *A History of Money from AD 800*, Toutledge & IEAA, London 1994

Cipolla, Carlo Maria, *Tre storie extra vaganti*, Il Mulino, Bologna 1994

Cipolla, Carlo Maria, *Clocks and Culture – 1300-1700*, Norton & Co, New York 1978

Cipolla, Carlo Maria, *Guns, Sails, and Empires*, Sunflowers University Press, Manhattan, Kansas 1987

Cipolla, Carlo Maria, *Literacy and development in the West*, Penguin Books, London 1969

Cipolla, Carlo Maria, *Conquistadores, pirati, mercatanti*, Il Mulino, Bologna 1996

Cipolla, Carlo Maria, *Before the Industrial Revolution*, Norton &Co, New York 1993

Cogliati Arano, Luisa *Tacuinum Sanitatis*, George Braziller, Inc. , New York 1976

Collin, Bruno et Véronique, *Histoire de la monnaie*, Trésor du Patrimoine, Paris 2003

Colomb, Christophe, *Œuvres complètes*, Ed. La Différence, Paris 1992

Colson, Bruno et Coutau-Bégarie, Hervé *Armées at Marines au temps d'Austerlitz et de Trafalgar*, Ed. Economica, Paris 2007

Crouzet-Pavan, Elisabeth, *Venise triomphante, les horizons d'un mythe*, Albin Michel, Paris 1999

Chungara Castro, Victor, *Tradiciones y Leyendas de Uyuni*, Ed. Leonardo, Uyuni, 2005

Dachner, Don & Dene, *Caribbean History*, Traveler's Press Inc., Dixon CA, 1995

d'Artigues Agnès & Rey-Valett, Hélène *Histoire économique du capitalisme industriel*, Ed. Vibert, Paris 2003

Delumeau, Jean, *L'alun de Rome*, SEVPEN, Paris 1961

Diamond, Jared, *Effondrement*, Gallimard, Paris 2006

Diamond, Jared, *Guns, Germs and Steel*, Norton & Co, New York 1999

Doumas, Christos, *Santorini*, Zadotike, Athens 1997

Duby, Georges, *Les temps des cathédrales*, Gallimard, Paris 1976

Ducellier, Alain, Kaplan, Michel & Martin, Bernadette & Micheau, Françoise, *Le Moyen Âge en rien : Bysance et l'Islam, Des Barbares aux Ottomans*, Hachette, Paris 2006

Durschmied, Erik, *The Hinge Factor*, Arcade Publishing, New York 2000

Durschmied, Erik, *The Hinges of Battle*, Coronet Books, London 2002

Egg, E *et al*, *Canons, histoire illustrée de l'artillerie*, Edita, Lausanne 1971

Elliott, J.H., *Imperial Spain – 1469-1716*, Penguin Books, London 1990

Elorrieta Salazar, Fernando, *Cusco et la vallée sacrée des Incas*, Edgar Elorrieta Salazar Ediciones, Cusco 2006

Encel, Frédéric, *L'art de la guerre par l'exemple*, Flammarion, Paris 2000

Fabris, Gianpaolo e Minestroni, Laura, *Valore e valori della marca*, Angeli, Milan 2004

Favier, Jean, *De l'or et des épices*, Fayard, Paris 1987

Favier, Jean, *Les grandes découvertes*, Fayard, Paris 1991

Fernandez-Armesto, Felipe, *Food : A History*, Pan Books, London 2001

Fernandez-Armesto, Felipe, Amerigo, *The Man who gave his Name to America*, Weidenfel & Nicolson, London 2006

Freese, Barbara, *Coal : a human history*, Arrow Books, London 2003

Galbraith John Kenneth, *Brève histoire de l'euphorie financière*, Seuil, Paris 1992

Galéazzi, Michel, *Lexique numismatique*, Bibliothèque des AST, Revigny 2005

Geisst, Charles R., *Wheels of Fortune*, John Wiley & Sons, New York 2002

Geisst, Charles R., *100 years of Wall Street*, McGraw Hill, New York 2000

Gelmi, Josef, *I papi*, Rizzoli, Milan 1986

Genaille, Robert, *La peinture hollandaise*, Ed. Pierre Ptsiné, Paris 1956

Geoffroy, Patrick, *La route de l'ambre*, Ed. du Felin, Paris 2002

Gibbon, Edward, *The History of the Decline and Fall of the Roman Empire*, Boston 1856

Grimal, Pierre, *Mythologies de la Méditerranée au Gange*, Larousse, Paris 1963

Gross, Daniel, *Forbes Greatest Business Stories of all Time*, J. Wiley & Sons, New York 1996

Hanke, Lewis and Gunar , Mendoza, *History of the Imperial City of Potosi*, Brown University , Providence 1965

Heers, Jacques, *La découverte de l'Amérique*, Ed. Complexe, Paris 1991

Heers, Jacques, *La ruée vers l'Amérique*, Ed. Complexe, Paris 1992

Henaff, Marcel, *Le prix de la vérité*, Seuil, Paris 1999

Henry, Gerard Marie *Les crises au XX siècle*, Belin, Paris 2003

Herrera, Adolfo, *El duro : studio de los reales de a ocho espagnoles*, RAH, Madrid 1914

Hibbert, Christopher, *Cities and Civizations*, Walcome Rain Ed., New York 1996

Hocquet, Jean Claude, *Venise et la mer – XII-XVIII siècle*, Fayard, Paris 2006

Hocquet, Jean Claude, *Le sel et la fortune de Venise*, PUF Lille, Lille 1978

Hobsbawm, Eric J., *L'ère du capital*, Pluriel, Arthème-Fayard, Paris 1978

Homer, Sidney & Sylla, Richard *A History of interest rates*, Rutgers University Press, London 1991

Hughes, Bettany, *Hellen of Troy : Goddess, Princess, Whore*, Knopf Publ., London 2005

Hugill, Peter J., *World Trade since 1431*, The John Hopkins University Press, Baltimore 1993

Hunt, Edwin & Murray, James, *A history of Business in Medieval Europe 1200-1500*, Cambridge University Press, Cambridge 1999

Huyghe, Edith et François-Bernard, *Les coureurs d'épices sur la route des Indes fabuleuses*, JC Lattès, Paris 1999

Huyghe, Edith et François-Bernard, *La route de la soie*, Payot, Paris 2006

Huyghe, Edith et François-Bernard, *Histoire des secrets*, Hazan, Paris 2000

Infelise, Mario, *Prima dei giornali*, Editori Laterza, Rome 2005

Iburg, Anne, *Les épices*, Gründ, Paris 2006

Keagan, John, *Histoire de la guerre*, Editions Dagorno, Paris 1996

Kindelberger, Charles, *Manias, Panics and Crashes*, Basic Books, New York 1989

Lane, F.C., *Venice, a Maritime Republic*, John Hopkins University, Baltimore 1973

Le Goff, Jacques, *Marchands et banquiers au Moyen Age*, PUF, Paris 1972

Le Goff, Jacques, *Un autre Moyen Âge*, Gallimard, Paris 2002

Le Rider, Georges, *Naissance de la Monnaie*, PUF, Paris 2001

Le Roy Ladurie, Emmanuel, *Histoire du climat dépuis l'an Mil*, Flammarion, Paris 1983

Lewis, Michael Arthur, *The Spanish Armada*, Crowell & Co, New York 1968

Lohmann Villena, Guillermo, *Plata del Perú, riqueza de Europa*, FECP, Lima 2004

Lopez Serrano, Alfredo, *Los cambios de siglo en la historia de Espagna : siglo XV-XX*, videoconferencias 2001

Luzzatto, Gino, *Storia economica dell'età moderna e contemporanea*, CEDAM, Padua 1960

Mackay, Charles, *Extraordinary Popular Delusions and the Madness of Crowds*, J. Wiley & Sons, Inc., New York 1996

Malaguzzi, Silvia, *Boire & Manger – traditions et symboles*, Hazan, Paris 2006

Magalhaes Godinho, Vitorino, *Les Découvertes*, Ed. Autrement, Paris 1990

Mamani-Ventura, *Sal y Salares Andinos*, Latinas Editores, Oruro Bolivia 2003

Manchester, William, *Les Armes des Krupp*, Robert Laffont, Paris 1970

Mann, Charles CLK, *1491, The Americas before Columbus*, Granta Books, London 2006

Martin, Colin & Parker, Geoffrey, *Le dossier de l'Invincible Armada*, Tallandier, Paris 1988

Massa, Alberto, *El ùltimo dia de Francisco Pizarro*, Alberto Massa Murazzi Ed., Lima 2003

Masson, Philippe, *De la mer et de stratégie*, Tallandier, Paris 1986

McMillan, John, *Du bazar à la corbeille*, Ed. Village Mondial, Paris 2003

Medina, Oscar, *Mystery of Inka Trail*, *Millenium Editores*, Cusco 2007

Micklethwait, John & Wooldridge, Adrian, *The Company*, Phoenix Paperback, London 2003

Mizon, Louis *L'indien, témoignages d'une fascination*, ELA Diffusion, Paris 1992

Mollat, Michel, *Les pauvres au Moyen Âge*, Ed. Complexe/Hachette, Paris 1978

Monnier, Philippe, *Venise au XVIII siècle*, Perrin & Cie, Paris 1907

Morineau, Michel, *Les grandes compagnies des Indes Orientales*, PUF, Paris 1994

Morris, Jan, *The Venetian Empire – a Sea Voyage*, Penguin Books, London 1990

Nani Moncenigo, Mario, *L'Arsenale di Venezia*, Ed. Filippi, Venice 1927

Needham, Joseph, *Science and Civilization in China*, Cambridge University Press, Cambridge 1954

Ortiz, Domingo, *Crisis y decadencia en la Espagna de los Asturias*, IES 6, Barcelona 1969

Panaghiotis, Christou et Papastamatis, Katharini, *Mythologie grecque*, Bonechi, Florence 2001

Panzac, Daniel, *La caravane maritime : Marins européens et marchands ottomans en Méditerranée (1680-1830)*, CNRS, Paris 2004

Pasquinelli, Barbara *Le geste et l'expression*, Ed. Hazan, Paris 2006

Pastoureau, Michel, *Les couleurs*, Ed. Du Panama, Paris 2006

Pastoureau, Michel, *Bleu, histoire d'une couleur*, Points, Paris 2006

Pelt, Jean-Marie, *La cannelle et le panda*, Fayard, Paris 1999

Perrier-Robert, Annie, *Le chocolat*, Editions du Chène, Hachette, Paris 2000

Petacco, Arrigo, *La croce e la mezzaluna : Lepanto 7 ottobre 1571*, Mondadori, Milan 2005

Petifils, Jean-Christian, *Fouquet*, Perrin, Paris 1998

Philibert, Myriam, *Mythologies*, EDL, Paris 2000

Pigafetta, Antonio, *Magellan, le premier tour du monde*, Tallandier, Paris 1999

Pirenne, Henri, *Storia economica e sociale del Medioevo*, Garzanti, Milan 1972

Pirenne, Henri, *Les grands courants de l'histoire universelle*, Ed. de la Baconnière, Neuchâtel 1947

Platt, Richard, *Corsaires et pirates*, Gallimard, Paris 1994

Ponce Sanginés, Carlos, *Tiwanaku y su fascinante desarollo cultural*, Producciones Cima, La Paz 2004

Porte, Rémy, *La mobilisation industrielle*, `14-18 Editions´, Paris 2005

Presta, Ana Maria, *Los Encomenderos de la Plata 1550-1600*, Banco Central de Reserva del Peru, Lima 2000

Petacco, Arrigo, *La Croce e la Mezzaluna. Lepanto 7 ottobre 1571*, Mondadori, Milano 2005

Preto, Paolo, *I servizi secreti di Venezia*, Il Saggiatore, Milan 2004

Preto, Paolo, *Persona per hora secreta*, Il Saggiatore, Milan 2006

Richardot, Philippe, *La fin de l'armée romaine 284-476*, Economica, Paris 2005

Richardson, Paul, *Indulgence : Around the World in Search of Chocolate*, Abacus-New Ed. London 2004

Ringrose, Kathrin, *Eunuchs and the social construction of gender in Byzantium*, The University of Chicago Press, Chicago, 2003

Roel Pineda, Virgilio, *Historia Social y Economica de la Colonia*, Herrera Editores, Lima 1999

Rostovtseff, Michel Ivanovic, *Histoire économique et sociale de l'Empire Romain*, Laffont, Paris 1988

Rowley, Antony, *L'histoire mondiale de la table*, Odile Jacob, Paris 2006

Russell, Lawrence Richard, *Battles*, Robinson, London 2002

Schurz, William Lytle, *The Manila Galleon*, Dutton Paperback, New York 1959

Sédillot, René, *Histoire de l'or*, Fayard, Paris 1972

Serrano Mangas, Fernando, *Los galeones de la Carrera de Indias*, EEHA, Seville 1985

Simonnot, Philippe, *Les Papes, l'Eglise et l'argent*, Bayard, Paris 2005

Simonnot, Philippe, *Vingt et un siècles d'économie*, Les belles lettres, Paris 2002

Sobel, Robert, *Panic on Wall Street*, Beard Books, Washington 1999

Sobel, Robert, *The Great Bull Market : Wall Street in the 1920s*, Northon & Co, New York 1968

Sombart, Werner, *Economic Life in the Modern Age*, New Brunswick, New York 2001

Sombart, Werner, *Luxus und Kapitalismus*, Dunker und Humblot, Munich 1922

Spence, Johnathan D., *Les palais de mémoire de Matteo Ricci*, Payot, Paris 1986

Strauss, Barry, *The Trojan War : a new History*, Simon and Schuster, New York 2006

Taube, Gehrard, *500 years of German cannons*, Schiffer Publishing, Atglen PA 2001

Tenenti, Alberto, *L'età moderna XVI-XVIII secolo*, Il Mulino, Bologna 2005

Tenenti, Alberto e Romano, Ruggero, *Storia universale dei popoli e delle civiltà*, Utet, Turin 1981

Thomas, Hugh , *Rivers of Gold*, Random House Ltd, London 2004

Torre, Silvio, *Colombo, un nuovo mondo a tavola*, IdeaLibri, Milan 2002

Toussaint-Samat, Maguelonne, *Histoire naturelle et morale de la nourriture*, Larousse, Paris 1997

Valéry, Valérie Françoise, *Les épices* Ed. Chène, Paris, 1998

Van Doren, Charles, *A History of Knowledge*, Randomhouse, New York 1992

Viallon, F. Marie, *Venise et la Porte Musulmane 1453-1566*, Ed. Economica, Paris 1995

Vilar, Pierre, *Oro e moneta nella storia*, Laterza, Bari 1971

Viller, Claude, *Les grands voyageurs*, Ed. Hors Collection, Presses de la Cité, Paris 1993

Vines, Stephen, *Market Panic*, John Wiley & Sons, London 2003

Watts, Sheledon, *Epidemics and History*, Yale University Press, New Haven 1999

White, Lynn, *Medieval Technology and Social change*, Galaxy Books, Oxford 1962

Wilmots-Vandendaele, *Le marché de l'or*, Economica, Paris 1985

Zorzi, Alvise, *La Repubblica del Leone – Storia di Venezia*, Rusconi, Milan 1979

Zorzi, Alvise, *Le Grand Canal*, Perrin, Paris 1994

Watin-Augouard, Jean, *Histoire des marques*, Eyrolles, Paris 2006

Weiss, Luigi, *I corrieri della Serenissima*, Elzeviro, Padova 2001

Willis, John E. Jr., *Lima, Pekin, Venise 1688 : une année dans le monde*, Ed. Autrement, Paris 2003

Journals
Annales, Histoire, Sciences Sociales
Historia (Monthly), Paris
Storia di Venezia Florence University Press
L'histoire (Monthly), Paris
The Economic History Review, London
Cahiers d'Histoire Mondiale, Paris
Cambridge Historical Journal, Cambridge
Bollettino dell'Istituto di Storia della Società e dello Stato Veneziano, Venice

Press
Il Sole 24 Ore, Milan
La Repubblica, Milan
L'Espresso, Milan
Le Figaro, Paris
L'Expansion, Paris
Les Echos, Paris
Le Monde, Paris
The Financial Times, London
International Herald Tribune, Paris

Internet
Various public and private sites

INDEX

Composé par MCP – N° 443351Y. – Dépôt légal : novembre 2007
Imprimé en France. - JOUVE, 11, bd de Sébastopol, 75001 PARIS